The History of Anglo-Japanese Relations, 1600–2000

The History of Anglo-Japanese Relations, 1600–2000

General Editors: **Chihiro Hosoya** and **Ian Nish**

The five volumes which make up the series *The History of Anglo-Japanese Relations, 1600–2000*, cover the relationship between these two island communities from the first contacts at the start of the seventeenth century through to the end of the present millennium. While the studies cover the Anglo-Japanese relationship over the past four centuries, they tend to concentrate on features of the past 150 years. The volumes have been prepared independently over the past five years by Japanese and non-Japanese scholars who have met to debate and discuss their papers. These studies analyse the rise and fall of these relations in four dimensions: political and diplomatic; economic and business; military an naval; and social and cultural.

Titles in the series:

The History of Anglo-Japanese Relations, 1600–2000
Series Standing Order ISBN 0–333–79224–6
(*outside North America only*)

You can receive future titles in this series as they are published by placing a standing order. Please contact your bookseller or, in case of difficulty, write to us at the address below with your name and address, the title of the series and the ISBN quoted above.

Customer Services Department, Macmillan Distribution Ltd, Houndmills, Basingstoke, Hampshire RG21 6XS, England

The History of Anglo-Japanese Relations, 1600–2000

Volume III: The Military Dimension

Edited by

Ian Gow
Professor of Asian Studies
University of Nottingham

and

Yoichi Hirama
Rear-Admiral (Retd)
Japanese Self-Defence Forces

with

John Chapman
Scottish Centre for War Studies
University of Glasgow

Published by
PALGRAVE MACMILLAN
Houndmills, Basingstoke, Hampshire RG21 6XS and
175 Fifth Avenue, New York, N.Y. 10010
Companies and representatives throughout the world

PALGRAVE MACMILLAN is the global academic imprint of the Palgrave
Macmillan division of St. Martin's Press, LLC and of Palgrave Macmillan Ltd.
Macmillan® is a registered trademark in the United States, United Kingdom
and other countries. Palgrave is a registered trademark in the European
Union and other countries.

ISBN 0–333–79196–7

This book is printed on paper suitable for recycling and
made from fully managed and sustained forest sources.

A catalogue record for this book is available from
the British Library.

A catalog record for this book is available from
the Library of Congress.

Printed and bound in Great Britain by
Antony Rowe Ltd, Chippenham and Eastbourne

Contents

Foreword

We write as chief coordinators of the Anglo-Japanese History Project, a project for studying the history of the relationship of these two countries from 1600 to 2000. The project originated in the statement of 31 August 1994 by Mr Tomiichi Murayama, on behalf of the coalition cabinet which he led. In this he announced the setting up of the Peace, Friendship and Exchange Initiative which would begin in 1995, the fiftieth anniversary of the end of the Asia-Pacific war. One part of the Initiative consisted of support for historical research, and particularly support for researchers in order 'to enable everyone to face squarely the facts of history'. The relationship between Japan and Britain was deemed to be one of the areas which came within the Initiative.

In order to implement this policy decision, the Japanese government announced that it would 'support the compilation of a series of volumes forming a comprehensive history of the UK–Japanese Relationship (Nichi-Ei kankeishi)'. The project was to be conducted by researchers from both Japan and the United Kingdom and to be funded over five years by a subvention administered by the Japan Society, London. Project offices were opened in London and Tokyo. After preliminary discussions in London and Tokyo in 1995, it was agreed that the project would aim at conducting academic research and publishing volumes covering four central fields in Anglo-Japanese historical relations. Coordinators from the Japanese and British sides were appointed as follows:

The Political-Diplomatic Dimension (2 volumes)
(editors Yoichi Kibata and Ian Nish)
The Military Dimension (1 volume)
(editors Ian Gow, Yoichi Hirama and John Chapman)
The Economic-Business Dimension (1 volume)
(editors Shinya Sugiyama and Janet Hunter)
The Social-Cultural Dimension (1 volume)
(editors Chushichi Tsuzuki and Gordon Daniels)
These coordinators, in turn, selected experts in these fields and commissioned them to conduct research and write chapters.

The first fruits of this research were discussed by both sides at Workshops held at the Civil Service College, Sunningdale, UK in July 1996, Shonan Village Centre, Hayama, Japan (September 1997), and Stephenson Hall, Sheffield University (August 1998). On these occasions draft chapters were presented by the contributors; and the discussion which ensued led to the revision of manuscripts.

It is too early for us to make sweeping generalizations about Anglo-Japanese relations over four centuries since the majority of papers from the four sections have not yet come in. But discussion at the workshops has pointed out the positive aspects of the relationship between the two countries, which has been strong enough to survive setbacks and even disasters. Just as Britain's naval actions at Shimonoseki and Kagoshima in the 1860s were followed by the years of the Anglo-Japanese Alliance (1902–23), so the dark years culminating in the Asia-Pacific war have been followed by the broadly favourable development of bilateral relations over the last 50 years, strengthened by wider common interests and deeper and more extensive exchanges in every field of activity. We recognize that there are problems outstanding between the two countries and hope that this series will make some contribution to their solution by clarifying some of the issues and will help to promote better understanding.

We as chief coordinators would like to thank the contributors who have devoted much time and effort to the Project. Thanks are due to the Japan Society (and the Tokyo office of the Project) for arranging its financial and administrative aspects. Finally, we are grateful for the cooperation of the officials of the Japanese Embassy, London, and the Japanese Ministry of Foreign Affairs. They have made it clear from the start that they would not take any part in the publication programme itself. What appears in these volumes is the work of independent scholars.

In conclusion, we should say that the joint project, which has been administered by a Steering Committee in London, presided over by Sir Sydney Giffard, and an Advisory Committee in Japan, has since its inauguration in 1995 been conducted most harmoniously.

CHIHIRO HOSOYA and IAN NISH

Preface

The volume consists of essays from a Japanese perspective by a team of Japanese researchers and from a British perspective by an international team of scholars. The international team comprised British researchers and British-trained Canadian and American researchers with a long-standing interest in Anglo-Japanese relations and military affairs.

Drafts of papers were exchanged and papers fully discussed and debated. However, they were all written independently and the editors have made no attempt to eliminate points of disagreement. Due to the large numbers of papers and the space limitations there have been some editorial cuts to respond to the differing lengths of English and Japanese texts. However, in the very sensitive essays by Pritchard, Flower and Kita it was agreed that these should be presented without editorial alterations and thus be exactly the same in both languages. The Kita essay was allowed greater length than other essays since it had been agreed by both sides at the beginning of the project that the Japanese side ought to be allowed to provide an essay in our volume. This was to permit a response to the two essays by Flower on POWs in the diplomatic volume and in our own volume.

We are grateful to the Japanese contributors for undertaking the double burden of arranging for the translation of the British papers into Japanese and for providing corrections or full translations to their English texts. We are very grateful to all the translators. The Japanese language version of these papers has been published by Tokyo University Press.

We would like to express our special thanks to Tadashi Kuramatsu in the London office and Philip Charrier in the Sheffield office for providing excellent administrative support in addition to contributing essays to the volume. The editors are also grateful to the Tokyo office team for their guidance and support, notably Professor Takahiko Tanaka, Ms Eriko Jibiki and Ms Yoshie Takamitsu. Likewise we are grateful to the London team for their patience, guidance and support. We benefited greatly from the advice of Mr Lewis Radbourne, OBE, joint chairman of the Japan Society, Sir Sydney Gifford and the hard work of Mrs Anne Hemingway and the staff of the Japan Society, London. In bringing these volumes to final publication, the editors wish to thank (publisher side to be inserted later Japanese and British) for their patience, professionalism and cordial cooperation.

Editors' Note and Acknowledgement

In view of the long period covered by this volume, the spelling of place-names, etc. has been left to the discretion of the contributors.

In common with Western bibliographical practices, the names of Japanese chapter authors are given with the family name second. In the main body of text, the usual Japanese style is adopted, with family names first.

We acknowledge the use of Crown Copyright material in the Public Record Office, Kew. Our contributors wish to thank a large number of librarians and archivists etc. in Japan, the Netherlands, Australia and the United Kingdom.

In all endnotes where books are published in Japan, the place of publication is Tokyo, unless otherwise specified.

List of Contributors

Yoshio Aizawa, National Institute for Defence Studies, Japan

Michio Asakawa, Tokyo Science University, Japan

John W.M. Chapman, University of Glasgow, Scotland

Philip Charrier, University of Regina, Canada

Takeshi Chida, Hiroshima International University, Japan

John Ferris, University of Calgary, Canada

Sybilla Flower, researcher on Japanese POW issues

Ian T.M. Gow, University of Nottingham, England

Sumio Hatano, Tsukuba University, Japan

Yoichi Hirama, formerly National Defence Academy, Japan

Yasuaki Imaizumi, ex-Military Attaché to the United Kingdom

A. Hamish Ion, Royal Military College of Canada

Yoshito Kita, Nihon University, Japan

Tadashi Kuramatsu, Aoyama Gakuin University, Japan

R. John Pritchard, researcher on the International Military Tribunal for the Far East

Haruo Tohmatsu, Tamagawa University, Japan

List of Abbreviations

ADM	Admiralty
ALP	Admiralty Library, Portsmouth
AWM	Australian War Memorial, Canberra
BL	British Library, London
CAB	Cabinet Office
CID	Committee of Imperial Defence
CIGS	Chief of the Imperial General Staff
COIS	Chief of Intelligence Staff
COS	Chiefs of Staff
DDMI	Deputy Director of Military Intelligence, War Office
DMO	Directorate of Military Operations, War Office
DMOI	Directorate of Military Operations & Intelligence, War Office
DNDO	Department of National Defence, Ottawa
DNI	Directorate of Naval Intelligence
FAA	Fleet Air Arm
FECB	Far Eastern Combined Bureau
FEDO	Far East Direction-Finding Organisation
GC&CS	Government Code & Cipher School
GFM	German Foreign Ministry
GOC	General Officer Commanding
HF–DF	High Frequency Direction-Finding
IJA	Imperial Japanese Army
IJN	Imperial Japanese Navy
JIC	Joint Intelligence Committee
MID	Military Intelligence Department
NAA	National Archives of Australia, Canberra
NAS	National Archives of Scotland, Edinburgh
NAW	National Archives, Washington DC
NLA	National Library of Australia, Canberra
NLS	National Library of Scotland, Edinburgh
NMM	National Maritime Museum
POW	Prisoners of War
PRO	Public Record Office, Kew
PUS	Permanent Under-Secretary of State
RAF	Royal Air Force
RAFM	RAF Museum, Hendon
RN	Royal Navy
RNAS	Royal Naval Air Service
RSS	Radio Security Service
WO	War Office

Part I
From Pupils to Partners

1
Days of Seclusion

A. Hamish Ion

For nearly two hundred years following the closure of the English Factory at Hirado in 1623, lack of command of the sea in eastern waters and events in Europe prevented the resumption of Anglo-Japanese relations. In 1793 the British government instructed Viscount Macartney to open relations after completing his mission to China. The outbreak of war with France stopped him from doing so. The war with France also ended voyages of exploration in the northern Pacific that had then been edging close to Japan. James Cook passed along the western side of Japan but did not land. In 1791, the *Argonaut* touched the coast of Niigata and in 1795–97 the *Providence* visited Hokkaido but was warned off.

During the Napoleonic Wars, Britain was too busy protecting shipping from French forces in the Indian Ocean and South China Sea to concern itself with Japan. But this changed when the Netherlands came under Napoleonic control. In 1808, Fleetwood Pellew (1789–1861), captain of the frigate HMS *Phaeton*, was sent on detached duty from Rear-Admiral William Drury's squadron off Macao to Nagasaki to look for Dutch ships. Not finding them, the *Phaeton* quickly sailed back to Macao Roads.[1] The capture of Mauritius in 1812 and the blockade of France ensured British mastery of the eastern seas. Throughout the nineteenth century no European power could effectively challenge the Royal Navy in the Indian Ocean and beyond. Yet, as far as Japan was concerned, British naval dominance in eastern waters brought little change. In 1814 and again in 1815 Sir Stamford Raffles, the governor of British-occupied Java, tried and failed to open East India Company trade with Japan. Peace in 1815 brought retrenchment and a return to voyages of exploration as in the late eighteenth century. The fringes around metropolitan Japan were visited. In 1816, HMS *Alceste*, HMS *Lycra* and the East Indian Company ship *General Hewitt* were sent to China as escort for the Amherst Embassy. Leaving Lord Amherst at Peiho, the *Alceste* and the *Lycra* made a number of useful surveys off the Korean coast and visited the Ryukyu Islands where the *Alceste* underwent repairs.[2] In June 1818, the brig *Brothers* entered Tokyo Bay. It was some nine years later, in

June 1827, that HMS *Blossom* surveyed Port Lloyd in the Bonin Islands on its way back to the Bering Straits where they hoped to contact the Franklin expedition.[3] The visit of Beechey to the Bonin Islands sparked interest in Hawaii and an English-speaking colony was established there in 1830. Yet British naval visits to the Bonin Islands did not resume until 1851 when HMS *Enterprise* visited the islands. A year later the survey brig HMS *Serpent* also visited the islands. In 1853, it was the turn of the US Navy to come to the islands, as they did for the next two years. At Naha, the Loochoo Naval Mission was established in 1846 by the medical missionary, Bernard Jean Bettelheim, and British warships visited in the late 1840s. The mistreatment of Bettelheim by the Naha authorities attracted the attention of Lord Palmerston and resulted in the visits of the *Pilot* in late 1849, *Reynard* in October 1850, and *Sphinx* in early 1852.[4] Bettelheim encountered difficulties but did manage to stay. Efforts to land in metropolitan Japan failed, as in the so-called Morrison Incident of 1837. In 1845, HMS *Samarang* entered Nagasaki harbour in order to take on provisions and received a welcome that was not unfriendly. It was not until 1853 that Perry managed to open up Japan to westerners. Following Perry, Rear-Admiral Sir James Stirling, without waiting for instructions from London, began negotiating the first British convention with the Japanese at Nagasaki in 1854.[5]

Stirling's actions were an exception to the rule and in opening Japan the Royal Navy's influence lay in 'policy execution rather than formulation'.[6] Britain's greater maritime power ensured she would benefit most from any treaty with Japan. Since the Crimean War was taking place, Stirling's major concern in 1854 was the Russian threat to Britain's position in China. He entered negotiations with the Japanese to forestall Russian use of Japanese ports and resources.[7] The Russians actually had little desire to challenge the Royal Navy in eastern seas during the Crimean War. However, the inactivity of Admiral Stirling in regard to taking the war to the Russians in Kamchatka was scathingly criticized by Edmund Fremantle, then serving as a midshipman aboard HMS *Spartan* on the East Indies and China Station.[8] In 1855, a British squadron under Commodore C.B.J. Elliot cruised in the Sea of Okhotsk and the Gulf of Tartary during which time *Spartan* and the British warships visited Hakodate.[9] September and October 1855 found the British ships further south as Admiral Stirling collected a sizeable force at Nagasaki to ratify the Convention signed the year before.[10] The Royal Navy force was joined by three French warships. Fremantle concluded that this was a force to overawe the Japanese, but that it could have been used to clear the Siberian coasts and capture everything Russian afloat.[11] The opening of the ports to British trade helped ensure that Japan's northern territories and islands did not fall into Russian hands. The Royal Navy perceived a real Russian threat from the north and they needed to prevent Russia, which was already in possession of northern Saghalien, from taking over southern Saghalien, Tsushima Island and Hokkaido. Visits to the Gulf of Tartary provided intelligence of Russian activities and served to maintain the territorial integrity of Japan. The surveys of the Japanese west coast that were undertaken by the Royal Navy in 1855, 1859 and 1860 were to keep watch on the Russians who were also conducting hydrographic surveys in the area. Such concerns were not evident when Lord Elgin arrived in Nagasaki and Edo in late summer 1858 to negotiate the British treaty with the Shogunate. The paddle steam frigate HMS *Retribution*, the gunboat HMS *Lee* and the steam yacht *Emperor* (Queen Victoria's gift to the Emperor) accompanied Elgin in HMS *Furious*. The strength of Elgin's flotilla was less than that of Stirling's three years before, but they were courteously received at Nagasaki and also at Edo. Visiting Nagasaki in HMS *Tribune*, F.M. Norman noted that 'these people were in reality highly civilised'.[12] These first contacts engendered respect for the Japanese among some British naval officers.[13]

The 1858 Treaty with Japan brought added responsibilities to the Royal Navy. They came at a time when the Royal Navy in East Indies and China waters still had ongoing problems stemming from the treaty to end the Second Anglo-Chinese War. Resolving this, there were now tensions on the China coast and interior from the Taiping Rebellion. Calls for Royal Navy assistance from the British Minister in Japan to protect diplomatic and consular personnel and provide transport to their posts or on fact-finding tours to Hokkaido stretched an already hard-pressed Royal Navy. In 1863, there were some 47 Royal Navy ships in China waters but only one, the flagship HMS *Euryalus*, was a steam frigate with 35 guns and only three others, *Encounter*, *Pearl* and *Scout*, were steam or screw corvettes of any significant naval power. The majority were relatively lightly armed gunboats. The lack of large and powerful warships made any attack on a fortified land position an even more risky undertaking. The China Squadron, although not a powerful force, was nevertheless until the turn of the century the strongest single naval force in East Asian waters. Fortuitously, problems on the China coast and in Japan in the early 1860s occurred at times that allowed the transfer of naval assets from one place to the other. This could be done with relative alacrity due to steam power and to the daring of admirals risking movement of forces, despite ongoing tensions, from the China coast to Japan or elsewhere.

The Royal Navy's problems were compounded by the fact that Sir James Hope as C-in-C East Indies and China (in 1865 the two areas were separated) commanded an enormous station extending from the Red Sea to the Bering Sea (the Australian area was made a separate command in 1859). Japan was an added responsibility. After 1865, the new China and Japan Station still extended to include Singapore and the Straits of Malacca. By this time, the naval station, however, consisted of four divisions: the Straits of Malacca at Singapore; South China; North China at Shanghai, and Japan under the Senior Officer at Yokohama.[14] Security of the Minister and his staff and the British communities at Japan's treaty ports was a constant concern in the first years after 1858. By 1861, the frequent assassination of Europeans in Japan led Rutherford Alcock, the British Minister in Japan, to feel that there were

> but one or two alternatives open to the Western Powers, either to withdraw their diplomatic agents, and cease all intercourse with the Japanese; or to maintain them in security by calling the Japanese rulers to account, and making them responsible for the lawless acts of their subjects.[15]

Rear-Admiral Hope downplayed these incidents and lacked sympathy for fellow Britons in Japan, but did bow to pressure to provide the Minister with a permanent British guard.[16] Hope clearly wanted to avoid armed conflict with the Japanese despite continuing attacks on individual westerners or even British Legation staff. It was Alcock and after him Lt. Colonel Neale who pressed for military action. Given the attitude of the Foreign Office, the Royal Navy now had to consider military operations against Japan. The question for Hope and his successor, Rear-Admiral Sir Augustus Leopold Küper, was how best to respond to the repeated attacks on British diplomats and merchants. Because of his more recent experiences in China and Japan, Hope, who was better able to judge the possible outcome of such a military operation against Japan than Küper, drew up the plans. The key to a successful blockade was to stop the rice supply entering Edo by gaining control of the Hakone Pass and blocking sea routes into and out of the Inland Sea. This was difficult but not impossible and the best means of coercion since most rice supplies to Edo were seaborne. As far as attacking the forts guarding Edo itself was concerned, it was thought that this would take all the gunboats on the China Station and as many heavy ships as were available. Because the murder of C. Lennox Richardson had already taken place when Hope put his ideas on paper about attacking the forts guarding Edo, he also raised the possibility that the gunboats could attack Satsuma, the domain responsible for the attack on Richardson.[17] Since the Edo forts were difficult to take, an attack on Satsuma was certainly militarily preferable. There was very considerable support on the China coast for an Anglo-Japanese War. In May 1863, *The North China Herald* in Shanghai saw it as retribution on the rulers, a war of liberation of the Japanese from feudalism and a war of diplomacy to ensure treaty rights.[18] Admiral Küper, concerned about the safety of the British communities in Yokohama and Nagasaki, wished to avoid a war which would destroy commerce. He also doubted whether the *daimyo* would be able to pay reparations after defeat. He warned that if he had to undertake coercive measures against the Japanese, 'it would lead to a protracted war, and . . . an expedition both Naval and Military on a much larger scale than any yet sent to China'.[19] Major-General W.G. Brown, commanding British ground forces in China, was also reluctant to use force against the Japanese and unwilling without direct orders from London to send troops to protect the Japanese treaty ports.[20] But the Foreign Secretary in London insisted that force should be used if demands for reparations were not met. In late December 1862, Earl Russell suggested that the *daimyo* of Satsuma be brought to account by blockading Kagoshima, by shelling his residence, if possible, and by seizing steamships purchased in Europe.[21] Within weeks, Küper was given permission to seize, detain and bring Japanese ships to port should reparations and satisfaction not be given by the Japanese. Despite the authority to use force, Küper remained cautious even as Anglo-Japanese relations worsened.[22] Küper was informed that large numbers of Japanese troops had been seen on the *Tokkaido* and earthworks were being thrown up close to Yokohama. In May, he found out that a new battery had been built on the shore at Nagasaki immediately opposite the British Consulate. Faced with an increasingly hostile situation, Küper felt that he could not guarantee the safety of foreign residents and advocated their evacuation from the treaty ports in the event of an outbreak of hostilities. He believed that both Nagasaki and Yokohama, surrounded by commanding heights, would have to be defended by a large military force. Similarly, the Admiral doubted the success of any attack that he could make with his very limited force. Küper noted that

> the principal cities and seats of Government are quite inaccessible to a naval force from the shallow waters surrounding them, and I should not have a sufficient force to oppose, on shore, the hundreds of thousands of armed and resolute men which it is in the power of Japan to produce at any point.[23]

Given his considerable reservations, Küper had no intention of bombarding Kagoshima when he arrived there in September 1863. Küper saw his task as that of supporting the diplomatic efforts of Lt. Colonel Neale, the acting Minister, in obtaining payment of the indemnity of £25 000 owed by the *daimyo* of Satsuma for the murder of Richardson. The action was precipitated by the Kagoshima batteries firing on anchored British warships following the British boarding of three Satsuma merchant ships to ensure payment of the indemnity.[24] This was completely unexpected by the British. There was clearly a lot of resentment toward Küper in the British ships about the way that the action had been allowed to end. Ernest Satow, a student interpreter at the British Legation who witnessed the action, noted their discontent, remarking that nearly everyone wanted to go in again and the demands would have been obtained and that it would now 'take a great deal more trouble and cost more lives'.[25] However, Ballard in his study of Japanese sea power was much more sympathetic to Küper's position, regarding his action a success.[26] In London, Küper's handling of the situation at Kagoshima was not generally approved of. He was later blamed in the

Commons for causing Kagoshima to burn, but this was part of an Opposition attack on government policy in general towards Japan.[27] He was also criticized because 'insufficient strategy was employed in the attack on the batteries'.[28] The question of using force against the Japanese did not disappear and the murder of Lt. Camus of the 3rd *Chasseurs d'Afrique* on 15 October 1863 outside Yokohama showed that the murdering ways of Japanese *samurai* had not stopped.[29] The possibility of more hostilities between Britain and Japan could not be overlooked. Major-General Sir John Michel and Hope were asked by the Admiralty to give their opinions as to the measures to be taken in the case of war. Michel believed the terrain of Japan to be essentially unfavourable to civilized military warfare, comparing it to Switzerland and 'extremely favourable to guerilla warfare'.[30] He did not think that it would difficult to capture either Edo or Osaka but considered that the taking of what he called Miaco [Kyoto] would be costly. Michel believed that 'the principal difficulties of a War in Japan would be the Commissariat and transport'.[31] Any British army operating in Japan would have to go to Bombay for mules, but could obtain the rest of its transport in China. Hope, more precise in his suggestions, was much concerned with the naval considerations of supporting a force of 12 000 infantry, 500 cavalry with artillery and 2000 coolies, a force all told of 15 175 with 1000 horses (500 for the cavalry and 500 transport). He estimated that the monthly cost of sustaining such a force would be £102 650 (using the data from the Chinese expedition), making war with Japan a very expensive business. In his reply to Michel and Hope, Küper also felt that virtually all supplies for an invading army would have to come from China or India. Küper, however, believed that Michel and Hope had underestimated the difficulties involved in capturing Edo, where the shallowness of the Bay prevented larger ships coming close to the shore and the Edo Fort moat prevented a boat approach.[32] Fortunately, however, it was not Edo but the simpler task of destroying the Choshu batteries on the Shimonoseki Straits that fell to Küper. Originally, he had planned in September 1863 to proceed to the Shimonoseki Straits from Kagoshima. Worried over the possible consequences of the bombardment of Kagoshima for the security of Yokohama, he changed his mind and decided to return immediately to the treaty port. It was not until August 1864 that Küper's multinational force was able to attack the Choshu positions along the Straits. Militarily more satisfactory than the earlier bombardment of Kagoshima, it was quite similar to actions against pirate lairs on the China coast.[33] It consisted of a naval bombardment followed by a landing to storm and destroy the enemy's batteries.[34] The victory assured the security of the foreign community in Yokohama, now garrisoned by British and French troops. Happily, the action against the Choshu batteries marked the end of major incidents between British and Japanese forces until the Second World War. Yet all was not conflict during this period. In January 1862, HMS *Odin* was tasked with transporting the

Japanese Embassy to Europe from Yokohama to Suez. The Japanese made a favourable impression on *Odin's* commanding officer and this provided the Royal Navy with a pleasant interlude during which relations with the Japanese were good.[35] Anglo-Japanese military relations during the late nineteenth century benefited from British naval aid in the building of Japan's navy, beginning with the Tracey Mission in 1867,[36] followed after the Meiji Restoration by the Douglas Mission[37] and a gaggle of later naval helpers and advisers, among whom Captain John Ingles stands out.[38] Indeed, British naval advisers to the Imperial Japanese Navy were only a small part of the contact between the British military and Japanese. As some of them like Tracey, Douglas and especially Arthur Wilson rose to high rank and held positions of influence, there is a temptation to exaggerate their influence on the development of Meiji Japan during their often brief stays.[39] Beyond advisers, there was considerable and constant contact between the British armed forces and the Japanese during the late nineteenth century. There were royal visits to Japan including that of the sailor son of Queen Victoria, the Duke of Edinburgh, in 1869 and later the grandsons of the Queen, the Dukes of Clarence and York (later King George V). Both trips were important in establishing Japanese court protocol for receiving foreign royal personages, as well as bringing the respective navies together. A British force remained at Yokohama to ensure Japanese good behaviour from 1862 until 1875.[40] A Royal Navy sick quarters continued to exist beyond the end of the century and coal and supply depots there and at Nagasaki catered to British warships that were constantly visiting Japanese ports. Much effort was expended to ensure an adequate supply of coal for British warships coming to Japan. Larger Royal Navy ships made use of the Japanese repair facilities at Yokosuka and Nagasaki. It became policy to rotate China Squadron ships so that crews could spend at least some part of their tour in Japanese waters away from the heat and tropical diseases of the more southerly areas of the Station.

The British Army was less concerned with Japan than the Navy. The British garrison in Yokohama played a significant role in the sporting and social life of the treaty settlement during the 1860s and 1870s. In an interview with Lt. Col. Fleetwood Richards and other officers of the Royal Marine battalion just prior to the final withdrawal of that unit from Japan, the Meiji Emperor remarked upon the cordial relations which had always existed between his officers and those of the battalion, and upon the benefit which the former had derived from their intercourse with the latter.[41] In fact, even though individual officers and men did have contact with the Japanese military, the British garrison in Yokohama was an opportunity missed to influence the development of the Meiji Army. In the early 1880s, one starts to find the first appreciations of the Japanese Army and Navy in professional military journals.[42]

From 1885, Major-General Palmer RE served in Japan and he remained there after his retirement from the British Army in 1887 until his death.

Palmer was responsible for the first major waterworks and other important engineering projects in Yokohama and was able to provide information about the Japanese Army. On a short leave to Japan in 1893, Captain G.J. Younghusband summed up the British military opinion of the Japanese Army when he described the soldiers in the Imperial Guard as being similar to the Gurkhas.[43] The Sino-Japanese War in 1894 saw British military observers sent to both sides. Among those who were with the Japanese Army was Captain N.W.H. Du Boulay of the Royal Artillery who was impressed by the Japanese.[44] Lt. Col. E.G. Barrow was another Army officer much impressed by the efficiency of the Japanese Army and prior to the war he stated that Japanese troops were superior to those of the Chinese. Reassuringly, however, he noted in 1895 that he ranked them alongside Indian Army sepoys and in fact viewed British Indian regimental officers as superior to the Japanese.[45] Like many other wars, the Sino-Japanese War supported and influenced views of different military thinkers in Britain and Vice-Admiral Colomb pointed out 'if it comes to a conclusion it will still be found shaping our naval and military policy till another war furnishes another set of experiments'.[46] The naval action of the Yalu caused Admiral of the Fleet Geoffrey Hornby to conclude merely that 'it is the best man that wins',[47] but a more sanguine commentator remarked 'Japan now stands before the world as a naval and military power of the second rank',[48] and that an alliance with them could turn the balance in a western struggle.

The growing strength of Japan after 1895 continued to attract attention. By the end of the Boxer Uprising, good relations had been established between the British and Japanese militaries. Nevertheless, for all the fortuitous results of Anglo-Japanese naval and military contact in terms of the transfer of ideas and technology or personal goodwill, the British presence in Japanese and East Asian waters was intended primarily to serve and to protect British interests. Despite its limited resources at their disposal, the China Squadron was able to achieve command of the eastern seas, ensuring that Britain still commanded them at the end of the century.

Notes

1. See W.G. Aston, 'H.M.S. "Phaeton" at Nagasaki in 1808', *Transactions of the Asiatic Society of Japan* [hereafter *TASJ*], vol. 7 (1878–79), pp. 323–36 and Public Record Office [hereafter PRO] Admiralty [ADM] 51/1952, Folder 6 HMS *Phaeton*, Captain's Log and ADM 1/181 25 June 1809, enclosure on Nagasaki.
2. For the voyage see John McLeod, *Voyage of H.M.S. Alceste to China, Corea, and the Island of Lewchew with an Account of her Shipwreck* (London: John Murray, 1819).
3. See Russell Robertson, 'The Bonin Islands', *TASJ*, vol. 4 (1875–76), pp. 111–42 and 113–18.
4. PRO: ADM 125/134, Loochoo Islands 1849–1852.

5. Grace Fox, *British Admirals and Chinese Pirates 1832–1869* (London: Kegan Paul, Trench, Trubner, 1940), p. 71.
6. W.G. Beasley, *Great Britain and the Opening of Japan 1834–1858* (London: Luzac, 1951), p. 200.
7. Grace Fox, *Britain and Japan 1858–1883* (Oxford: Clarendon Press, 1969), p. 11.
8. Edmund Fremantle, *The Navy as I Have Known It 1849–1899* (London: Cassell, 1904), p. 89.
9. Ibid., p. 106.
10. Beasley, *Great Britain and the Opening of Japan*, pp. 136–7.
11. Fremantle, *The Navy as I Have Known It*, p. 107.
12. 'A Cruise in Japanese Waters', *Blackwood's Edinburgh Magazine*, vol. LXXXIV, no. DXVIII (December 1858), pp. 635–46, especially 641.
13. Francis Martin Norman, 'Martello Tower', in *China and the Pacific in H.M.S. 'Tribune' 1856–60* (London: George Allen, 1902), p. 236.
14. Fox, *British Admirals and Chinese Pirates*, pp. 62–71.
15. PRO: ADM 125/116: Alcock to Hope, 8 July 1861.
16. Ibid., Commander in Chief: Report on the State of our Relations with Japan.
17. See PRO: ADM 1/5790, Part 2. Hope to Paget, 18 October 1862.
18. *The North China Herald*, 23 May 1863.
19. PRO: ADM1/5824, Küper to Admiralty, 28 April 1863.
20. PRO: ADM 125/117, Brown to Neale, 12 May 1863.
21. Ibid., Russell to Neale, 24 December 1862.
22. Ibid., Romaine to Küper, 10 January 1863.
23. PRO: ADM 1/5824: Küper to Admiralty, 28 April 1863.
24. Admiral Sir Charles Dundas of Dundas KCMG, *An Admiral's Yarns: Stray Memories of 50 Years* (London: Herbert Jenkins, 1922), p. 35.
25. PRO 30/33/15/1, Satow Diaries, 13 September 1863.
26. G.A. Ballard, *The Influence of the Sea on the Political History of Japan* (London: John Murray, 1921), pp. 100–1.
27. Ballard, *The Influence of the Sea*; Clowes, vol. 7, p. 200 and Grace Fox, *Britain and Japan, 1858–1883*, pp. 116–19; see also *The Japan Herald*, 16 April 1864.
28. Dundas, *An Admiral's Yarns*, p. 35.
29. *The Japan Herald*, 17 October 1863.
30. PRO: ADM 125/118: Paget to Küper, 3 February 1864 and memoranda of Michel and Hope.
31. Ibid.
32. Ibid., Küper to Admiralty, 13 June 1864.
33. PRO: ADM1/5876: Alcock to Küper, 16 August 1864, enclosure 18 August Memorandum.
34. Two Admirals Admiral of the Fleet Sir Fairfax Moresby, G.C.B., K.T., D.C.L. (1786–1877) and His Son, John Moresby, *A Record of Life and Service in the British Navy for a Hundred Years* (London: John Murray, 1909), pp. 234–49.
35. See PRO: ADM 125/116: Hay to Hope, 21 January 1862.
36. For a description of the Tracey Mission, see Sir Edward E. Bradford, *Life of Admiral of the Fleet Sir Arthur Knyvet Wilson Bart., V.C. G.C.B., O.M., G.C.V.O.* (London: John Murray, 1923), pp. 22–7.
37. For the Douglas Mission, see John Curtis Perry, *Japan as a Naval Power*, pp. 381ff. See also Archibald C. Douglas, 'The Genesis of Japan's Navy', *Transactions and Proceedings, The Japan Society, London*, XXXVI (1938–39), pp. 19–28.
38. See Fox, *Britain and Japan 1858–1883*, pp. 263–8.
39. For a brief account of Ingles' influence on the Imperial Japanese Navy, see David

C. Evans and Mark R. Peattie, *Kaigun: Strategy, Tactics, and Technology in the Imperial Japanese Navy, 1887–1941* (Annapolis, MD: Naval Institute Press, 1997), pp. 12–13, 36 and 48–9.

40. PRO: ADM 201/45, Part 2: Sir Harry Parkes to Colonel Fleetwood Richards, 27 February 1875. For British and French garrisons in Yokohama, see Yokohama Kaiko Shiryo Kan, *Shiryo de tadoru Meiji Ishin Ki no Yokohama Eibu Chyton Gun* (Yokohama: Yokohama Kaiko Shiryo Fukyu Kyokai, 1993).

41. *The Japan Weekly Mail*, 27 February 1875.

42. See, for instance, 'The Army and Navy of Japan', *Royal Engineers Journal*, vol. 3 (1 January 1883) p. 12; 'Japan as a Fighting Power', *Royal Engineers Journal*, vol. 15 (1 May 1885), pp. 115–16.

43. Captain G.J. Younghusband, *On Short Leave to Japan* (London: Sampson Low, Marston, 1894), p. 214.

44. See Captain N.W.H. Du Boulay, 'The Chino-Japanese War', *Royal Artillery Journal*, vol. 22 (1896), pp. 377–98.

45. Lt. Colonel E.G. Barrow, 'Military Japan After the War', *The United Service Magazine*, vol. 12 (1895–96), no. 803 (October 1895), pp. 13–20 and 16–17.

46. P.H. Colomb, 'The Functions of Armies and Navies: a Demurrer to Colonel Maurice's Pleadings', *United Service Magazine*, New Series vol. 10 (1894–95), pp. 220–226, especially p. 222.

47. Admiral of the Fleet, Sir G. Phipps Hornby, 'The Yalu Action', *The United Service Magazine*, vol. 10 (1894–95), pp. 137–41, especially p. 141.

48. H.W. Wilson, 'England and the New Japan', *The United Service Magazine*, vol. 11 (1895), pp. 109–22, especially p. 113 and Captain R.J.B. Mair, 'The Growing Strength of Japan', *Royal Engineers Journal*, vol. 29 (March 1899), pp. 55–6.

2
Anglo-Japanese Military Relations, 1800–1900

Michio Asakawa

British military activities during the Bakumatsu period

Japanese isolationist policy, firmly maintained under the Tokugawa Shogunate for over two hundred years, ended with Commodore Matthew Perry's visit and the conclusion, on 31 March 1854, of the Treaty of Kanagawa (the Japan–US Friendship Treaty). Six months later, on 14 October, Japan and Britain signed a similar friendship treaty which established diplomatic relations between the two countries.

After 1750, the Western Powers had tried to open Japan for the sake of their commercial interests. Following the friendship treaties of 1854, five Western Powers – the United States, Britain, Russia, the Netherlands, and France – now pressed Japan to sign commercial treaties. Unfortunately, by exercising the 'mode of appealing to the feelings most likely to influence a Japanese – national pride and fears of aggression',[1] their plans ironically backfired and excited a spirit of xenophobic nationalism in Japan.

This ideological trend in Japan crystallized into the *Sonno-Joi* movement, which criticized the Shogunate's conservative policies and sparked a series of attachs on western residents in Japan, during which westerners suffered more than twenty cases of violence, including murders.[2] Raids on Britain's temporary legation and the Imperial-ordered shelling of western ships further complicated Japan's diplomatic relations. In retaliation against *Joi* terrorism, Britain undertook military action against Japan to extract from the Shogunate a reliable guarantee of its treaty obligations and protection of westerners.[3]

The *Tozen-Ji* Affair and British blockade plans

London appointed Sir Rutherford Alcock as British Consul-General and diplomatic representative to Japan. After arriving in Edo (present-day Tokyo), Alcock opened a temporary legation at the *Tozen-Ji* Temple in Takanawa on 26 June 1859. On 5 July 1861 14 stipendless *samurai* from the Mito domain attacked the temple, injuring two British citizens, a secretary and a consul resident in Nagasaki. On 26 June 1862, a retainer from the Matsumoto domain who was one the guards at the *Tozen-Ji* Temple tried but failed to assassinate E. John Neale, the British minister extraordinary. The assassin killed himself after slaughtering two British soldiers. These two raids on their temporary legation hardened British attitudes towards the Shogunate. Neale ordered Sir James Hope, the commander of the East Indies Fleet, to plan an armed blockade against Japan. Referring to the necessity of forcibly extracting reparations from the Japanese government, Neale told the admiral to lead a squadron sufficient to blockade Edo, Nagasaki, and the Inner Sea to Edo, and to demand terms under an ultimatum. If the Shogunal government refused these terms, the admiral was to go to Osaka and negotiate directly with the Imperial Court. If those negotiations failed, Hope's vessels were to blockade all ports on the southern coast of Japan and to continue that blockade until ordered by London to discontinue it. He was to inform the government of the consequences should it refuse London's terms. If the blockade proved ineffective, Neale's orders included the possibility of destroying, as expedient, the batteries in front of Edo and along other parts of Japan's coasts.[4] Hope ordered Admiral Augustus L. Küper to investigate the possibilities of such a blockade, and he sent a concrete blockade plan to the vice-minister of the Navy on 18 October 1862. Britain's 'gunboat policy',[5] supported by seizing command of the seas around Japan, became increasingly effective in forcibly resolving its diplomatic complications with Japan.

The Namamugi Affair and the Anglo-Satsuma War at Kagoshima

A party of Lord Hisamitsu Shimazu of the Satsuma domain killed three Englishmen in Namamugi near Kanagawa-shuku on 14 September 1862. Britain vigorously protested about this ruthless, daytime assault on its unarmed citizens exercising their treaty rights on a public road.[6] The British government demanded an apology and a £100000 indemnity from the Shogunate, plus punishment of the killers and a £25000 compensation from the Satsuma domain. To impose a prompt solution with Dutch and French help, Britain put on a military demonstration by gathering their men-of-war in the Bay of Edo.[7]

After the Shogunal government accepted British demands on 6 August 1863, Britain sent seven men-of-war to Kagoshima, the capital of the Satsuma domain, for direct negotiations. Satsuma meanwhile expected British retaliation after the Namamugi Affair and had strengthened its defences by positioning 85 diverse cannon in ten of its batteries.[8] The gun battle between the British squadron and the Satsuma forces lasted from 15 to 16 August 1863. The British weapons, including 24 Armstrong, breech-loading, rifled guns[9] out of 89 on seven ships,[10] were far superior to Satsuma's. The narrow Bay of Kagoshima, however, limited the effectiveness of the British cannon, which were more suitable to long-range action. The close-ranged exchange as well as bad weather lent an advantage to Satsuma. The British squadron suffered 63 casualties, including 13 fatalities. Satsuma also endured considerable damage. The British bombardment destroyed Satsuma's batteries and the *Shuseikan* [armoury]; a part of the castle town burned; and there were 19 casualties, including five killed. From their temporary retreat in Yokohama, on 17 August the British threatened to return with their fleet. So menaced, Satsuma opened direct negotiations and accepted peace with Britain.

Bombardment of foreign ships and the Anglo-Choshu War at Shimonoseki

The *Sonno-joi* movement in Kyoto sought sufficient political legitimacy to impeach the Shogunate's diplomatic policies by appealing to the Imperial Court whose sentiments inclined to rejecting the opening up of Japan. In December 1862, the Imperial Court sent a messenger to Edo to press the Shogunate to carry out *Joi* and expel the 'barbarians'. Shogun Iemochi during his visit to Kyoto in the following year set the date for *Joi* action as 25 June 1863.

With the deadline for the *Joi* execution, the Choshu domain began to bombard western ships. Choshu attacked ships of the United States, France, and the Netherlands, which were sailing through the Strait of Shimonoseki. In retaliation, the United States first sent its men-of-war to the Strait. On 16 July 1863, Americans attacked Choshu's warships, sinking two and destroying one. France followed suit and dispatched two of its men-of-war. On 20 July, they bombarded the Maeda battery and landed 250 soldiers to disable it.

The Tottori domain also carried out the *Joi* order by attacking British ships at Tenpozan in Osaka on 29 July. The Tottori's *Joi* action, however, was limited to 'firing five cannon balls. They did not reach the British ships. The British left without retaliation'.[11] Fortunately, Britain exercised restraint over this incident. This was a magnanimous action given that, pressured by the Imperial Court on 24 June 1863, the Shogunate had announced the closure of Japanese ports to western ships. The Imperial Court further commended the domains for their *Joi* activities and ordered more. Thus, despite damage from American and French men-of-war, Choshu maintained its xenophobic policy and continued to blockade the Strait of Shimonoseki. This considerably irritated the Great Powers and triggered talks among the ministers of Britain, the United States, France, and the Netherlands. On 22 July 1863, they jointly agreed to impose armed sanctions against the Choshu domain, at least partly to discourage xenophobic attitudes in Japan. For over a year, the four countries held off imposing armed sanctions against Choshu. But on 22 July 1864, they formulated a concrete plan to attack Shimonoseki, and on 28–9 August, an allied fleet gathered off Himeshima in the Bungo domain. Admiral Küper of the Royal Navy led the combined fleet of nine British, one American, three French, and four Dutch ships, 17 vessels in all.[12]

Recalling the British experience in fighting at short-range against Satsuma, the Allied Powers planned Choshu's defeat – and the destruction of *Joi* activities – by making full use of their superior firepower, out-range tactics, and marine forces to conquer Choshu's batteries.[13] Choshu, meanwhile, strengthened its defences by placing seventy cannon in ten of its batteries and by garrisoning them with about 2000 soldiers.[14] However, Choshu's military, saddled with older weapons and insufficient facilities including its batteries, proved no match in its fight against the superior Allied fleet. The four-power Allied fleet directly attacked Choshu from 5 to 8 September 1864. Naval shelling and a marine landing put Choshu's batteries out of action. The Choshu domain suffered 14 deaths and over forty wounded.[15] When the Allied powers had seized more than sixty guns to deprive the domain of its ability to continue the fight, Choshu accepted peace on 14 September.

Choshu's loss of the Bakan War proved afresh the limitations of the militant *Joi* movement. The Allied powers used their victory to force the Shogunate to reconsider its decision to close Japan's ports as well as to obtain Imperial approval for the pending commercial treaties. On 4 November 1865, ministers from Britain, the USA, France and the Netherlands brought nine men-of-war – five British, three French, and one Dutch – to Hyogo. Thus backed, they presented their terms and forced Japan to accept their diplomatic demands, including those regarding the commercial treaty. The Great Powers believed that the armed conflict against the western countries and the domestic strife in Japan derived from the attitude of the Imperial Court, which had refused to approve the treaties signed by the Shogunate. The Western Powers had resorted to force, at least in part, to put military pressure directly on Emperor Komei who stood at the head of the *Joi* movement.[16]

In response, the Court issued an instruction on 22 November 1865, 'to take appropriate measures concerning the treaties while the Court is in the ratification process'.[17] Eight years after their conclusion, Japan's commercial treaties with the Western Powers finally received Imperial ratification. The *Sonno-Joi* movement, which had been impeaching the Shogunate for signing such treaties without Court approval, thereafter lost its legitimizing cause and quickly declined.

Britain and the military reforms under the Shogunate

The *Sonno-Joi* activities – including the murders of western residents and the attacks on western ships under the patronage of the Imperial authority – had seriously debased the Shogunate's diplomatic credit. After the conclusion of the commercial treaties, the Shogunate had to permit the stationing of British and French troops in Yokohama under the pretext of protecting western residents. Meanwhile, in order to build up its military strength against anti-Shogunate *Sonno-Joi* activities, the Shogunate launched its own military reforms. The Shogunate's *Bunkyu* Military Reform originally attempted to reorganize the existing military system into a modern military force by following translated Dutch manuals. Such methods, however, soon proved inadequate and drove the Shogunate to seek direct guidance from western military advisers. The Shogunate's military reforms during the Keio period (1865–68) proceeded under the direction of western advisors: French for the Army and British for the Navy.

Garrison forces in Yokohama

Britain began stationing its armed forces in Japan in 1861 immediately after the opening up of Japan's ports. These troops only guarded the British legation, and were consequently few in number. The full-scale stationing of British and French forces began in 1863 after the delegates of those countries on 25 May had gained the Shogunate's permission, which read: 'the foreign representatives, that is, those of Britain and France, should take measures to defend Yokohama from attack by the anti-foreign party'.[18] Earlier, the Shogunate had handed a letter to Britain which read, 'We understand your need to protect your residents in Japan and their properties.'[19] The Shogunal government at this point believed that the garrisoning of western military forces in Japan only be a temporary measure.

Disregarding the Shogunate's hopes for their garrisons, Britain and France 'demanded expansion of various facilities and enlargement of areas, and subsequently constructed almost permanent military camps'.[20] The Japanese called for the complete withdrawal of these foreign troops throughout the Restoration period and their removal remained a major diplomatic task for the Meiji government. The British forces in Yokohama consisted mainly of army units transferred from Hong Kong, Shanghai, and South Africa, plus some from the Royal Marines.[21] In 1864 the forces garrisoned in Japan reached their peak in strength, numbering more than 3000 British and French troops. The *Joi* movement was then at its most radical. Throughout the late Tokugawa and early Meiji periods, approximately 1000 men, about 800 of whom were from Britain, were permanently stationed in Yokohama. Those numbers started to decrease after 1872 and the last were withdrawn in 1875.[22]

The approach to military instruction in the Army

Although the British and French troops in Yokohama were objected to by the Shogunate, in the end the British garrison pioneered the model for modernizing the Shogunate's Army and its military reforms. During the *Bunkyu* reforms, for the first time the Shogunate organized its army with infantry, cavalry, and artillery. The reality, however, left much to be desired and was criticized as a 'paper army'[23] built 'by completely imitating translated manuals and being sufficient only to keep up appearances'.[24]

In October 1864, the Shogunal Army, just as its Navy as discussed below, began talking about the possibility of sending students to the Netherlands to obtain advanced, western military skills. Within the Shogun's administration, the Elders aborted this plan based upon the opinion of the Foreign Magistrate. As an alternative, he ordered that the Army 'get an understanding to have the British Army stationed in Yokohama train the Shogunate's Army'.[25] Sixty Japanese soldiers, including twenty officers and forty enlisted men under the control of the Kanagawa Magistrate, first received British training in Yokohama. Hayashi Hyakuro, an officer and artillery instructor, led the Japanese soldiers.[26] The Second Battalion of the 20th Foot Regiment transferred from Hong Kong, and undertook the training of the Japanese soldiers. In November 1864, the Kanagawa Magistrate paid Lieutenant-Colonel H. R. Browne, commanding officer of the Second Battalion, 'to reward their efforts at instructing rifle drill to our soldiers'.[27] On 30 November 1864, Shogunal councilors officially asked the British minister if his men would offer military instruction to Japan's soldiers. The British agreed on 23 December.[28] Thus the Shogunate's Army under Kubota Sentaro, chief of the officers in the Kanagawa Magistracy, began to receive full-scale training from the British garrisoned in Yokohama. British instruction emphasized drills based on the text, *British Infantry Tactics* (1862 edn) which prepared soldiers for muzzle-loading rifle tactics.[29] Around November 1865, the Shogunate organized 'one infantry battalion, one artillery platoon, and a music band modeled on British organization', dressed in British 'scarlet woolen clothing'. They were assigned to guard southern Nishinomaru in Edo under a system of monthly shifts.[30]

Against the wishes of the Shogunate, the British did not train officers at this time. Even an English teacher, who was visiting the British garrison to answer questions regarding military study, criticized this situation: 'Suddenly the training has been limited to handling of rifles and bayonets, and has made little progress.'[31] The Shogunate, which had prepared for officer education by opening an English-language training centre, was disappointed. England was reluctant to instruct officers partly because its forces in Yokohama, one of its garrisons in the Far East, lacked a staff member who was suitably qualified to train officers. Further, Britain had a political consideration: 'It could not be a desirable policy for Great Britain to endeavour to bolster up a decaying power.'[32] Taking advantage of its diplomatic rapprochement with France, the Shogunate changed its military system to one based on French assistance. At the beginning of 1866, the Shogunate successfully invited a group of military instructors from France. The officers and enlisted under the Kanagawa Magistrate who had received British training were now transferred to the control of the Army Magistrate. On 15 June 1865, 538 officers were admitted as guards for westerners, and over 1000

enlisted as infantrymen.[33] Through these men the fruits of the British training were absorbed into the Shogunal Army.[34]

The employment of naval advisers

Soon after Perry's visit in 1853, the Tokugawa Shogunate began to build a
modern navy by requesting the sale of men-of-war and technological education from the Netherlands. Step-by-step, the Shogunate consolidated the
foundation for its Navy during the Ansei period (1854–60) through Dutch
naval training on three separate occasions and through Dutch gifts and sale
of four men-of-war.[35] The Dutch training took place in Nagasaki, but on 6
September 1857 the Shogunate decided to set up a naval training centre in
Edo in order to give its own education to Tokugawa's vassals. The naval training centre, the *Gunkan Kyoju-sho*, became the naval sailing training centre,
the *Gunkan Soren-jo*, in 1859. By 1866, it had grown into a naval academy,
the *Kaigun-sho*. The Shogunate used these institutions to educate its vassals
in order to create a modern Japanese navy. Parallel with its request to the
Netherlands to build a modern warship, the *Kaiyo-maru*, the Shogunate produced a plan to send naval students to the Netherlands.[36] On 1 November
1862, nine military students and six engineers departed from Nagasaki for
the Netherlands. In addition, a naval sailing training centre, the *Kaigun
Soren-jo*, was founded in Kobe in June 1863 based upon Katsu Rintaro's
conception. The centre was open for volunteers from the various domains.
Nine months later, however, in December 1864, the Shogunate ordered its
closure.[37]

Throughout the Keio period (1865–68), the Shogunate consolidated its
naval organization and strengthened its navy by purchasing large war
vessels. Organizational advances increased the need to obtain technical
training from the advanced countries in the West. The Shogunate moved
ahead with plans for inviting foreign military advisers to assist in naval
training and asked Britain to send instructors. Although Britain had been
quite reluctant to offer officer training for the Shogunal Army, London now
felt threatened by the diplomatic rapprochement drawing the Shogun
and France closer together. As a result, London vigorously solicited the
Shogunate to accept British advisers. At the suggestion of the French
Minister, Leon Roches, who wished to maintain a balance of power in Japan
between British and France, the Shogunate accepted British assistance.

Seventeen military advisors in the British Naval Mission under Commander Richard E. Tracey arrived in Japan on 24 October 1867.[38] The Shogunate
used the *Kaigun-sho* naval academy as a training centre and built additional
rooms for classes and students. The government furthered naval officer education by offering various subjects on sailing, rifled artillery, sabre techniques, and navigation. Instruction included drills on board the battleship
Choyo.[39] Seventy-one students entered the dormitory in November 1868.
But, based on the British declaration of neutrality on 18 February 1868, at

the outbreak of the Japanese Civil War – the *Boshin* War – the British minister ordered Britain's military advisers to withdraw. Because all the students soon left the dormitory, the Shogunate's programme of naval training ended.

Britain and the establishment of Meiji military forces

The Imperial Restoration of 3 January 1868 abolished the Tokugawa Shogunate and established the Restoration government. An armed conflict between the domains loyal to the Shogunate and those of the new government broke out in Toba and Fushimi in Kyoto on 27 January. These original skirmishes developed into the *Boshin* War. The Restoration government consolidated its position as a national government during this year-long civil war. From the Shogunate, the new government inherited a political structure, a confederacy of local domains – as one historian has put it: 'The centralized feudalism under the Imperial Court replaced the one under the Shogunate.'[40] With *Haihan Chiken*, the abolition of domains and the creation of a new prefectural system on 29 August 1871, the Meiji government began building its framework as a centralized, national state. In this process, the immediate military task Japan's central government faced was one of creating military forces on a national level by overriding the traditional autonomy of the feudal domains.

Britain and the Japanese Army before military standardization

To win the *Boshin* War, the Restoration government drew upon the military power of a confederation uniting 118 domains which provided more than 117000 men.[41] The Emperor – 'the leader of the allied domains'[42] – gave court nobles temporary authority as military commanders under titles such as *Seii Taishogun* and *Tosei Daisotoku*. They controlled the armed forces. When the domain soldiers were mobilized, the new government ordered them 'to adopt the Western style of drill'.[43] and to develop forces that could fight modern wars. By the end of the Tokugawa period and using translated western textbooks, many domains had already started experimenting to modernize their forces. During the period 1864–68 diverse domains had voluntarily adopted Dutch, British, or French tactics to cope with tactical manoeuvres necessary for muzzle-loading Minie Rifles. British military technology and knowledge were introduced to Japan after 1864. The Satsuma and Saga domains, which had led the armed struggle against the Shogunate in the *Boshin* War, also led the way in adopting the British military model.

Meanwhile those domains had begun to import regularly British weapons such as rifles and cannon. Some even attempted to copy these weapons. Most noteworthy was the Saga domain's efforts to copy the Armstrong, breech-loading rifle. Saga imported six-, nine- and twelve-pound Armstrong breech-loading field rifles.[44] By 1867, the domain had successfully reproduced one six-pounder and one nine-pounder.[45] The Saga domain actually deployed two of the six-pound Armstrong breech-loading, field rifles in the *Boshin* War.[46] It used them against the *Shogi-tai* troops in Ueno and the besieged army in Aizu. Throughout the *Boshin* War, the British military system spread over many domains partly because those royal domains which had adopted the British system had seized military leadership in the new government. Further, Britain's benevolent neutrality on behalf of the anti-Shogunate forces contributed to the rapid penetration of the British military system in Japan. Furthermore, the main troops under the direct control of the Restoration government, such as the Totsugawa Imperial Guard [47] and the *Boshin* Conscripted Force,[48] also seem to have adopted British formations and training. Such examples show that the British military system had become standard in the Japanese Army already by 1868–69.[49]

Many domains modelled their drills and training on the *Field Exercise and Evolutions of Infantry* (1862), a British manual for muzzle-loading fire arms.[50] They naturally desired to import the British Enfield rifles which the manual depicted over other models of guns.[51] Larger domains with annual incomes greater than 100 000 *koku* (rice-related measurement) such as Satsuma, Saga, Kanazawa, Hiroshima, Tottori, Kumamoto, Fukui, and others later adopted *Field Exercise and Evolutions of Infantry* (1867), a British manual book for Snyder breech-loading rifles. As the new government debated the method of military standardization, the Satsuma domain especially strongly supported the adoption of the British system for its superiority of manoeuvre.[52] This debate, which also reflected the power struggle between Satsuma and Choshu, was not easily resolved. Choshu's politicians insisted on basing army education on the French system and continuing the work of the French military advisers who had been invited by the old Shogunate government. Through discussions in the House of Representatives, they rallied the support of various domains for the French model of military standardization. On 25 October 1870, the government announced the mandatory adoption of the French military system by every domain, thereby laying the foundation for the modern development of the Japanese Army on the French model.

British influence on the naval establishment

The new government after the Restoration built the foundation for a navy by setting up its ministerial bureaucracy under the *Sanshoku*, 'three administrative positions'. In the beginning, the government lacked sea power under its direct control. The State jury-rigged its naval strength by requisitioning warships and other vessels from the feudal domains.[53] During the *Boshin* War, the government reinforced its naval power by confiscating the Shogunate's ships, by receiving donations from various domains and by purchasing ships from foreign countries. As a result of these actions, by the first half of 1869, the government's military administrative office had acquired

19 vessels, comprising ten warships and nine transports.[54] Japan's naval power in this period consisted of a dual structure between the new government and the various domains. Twenty-eight domains possessed a total of 83 ships and men-of-war,[55] including a fair number of obsolete vessels. Only the large domains such as Satsuma, Saga, Choshu, Tosa, Kurume, Kumamoto, Kanazawa, Hiroshima, and Fukuoka with incomes greater than 100000 *koku* had legitimate naval organizations.

The unification of these naval forces by the new government took its course relatively smoothly, in contrast to the inter-domain power struggles seen in establishing Japan's Army. On 19 October 1870, the government issued a decree on the 'the domain system' which clearly stated that the central government would control the Japanese Navy 'with naval funds supplied by the domains'.[56] Thus, one-by-one, the naval force of each domain was dissolved even before the *Haihan Chiken* reorganization, which fundamentally uprooted local power bases by abolishing the feudal domain system. In the form of offerings to the Imperial Court, the new government absorbed the ships and warships from those domains and placed them under its control.

The new government made progress in constructing a navy by assimilating various opinions from the different domains gathered through House of Representatives discussions regarding adopting a British model, personnel training and related matters. The urgent task was to build a naval educational system. Officer education in the Japanese Navy began with the *Kaigun Soren-jo* (Naval Training Centre) opened on 22 October 1869. Despite a couple of name changes, the government gradually improved the quality of education at the centre. It was called the *Kaigun Heigaku-ryo* (Naval Study Centre) between 1869 and 1876 and the *Kaigun Heigakko* (Naval Academy) between 1876 and 1945.

The personnel of the Naval Study Centre in 1870, for instance, consisted of 22 former Shogunate vassals from the Shizuoka domain out of the total of 55 men.[57] Despite the new government's policy of adopting the British naval system, mixed at the beginning with the Dutch system, the new Navy showed the legacy of the Shogunate Navy just as the new Japanese Army had retained continuity with the Shogunate period. The Naval Study Centre also employed foreign instructors to teach advanced military knowledge. The *Oyatoi* instructors included many British naval officers and played a leading role in setting up various courses including foreign languages, military discipline, artillery tactics, navigation, and military music, as well as setting up a Marine Corps.[58]

A particularly important development was the attempt to found a Marine Corps based on the suggestion of Lieutenant George Albert Hawes and the instruction of Lieutenant Francis Brinkley, both of the Royal Navy. This development seems to have begun around the time of *Haihan Chiken* in 1871. The government recruited all of its officers and junior officers from the various domains. This Marine Corps was designed to include 'guards and field artillery troops necessary for ceremonies'[59] and therefore its total of 1390 men included artillery, infantry, a music band, a drummer band, translators, and surgeons.[60] In November 1871, an educational programme to train Marine Corps officers began with the enlistment of 'artillery students'. On 4 April 1872, those students were reassigned to the Naval Study Centre. Because the Hojutsu *Seito Gakusha* – the artillery school for the Marine Corps – was created on 13 August 1872, they were brought under the control of the Marine headquarters. This educational organ was renamed *Kaihei Shikan Gakko* (the Marine Corps Academy) on 23 September 1875. When the Marine Corps was abolished in July of the next year, the Marine Corps Academy lost its independent educational function. The Academy was eventually reorganized into the Naval Academy in August 1877.[61] Although the Marine Corps of the Japanese Navy lasted only a little over five years, it had gone through 'artillery and rifle training'[62] modelled after the training of the British Marine Corps. The government sent its small-scale, marine forces to the Saga Rebellion (1874), the Taiwan Expedition (1874), the Kanghwa Affair (1875), and also on other operations.

Having employed foreign instructors, the Naval Study Centre also requested military advisers from the West just as those the Shogunate had attempted to bring in. Through diplomatic channels, Britain agreed to send a group of naval advisers, the 'Douglas Mission'. Thirty-four advisers under Commander Archibald Lucius Douglas RN arrived in Japan on 27 July 1873. Upon his arrival at the Naval Study Centre, he steadily eliminated Dutch elements from its educational system, and on 30 September 1873, he revised the Centre's regulations 'to follow British Navy regulations'. He also added an engineering department in October 1873, and organized an ocean voyage on the *Tsukuba* as a training ship. He hired Basil H. Chamberlain to strengthen English-language education.[63] The long-lasting British tradition in the Japanese Navy is the legacy of this Douglas Mission. A contemporary Japanese commented on their achievements:

Douglas is a favorable person with a majestic appearance and an ability to create a harmonious atmosphere. He himself is an outstanding sailor, and his men are all selected on their merit. His instruction to our students is limited, mostly practical with no strategic theorizing. However, the education in the Imperial Navy henceforth improved its prestige, and those British teachers greatly contributed to it in organizing its educational system, developing its curriculum, etc.[64]

Douglas returned to England on 25 July 1875 and was succeeded by Lieutenant Charles W. Jones. Of the other members, 14 returned home in 1876 when their contracts expired. Those who renewed contracts stayed in Japan for a while and continuously participated in naval education.

One-by-one these British advisers returned home, and their number decreased.

Britain's and Japan's overseas expansion

The new Meiji government established by the Imperial Restoration propelled national unification of Japan's military power through *Haihan Chiken*. The main objective of this military reform reads, 'its immediate object is to maintain domestic order, and its future objective is overseas expansion'.[65] The reform recognized the threat from the 'powerful enemy in the north', Russia. Japan's modern armaments program, nonetheless, started out emphasizing 'internal, defensive, and passive objectives'.[66]

On 4 April 1872, the *Hyobu-sho* (Military Department) which 'controlled both the Navy and the Army'[67] was abolished. The Departments of Army and Navy became independent from each other and each steadily built up its own institutional system. At this point, Japan's military strength was used mainly to suppress uprisings and rebellions by members of the dissatisfied former *samurai* class. The maintenance of domestic peace in Japan remained its military priority until the end of the Satsuma Rebellion in 1877.

Meanwhile, Japan conducted limited overseas ventures. In 1874, Japan carried out its first overseas expedition to Taiwan. Then, in the Kanghwa Affair of 1875, Japan used gunboat diplomacy forcibly to open up Korea. The next year Japan established diplomatic relations with Korea. Because organized anti-government uprisings declined after the Satsuma Rebellion, Japan more actively intervened in Korea, using Korea's civil wars of 1882 and 1884 as pretexts to dispatch its troops to the peninsula. This inevitably increased the friction with Qing China over control of Korea.

Britain and the increase of Japanese armaments against Qing China

In earlier times, Japan's military had emphasized its function in maintaining domestic order. As Sino-Japanese relations had become strained over Korea, however, the military increasingly considered the need to fight foreign wars. Japan saw China as its potential enemy over hegemony in East Asia and began military planning and preparations for a possible Sino-Japanese war.[68] Receiving the Imperial edict on 22 December 1882, the prime minister ordered the Army and Navy ministries to increase their armaments. After 1883, the government ordered the Army and the Navy to increase the number of soldiers and to build new warships, annually appropriating ¥1 500 000 for the Army – an extra ¥240 000 was allocated for batteries at Tokyo Bay – and ¥3 000 000 for the Navy.[69]

To build 'a foundation sufficient to raise about 200 000 soldiers in case of a war',[70] the Army drew a plan to set up six divisions in each *chindai* (the organizational unit of the old military system) and one division in the Imperial Guard. With the abolition of *chindai* and the implementation of a divisional organization, this plan became reality on 12 May 1888. As a result, seven divisions consisting of 14 infantry brigades (28 regiments), two cavalry battalions, seven artillery regiments, six battalions, one company of engineer corps, and six battalions of transportation corps were set up.[71] Army regulations regarding organization, equipment, tactics, and other important matters, paralleled this arms expansion and gradually changed the character of the Japanese Army from the French to the Prussian style. By the beginning of the 1890s, the Japanese Army had adopted the Prussian models of conscription, military education, and manuals.

The Navy worked out an industrial plan worth a total of ¥26 640 000 for an eight-year period between 1883 and 1891.[72] A draft for equipment standards for vessels was drawn up and received Imperial approval. Further, the five-year programme of the second naval expansion included the plan to build 46 ships and was submitted to the Cabinet Council in 1888. This plan, however, was rejected for financial reasons, and only one cruiser, one gunboat, and three torpedo boats were newly built.

The naval construction plan to prepare for a war with China was discussed as a budget issue in the first Diet of 1890. Although heated discussions sometimes caused complications, construction costs were continuously provided for despite the burden that this placed on national finances. Consequently, the level of Japan's military strength right before the Sino-Japanese War included 28 military vessels with a total displacement of 57 632 tons and 24 torpedo boats, displacing 1475 tons.[73] In addition, six warships displacing 33 330 tons and two torpedo boats totalling 165 tons were already under construction.[74] Among these vessels, Japan had bought three ships from Britain: the *Fuso* – an ironclad corvette, the *Kongo* – an iron-belted corvette, and the *Hiei* – another iron-belted corvette. These ships had been ordered in 1875. During the process of military expansion against China, Japan also placed an order with Britain for an additional four cruisers: the *Naniwa*, *Takachiho*, *Chikushi* and *Yamato*.

All of these British vessels were deployed as capital ships of the Japanese Navy during the Sino-Japanese War. British influence on the Japanese Navy, however, was not limited to the material. It also extended to the technical. Japan invited Captain John Ingles RN as an instructor for naval tactical training in the process of Japan's military preparations against China. He was appointed as an instructor at the *Kaigun Daigakko* (Naval War College), which was opened in August 1888.

By the beginning of 1894, and after more than ten years of effort, Japan had generally completed its military preparations against China. Now the government endeavoured to consolidate national unity supporting the first full-scale foreign expedition by building a national consensus favoring a Sino-Japanese war.

The Sino-Japanese War

Qing China had also been modernizing its military forces through the 'Self-Strengthening' movement of the 1860s. In fact, China possessed a numerically stronger army and navy than Japan at the beginning of the 1890s. Before the outbreak of war, the Chinese Army already had 350000 men under arms consisting of 862 units of infantry (including artillery and engineering corps) and 192 units of cavalry. In addition, the Chinese Army had newly recruited another 630000 men.[75] They, however, clearly showed deficiencies in modernizing the Army's training and equipment. Further, the Chinese organized their new forces – the *Xian jun* Army, the *Huai jun* Army, the *Fan jun* Army, and the *Lian jun* Army – to coexist without sufficient unification of their chains of command with China's traditional troops, such as the Manchurian *Baqi* and the *Luying* troops.[76] The Japanese Army investigated and confirmed the situation of the Chinese Army beforehand. Being confident of defeating the larger numbers of China's Army as a result of their own superior organization and equipment, the Japanese Army advocated a war with China.

China's Navy, in contrast, posed a considerable threat to Japan. With armoured turret ships of 7000 tons displacement such as the *Ding yuan* and *Zhen yuan*, it had a history of naval expansion under British tutelage. Before the war, the Chinese Navy had been organized in four fleets – *Peiyang*, *Nanyang*, *Fujian*, and *Guangdong* – and it possessed 82 warships and 25 torpedo boats, displacing a total of 850000 tons.[77] The *Peiyang* Fleet, with 22 war vessels and 12 torpedo boats, under Commander Ding Ru-chang became China's main fleet during the Sino-Japanese War. Having Captain W.H. Lang RN as its general instructor, the *Peiyang* Fleet had adopted the *Peiyang* Fleet Regulations in September 1888 and pursued tactics based on British systems.[78] The Japanese Navy was aware of its inferiority vis-à-vis the Chinese. Taking Captain Ingles' suggestion, to compete with the so-called 'Quarter-line' formation, the leading tactic in naval warfare at the time, they decided to use the 'Single-vertical' formation.[79] Accordingly, the Japanese planned 'to increase the speed of the fleet, close on the enemy quickly, and shoot quick-firing guns'.[80] Japan's naval preparations against China therefore stressed increasing the speed of its military vessels and equipping them with quick-firing guns.

During the Sino-Japanese War, Japanese warships maintained an average speed of 13.9 knots, which exceeded the Chinese average (11.8). Japan also mounted 217 quick-firing guns on its fleets, which overpowered the 22 quick-firing guns of the Chinese fleets.[81] The main armament among those quick-firing guns was the 12-cm gun, which had been developed by the Armstrong Company in 1887. This new, powerful, medium-calibre gun could fire every 20 seconds, which exceeded Krupp's 12 cm quick-firing gun's rate of every 90 seconds.[82] Japan declared war on China on 1 August 1894.

To open the war, Japan planned a two-stage operation. In the first stage, Japanese forces were to hold the Chinese Army on the Korean peninsula and attempt to acquire control over the Yellow Sea and the Gulf of Po Hai. Based upon those successes the Japanese Army was then to fight a decisive battle on the Zhili plateau.[83] From the war's onset, Japan's Army overwhelmed the Chinese forces and pushed them out of the Korean Peninsula in less than three months. Once it invaded Chinese territory, however, the Japanese Army faced a hard fight in southern Manchuria partly because of the region's very severe winter. The land operations ended with Japan's victory after the Battle of Tianzhuangtai in March 1895, and the Japanese Army did not have to carry out the second stage of its operational plan.

Meanwhile, in order to secure control of the sea, Japan's Navy planned to destroy the *Peiyang* Fleet quickly. Japan was cautious about fighting a decisive battle with an apparently superior enemy. For almost two months after the Battle of Fengdao on 25 July 1894, the Japanese combined fleet was engaged mainly in transporting Japanese Army soldiers. The decisive battle between the Japanese and Chinese main fleets was fought on 17 September 1894. The Chinese Fleet possessed clearly superior material forces. Twelve Japanese vessels, in fact, fought against 14 Chinese ships, including four large ships like the *Ding yuan* and *Zhen yuan*. The Chinese ships were also equipped with 21 large calibre guns of more than 20 cm. while the Japanese ships had only 11.[84] In contrast, Japan exploited its fleet's faster average speed and its quick-firing guns. The Japanese Fleet deftly deployed into a 'single-vertical' formation and destroyed the bunched Chinese ships one-by-one. With this victory, Japan had seized command of the Yellow Sea. The *Peiyang* Fleet had suffered a crushing defeat with three ships sunk, one burned, and seven damaged. The Japanese Fleet lost no vessels and suffered only relatively minor damage.[85] Modern military experts have analysed the causes behind the seemingly stronger *Peiyang* Fleet's defeat at the hands of the newly-built Japanese Navy at the Battle of the Yellow Sea. They point to the low standards of training, lax military discipline, poor lines of communications in the rear, and the unqualified officers in the *Peiyang* Fleet as its main weaknesses.[86]

The Japanese victory at the Battle of the Yellow Sea changed western opinion towards Japan from one 'seemingly critical toward our country'[87] at the beginning of the war to a pro-Japanese one. Anglo-Chinese relations, which had been so close that 'other countries could anticipate the possibility of Britain taking direct action over any crisis for China',[88] were now transformed. This change formed a favourable environment for Japan in the international community. In January and February 1895, the Japanese Navy, in cooperation with the Japanese Army's land operations, attacked Weihaiwei to destroy the remaining forces of the *Peiyang* Fleet. China lost torpedo boats and three large vessels, including the *Ding yuan*, in the course of this campaign.[89] Commander Ding Ru-Chang killed himself on 17

February after surrendering to Japan. After the *Peiyang* Fleet had been annihilated, China inclined towards peace with Japan by appointing Li Hong-zhang as a plenipotentiary. Negotiations between the two countries proceeded to an armistice agreement on 30 March 1895. The Sino-Japanese War ended with the conclusion of the Treaty of Shimonoseki on 17 April.

The Boxer Rebellion

With the Treaty of Shimonoseki Japan achieved its primary objective of eliminating Chinese influence in Korea and additionally acquired concessions in the Liaodong Peninsula, Taiwan, and the Penghu Islands, plus a military indemnity of 200 million taels (¥300 million).[90] To lessen Japan's demands, at the end of the war China solicited the intervention of the Great Powers. On 23 April 1895, co-operation among Russia, Germany, and France (the Triple Intervention), prevented Japan from receiving the treaty concession of the Liaodong Peninsula. China's reliance on western countries, however, backfired because it accelerated their disregard for China's sovereignty and territorial integrity. The door was opened to further acquisitions of Chinese concessions by the Great Powers. The Triple Intervention against Japan, at the same time, spurred anti-Russian sentiments among the Japanese people. Under the slogan of '*Gashin Shotan*' ('Sleeping on a Bed of Nails'), Japan further increased its military strength and preparations for a coming war against the potential enemy, Russia.

Meanwhile, responding to several requests from Britain, on 15 June 1900, Japan sent special forces troops and on June 26 added the 5th Division in answer to the Chinese Boxer Rebellion.[91] Japan, Britain, the United States, Russia, France, Germany, Austria and Italy sent troops to China to suppress the anti-western movement. It was the first opportunity for Japan's armed forces to participate in military operations alongside western forces. Because Japan had sent its soldiers at British request, Japan tended to co-operate closely with Britain and the United States in their military effort.[92] The Japanese military in general received high marks from its allies. A contemporary celebrated the

> brave action, and the humane and disciplined attitude of our troops, which were clearly displayed before the eyes of the Allied forces. The reputation of our soldiers was introduced to the peoples of the West and we Japanese astounded the world as a people who would develop in the future and who deserved and respect and admiration.[93]

After Beijing's occupation by the Allied forces on 14 August 1900, China agreed to peace talks, and the Boxer Protocol[94] was signed on 7 September 1901 to end the rebellion. The protocol demanded that the Qing government pay an indemnity of 450 million taels and approve the stationing of western troops in China. These concessions dramatically expanded the power of western countries in China. Russia's recent occupation of Manchuria had especially strained relations with Japan over control of Korea. Sharing strategic interests against the Tsarist threat in northern China, Japan strengthened its diplomatic partnership with Britain and embarked on a path of military confrontation with Russia.

Japan's military preparations against Russia

The Japanese legislature had already begun drawing up a plan for an arms expansion against Russia around the time that the outcome of the Sino-Japanese War had become evident. The Triple Intervention, however, spurred Japan towards its military preparations. Passing its approval in the Ninth Diet, Japan began massively expanding the Army and Navy after the 1896 fiscal year. The Japanese Army, according to the plan, was scheduled to increase by six divisions, two cavalry brigades, and two artillery brigades – all to be completed within three years.[95]

The Japanese Navy went through three naval construction plans and came to possess 'six battleships, six armoured cruisers, twelve cruisers, other destroyers, torpedo boats, etc., a total of 152 ships'.[96] Its objective was to create 'one fully-equipped, strategic fleet with a nucleus of six battleships, six armoured cruisers, with lighter auxiliary units of second- and third-class cruisers, destroyers, torpedo boats, etc., completely equipped with stan-dardized vessel types, speed, gun types, number of guns, etc.'[97] This new Japanese fleet was also known as the '6:6 Fleet' (that is, six battleships and six cruisers), and was mostly completed by the time of the outbreak of the Russo-Japanese War.

On its main capital ships Japan uniformly adopted various guns made by Armstrongs. The warships were equipped with Armstrong 40-calibre, 12-inch guns as main weapons and Armstrong 40 calibre, 6-inch, quick-firing guns in their secondary batteries. The armoured cruisers were equipped with Armstrong 45 calibre, 8-inch guns as main weapons and Armsrong 40 calibre, 6-inch, quick-firing guns in their secondary batteries.[98] The Japanese Fleet also possessed superior average speed compared to Russia's fleets. In their main fleets, first-class Japanese vessels maintained 18.0 knots on average, while the Russians to make only 17.6 knots. Japanese cruisers maintained 20.5 knots on average compared to 19.8 knots for the Russians.[99] Moreover, those Japanese ships of the '6:6 Fleet' were powerful and new, having been built between 1897 and 1902. The overall quality of the Japanese naval personnel, including their commanders' abilities and their sailors' general military skills, proved superior to that of the Russian Navy. Japan effectively executed tactics of 'winning the battle by returning fire from its main batteries at 4000 to 5000-meters-distance'[100] in sea battles during the Russo-Japanese War, which unexpectedly launched a new epoch in the history of naval warfare.

Support from Britain, especially in checking Russia's southward expansion, played its part in increasing Japan's naval power. When the Anglo-Japanese Alliance was signed in 1902, Japan's naval power had grown to rank fourth in the world, behind Britain, France, and Russia.[101] The Anglo-Japanese Alliance had been signed 'not to fight Russia . . . but to develop Japan's cooperation and commerce with Russia.'[102] Japan's primary objective in its diplomatic negotiations was to extort compromise from Russia on the Manchurian and Korean issues over which the interests of the two powers were colliding, and to eliminate Russia's military threat to Japan. Russia's military occupation of Manchuria in 1901 was the flashpoint of controversy. Although the conclusion of the Anglo-Japanese Alliance had temporarily secured Russia's promise to withdraw from Manchuria, Russia's failure to fulfill its word eventually drove Japan to initiate the Russo-Japanese War.

Notes

1. Rutherford Alcock, *The Capital of the Tycoon*, vol. 1 (London: Longmans, Green & Co., 1863), p. 211.
2. For official Japanese records of these incidents refer to the Japanese Ministry of Foreign Affairs file *Zoku Tsushin Zenran Ruishu no Bu, Bokomon*.
3. For detailed planning see Ishii Takashi, 'Bakumatsu ni Okeru Eikoku Kaigun no Nihon Engan Fu-sa Keikaku, Pt 1 and Pt 2 *Rekishi Chiri* 76 (Nos 7/8/1949, nos 1 & 2).
4. Ibid., (no. 1), pp. 41–2.
5. Ishii Takashi, *Bakumatsu no Gaiko* (Sanichi Shobo, 1948), p. 96.
6. Otsuka Takematsu, *Bakumatsu no Gaiko* (Iwanami Shoten, 1934), p. 53.
7. Kajima Morinosuke, *Nichi-Ei Gaikoshi* (Kajima Kenkyu-jo, 1957), p. 23.
8. Koshaku Shimazu-ke Hensan-jo, *Satsu-han Kaigun Shi* (Hara Shobo, 1968), vol. 2, pp. 428–9.
9. 'Kagoshima-wannai Hogeki ni shiyo seshi Armstrong-ho nitsuki Eikoku no Hokoku', ibid., vol. 2, pp. 521–33. The report recorded that 13 of the Armstrong rifled guns broke down during the battle. These weapons, nonetheless, impressed the Japanese with their power and effectiveness during the Anglo-Satsuma War. In 1864, Kawamoto Komin published at Roshi-kan a translation of an excerpt on Armstrong breech-loading, rifled guns by Howard Douglas, *A Treatise on Naval Gunnery* (1860) as *Amusutoron Shinpo Zusetsu*. The demonstrations of the power of the new weapon also encouraged the Shogunate and the Saga domain to import and reproduce the guns.
10. Hara Takeshi, *Bakumatsu Kaiboshi no Kenkyu* (Meicho Shuppan, 1988), p. 66.
11. Tottori-han Shi Hensan-jo, *Tottori-han Shi* (Tottori: Tottori-ken, 1969–70), vol. 1, p. 111.
12. Ernest Satow, *A Diplomat in Japan* (London: Seeley, Service & Co., 1921), pp. 102–3.
13. Hara, *Bakumatsu Kaiboshi*, p. 80.
14. Suematsu Kencho, *Bocho Kaitenshi* (Kashiwa Shobo, 1967), vol. 1, p. 667.
15. Ibid., pp. 102–3.
16. Ishi Kanji, *Taikei Nihon no Rekishi* (Shogakukan, 1993), p. 161.

17. Gaimu-sho, *Nihon Gaiko Nenpyo narabini Shuyo Bunsho* (Kokusai Rengo Kyokai, 1955), p. 28.
18. Satow, *A Diplomat in Japan*, pp. 77–8.
19. Yokohama-shi (ed.), *Yokohama-shi Shi* (Kanagawa: Yokohama-shi, 1964), Shiryo-hen vol. 3, p. 367.
20. Yokohama-shi (ed.), *Yokohama-shi Shi* (Kanagawa: Yokohama-shi, 1959), vol. 2, p. 805.
21. See Hara Tomio, *Bakumatsu Ishin-ki no Gaiatsu to Teiko* (Azekura Shobo, 1977).
22. Yokohama Kaiko Shiryokan (ed.), *Shiryo de Tadoru Meiji Ishin-ki no Yokohama Ei-Futsu chuton-gun* (Kanagawa: Yokohama Kaiko Shiryo Fukyu Kyokai, 1995), p. 272.
23. Katsu Awa, *Rikugun Rekishi* (Rikugun-sho Sosai-kyoku, 1889), chapter 24, p. 5.
24. Kurimoto Joun, *Hoan Iko* (Tokyo: Shogabo, 1900), p. 109.
25. Katsu, *Rikugun Rekishi*, chapter 24, p. 6.
26. Hitsuka Ryu, *Yokohama Kaiko Goju-nen Shi* (Kanagawa: Yokohama Shoko Kaigo-sho, 1909), vol. 1, pp. 338–9.
27. Ishin Shiryo Hensan Jimu-kyoku (ed.), *Ishin Shiryo Koyo* (Meguro Shoten, 1940), vol. 5, p. 616.
28. Kikakegawa Hiromasa, 'Bakumatsu-ki no Rikugun Kyoiku ni tsuite – Eikoku Rikugun Densho o Chushin ni', *Gunji-shi Gaku*, no. 79 (December 1984), p. 52.
29. With the introduction of British training, Akamatsu Kosaburo translated the manual *Field Exercises and Evolutions of Infantry* of 1862 fully into Japanese as *Eikoku Hohei Renpo* (Shimosone Keiko-ba, 1865).
30. Ota Hisayoshi, *Yokohama Enkaku-shi* (privately published, 1892), p. 90. About 800 soldiers who had received British training under the Kanagawa Magistrate took part in a joint exercise with British garrison forces on 21 March 1866. See John R. Black, *Young Japan: Yokohama and Yedo, 1858–79* (London: Oxford University Press, 1968), vol. 1, p. 412.
31. Katsu, *Rikugun Rekishi*, chaps. pp. 21 and 24.
32. Satow, *A Diplomat in Japan*, p. 147.
33. Yoshino Masayasu, *Kaei-Meiji Nenkan-roku* (Gannan-do, 1968), vol. 2, p. 1217.
34. Furuya Sakuzaemon, who had been reassigned as an officer under the Kanagawa Magistrate into the Shogunal infantry, translated two British military texts on tactics and there was also a manual published for the command of the Shogunal rifle corps. See *Hohei Soren Seikai* (Chinsho Kubota, 1866); *Eikoku Hohei Soren Zukai* (unrecorded, 1868); and anon., *Eishiki Soren Hohei Reishi* (Ju-tai Kata, 1867).
35. See Mizuta Nobutoshi, *Bakamatsu ni okeru Waga Kaigun to Oranda* (Yushu-kai, 1929) and Fujii Tetsuroi, *Nagasaki Denshu-jo* (Chuo Koron-sha, 1991).
36. Katsu Awa, 'Kaigun Rekishi', in *Katsu Kaishu Zenshu* (Kaizo-sha, 1928), vol. 8, pp. 459–61.
37. Kaigun Kyoiku Honbu (ed.), *Teikoku Kaigun Kyoiku-shi* (Hara Shobo, 1983–84), vol. 1, p. 6.
38. Shinohara Hiroshi, *Kaigun Soetsu-shi* (Libroport, 1986), p. 141.
39. Documents in Katsu, *Katsu Kaishu Zenshu*, vol. 8, pp. 368–77, sketch the Shogunate's naval training by British military advisers.
40. Fukushima Masao, *Chiso Kaisei* (Yoshikawa Kobun-kan, 1986), p. 56.
41. This total is recorded in *Kakuhan Senko Roku* in Kokuritsu Kobunsho Kan.
42. Shihara Yasuzo, *Meiji Seishi* (Fuzan-bo, 1892), vol. 1, p. 117.
43. Tottori-han Shi Hensan-jo, *Tottori-han Shi*, vol. 3, p. 234.
44. Sugimoto Isao et al. (eds), *Bakumatsu Gunji Gijutsu no Kiseki: Saga-Han Shiryo*, 'Matsuno Rakuyo' (Kyoto: Shibunkaku Shuppan, 1987), pp. 293–4, 333. The

Shogunate also imported 12-pound, Armstrong breech-loading field guns in May 1867.

See Gaimusho Gaiko Shiryo Kan, *Zoku Tsushin Zenran, Ruishu no Bu, Buki Mon, Eisho yori Kobai Taiho Daika Ikken* (1867).

45. Ohashi Shuji, *Bakumatsu Meiji Seitetsu Ron* (Agune, 1991), p. 55.
46. Hideshima Naritada, *Saga-han Ju-Ho Enkaku-shi* (Saga: Hizen Shidan-kai, 1934), p. 301.
47. *Rikugun Kyoiku-shi, Meiji Bekki Dai Ikkan-ko,* NIDS.
48. Tottori-han Shi Hensan-jo, *Tottori-han shi,* vol. 3, p. 247.
49. The various domains chose different western countries as the sources of their tactical textbooks for the military organization and the training of key infantry forces. Though it is difficult to discover the choices made by every domain, the records of the Imperial drill at Komabano show that 36, or over half, the domains out of a total of 59 and six corps of government soldiers had adopted the British model. This contrasted with the 12 domains which had turned to the Dutch and 13 to the French. *Komabano Rentai Tairen-ki,* in NIDS.
50. There are several Japanese translations of *Field Exercises and Evolutions of Infantry* of 1862: Akamatsu Kosaburo and Asazu Tominosuke, *Eikoku Hohei Renpo* (Shimosone Keiko-ba, 1865); Uriu Sanshin, *Hoso Shinsho* (Nanetsu Heigaku-sho, 1866); Akamatsu Kosaburo, *Jutei Eikoku Hohei Renpo* (Satsuma-han, 1867); Akamatsu Kosaburo and Asazu Tominosuke, *Eikoku Hohei Renpo* (unrecorded, 1868).
51. When the feudal domains were abolished, the *Hyobu-sho* confiscated small arms. Enfields made up 53123 of the 181012 rifles collected. Rikugun-sho, *Heiki Enkaku-shi* (Tokyo: Rikugun-sho, 1913), vol. 1, pp. 4, 37.
52. The French military system, which had been adopted by domains such as Choshu, was still based on muzzle-loading rifles (*Field Tactics for Light Infantry,* 1863 edition) and was identical to the French training under the Shogunate. There are additional translations of *Field Exercise and Evolutions of Infantry* (1867 edition) which used Snyder breech-loading rifles: Uriu Sanshin, *Hohei Shinsho Zoho* (Chikuhoro, 1868); Hashizume Kanichi, *Eikoku Hoso Shinsho* (unrecorded, 1868); Awazu Keijiro, *Eikoku Bisenju Renpei Shinshiki* (Heiganshi Keiko-jo, 1869). Snyder rifles remained the standard weapon in the Japanese Army even after standardization with the French system and remained as reserve weapon when superseded by the Japanese-produced Murata bolt-action rifle distributed to all forces in 1886.
53. See Kaigun-Sho (ed.), *Kaigun Seido enkaku* (Hara Shobo, 1971), especially vol. 2 for the early development of the naval bureaucracy.
54. Koshaku Shimazu-ke Hensan-jo (ed.), *Satsuhan Kaigun-shi,* vol. 3, pp. 1071–3.
55. Ibid., pp. 1074–82.
56. 4.5 per cent of the current *koku* income. Shushi-Kyoku (ed.), *Meiji-shi Yo* (Goyo Inko-jo, 1876), chapter 4, p. 54.
57. Kaigun Heigakko (ed.), *Kaigun Heigakko Enkaku* (Hara Shobo, 1968), pp. 13–17.
58. Shinohara, *Kaigun Sosetsu-shi,* pp. 219–43 for more information on the employment of *Oyatoi* in the Navy.
59. Yamaguchi Kiyomatsu, *Nihon Kaigun Rikusentai-shi* (Daishin-sha, 1943), p. 55.
60. Sawa Kannojo, *Kaigun Nanaju-nen-shi Dan* (Bunsei Doshi-sha, 1942), pp. 247–8.
61. See Kaigun Kyoiku Honbu (ed.), *Teikoku Kaigun Kyoiku-shi* (Hara Shobo, 1983–84), vol. 7, pp. 543–56 on the development of naval training institutions at this date.
62. See Kaigun Yu-Shu Kai (ed.), *Kinsei Teikoku Kaigun-shi Yo* (Hara Shobo, 1974), p. 125. As a textbook for the Japanese Marine Corps, Brickley (trans.), *Eikoku*

Jutai Renpo, Writings of Hattori Motonosuke and Tamaki Shozo (Seika-do, 1871) was published.

63. See Kaigun Kyoiku Honbu (ed.), *Teikoku Kaigun Kyoiku-shi*, vol. 1, pp. 182–209 for more detail on the Douglas Mission.
64. Ibid., p. 188.
65. Oyama Azusa (ed.), *Yamagata Aritomo Iken-sho* (Hara Shobo, 1966), pp. 43–6.
66. Matsushita Yoshio, *Meiji no Guntai* (Shibun-do, 1963), p. 12.
67. Boei-cho Boei Kenkyu-jo Senshi-bu, *Senshi Sosho: Rikugun Gunsenbi* (Asagumo Shinbunsha, 1979), p. 4.
68. NIDS (ed.), *Daihonei Rikugun-bu 1* (Asagumo Shinbunsha, 1967), pp. 18–19.
69. Watanabe Ikujiro, *Kiso Shiryo: Kogun Kensetsu-shi* (Kyoritsu Shuppan, 1944), pp. 209–12.
70. Ibid., p. 228.
71. Rikugun-sho (ed.), *Rikugun Enkaku Yoran* (Rikugun-sho, 1890), pp. 83–5.
72. See Sato Ichiro, *Kaigun Goju-nen shi* (Masu Shobo, 1943), pp. 95–107 for more details of naval expansion during this period.
73. Ogasawara Chosei, *Nihon Teikoku Kaijo Kenryoku-shi Kogi* (Shunyo-do, 1904), pp. 367–8.
74. Kaigun Yushu-kai (ed.), *Kinsei Teikoku Kaigun-shi Yo*, p. 211.
75. Sanbohonbu (ed.), *Nisshin Senshi* (Tokyo Insatsu Kabushiki-Gaisha, 1904), vol. 1, p. 57.
76. Zhan Yu-tian et al., *Zhon guo jindai junshi-shi* (Shenyang: Liaoning renmin chuban-she, 1983), p. 255.
77. Sanbohonbu (ed.), *Nisshin Senshi*, vol. 1, pp. 58–9.
78. Zhan Yu-tian et al., *Zhon guo jindai junshi-shi*, pp. 275–8.
79. NIDS (ed.), *Kaigun Gunsenbi* (Asagumo Shinbun-sha, 1967), pp. 108–12.
80. Shinohara, *Kaigun Sosetsu-shi*, pp. 379–81.
81. Ogasawara, *Nihon Teikoku Kaijo Kenryoku-shi Kogi*, pp. 367–8.
82. Kogakkai, *Meiji Kogyo-shi: Kahei, Tekko-hen* (Kogakkai Hakko-jo, 1929), p. 120.
83. Sanbohonbu (ed.), *Nisshin Senshi*, vol. 1, pp. 177–8.
84. Kaigun Yushu-kai (ed.), *Kindai Teikoku Kaigun-shi Yo*, p. 598.
85. Sanbohonbu (ed.), *Nisshin Senshi*, vol. 2, p. 250.
86. Xu Hua, 'Luelun beiyang haijun fumie de neibu yuanin', Junshi kexueyuan zhanlue yanjiubu, *Zhongguo jindai junshi lunwenji* (Beijing: Junshi kexue chubanshe, 1987), pp. 198–212.
87. Ogasawara, *Nihon Teikoku Kaijo Kenryoku-shi Kogi*, p. 439.
88. Tanaka Hiromi, 'Nisshin Ryokoku no Tairitsu to Kaisen eno Kiseki', in Kuwata Etu (ed.), *Kindai Nihon Senso-shi: Nisshin, Nichiro Senso* (Dodai Keizai Kondan-kai, 1995), vol. 1, p. 133.
89. Sanbohonbu (ed.), *Nisshin Senshi*, vol. 6, p. 165.
90. Gaimusho, *Nihon Gaiko Nenpyo narabini Shuyo Bunsho*, vol. 1, pp. 165–9.
91. See Gaimusho, *Nihon Gaiko Bunsho vol. 33, Hokushin Jihen* (Nihon Kokusai Rengo Kyokai, 1956).
92. Kawano Mitsuaki, 'Hokushin Jihen', in Kuwata, *Kindai Nihon Senso-shi*, vol. 1, p. 389.
93. Sugahara Sagae, *Hokushin Jihen-shi Yo* (Kaiko-sha, 1926) p. 128.
94. Gaimusho, *Nihon Gaiko Nenryo narabini Shuyo Bunsho*, vol. 1, pp. 196–8.
95. Matsushita Yoshio (ed.), *Yamagata Aritomo: Rikugun Enkaku-shi* (Nihon Hyoron-sha, 1942), p. 75.
96. Sato, *Kaigun Goju-nen Shi*, pp. 190–1.
97. Koyama Hirotake, *Kindai Nihon Gunji-shi Gaisetsu* (Ito Shoten, 1944), p. 389.

98. Kogakkai, *Meiji Kogyo-shi*, p. 122. See also Mayuzumi Haruo, *Kanpo Shageki no Rekishi* (Hara Shobo, 1977).

99. Koyama, *Kindai Nihon Gunji-shi Gaisetsu*, p. 432.

100. Fujiwara Akira, *Nihon Gunji-shi* (Nihon Hyoron-sha, 1987), vol. 1, p. 119.

101. Koike Inokazu, *Zusetsu Soran: Kaigun-shi Jiten* (Kokusho Kanko-kai, 1985), p. 24.

102. Kajima Morinosuke, *Nihon Gaiko-shi*, p. 269.

3

The Royal Navy and Japan, 1900–1920: Strategic Re-evaluation of the IJN

Ian T.M. Gow

Naval interest in Japan in the first two decades of the twentieth century embraced a variety of interests. The IJN, in terms of men and material, owed a great deal to British influence and thus there was a continuing interest in a former pupil. The high dependence on British technology, in terms of ships and equipment, also meant that in both peacetime and wartime Japan acted as a testbed for technology and operations which greatly interested British naval planners. The tremendous growth of the IJN, plus its victory over China, created a new non-European naval force in the Far East and forced the RN to evaluate Japan as either an opportunity or a threat. This period is dominated by seeing Japan as an opportunity but suspicions still existed and the threat from Japan, whether used as a budgetary/hypothetical or as a potential enemy, was always there and emerged in naval planning towards the end of this period. Naval policy for Japan was in many respects a subset of diplomatic and trade relations with the region and thus the Cabinet (especially the Prime Minister), Foreign Office, Treasury and even the Colonial Office exerted considerable influence. The political head of the Navy, the First Lord, was a civilian and a cabinet minister. He normally had no experience or even knowledge of naval affairs. Some, such as Lord Selborne, and especially Churchill, developed very considerable expertise on naval matters and thus exerted influence on both politicians and professional naval officers. The senior naval officer, the First Sea Lord, held responsibility for strategy and policy. He worked closely with the First Lord and also with the Committee of Imperial Defence (CID). CID views on naval matters were not necessarily the views of the Admiralty but often reflected a working compromise. Nevertheless, generally the Admiralty had the greater say on Far Eastern/Pacific matters, which were regarded as essentially a naval responsibility. There was a Deputy Chief of the Naval Staff (DCNS) and an Assistant Chief of the Naval Staff (ACNS). The Naval Intelligence Division was another key organization headed by the Director of Naval Intelligence (DNI), a powerful figure privy to intelligence from all branches. He was often destined for higher rank within the Navy and also provided a rather discrete naval influence when, as was frequently the case, he was promoted to secretary to the CID. Naval perspectives on Japan came from a variety of sources especially the C-in-C China/Eastern Fleet and the various naval attachés in Japan. On many occasions the former used a Japanese threat to try to increase or at least prevent a decrease in the size of his fleet and provided the basic views from the region. Foreign Office views were also taken into account, as well as intelligence and opinion from the Empire. In addition, several senior officers had had considerable experience (if not up-to-date personal knowledge) of working directly with the Japanese earlier in their career. These included First Lords such as Beatty and Chatfield and admirals such as Wilson, Douglas and Ingles who had taught in Japan and retained contacts after returning home, and their insights were extremely valuable. One should note that the quality of naval attachés was particularly high, many achieving flag rank and some becoming DNI.

At the end of the nineteenth century the RN was faced with major challenges to its Two Power standard, and more especially its ability to maintain global supremacy and indeed even theatre supremacy in the Far East. The German Navy Acts from 1898 shifted the focus towards concentrating the fleet in European waters. The seizure of Port Arthur in 1897 by the Russians, and their decision to dispatch first-class units there plus the actions of the French, Russia's allies, who invested heavily that same year in armoured cruisers for its Far Eastern interests, created a naval race in Far Eastern waters. The Admiralty initially tried to resolve this by augmenting the China Squadron with armoured warships. However, British naval responses to the naval threats were greatly handicapped by the twin problems of budgets and manpower. In addition to these potential threats from European powers – German naval potential drew the navy back to the North Sea and Atlantic whilst Franco-Russian developments drew ships to the Far East and there was also the need to allocate increased naval support during the South African War – was the emergence of a new regional naval power, Japan. Fresh from victory over China, Japan was also engaged in a naval race with Russia greatly accelerated by the transfer of first-class units of the Baltic Fleet to Port Arthur. This growth of the IJN, former pupils, further reduced the RN's credible superiority in this theatre. The appointment of a naval attaché dedicated to the USA and Japan in 1899 was followed by a request for an extension of the period in Japan by a year. Ernest Satow, supporting an extension and indeed an attaché dedicated to Japan, indicated that Russia, Germany, France and Germany all had naval attachés there. Until the departure of the Ingles mission in 1897 there had been RN instructor officers in Japan attached to the IJN and this may have sufficed and also been rather cost-effective. There was now clearly a need to monitor the progress of this former pupil and also a growing unease at the growth and expertise of the IJN in the Far East. However, an alliance now emerged as an opportunity to ensure eastern security, concentrate naval units in Europe and also achieve economies. In 1900 during the Boxer disturbances in China, the RN operated alongside IJN units. Admiral Seymour, C-in-C China Squadron, arrived in late May 1900 and was concerned for British nationals as the scale of Boxer disturbances grew. The British ships were joined by those of seven other nations, including the Japanese. Seymour landed an eight-nation force from these ships on 10 June and included IJN personnel under his command. This force also included future First Sea Lords, Jellicoe and Beatty, who were to play major roles in naval policy towards Japan in the inter-war period. The expedition failed, but RN officers were impressed by the reliability and courage of IJN personnel. Jellicoe was later to state, rather prophetically concerning the Russians: 'The Japs are doing splendidly in the fighting and they are as pleased as possible fighting alongside our men. They are opening the eyes of the Russians who will not be so anxious to go to war with them after what they have seen of then I fancy.'[1] In addition, the multinational naval force which took part in the capture of the Taku Forts included IJN vessels. This force, under a Senior Officers Council, with only eight small gunboats capable of operating in shallow waters, captured four new German-built Chinese destroyers of vastly superior power and also captured the forts. Whilst hardly major naval activities, they do show the IJN working closely with the RN and performing extremely well. These events, plus the actions of Japanese volunteers and Japanese army units, clearly impressed British naval and military planners, current and future. This may have further fuelled the idea of a possible alliance with Japan in Far Eastern waters to combat the growing combined Russian and French threat to both the RN and the IJN.[2] The Admiralty had recognized the need to monitor the IJN more effectively in 1899 by appointing a third naval attaché exclusively devoted to the United States and Japan. The first reports concerning the 1900 mobilization of the whole Japanese fleet, the first since 1894, were reported by Captain Ottley, although details were scant given the secrecy surrounding these events. His report can be interpreted as indicating a slightly more helpful attitude to the British naval officers than to German and other foreign attachés but nevertheless he also felt excluded. Ottley indicated that the Japanese, whilst in possession of fine modern ships and having little doubt that they were individually efficient, doubted their ability in terms of 'tactical handling and Squadron work' and in fleet manoeuvres. He indicated they were 'secretive beyond words' and that he required a longer stay to obtain better information and to master the language.[3] The DNI Admiral Custance responded positively, recommending he be allowed to stay a year in Japan and stating 'it is believed to be of much importance that HM government should have this knowledge at their disposal'.[4]

The first Anglo-Japanese Alliance

This period showed a marked deterioration in the British naval situation in the Far East. From a position of superiority over Russia and China in 1898, the RN was now outnumbered and outgunned. By April 1901, Russia had placed five of her new battleships in the Far East, continued to build up Port Arthur and promised further reinforcements in the shape of battleships and cruisers as well as other smaller ships. The French had also sent new cruisers to the Asia-Pacific region. The RN had only four battleships against the combined Russian and French and, of course, the emergence of German naval power there too, possible as part of a triple coalition, greatly exacerbated the problem. Alliance suggestions, with the US or Germany, had been considered for some years, but increasingly Japan appeared as the best option. The Admiralty, battling with the Treasury, admitted in Parliament that they could not meet their worldwide obligations. They now switched from scraping together funds to strengthen the increasingly vulnerable China Fleet to alliance politics and to Japan. Admiral Custance had alerted the First Lord of the Admiralty to the growth of the IJN and the RN's growing vulnerability in the Far East. Selborne prepared a memorandum for the Cabinet advocating an alliance with Japan. He baldly stated that the British in a few months' time would only have four battleships and 16 cruisers as against a Franco-Russian combination of seven first-class, two second-class battleships and 20 cruisers.[5] Selborne, aware of the budgetary problems, saw an alliance as a means of avoiding the massive costs of building and manning an expanded China Fleet and also of reducing dramatically the costs of repairs, docking and coaling which they would incur if they improved Hong Kong. The Japanese responded positively to a Foreign Office approach. In all of the preliminaries, the naval thinking seems to have been done by the DNI and the civilian First Lord, indicating that the *raison d'être* was politico-financial rather than strategic. Selborne's belief was that only diplomacy and alliances could actually rescue the Admiralty from its predicament in the Far East. It soon became evident that whilst both sides wished for naval benefits from this naval-based alliance, they sought different things. The IJN's building programme had effectively been stopped due to lack of funds in 1902 and it saw the RN helping them to meet the Russian Pacific Fleet threat whilst the British saw the addition of IJN forces as a way of preventing further increases in China Squadron expenditure and even a reduction in the British commitment to that station. The naval underpinning of this alliance necessitated special naval agreements attached as secret notes. Differences in the interpretations of the two sides were immediately apparent. The British aimed to avoid Japanese efforts to bind them to keep a considerable naval force at all times in the Far East and also avoided mentioning specific figures. The Admiralty, driven by the need to avoid binding commitments to an ally in any one theatre, hoped for at the very least an undertaking that the combined forces of Japan and Britain would remain superior to that of any two powers combined. The British took offence and basically threatened the Japanese that their attitude might prejudice the negotiations. They indicated, despite the fact that they had initiated a naval alliance proposal in their own interests, that it was too one-sided and too hard on the British side. Japan responded by suggesting that each power should in future maintain a fleet superior to the oriental fleet of any third power. The Admiralty sought and obtained an agreed clause which could be interpreted so as to permit them to alter the naval commitment as they saw fit and in accordance with their perception of their own needs. The final agreed version therefore read.

> At the present moment Japan and Great Britain are each of them maintaining in the *Extreme East* a naval force superior in strength to that of any other power. [Each Ally] has *no intention* of relaxing her efforts to *maintain, so far as may be possible, available for concentration in the waters of the Extreme east* a naval force superior to that of *any third power.*[6]
> (emphasis mine)

'Available for concentration' here clearly implied bringing ships from other stations (Australia, East Indies, Pacific) or even a 'fleet' from European waters. Moreover, it was now a statement of intent (no intention) rather than a full-blooded commitment and it was not in the main, public text. In addition it is worth noting that it now read 'any power', no doubt influenced by the fact that Britain had signed an entente with France and this clause was now aimed at the Russians alone. It was, however, accepted by the Japanese and this, together with the peacetime co-operation clauses, clearly benefited the RN greatly.

The various agreements on matters such as signals and codes were agreed easily, but there were more complex discussions required on such key issues as assemblies of fleets and most important of all the issue of 'command'. In December 1902, the naval attaché in Tokyo reported on the two conferences that had occurred since the signing of the treaty.[7] He pointed out that the difficulties of alliance strategic and tactical planning meant that two different naval forces working together would be thought of as inferior to a similar-sized force of a single power (under a single command). It had been agreed earlier that there should be no overall C-in-C, One wonders whether the British were sensitive to the snub given to the Japanese Army in the Boxer Incident when the Japanese were passed over for a German C-in-C for the relief of Tientsin. There is reason to believe that were the British in a larger concentration in the theatre they would have pushed for a British C-in-C. Prince Louis of Battenberg in 1903 had commented on this stating 'in a combined fleet of equal parts this country's claims to leadership stand on a different footing to the time when we only provided a smaller portion'.[8]

However, the matter appeared closed until the early months of the Russo-Japanese War when the naval attaché raised the issue again.[9] Prior to the outbreak of the war, the Admiralty had already received complaints from the Japanese that the British were not keeping to the agreements.[10] First, however, we must examine the naval aspects of the Russo-Japanese War and its impact on Anglo-Japanese relations.

The Royal Navy and the Russo-Japanese War

Britain was only required to come to Japan's aid in the conflict with Russia if Russia combined with another power or if Japanese territory proper was attacked. However, naval assistance before and during the war was indirectly forthcoming and did assist the Japanese. Immediately prior to the war Russia outbid Japan for battleships being built in British yards for Chile. The RN purchased these ships in order to prevent Russia obtaining them, but felt unable to allow Japan to buy them from her. The Admiralty then negotiated with the Italian shipyard building two more battleships for Argentina and acted as agent on behalf of the Japanese. These ships arrived in Asian waters just as the conflict started. Britain also acted to prevent Russian armed merchantmen from passing through the Dardanelles, refused Russians logistical support, passed intelligence on the movements of the Russian Baltic fleet and at one point mobilized the Mediterranean Fleet when a British trawler mistaken for a Japanese MTB was sunk. Perhaps the most important support for Japan was the exercise of 'silent power' – namely the fact that the naval agreements ensured, as a by-product, that the cost of Russian support against Japan by another power brought the world's most powerful navy, the Royal Navy, in on the side of Japan.

The war, however, was of immense benefit to the RN. It was a means to assess IJN personnel, technology and strategy and they were very keen to get officers aboard IJN ships. They encountered some resistance since the Japanese feared that any future credit might be put down to having RN staff aboard. However, they did eventually agree and RN officers observed from Japanese ships in every major naval encounter. Their reports were read widely at home, including by the King.[11] In addition, after the war the naval attachés were able to obtain naval assessments in Japanese that they promised to keep confidential. This is why Corbett's *Confidential – Maritime Operations of the Russo-Japanese War 1904–5*, volume 1 had only six copies made – it was not widely distributed and was kept from the Japanese.[12] The war acted as a major testbed for naval thinking on the whole range of naval tactics and technology although, of course, planners drew both positive and negative lessons depending on their agenda. There was certainly evidence that leading naval planners doubted Japan's ability to defeat the Russian navy, but there is also no doubt that they were quick to claim some of the credit for the IJN's performance and the IJN did acknowledge publicly its debt to the RN. The opportunity for very able naval officers to observe at first-hand the IJN at war resulted in a more positive view of the Japanese.[13] Troubridge criticized Togo for not following through and being risk-averse, something he himself was court-martialled for in the First World War and ironically cited this action in a more positive light.[14] Perhaps the most important statement he made, which gathered some support within the Admiralty, was that the Japanese had proved themselves and therefore were capable of being put in charge of RN units in joint operations under the alliance.[15] For the cash-starved Admiralty the elimination, for a time at least, of the Russian threat was a major bonus and not only avoided increased expenditure on the China Station, which a Russian victory would have necessitated, but actually offered a chance to reduce commitment to that station. As soon as the war ended the British recalled their battleships from the China Station, replacing them with four armoured cruisers to match France, the Anglo-French *entente* not withstanding, still leaving the RN superior to the French, Germans, Russians and Americans combined.

The second Anglo-Japanese Alliance

The elimination of the Russian threat, the *entente* with France and the limited presence of German and American ships on the China Station at this time made the extension of the alliance in its present form less attractive than hitherto. The Russian naval threat was eliminated but the land threat remained. British policymakers, supported by the Admiralty, saw this as an opportunity to barter naval support to Japan in the event of a rebuilt Russian fleet for army support for India. Admiralty documents supported a suggestion for 150000 men for the Indian frontier.[16] The reluctance of the Japanese to agree to extending support for Britain's Asian interests beyond the Far East resulted in the naval agreements being deleted. A more general agreement on military and naval (in that order) discussions was agreed. Moreover, the British commitment was now against any European Power thus possibly contributing to a further Japanese naval build-up against the USN, which in turn worried the Admiralty but worried Dominion defence planners even more. This exclusion of the United States was as much to prevent a need to match the US Navy in the Far East as any clear pro-American stance by the Admiralty. However, it did now cover conflict with one power rather than a coalition and thus increased the naval security of Japan against a war of revenge by Russia. The vagueness of the agreement allowed Britain to avoid further embarrassing questions regarding the number and type of ships committed to the China Station. From this period on, naval security for British interests in the region rested more and more with the expanding and ever more confident IJN, further fanning fears within Australian and New Zealand of the growing Japanese naval threat.

As with the first alliance there was a necessity for further talks regarding important issues relating to joint operations such as signals, codes, and again the sensitive issue of command. Admiralty documents did in fact state: 'In the Far East, therefore, it is but natural that any combined Anglo-Japanese naval forces should be commanded by a Japanese Naval officer.'[17] It was a major concession and British ships were placed under Japanese command during the First World War.

Increased respect for IJN abilities was counterbalanced by a growing perception that the Alliance would not last forever and that the pace of IJN growth might be a future threat to British interests in the region. This may have been further fuelled by a German naval build-up reminding British defence planners that the Japanese Army was pro-German. The Japanese, although shifting to a greater dependence on their own yards for ships and equipment still depended very heavily on British research and development and Admiral Yamamoto had clear instructions to obtain a full exchange on 'education and research' when carrying out the naval discussions following the Second Alliance.[18] The Admiralty was increasingly reluctant to open-ended exchange and Japanese requests for joint exercises were rejected and naval attachés were given clear instructions not to ask for Japanese information if that allowed the Japanese to ask for information in return.[19]

The First Sea Lord Fisher, always suspicious of the Japanese and fearful they would soon become a potential foe, angrily criticized them for obtaining too much knowledge but did personally relent when the IJN asked for information on experimental larger guns and then allowed them to be ordered for the Kongo making it pound for pound more powerful than the British ships of that class.[20] This growing caution within the RN perhaps reflected a general trend towards more secrecy in naval affairs in terms of new technologies. However, it may also have reflected increased concerns in Australia and New Zealand (as well as Malayan Command) fuelled by the reduction in the China Fleet and the growth of the IJN. Finally, even before the renewal of the Anglo-Japanese Alliance in 1911, the CID had produced a document considering the termination of the alliance and a need to 'reinforce the China Fleet in order to neutralise the danger from a preponderant Japanese fleet in the China Seas'.[21] It is also no coincidence that the Admiralty, still struggling with the Exchequer for funds, should now consider various options for an Imperial Navy or greater support from them for a combined naval presence against Japan. Whilst one cannot eliminate the possibility that scaremongering within the Admiralty in the pursuit of increased budgets (Japan as a budgetary enemy) played its part, there can be no doubt that the British Empire was increasingly viewing Japan as a potential enemy. In May 1911, in the very year that the third alliance was to be signed, the CID considered a 'hostile Japan in the absence of the alliance as most likely to attack if Britain were bogged down in a European Conflict'.[22]

The Third Alliance was essentially an extension of the second and naval matters were not really discussed directly. However, the British exclusion of countries with whom they had an Arbitration Treaty (namely the USA) sent a very clear signal indeed that Britain not only was excluding conflict with the United States but also would not come to Japan's aid if the primary potential enemy of the IJN, the USN, declared war with Japan. This undoubtedly triggered a further acceleration of Japanese naval building and the so-called 8–8 Fleet in turn further increased British and Imperial concerns about the Japanese naval threat. Increasingly, the alliance began to look more a negative control device allowing Britain to exert some control on Japanese ambitions in Asia. It also undoubtedly fanned Japanese fears, even within the IJN, of a future Anglo-American coalition against the Japanese.

Naval co-operation in the First World War

Britain's first approaches to the Japanese over the war with Germany reflected both her realization of the need for Japanese naval assistance and her suspicions of Japanese naval and imperial aspirations in the Asia-Pacific region. Initially, it was felt that the Far East could be kept out of the war and Japanese naval assistance would only be required if Hong Kong or Weihaiwei were attacked. However, it soon became apparent that the weaknesses of the China Fleet, together with the presence of powerful and mobile German forces, exposed the inability of the RN to blockade Tsingtao, protect shipping and chase German vessels now loose in the region. The first request, bringing with it the necessity for Japan to actually declare war, was for help in protecting British trading interests by chasing down armed merchantmen off China and the surrounding seas which the limited resources of the RN couldn't deal with.[23] This initial request set the scene for an unseemly debate over British efforts to limit the scope of the IJN and created an atmosphere of Anglo-Japanese mistrust which was to recur continuously throughout the war. The Admiralty was most concerned about American fears of an expansionist Japanese naval presence in the Pacific region, whereas British interests were also concerned about the attitude of China if German territories in China were captured by the Japanese. In addition, the Americans and the Australian and New Zealand defence planners were frightened of the possibility of Japan acquiring bases in the Western Pacific north of the equator or worst still south of the equator. Japan refused to allow limitations on her navy's scope of operations and throughout the war she used her naval contribution as a lever in various negotiations over China and anti-Japanese discrimination within the dominions. The Foreign Office desperately tried to limit the Japanese scope of operations, even issuing a public statement without the approval of the Japanese government.[24] The first request for concrete help, however, was for Japanese naval officers under training in England to be placed aboard British ships on the western coast of the USA. The Japanese response was a rather pointed remark that the

Admiralty seemed in this case rather less willing to limit the scope of IJN activity![25] The inconsistent behaviour of British policymakers, in first suggesting no help, then only if asked, then concrete help but limited scope and then withdrawing even that request did nothing to reduce a sense of mutual distrust. However, the Japanese, and especially the IJN, seemed keen to participate in the war. The IJN had been scandalized by the Siemens Affair and this was a chance to win back public support, possibly win greater naval appropriations, breaking the deadlock over army versus navy funding. It would also expand their sphere of operations and help their former mentors. British ships, the battleship *Triumph* and the destroyer *Usk*, were placed under the C-in-C, Second Squadron IJN, for the attack on Tsingtao and there was none of the tensions and criticisms of British contributions which bedevilled the army role both at the time and later in the war. British and Canadian ships also served under Admiral Moriyama off the US and Canadian coasts. This was clearly the first time that RN ships served under a Japanese naval officer. Given the RN's adamant refusal to serve under officers of the Indian Navy, this was a major coup for an Asian nation. Japan also assisted with the chase for the *Emden*, and provided escorts for ANZAC forces, but this was limited co-operation narrowly defined. The IJN also contributed in the Indian Ocean. By the end of 1914, the war in the Far East was effectively over. However, tensions continued to escalate over the Japanese occupation of the Mariana, Caroline and Marshall Islands and especially over Yap, which the Australians were determined to occupy. In the end, the Admiralty, which never rated the island groups as any threat conceded Japanese occupation and even, by default, accepted their insistence that she retain them after the war.[26] However, despite the fact even an interpretation of the spirit of the alliance precluded Japanese help outside the Far East and India, the British were forced to request the despatch of a division of the Japanese battlefleet in September and even offered to pay for the expenditure. The request was refused and in November naval aid in the form of a contribution to the Baltic campaign was also refused. Whereas the more astute Japan-watchers clearly understood Japan's reasons for refusing, such responses were interpreted most negatively and contributed further to suspicions that Japanese naval contributions were first in Japan's interests and only secondarily to help her alliance partner. The Japanese, however, had made it clear that major naval units would be sent if Britain itself was invaded.[27] In early 1916 the Admiralty tried again to solicit naval contributions for the European theatre, asked this time for destroyers rather than battleships for the Mediterranean or possibly Home waters. Before the Japanese had time to fully consider this request much less decline it, the request was changed to a cruiser squadron to the Indian Ocean and a small force of destroyers to the Malacca Straits. The Japanese responded with the offer of four cruisers and four destroyers. They also dispatched a flotilla of destroyers and some cruisers to work with the British in patrolling the Indian

Ocean and Australian waters. With the exception of Indian concerns about turning the Indian Ocean into a Japanese lake, these efforts were well received by the Admiralty although the efforts by the Japanese to link in some way this naval support to pressure on the dominions regarding discrimination and trade issues caused some headaches for the Foreign and Colonial Offices. One highly sensitive issue concerned the Admiralty suspicion of the linkage between Japanese merchant shipping and the Indian nationalist movement. Jellicoe refers to it frequently in his letters, as does Beatty.[28] When the C-in-C China dispatched ships to intercept Japanese merchant vessels in a zone patrolled by the IJN he thus managed to insult an ally by boarding their ships and also offended the IJN. The Japanese response was immediate and threatened that a continuance of such activity would halt further naval support to the RN.[29] Japan did respond with further support in the Indian Ocean, but its most visible and most praised contribution was its offer of support in European waters when it responded very favourably to a request for a destroyer flotilla to be sent to the Mediterranean. This naval assistance, including a cruiser, was placed at the full disposal but emphatically not under the command of the British C-in-C at Malta. Two Japanese crews also manned two British destroyers and these efforts raised RN evaluations of IJN officers and men. Japan also dispatched in that year light cruisers off the Cape of Good Hope and off Singapore. Later in July 1917 the Admiralty found its battlecruisers totally outclassed by the Germans and requested the Japanese allow them to purchase two Japanese battlecruisers to be attached to the Grand Fleet, but this request was refused and again in October 1917 C-in-C Malta unsuccessfully requested one IJN battlecruiser for the Aegean Squadron to combat the *Goeben*.[30] The US entry into the war brought a bizarre twist to the requests for Japanese cruisers. They had heard wrongly that the British intended to transfer five capital ships to the Japanese at the end of the war.[31] On 18 August, the USN proposed four Japanese battlecruisers on the American Atlantic coast.[32] The American fears of the Japanese had been discussed by their Director of Plans in November 1917 and he suggested that their fears could be alleviated by the dispatch of battlecruisers to Europe with a promise to return one or more at the end of the war if they should be lost in action.[33] The Japanese naval contribution to the war was considerable, although clearly the failure to accept limitations on their scope of operations and the refusal of a number of requests for ships, especially ships outside of the Far East or Pacific areas, engendered British criticism during and even after the war. However, many of these criticisms were really directed at the Japanese government rather than the IJN itself. Time and again political ramifications were stated as the reasons for refusals for further naval support, although there was a faction in the IJN against dispatching any ships to European waters. In 1916 and 1917 the First Sea Lord Jellicoe, in stark contrast to his political master and First Lord Churchill (who praised the Japanese contributions), was very harsh in criticizing the Japanese and wrote to Admiral Beatty in July 1917 that the Japanese government and even the IJN were not helpful on the traffic of 'Indian seditionists' to and from Japan by Japanese merchant ships. He added, 'nevertheless, apart from the selling of guns and ammunition to the Russians, Japan is not taking a full share of the war'.[34] A few weeks later he again wrote to Beatty stating 'Japan again is being pressed for help . . . but the Japanese are not inclined to do anything for the cause'. Interestingly, Jellicoe later suggested the Admiralty purchase two Japanese battlecruisers to be crewed by the RN giving as his reason that such ships crewed by Japanese would be no match for the Germans.[35] In December 1917, the C-in-C China commented negatively on the Japanese squadron of destroyers, stating that it would be most unwise to employ them in the Aegean 'owing to their want of sound ideas in working in co-operation with our ships'.[36] This was to prove totally unfounded and the IJN performed excellently and were extremely co-operative and supportive of British and Allied efforts in the Mediterranean. Their efforts in rescuing survivors from sinking ships brought high praise. The C-in-C Malta judged them superior to the French and the Italians. The IJN, he stated, kept their ships in highly serviceable condition and went to sea far more than the Italians and the French.[37] In fact, they spent more time at sea than the RN.[38] He went on later to state that Rear-Admiral Sato and his men presented no problems whatsoever, comparing them most favourably to the lacklustre French and Italians. He noted that the French and the Italians were hopeless, the Greeks not worth mentioning, the Americans were not involved in this area but 'the Japanese are of course splendid, but their numbers are small'.[39] Their efforts were later highly praised in the British press. However, although much praised by local commanders, especially for their work in the Mediterranean, much of what they did was at the ship or small unit level and Japanese ships had little opportunity to show their mettle in actual fighting, such as in fleet manoeuvres.

The final area where Japanese and British naval units worked together was at Vladivostok in the early stages of the Siberian Intervention. Anglo-Japanese discussions on the nature of the intervention reflected again the underlying distrust at the political level. This was exacerbated by British discussions with the Americans without first consulting the Japanese. The dispatch of HMS *Suffolk* to Hong Kong and then via Japan to Vladivostok caused the two navies to be involved in a race to get their ships to Siberia first. The Japanese won and had two cruisers there prior to the arrival of HMS *Suffolk*. The tensions were clearly felt by the British commander who was refused upgrading to Commodore to deal with the other admirals present and his initial comments on the Japanese naval presence were negative.[40] However, the cause of the tensions was political and not professional. In this delicate situation Admiral Kato Kanji landed marines and Captain Payne supported him by landing marines, too. However, after the initial tensions the two sides worked together most harmoniously and Payne reported back after some months that Admiral Kato had been highly co-operative and this ought to be passed back through official channels.[41]

Japanese naval officers were involved in the lengthy discussions at the end of the war in the Allied Naval Council and did complain about being left out of discussions at times, but overall relations remained cordial and co-operative. Perhaps in this period the only concerns raised were intelligence reports that the Japanese Technical Naval Mission in Europe was negotiating with the Germans for technical help and the possible construction of submarines.[42] This may also have indicated that the Japanese were aware that should the Anglo-Japanese Alliance be discontinued, the IJN still needed a western source of scientific and technological expertise on the grounds that the British would be even less inclined to pass on such information than hitherto. The British government and Admiralty now began to consider the possible discontinuance of the Alliance. In addition, the growth of the IJN quantitatively and qualitatively together with the need to compete with or placate the Americans, to placate the Imperial territories and obtain their financial support, the advances in technology (coal to oil burning) which caused problems for both getting a fleet to the Far East and even maintaining it whilst there, placed Admiralty planners in a quandary regarding their global and regional Far Eastern role. In the years leading up to the First World War suggestions of a war with Japan were either using the IJN as a budgetary/hypothetical enemy or to placate nervous imperial concerns but planning now became focused on Japan as the potential, most likely enemy and the major threat to Britain's Far Eastern Interests. The dilemmas of choosing between the strengthening of the China Fleet, using the Fleet as a holding action until the main fleet arrived, creating an Imperial or Pacific Fleet or Imperial Squadron with financial support from the dominions all had to be considered against the option of continuing an alliance now no longer capable of being used to restrain the Japanese. The Alliance could possibly be used as a means of constraining the Americans or alternatively abrogation might open up co-operation with an ever more competitive USN. The years 1919–20, before the feelers for a naval disarmament conference, were difficult for British naval policymakers. In 1919, there were two major developments indicative of British and Imperial attitudes to the Japanese naval threat. The first of these was the dispatch of former First Sea Lord Jellicoe on an Imperial Mission, ostensibly under the guidance of the Admiralty. Jellicoe, increasingly distrustful of Japan, focused on naval planning to defend the Empire especially to prevent an invasion of Australia and NZ rather than focusing just on the China/Asian mainland (India) issues. He perhaps optimistically assumed that the China Squadron would shortly be strengthened and combining all ships in the region under a Pacific Fleet with a harbour in northern New Guinea. Jellicoe sought to obtain moral financial support for this force to deal with the IJN as Japan was 'our probable and indeed obvious enemy'.[43] He went on to state to the Dominions and to the Admiralty that 'Japan is the only nation in the Far East which would be in a position to inflict permanent damage on the Empire'.[44] He counselled it was 'very unwise' to rely on the alliance and take no steps for naval defence, indicated how history told us of 'allies turning into enemies in a very short space of time'. He concluded that it was inevitable that the interests of the British Empire and Japan must inevitably clash and 'for this reason the potential enemy in the Pacific is taken as Japan'.[45] This perspective is in line with the emergence of a naval mindset that indicated that even if the alliance did continue in some form an advanced base to combat a threat with Japan was still necessary. Meanwhile back at home in October 1919, the Admiralty informed the War Cabinet that it anticipated the non-renewal of the Alliance and stated that it was unlikely to be able to maintain a fleet equal to Japan's in the Far East. In case of war, the RN would be inferior 'for a time' adding that in the worst case, a period of three months was needed 'before our naval superiority could be established'. It suggested concentrating Far Eastern naval forces at Singapore, which it was improbable the Japanese would attack prior to arrival of the main fleet from Britain.[46] This clearly indicates that Japan, even in a year when it was an ally in war and an alliance partner, had become the potential enemy in naval planning. With her finances in a parlous state, Britain's defence planners now looked to measures to combat the Far Eastern threat from Japan. By February 1920 the possibility of avoiding the clash through continuing the Alliance seems to have been discarded by the Admiralty which now opined that it was 'neither necessary nor desirable . . . in its present form'.[47] The RN knew that without considerable increases in naval expenditure, which were unlikely, the ability to coerce Japan in the Far East was practically non-existent. Naval arms control seemed to offer a possible solution.

Notes

1. Rt. Hon. the Earl Jellicoe, *The Boxer Rebellion* (The Fifth Wellington Lecture, University of Southampton, 1993), p. 18.
2. Ibid., p. 19.
3. Ottley to Custance, 12 April 1900: PRO: ADM1/7488/5750.
4. Ibid., Custance to Admiralty, 12 May 1900.
5. Ian Nish, *The Anglo-Japanese Alliance: the Diplomacy of Two Island Empires 1894–1907* (London: Athlone Press, 1966), p. 174.
6. Ibid., p. 218: author's emphasis.
7. Troubridge to Battenberg (DNI), 24 December 1902: PRO: ADM116/1231B.
8. Battenberg paper, 10 December 1903: ADM1/7652.
9. Troubridge to Admiralty, 27 April 1904: ADM116/1231C.

10. I. Nish, 'Naval Thinking on the Anglo-Japanese Alliance 1900–1904', *Hogaku Kenkyu* (Keio University), vol. 56, no. 3 (1971), p. 13.

11. P. Towle, 'The Evaluation of the Experience of the Russo-Japanese War', in B. Ranft (ed.), *Technical Change and British Naval Policy 1860–1939* (London: Hodder & Stoughton, 1977), p. 67.

12. D.M. Schurman, *Julian S. Corbett 1854–1922* (London: Royal Historical Society, 1981), p. 140. The story of the History is covered on pp. 131–51.

13. P. Towle, 'British Estimates of Japanese Military Power, 1900–1914', in P. Towle (ed.), *Estimating Foreign Military Power* (London: Croom Helm, 1982), pp. 129–31.

14. E.R. Lumby (ed.), *Policy and Operations in the Mediterranean, 1912–1914* (Ashgate, England: Navy Records Society, 1970), vol. 115, pp. 251–2.

15. 8 June 1904: PRO: ADM 116/1231B.

16. Ballard/Ottley, 'Remarks as to the Future of the Anglo-Japanese Alliance', 4.4.1905: ADM116/1231C.

17. 'Admiralty Memorandum on Forthcoming Conference between British and Japanese Naval Officers regarding Naval Co-operation in War', 11 May 1905: ibid.

18. Nish, *The Anglo-Japanese Alliance*, p. 357.

19. Controller to Fisher, 15 October 1909: PRO: ADM 116/1231C.

20. Kato Kanji Denki Hensankai, *Kato Kanji Taisho Den* (Tokyo: Kato Kanji Taisho denki Hensankai, 1941), p. 542.

21. Ibid., p. 4.

22. I. Nish, *Alliance In Decline: a Study in Anglo-Japanese Relations 1908–23* (London: Athlone, 1972), chapter 7 pp. 115–31, remains the definitive analysis of this important series of negotiations. Both volumes by Nish cover the naval aspects of Anglo-Japanese relations extremely well.

23. Ibid., pp. 124–5.

24. Ibid., p. 122.

25. Ibid., pp. 143–6.

26. See Peter Lowe, *Great Britain and Japan, 1911–1915* (London: Macmillan, 1969), pp. 198–207.

27. *The Jellicoe Papers*, p. 135.

28. Nish, *Alliance in Decline*, p. 185.

29. Calthorpe to Admiralty: PRO: ADM137/1413.

30. US Office of Naval Operations to Benson, 7 October 1918 in M. Simpson (ed.), *Anglo-American Naval Relations, 1917–1918* (Navy Records Society, 1991), vol. 130, pp. 541ff.

31. Ibid., p. 349: Memorandum by US Planning Section, 10 August 1918.

32. Ibid., pp. 334–5: Memorandum by the Director of Plans (RN), 19 November 1917.

33. *Jellicoe Papers*, pp. 335–6.

34. Ibid., p. 136: Jellicoe to Beatty, 4 January 1917.

35. Ibid., p. 185: Jellicoe to Geddes, 21 July 1917.

36. 'Post-War Naval Policy', Long to Admiralty, 21 February 1917; minutes by G. Hope, 23 February 1917 in P. Halpern (ed.), *The Royal Navy in the Mediterranean 1915–1918* (Navy Records Society, 1987), vol. 126, p. 236.

37. Ibid., p. 282: Ballard to Admiralty, 21 August 1917.

38. Ibid., p. 469: Dickens to Dewar, 9 May 1918.

39. Ibid., p. 236.

40. Rear-Admiral Hong Kong to Admiralty, 17 January 1918.

41. Commanding officer, HMS *Suffolk* to Admiralty, 9 July 1918: B68/4. PRO

42. For a full analysis see J.W.M. Chapman, 'Japan and German Naval Policy,

1919–45', in J. Kreiner (ed.), *Deutschland–Japan Historische Kontakte Sonderdruck* (Bonn: Bouvier, 1984), pp. 211–64.

43. *Jellicoe Papers*, p. 267.
44. Jellicoe, 'The Naval Situation in Far Eastern Waters', *The Jellicoe Papers*, p. 346.
45. Ibid., p. 347.
46. 'Naval Situation in the Far East', Admiralty Memorandum for War Cabinet, 21 October 1919, in N. Tracy (ed.), *Collective Defence of the Empire, 1900–1940* (London: Navy Records Society), vol. 136, p. 263.
47. Nish, *Alliance in Decline*, p. 297.

4

The Anglo-Japanese Alliance and the First World War

Yoichi Hirama

The occupation of Tsingtao

On entering the war, the Tsingtao operation was carried out. On 23–4 September 870 soldiers from the South Wales Borderers Second Battalion stationed in northern China under the command of Brigadier N.W. Barnardiston, landed. The Japanese side assumed that the British troops' first battle would be around Mount Shihmen three days after they landed. But this plan was cancelled by the British who proposed to stay at Puli from the 25th and to prepare for battle there. After the battles at Kushan and Fushan, the British acquired half of the 36th Indian (Sikh) Regiment of 450 men and reached the front line. Thereafter, for a month the British and the Japanese prepared for a full-scale offensive which they launched on 31 October. But the British force did not move.[1] The Japanese units concluded 'it was hard to trust you as war comrades if you permit only our troops to engage in the fighting at this time', that 'the British army was baggage' and that it was 'no more than decoration on the battlefield'.[2] Consequently, Japanese newspapers and magazines reported that: British soldiers were different in nature from Japanese soldiers and were excessively 'elegant' (cautious) when it came to launching joint operations. Only when nothing happened were British soldiers wonderful and it was like taking a lady on a trip. However, such a lady can be a burden and lead to total disaster for a force when the enemy appears. Such reports, when reported back to Britain, generated considerable revertment among the British public.[3]

On the other hand, the Royal Navy dispatched an old battleship *Triumph*, a destroyer *Usk*, and the *Delta*, a hospital ship. The *Triumph* which had 10-inch guns was, although old, great support for the blockade in terms of fire-power and in landings greatly aiding the IJN which was short of shells. Lieut. Cdr. Yamanashi Katsunoshin, who was dispatched to China Squadron Head-quarters, had great respect for the British commanders' indomitable spirits, their continuous observation of the whole situation and the organization and training on board their ships. Captain Yoshida Seifu, involved in the joint operation as chief of staff at the IJN Second Fleet, praised British preparations, stating that 'during this battle, the British ships did not use gun plugs even in heavy rain. Every evening the electric circuits of each gun were checked. The scrupulous attention to detail was impressive.'[4] This praise reflects clearly the view that RN morale and fighting sprit was higher and more positive than that of the British Army who were merely participating because of political considerations.[5] Although possibly diplomatic language, the Japanese side evaluated RN operations as 'entirely successful' and highly valued its effectiveness and full of good faith.[6]

As Tsingtao collapsed and the German Eastern Squadron lost its base, the objectives of the joint Anglo-Japanese naval operations were achieved. According to the British official naval history of the war, 'the Tsingtao operation did not only bring special benefit to Japan but also performed the utmost and best service she could render to the Alliance'.[7] However, the British Consul, Sir John Pratt, resident in Tsinan recalled that the dispatch to Shantung was a perfect farce for the British. Professor Ian Nish has also written that the Tsingtao operation brought condemnation rather than satisfaction between Japan and Britain until the war ended.[8] The British political goal of increasing its reputation and its influence in China was not achieved. Moreover, the fact that IJA made light of the British Army's contribution was constantly repeated. This was all reported to Britain and caused strains on Anglo-Japanese relations which contributed to the later breakdown in relations between the two countries.

Occupation of the South Sea Islands

Although the IJN wished to acquire the South Sea Islands, they stated: 'we are suspending our Southern advance and will observe and await developments in the situation.'[9] This was due to anti-Japanese feelings in the USA; and the request by the British government for Japan to limit her theatre of operations. Furthermore, Japanese government policy was that the occupation of Kiaochow Bay would be the main operation. On 13 August, a report came through the IJN attaché in London, Captain Abo Kiyotane, attending a celebration for Japan's participation to the War, that the IJN were being asked to dispatch the cruiser *Izumo* to Mexico and to Esquimault due to the shortage of naval forces covering the security of the coasts.[10] This was outside Japan's 'limited' theatre of operations and prompted Foreign Minister Kato Takaaki to assert to Ambassador Sir William C. Greene in Tokyo that the 'limited theatre of operations' could not be included in the final notification. In addition, the minister protested, 'it [the request] is against the limitation suggested [by the Foreign Office] . . . nowadays, it seems that the communication among authorities in your country is unreliable'.[11] Then, Kato instructed Ambassador Inoue Kaoru that due to differences between the Foreign Office and the Admiralty and the contradictory demands of the

Foreign Office and the C-in-C China Squadron 'agreeing that the IJN and the RN exchange two of their ships', that Japan oppose proposals.[12] Later on 18 August, Admiral Sir Thomas M. Jerram, C-in-C China Squadron, reported that the German Eastern Squadron would gather at Yap in the Marshall Islands. On hearing this, the IJN judged that 'our assertion regarding the theatre of operation was acceptable to Britain'. Thus the IJN instructed its Third Squadron to take 'immediate action to secure the route from the south of Shanghai to the north of Hong Kong and protect commerce' and instructed the captains of the cruisers *Ibuki* and *Chikuma* to head for Hong Kong and carry out joint operations with the China Squadron. The IJN also commanded the captain of the cruiser *Izumo* that in order to maintain security off the North American coast, which was outside the 'limited theatre', he make Esquimault his base and 'protect the commerce of the Empire and our friends at the North American coast – Immediate action'.[13]

Furthermore, it was reported that the Admiralty directly requested Cdr. Sakurai Masakiyo, stationed as an assistant attaché in London, to request the IJN to dispatch battlecruiser *Ibuki* and two cruisers to surround and destroy the German Eastern Squadron: 'although if [the request] were to be directed by the Foreign Ministry, I would be afraid to lose a chance otherwise'. On 19 August, Cdr. Yamanashi reported the British request for additional ships to be dispatched. This request without Foreign Office instructions was considered by Admiral Jerram, who decided 'there would be no need to ask the British government's intention or consult with the Ambassador in Tokyo'.[14] Under such changed conditions, the IJN now determined to send one unit because of the Admiralty requests and the battleship *Satsuma* commanded by Rear-Admiral Matsumura Tatsuo led the 2nd Southern Squadron, comprising the second-class cruisers *Hirado* and *Yahagi*. By this reorganization, the Southern squadron *Asama*, *Kurama* and *Tsukuba*, commanded by Yamaya Tanin, were renamed 1st Southern Squadron. These units were directed to co-operate with the Australian Squadron. The 1st Southern Squadron in particular was directed to 'stay at the Eastern Caroline Islands as a temporary base and continue preparations until something happens at the Marshall Islands'. Responding to these instructions, Admiral Yamaya organized a combined landing party to scout the situation on Yap. He indicated: 'this activity is not to occupy enemy territory permanently. If the Germans appear, we will declare this island is under the Japanese Empire's authority. As soon as the scouting mission finishes, we will leave the island and return to the ship by four o'clock in the afternoon'. On the morning of 29 September, the unit landed at Yap without any resistance and 'flew our flag after lowering the German national flag'. The unit declared to the German governor on the island that the island 'would be under our authority as long as the German squadron keeps appearing' and then the unit seized official documents and weapons. After lowering the naval flag, the unit went back to the ship at 3:10 p.m.[15]

However, as 'the time was ripe for consideration of the South Seas Islands under German control', on 2 October the Japanese Cabinet debated whether the South Sea Islands should be occupied temporarily or permanently. It was decided that the decision to opt for permanent occupation or not would 'be determined depending on the subsequent situation' and for the time being temporary occupation was agreed. Three days after the cabinet decision, the IJN issued instructions to the 1st and 2nd Southern Squadrons 'to occupy key locations on the islands and place a garrison there'. The garrison 'will be replaced by troops dispatched from Japan at an opportune moment'.[16]

At that time, the German Eastern Squadron was situated in the South Seas Islands area and the *Emden* was directed to the Indian Ocean to maximize the threat and damage to Allied marine traffic. As the First Lord of the Admiralty Winston S. Churchill said, 'warships flying the Japanese flag committed themselves to escorts for most of the transportation in the Pacific and the Indian Ocean'.[17] In fact, the IJN dispatched the battleship *Satsuma*, the cruisers *Kurama*, *Tsukuba*, *Hirado*, *Yahagi*, *Nisshin* and *Kasuga* plus two destroyers to the Southern Pacific from Canada in order to surround the German Eastern Squadron at the Admiralty's request. The IJN also dispatched the cruisers *Ibuki*, *Chikuma* and *Nishin* to the Indian Ocean to deal with the *Emden*. Britain now had to rely totally on the IJN for the security of the Pacific and Indian Oceans and therefore had no reason or indeed power to limit the activities of the IJN.

The RN may have been concerned that the willingness of the IJN to co-operate would evaporate if the attempts, at the outbreak of the war, to limit the IJN's sphere of operations had remained in place. Churchill's telegram of 2 October recognized 'the crucial contribution' of the IJN and reiterated an expectation of strong and continuous support. The telegram was sent under the name of the Admiralty and the RN greatly appreciated not only the main goal of the Japanese fleet in destroying Germany's key bases in the Pacific but also the IJN's unlimited support in areas such as searching for the enemy's fleets, protecting commerce and providing troop escorts ships. In addition, in the congratulatory telegram celebrating the victory at the Battle of the Falklands from Navy Minister Yashiro Rokuro, Churchill expressed British gratitude for IJN support that

> we finally have victory in our hands after four months of joint operations . . . due to the strong and continuous support by the Japanese navy. We ensured the peace in a vast area of the sea from Mozambique to South American Continent as the result of destroying the German Eastern squadron. Taking this opportunity, we as the representatives of British and Australian navies would like to express our appreciation for the unlimited and precious support by Japanese Navy.[18]

Occupation of the South Seas Islands and mistakes by the UK and Australia

The South Seas Islands were occupied by the IJN due to both to an unfavourable situation for Britain at this time in the war and to the strong desire and willingness of the IJN to occupy the islands. Yet this 'temporary' occupation of the islands was later to cause misunderstanding when the RN adopted the strategy of reducing its naval power in the Far East. The British China Squadron lacked the ships and power to pursue the German Eastern Squadron alone. On top of that, Churchill's operational leadership was flawed after the outbreak of the war. By assuming that the German Squadron would return to Tsingtao for supplies, the C-in-C China Squadron was going to carry out a plan to advance to a point that would prevent the German Squadron from returning. However, Churchill ordered Admiral Jerram that all ships stationed in the Far East should meet at Hong Kong, just before an order was to be carried out. Therefore, the deployment off Tsingtao was cancelled and all ships gathered at Hong Kong, 1000 miles south of Tsingtao.[19]

Afterwards Jerome went into action off the River Yangtse to try and block supply ships from Tsingtao. But the British squadron arrived after coal and supply ships had left. Admiral von Spee therefore gained vital supplies to sustain long-term operations from more than ten supply ships. If Churchill had considered the anxieties of residents and had not ordered the concentration of ships at Hong Kong, the German squadron would not have been able to gather so many supply ships at Pagan Island and its activities would have been greatly limited, according to Peter Lowe: 'Regarding Jerram's utilisation of his ships, Captain T.G. Forthingham blamed too much emphasis on planning to attack Yap and an underestimation of the ability of German supply ships in Tsingtao to support the German Eastern Squadron thus precipitating long-term activity by the German Squadron.'[20]

As mentioned above, the dispersion of Anglo-Japanese naval units was the result of the Hong Kong concentration command by Churchill, and Admiral Jerram's misjudgment of the German Squadron leaving for the Indian Ocean. 'Destruction' as the first priority of naval strategy and the inappropriate use of their own naval units by Australia and New Zealand. These mistakes gave great freedom of action to the Germans, invalidated the limited theatre of operations of the IJN and provided the IJN with a good reason to occupy Yap.

On the other hand, the RN did not land on Yap but bombarded it on 11 August and again on 12 September since it was reported by Ambassador Greene that an Australian force would be sent there and the IJN did not have a plan of occupation.[21] The situation of Yap Island was unclear to Jerram. Although the communication facilities were destroyed, there was always a possibility that the system had been temporarily repaired and was being used. Thus, the 2nd Southern Squadron had been asked to investigate and landed temporarily when it was passing there. Having received a telegraph from Britain that the Australian force had been dispatched, the admiral Matsumura, Commander of the 2nd Southern Squadron, was directed to 'complete the procedure of the transfer of the Island'.[22]

However, a mistake by the Australian Minister of Defence George P. Pearce altered things completely. Pearce misinterpreted the telegraph 'Yap and others' as Yap and all of other Pacific Islands under German suzerainty. He announced that the Japanese government had agreed to transfer these islands to Australia and Australian forces would be sent to occupy these islands until the end of the war.[23] When he saw this newspaper report, Foreign Minister Kato informed Ambassador Inoue that it was only Yap that would be immediately transferred and that 'the British authorities should attend to instructing Australian officials to correct the misunderstanding'.[24] Ambassador Inoue visited Foreign Secretary Edward Grey and passed on this message on the 24th. But, two days previously a telegram had arrived stating that the IJN objected to the transfer of Angaur and Yap. Therefore, the dispatch of an Australian force might now cause friction between Britain and Japan. The Japanese occupation of Yap was only for military purposes and Foreign Minister Kato also agreed that the resolution of the territorial matter could be solved at the end of the war. Therefore, the decision to dispatch an Australian force should be reconsidered in order to maintain a smooth relationship between Japan and Britain, according to Greene's telegram.[25] In addition, the RN lost two cruisers, the *Monmouth* and the *Good Hope*, when Rear-Admiral Sir Christopher Cradock was defeated by the German Eastern Squadron at Coronel off the South-West American coast on 1 November. The RN now had to ask the IJN for support in order to seek out and attack the German Eastern Squadron. Faced with such a difficult war situation, Churchill sent Colonial Secretary Lewis V. Harcourt a message:

> I am sure that there is no reason to make Japanese navy repulse from the Yap Island and this occupation is just military but not political. Australia may push us for this matter but I would like you to hold it down. Naval Ministry has gained the efforts by Japanese navy's generous support and would oppose any activity that might possibly cause misgivings or unpleasant to Japanese navy. At this moment, we cannot afford to send cruisers to the Yap Islands. It is also impossible to change our current plan.[26]

Harcourt on the 23rd and Foreign Minister Grey on the 26th wrote separately to Governor-General Ronald M. Ferguson of Australia expressing the following opinion: co-operation between Japan and UK is mutually beneficial for both countries and the Japanese navy's support is sincere. The occupation of the German territories in the South Seas is in order to achieve the military goal and military consideration has to be taken seriously during the war. Sending your force to Angaur and Yap should be cancelled, as these territorial matters will be determined after the war.[27] On 6 December, Harcourt also informed Ferguson as follows:

> currently the Japanese navy's support is indispensable for our navy which is short of strength while the Japanese government are strongly opposed since the IJN has given so much support but gained nothing. I would like you to convince other ministers to agree to give Japan the islands north of the equator since you will have the Solomon Islands and others south of the equator.[28]

Thus Australia, through Defence Minister Pearce's misunderstanding, lost not only Yap but also all the South Pacific islands north of the equator, and this created a great territorial opportunity for Japan.

The rebellion of Indian soldiers stationed in Singapore

Five days after Ambassador Greene had protested to Foreign Ministry Kato against article 5 of the '21 Demands' on China, on the afternoon of 15 February 1915, a rebellion of Indian soldiers stationed in Singapore occurred at the Alexandria Barracks. A small party of about 25 Indian soldiers stole weapons and ammunition and attacked the prison camp where Germans were housed. They killed the commandant and officers there, stole weapons and gave them to German prisoners. Then, the soldiers (now numbering about 400) advanced into the town and some 17 white men and women were killed. In the late afternoon, around 5:00 p.m., this force was repulsed by a force comprising 85 soldiers of the Sultan of Johore's private army and white volunteers, but the barracks were surrounded and attacked. By that time, most of the British units in Singapore had been dispatched to the European front and those left behind consisted of only 550 soldiers, including the Sultan of Johore's soldiers, while only one gunboat, the *Cadmus*, was available. Under such circumstances, the Governor-General and Admiral Jerram, C-in-C China Squadron made a request to the Japanese Consul Fujii Minoru and Lt. Cdr. Araki Jiro, on the staff of the British China Squadron, for volunteers and ships. Consul Fujii arranged a civilian and sent 104 volunteer soldiers on 16 February. On receiving the telegram about the rebellion in Singapore, Rear-Admiral Tsuchiya Kanemitsu, C-in-C of the IJN Third Fleet, aboard the cruiser *Tsushima* heading for Hong Kong, immediately rerouted to Singapore and also directed the cruiser *Otowa*, stationed to watch for escaping German merchant ships off Manila Bay, at the request of the RN, to head immediately for Singapore. The *Otowa* reached Singapore on the evening of the 17th and landed 82 marines. On the next morning, these troops, together with men from the *Cadmus*, attacked the rebels' base, the Alexandria Barracks. After occupying this without resistance, these units defeated the mutineers, arrested 12 Indian soldiers and passed them over to the RN authorities. As soon as the *Tsushima* arrived in port, a combined force from the *Otowa* and *Tsushima* comprising 156 men was landed and they carried out city patrols and provided escorts to the hospitals, the Alexandria Barracks, and the warehouses from 17–21 February. The number of soldiers dispatched to crush the riot was 440 British soldiers (90 from the *Cadmus*, 200 regular soldiers and 150 volunteers), 344 Japanese (including 186 volunteers), 190 French and 42 Russians. The reliable force available immediately after the riots happened was 344 Japanese soldiers (158 from military units), the French *Montcalm*'s 187 men and 42 men from the Russian merchant cruiser *Orel* which had arrived in port the following morning. At the time the rebellion broke out, its cause was unknown. Until 600 soldiers of the 4th Infantry arrived from Rangoon, the force was small. Thus the RN was forced to rely on the IJN as the main force for the assault on the Alexandra Barracks and for escort duties after its occupation.[29] The rebellion was considered to be part of a German worldwide conspiracy. Under these circumstances, Admiral Jerram pointed out that 'the situation is very serious and inevitably a great anxiety', and IJN ships patrolled threatening areas because 'people were restless after the riot'. For all these reasons, 'the existence of Japanese navy must have been of "Utmost Value" to Britain'.[30] On 25 February, when a standing-down ceremony was held, the Governor-General praised the IJN by citing Churchill's speech in Parliament where he stated 'your fleets are "the most effective fleets" in the Pacific'.[31] This incident showed clearly the extent to which British security in East Asia was dependent on the IJN at sea and on land.

The dispatch of the 2nd Special Squadron to the Mediterranean

In 1916, Germany reinforced its submarine operations against commercial shipping and inflicted even greater damage. On 18 December 1916, the Admiralty again requested Japan's Foreign Ministry to provide ships. They requested two of the four cruisers of the 1st Special Squadron at Singapore to be sent to Capetown and four destroyers from this same squadron to be sent to the Mediterranean.[32] This request caused 'a great deal of concern within the IJN. They were advised by the Rear-Admiral Akiyama Saneyuki that the allies needed further co-operation.' The cabinet agreed to the request with the following conditions: Japanese shipping was also being sunk and the IJN had to consider their own duty to protect themselves and therefore any further requests would be rejected. As to the destroyer unit (four ships), there was the fear that they would be placed under British command. The cruiser and the two destroyer units had to be under independent (IJN) command. The decisions received cabinet approval on 10 December, but with the condition that the Japanese occupation of the South Seas Islands be approved.[33] Meanwhile three days prior to the cabinet decision, the IJN had instructed Rear-Admiral Sato Kozo to board the cruiser *Akashi* and 10th and 11th destroyer units (8 destroyers) and depart for Malta on 18 February 1917. They arrived at Malta on 13 April via Colombo and Port Said. After that there was a request from King George V and the IJN sent the 15th Destroyer unit by 1 June. Thus the 2nd Special Squadron at Malta now comprised 17 ships, one cruiser, 12 destroyers, plus two destroyers and two sloops on loan from the British.

The 2nd Special Squadron was based at Malta. This unit carried out direct escort duties for the most important (troop) transport vessels of the allied armies on the Alexandria–Malta–Marseilles, the Alexandria–Taranto and the Malta–Salonika routes. They were under the British C-in-C Mediterranean who controlled transport, escorts and anti-submarine operations. There were some 348 escort trips with the total number of escorted ships reaching 788 and the number of soldiers transported was around 700 000 (see Table 4.1). This unit containing the IJN ships contributed greatly to the war effort through these activities as well as saving the lives of some 7075 people from damaged and sinking ships.[34]

In the Mediterranean, there were anti-submarine ships from UK, France, Italy, Japan and USA. The report by the C-in-C Mediterranean, G.C. Dickens, to the Admiralty described the Italian Navy as 'inefficient and incapable of anti-submarine in terms of offence and defence. The Italians limited themselves to defence off their own coast. Therefore we cannot rely on its support.' The French Navy, he said, had a positive attitude but a problem with its organization. Hence, its operations could not be trusted and lacked military common sense. The Japanese Navy was wonderful but small, whilst the Greek Navy was almost totally discounted. The US Navy was active from Gibraltar to the Atlantic and so unavailable for activities in this theatre of operations.[35] Although escort duty was the main task for the IJN, the contribution may have been exaggerated since the size of the units was small and not one submarine was sunk. Nevertheless, the IJN escorted

Table 4.1 Number of Allied ships escorted by the Japanese Second Squadron

Country	Warships	Transports
Britain	21	623
France		100
Italy		18
Others		26

100000 soldiers from Alexandria to Marseilles between mid-April and mid-June 1918 and also escorted Allied troops from Egypt to Salonika at the end of September. These efforts may well have had a considerable influence on easing the tense military situation of the Allied armies at the time.[36] The following was reported to the Admiralty by Rear-Admiral George A. Ballard, Commodore of the Malta naval base:

> we often have conflicts with French and Italian navies about the policy of operation. But Commander Satô always responds to our requests so that there is no problem between the Japanese navy and us, which is satisfying. The support of Japanese fleets is precious. The net working rate of French navy is low comparing to British while the Italian Navy is much lower than French. But the Japanese navy is different.

The C-in-C Mediterranean, G.C. Dickens, reported: 'Commander Sato always prepares his fleets to respond to my request and his officers always practice their duty perfectly. . . . Needless to say, Japanese ships are wonderful.'[37] The active duty rate (days at sea) for ships (the number of actions/30 days as one month) of Allied destroyers reached a maximum of 60 per cent for the RN, 45 per cent for France and Italy, but the level for IJN units reached 72 per cent. The number of days at sea reached 25–26 days per month and the cruise average was 6000 miles per month. A number of events were recorded in the official naval war history: when lightning hit the *Transylvania*, 'in spite of the danger from the lightning they (IJN) performed courageously' and saved 3000 of the 3600 passengers and crew. Similarly, when lightning struck the *Multin*, 'the unit saved all but one of the 664 people on board because of their skilful operation'. The *Times* evaluated most highly the IJN ships' speedy and courageous actions and concern: 'Speedy arrival and seamanlike handling' and 'Good seamanship and the greatest rapidity of action.'[38] The activity of these IJN ships stationed in the Mediterranean made a significant contribution to the fighting of the Allied forces.

When Japan had received the request to dispatch ships to the Mediterranean, they demanded that Britain guarantee to support the Japanese occupation of Shantung and the South Sea Islands at the peace conference: 'the previous cabinet limited the theatre of operations of our navy so that we refused to dispatch ships. In consideration of this the present cabinet needs a strong case to back a decision (to dispatch).' In these negotiations, Ambassador Chinda Sutemi 'implied that the issue of the dispatch will result in a deadlock' without this guarantee. Japan then obtained a guarantee from Britain which would provide 'support for the request that Japan submit regarding to Shantung and Islands of German territories north of the equator'.[39] The strong desire to occupy German Pacific

Islands therefore influenced the decision to dispatch IJN ships to the Mediterranean.

Anti-Japanese criticism by Britain

To borrow the words of the *Genrô* (Elder stateman), Inoue Kaoru, 'the First World War was a miracle for the development and fortune of Japan in the new Taisho era'. However, in Britain there was great distrust and dissatisfaction regarding Japan's role in the war. Japan was perceived as having hesitated to co-operate and seemingly demanding reward for such requests, despite being an ally. Captain Edward H. Rymer RN noted this dissatisfaction in his report on 'The present situation of Japan' as follows:

> Japanese politicians claim that the alliance between Japan and UK is 'the Keystone' of Japanese diplomacy. But Japanese basic rules for this war are, first of all, pursuing the most economical benefit, and next considering international relations after the war. That is to not cause strong anti-Japanese feelings in Germany. Thus, support for the allies would be made minimally. These two rules control every activity by Japan. Although pro-German feelings are too much, it is because Japanese leading academics, doctors and lawyers learned from Germany and Japanese military was modeled on the German military. Especially, the defeat of the German military would devalue the evaluation of Japanese military and this would be unpleasant. But, why have Japanese applied German customs and methods? That is because Japanese consider that applying German methods is the most convenient way to make money. Hence, it is a mistake that Japanese are pro-German. Every Japanese is an absolute Japanophile – an egoist who thinks about only himself and has no feeling of sacrificing himself for other countries. Japan does not accept the request of dispatching fleets because dispatch would affect trading and lose benefit. Dispatch is against the first rule that is to pursue the maximum benefit. Japanese are not interested in us pointing out that Japan is not an undeveloped country in East Asia but has a lot of responsibilities as a member of the western camp. If we strongly suggest how Britain should support Japan, what Japan should do as an ally, and that Japan should have an obligation as an ally, Japan would desert us. If Britain concedes and begs for their support, the wise Japanese would become complacent inwardly with doing well or the ignorant Japanese would simply increase his confidence and escalate his demand . . . Japan was spellbound by money and blinded by the dream of being the leader in the Pacific.[40]

In addition to this, the British government received many anti-Japanese criticisms and complaints not only from Ambassadors in Japan and China but also residents there (especially traders). There were numerous complaints of Japanese interference and limits placed on British traders resident in China, pro-German speeches by high-ranking government officials, Japanese academics and journalists supporting Indian independence activists, and entry and trading limitations in the South Seas Islands. According to Ambassador Greene, who spent four years in Japan during the war and dealt with four Japanese Foreign Ministers (Kato Takaaki, Honno Ichiro, Goto Shunpei and Ishii Kikujiro), all adopted the same style of response to British requests for co-operation. That is, they either rejected the requests immediately, rejected by saying that they would answer later or waited for time to run out by saying that they have not yet considered and thus reject.[41] The collection of British formal complaints towards such Japanese attitudes might best be shown by the 'Memorandum on Anglo-Japanese Relations' distributed at the Imperial Conference held in March 1917, one year before the end of the war. The memorandum noted the following:

The Japanese possess fanatic love of the nation, national aggression and individualistic brutality and is full of deception. Japan is an aggressor nation by nature. The Japanese believe that they have a great political potential in the future. They were taught the idea of superiority and that they are more superior race than any other races such as the yellow-skinned race and the brown race. And, they consider it a moral obligation that they force their own culture upon neighbouring countries. Is there any room for harmonizing such Japanese aggressive ambition and British appropriate demand? Japan and Britain are so far apart in terms of morality. As long as British ideals and Japanese ambition are different, it is impossible to build a common foundation between the two countries. As Japanese education, commerce, organisation and rules have followed the German system, consequently Japanese characteristics mirror the German-style. It is not an exaggeration that Japan will become the Eastern version of Prussia. It has been said that Japan has to expand. That is true. However, why doesn't Japan develop Korea, Taiwan, Manchuria and Sakhalin? These districts should absorb the increasing population of Japan. Regarding resources, Japan's political aims in part involves the fall of the British Empire so that there is no common purpose of co-operation between Japan and Britain. If we cannot approve of such Japanese ambition, we must determine that the time will come to stop Japanese ambition by military force. The Alliance between Japan and Britain is built on sand. Sooner or later, it is necessary to determine whether to take action to stop expansion of Japan and become the faithful nation that took an honourable and moderate course for the world, or whether to take action against Japan by basically considering it as the eastern version of Prussia. This alliance is the result of two racially and culturally different countries bound by the fragile paper of a written provision.[42]

The Japanese responses and the background

As Captain Rymer pointed out, the Japanese Constitution was modelled on that of Germany and many Germans were invited to visit Japan. In addition, a great number of Japanese who had studied in Germany occupied important positions in government at this time. In addition, the IJA, which had a great influence on domestic politics, was modelled on the German system and had an underlying pro-German feeling as well as an admiration for the German system. On top of all this there was, semi-officially, a strong admiration for the German ability to put up such a good fight against the Allied armies. In addition to this pro-German feeling, there was an ongoing controversy over the Anglo-Japanese Alliance amongst Japanese leaders over those areas where the national interests of Japan were clearly in conflict with those of Britain.

The Anglo-Japanese Alliance had been a pivotal element in Japanese foreign policy since the Russo-Japanese War. However, in 1907 a trade agreement was concluded with Russia, originally a target of the Alliance. This caused a rift between Japan and Russia on the one hand and Britain and the USA over the Chinai Railway. In 1911, the third Anglo-Japanese revised agreement specifically excluded the USA. Japan had opposed Britain over the demand for guarantees regarding the occupation of the Kuanwai railway during the 1911 revolution. The pursuit of advantage in China led to serious antagonism between Japan and Britain. Therefore there was a movement to discard the alliance because of a growing distrust in its feasibility. One of the central aims of the Anglo-Japanese Alliance had been to maintain common benefits on China by protecting the independence and the territory of the Qing dynasty and equal commercial opportunities for the Allies. Yet when British attention was distracted away from China after the outbreak of the war, Japan certainly strengthened its foundations for business in China. There were only 966 offices of Japanese trading companies prior to the outbreak of the war, but the number had increased to 4483 in 1918 when the war ended.[43] When Britain protested and challenged such an aggressive expansion into China by the Japanese, they in turn protested that Britain had 'no obligation to support' Japan in the event of a US–Japan war whilst Japan had an obligation to protect India. As the Alliance increasingly was viewed as of 'small benefit for Japan but a great benefit for Britain',[44] arguments concerning revision or abrogation of the Alliance increasingly appeared in public in Japan.

Ultranationalist movements such as the *Genyosha* and *Kokuryukai* had emerged at the time of Japanese modernization. Such nationalist feelings were influenced by race-related and independence-related activities of Asian peoples triggered by the Japanese victory in the Russo-Japanese War. Opposed to the invasion of Asia by the Western Powers, this Japanese nationalism developed a new principle that Asian races should help each other against the white races. Especially as Germany supported the Guadal party (the independence group) financially in order to cause confusion in India, the Indian independence group became very active. In 1915, July Indian Independence hardliners Bhagwan Singh and Raj Bihari Bose defected to Japan as Britain tightened controls in India. When the British government requested the extradition of these activists, the Japanese government nearly agreed. But Inukai Tsuyoshi (*Kokumin-to*), Tokonami Takejiro (*Seiyukai*), Terao Toru (Professor of Tokyo University), Oyama Mituru (*Genyosha*), Uchida Ryouhei (*Kokuryukai*), Okawa Shumei (India researcher), journalists from the *Asahi*, *Yamato* and *Kokumin* newspapers and so forth sympathized with the Indian activists and protected them.[45] The *Yamato* newspaper criticized the government, stating that there was no clause concerning the transfer of criminals within the Alliance agreement. Even if the government had ordered these activists to be deported there would be only five days to leave and there were only steamer services to Shanghai and Hong Kong during this time. Hence, a deportation order whilst 'formally expelling' them was actually the transportation of criminals and 'expelling foreigners for such hollow reasoning is a disgrace to national dignity and national sovereignty'. In addition, the *Yamato* newspaper interviewed these Indians and reported that the IJN had supported the suppression of the Indian revolt at Singapore: 'the Japanese dispatched to the units stated they had never dreamed of firing on rioting soldiers'. Such actions, the newspaper reported, would have a 'serious detrimental influence' on 100 million Indians and their later feelings towards Japan. 'Japanese citizens should keep this in mind'.[46]

Meanwhile, the Indian Taraknath Das asserted that China, Japan and India should join together in a united Eastern peoples and needed to prepare for coping with western colonization and 'race competition in the future'. Although Japan had alliances with European countries, Professor Fang Chun-zong at St John University in Shanghai questioned whether Japan would still manage to continue the alliance. He asserted that the alliance between Japan and European countries was a mistake and that Japan should act for Asia with Asians. The issue of racial discrimination in USA and Australia reinforced this assertion which was increasingly popular in Japan. The argument advanced was as follows: 'Japan alone fighting against the Great Powers of Europe would lead to its extinction. However, it is impossible for Japan to gain a real friend (ally) in Europe. Consequently, it is natural for Japan to seek its real friend in Asia.'[47] This Asian principle of acting 'with Asians' increasingly separated Japan and made it a less active supporter of Britain.

Although there were numerous British criticisms of Japanese co-operation with Britain during the war, I should like to evaluate this by reference to 'Memorandum on Anglo-Japanese Relations' at the 1917 Imperial Conference mentioned above. This report was distributed at the conference and shows the overall evaluation from a British perspective of the Japanese contribution during wartime.

1. Benefits Japan gained from the Anglo-Japanese Alliance
- Secured the German right to the Shantung Peninsula and the German-held South Seas Islands north of the equator.
- Acquired the transfer of the Northern China railway and the fishery rights along the coast of Russia. Gained some privileges from the agreement between Russia and Japan but weakened the Anglo-Japanese Alliance.
- Acquired the right for Japanese doctors to provide medical treatment in the Malay Peninsula.
- Gained significant benefits from exporting weapons and ammunition to the Allies.
- Accelerated industrial development.
- Ensured the Japanese economic position by increasing exports towards India, Australia, South Africa and Thailand while European countries were too involved in the war.
- Gained 'a free hand' in China by supporting the southern military clique in China.

2. Unfaithful actions as an ally
- Protected Indian independent activists in Japan and failed to co-operate with British investigations.
- Took no appropriate measures to stop German commercial activities until the end of 1916.
- Did not make any effort to reduce trading with Germany through neutral nations.
- Did not restrain the protest against the Anglo-Japanese Alliance and created a negative influence on neutral nations.
- Totally ignored the need to secure the raw materials Britain needed and furthermore demanded from Britain repeatedly war supplies such as iron and gold.
- Did not co-operate with British attempts to limit the import of unnecessary supplies but obstructed these efforts.
- Made great efforts to weaken the British position in China and succeeded.

3. Contributions as an ally
- Occupied Tsingtao and destroyed the German base in the Far East.
- Occupied the German South Seas Islands and destroyed German support bases.
- Carried out joint operations such as escorting ANZAC troops to Europe as well as helping to seek out and attack and destroy the German Eastern Squadron.
- Sent two cruisers to the Indian Ocean and a destroyer to Singapore.

Later agreed to dispatch two cruisers to Capetown and one cruisers and 12 destroyers were sent to the Mediterranean.

- Supplied weapons and ammunition to Allied countries, especially Russia.
- Accepted government bonds from Britain and Russia (later France).
- Escorted gold from Vladivostok to Canada twice (note: additional two escorts followed).

When asked in the USA his views on the Alliance, Foreign Secretary Sir Arthur J. Balfour recalled 'there were almost no cases where Japan did not co-operate with British requests'. Again, Foreign Secretary Grey evaluated the actions of Japan during the war as follows: 'during the last year that I served as Foreign Secretary Japan was always fair in her obligations as an ally and in sharing the benefits. The Japanese government and Ambassadors stationed in UK were honourable and faithful allies.' The First World War was 'a great opportunity' for Japan to expand its territories. 'If there were any European country like Japan which had surplus population and if they needed territories, it is doubtful that they (the European countries) would have managed to control themselves in the face of such an immediate opportunity as Japan did.'[48] However, Britain believed that Japanese journalism, which reported carelessly and sensationally and instigated anti-British feelings, was actually controlled by the Japanese government. Thus, as described above, Britain always suspected that the Japanese were not keeping faith with them. In addition, Japan continued to pursue its own national interests, such as territorial rights and territorial expansion. Japan at that time was also affected by the active psychological game being played by the Germans who hoped to make Japan desert the Allies. In the self-governing dominions of the Allied countries, in the USA and in the UK, there was racial discrimination towards the Japanese. The Dominions refused to sign the Anglo-Japanese Treaty of Commerce and Navigation. There was also an incident during which the cruiser *Yahagi* was fired upon from a coastal fort when entering Fremantle after her patrol duties.[49] Under such circumstances Japan's responses were not necessarily unfaithful, as Foreign Secretary Grey pointed out.

Certainly Japan repeatedly claimed the possession of the German Pacific Islands and obtained it. But Britain and her dominions got not only African German colony, but also the Pacific Islands south of the equator, New Guinea, New Britain, Solomon Islands and Samoa. While, Japan got only the North of German Pacific Islands which are just 'a piece of bread waste' for Japan.

During the war, the IJN established sea control of the Pacific and Indian Ocean completely, and without Japanese assistance, Great Britain would have lost control of the Pacific and Indian sea line of communication. In the Mediterranean, at its peak strength in 1917, the Japanese flotilla numbered 17 warships. But after the war, why did British and the Allies so quickly forget Japan's assistance, and why has western naval history neglected this Japanese contribution to the Allies? The most obvious reason was the situation in the Pacific after the war. After the war, The German threat to Britain's Far East possessions had been removed and the nascent Soviet Union was no longer threatening India. 'The common enemy' had disappeared and Japan became Britain's 'Most likely enemy in future conflict'.[50]

Hostile views of Japan prevailed during the war fuelled by German propaganda based on a racial animosity towards the Japanese. This did not diminish during the struggle, despite Japan's assistance to the British and Americans. Beside racial prejudice, the naval rivalry of the Royal Navy and United States Navy quickly re-emerged. In the Mediterranean while escorting British troops, Japanese destroyers were not leased the submarine detection device, and Japanese liaison officers were not allowed to deal with crypt analysis.

In Australia, Japanese devotions and services were denied by the First Naval Member and a report of the 'Misleading Reference to Japanese Naval Action in the Pacific Ocean during the War' was submitted to Prime Minister William M. Hughes.[51] Given these events, it is perhaps not so surprising that the record of Japanese assistance quickly and completely disappeared from western naval history after the war.

Then at the peace conference, the clause for abolishing racial discrimination was rejected because of opposition from the British dominions of Canada and Australia. The unfavourable Japanese naval ratio was compelled by an apparent conspiracy by the USA and Britain at the Washington Conference, and the fortification of Singapore immediately after the cancellation of the Alliance suggested an image of an 'ungrateful Britain' to the Japanese people.[52] The reason for these aggravated anti-British feeling is explained by the Japanese navy as follows:

Until the First World War, Britain took full advantage of its relationship with Japan, fully employing Japan's military strength and goodwill at all times, including the period of Imperial Russia's aggression to China, restraining the Indian independence movement, blocking China's anti-foreign activities, and protecting its dominions after it concentrated its fleets in the North Sea. Once peace resumed, however, its attitude suddenly changed and Britain refused to grant Japan even the slightest concessions. This led to Japanese isolation at the Washington Conference. The return of Shantung, the annulment of the Anglo-Japanese Alliance, the conclusion of the Nine Power Treaty, and eventually to all-out suppression of Japanese trade.[53]

Thus, both Japan and Britain took their separate paths on a collision course to disaster.

Notes

1. Rikugun Sanbo Honbu (ed.), *Hi Taisho 3 Nen Nichidoku Senshi (Secret History of the German–Japanese War of 1914)*, 2 vols (Rikugun Sanbo Honbu, 1916), vol. 1, pp. 81, 332 and 472.
2. Rikugun Sanbo Honbu (ed.), *Taisho 3 Nen Seneki Shoken Shu (Collection of the Reports and Observations on the War of 1914)* (Rikugun Sanbo Honbu, 1915), p. 102, NIDS.
3. Doc. No. 345, Abstract of Newspaper, August 1918, FO371-3816, PRO.
4. Sakano Junji (ed.), *Takarabe Nitsuki Kaigun Jikan Jidai (Diary of Takarabe: Navy Vice Minister Era)*, 2 vols (Yamakawa Shutsupan, 1983), vol. 2, p. 374; Capt. Yosida Seifu, *Dai 1 and Dai 2 Kantai Senji Nitsuki (War Diary of First and Second Fleet)*, NIDS.
5. Osaka Asahi Shinbunsha (ed.), *Chintao Senki Hokushin Kansenki (Boxer's Rebellion and Capture of Tsingtao)* (Senki Meicho Kankokai, 1930), p. 32.
6. Letter from Capt. Rymer to Admiral Yashiro, Nichiei Kaigun Kosho Tuzuri: Taisho 3–6 Nen (Document File of Anglo-Japanese Naval Negotiation File of 1914 to 17; hereafter cited as Kosho Tuzuri), NIDS.
7. Julian S. Corbett, *History of the Great War: Naval Operations* (London: Longmans, Green and Co.), vol. I, p. 279.
8. John T. Pratt, *War and Politics in China* (London: Jonathan Cape Ltd, 1942), p. 137; Ian H. Nish, *Alliance in Decline: a study in Anglo-Japanese Relations 1908–1923* (London: The Athlone Press, 1972), pp. 132, 139.
9. Kaigun Gunrebu (ed.), *Kimitsu Taisho 3-4 Nen Seneki Kaigun Senshi (Top Secret Naval Operation of 1914 to 15* (hereafter cited as Kaigun Senshi) (Kaigun Gunreibu, 1919), vol. 1, p. 257.
10. Ibid., pp. 400–1.
11. Gaimusho (ed.), *Nihon Gaiko Bunsho Taisho 3 Nen, vol. 3* (hereafter *NGB Taisho 3-3*) (Gaimusho, 1966), p. 147.
12. *NGB Taisho 3-3*, pp. 147, 167.
13. *Kaigun Senshi 3-4 Nen*, vol. 1, pp. 241–3, 258–9.
14. Ibid., pp. 438, 452.
15. Ibid., pp. 286–8.
16. Ibid., p. 320, also refer to vol. 5, pp. 141–230.
17. Winston S. Churchill, *The World Crisis 1911–1914* (London: Thornton Butterworth Ltd., 1923), vol. III, p. 299.
18. Message from Churchill to Yashiro, 17 October 1914, Kosho Tuzuri, p. 60, Martin Gilbert (ed.), *Winston S. Churchill: Documents July 1914–December 1916* (London: William Heinemann Ltd, 1975), vol. 3, Part 1, pp. 247–8, 301–2.
19. Corbett, *History of the Great War*, pp. 146–7.
20. Peter Lowe, *Great Britain and Japan, 1911–1915: a Study of British Far Eastern Policy* (London: Macmillan, 1969), p. 176; Thomas G. Forthingham, *The Naval History of the World War, Offensive Operations 1914–15* (Cambridge, MA: Harvard University Press, 1925), pp. 96–8.
21. Greene to Kato, 12 October 1914, in Ann Trotter (ed.), *British Documents on Foreign Affairs: Reports and Papers from the Foreign Office Confidential Print, Part 3: From the First to the Second World War Series E, Asia, 1914–1939, Japan August 1914–1915* (hereafter cited as *BDFA*) (University Publications of America, 1991) (hereafter *BDFA III-1*), p. 84; ibid., *NGB Taisho 3-3*, p. 668, Telegram from Naval Office Melbourne (25 November 1914), ibid., Kosho Tuzuri.
22. *Kaigun Senshi*, vol. 1, pp. 498–9.

23. Ibid., *NGB Taisho 3-3*, p. 670.
24. Ibid., *Gaigun Senshi 3-4 Nen*, vol. 1, pp. 498–9.
25. Ibid., *NGB Taisho, 3-3*, p. 672, Doc. 74103, Greene to Grey (21 November 1914), G1: Governor's Records, N18: NZA.
26. Churchill to Harcourt (18 October 1914), Gilbert, *Winston S. Churchill: Documents*, vol. 3, part 1, p. 203.
27. Doc. 330, Doc. 329, *BDFA II-1*, p. 136, Telegram Sir Edward Grey (25 November 1914), Ibid., *Kankei Tuzuri*.
28. Harcourt to Ferguson (6 December 1914), Nova Papers, No. 4, ANA.
29. *NGB Taisho 4-3*, pp. 1194–1205, *Kaigun-Senshi 3-4 Nen*, vol. 4, pp. 380–8; 'Indohei no Bodo ni Kanshi Houkoku' (Report on Indian rebellion), *Taisho 4-Nen Kobun Biko (Official Documents of Supplement 1915)*, vol. 116, refer also to Jerram Papers General Letter No. 36, Jerram to Admiralty, 27 February 1915, NMM.
30. Letter from Greene to Kato, *Kankei Tuzuri*, NIDS.
31. 'Indohei no Bodo ni kanshi Hokoku', p. 1202.
32. Doc. No. 96, No. 102, *NGB Taisho 6 Nen*, vol. 3, p. 99, Doc. No. 217, Greene to Balfour, 27 January 1917, *BDFA vol. II, Part 2*, p. 196.
33. Kaigun-Senshi Furoku Kmitu Hokan (Top Secret Supplementary File of the Naval Operation), pp. 24–30.
34. *Kaigun Senshi 4-9 Nen*, vol. 2, pp. 288–313, Dai 2 Tokumu Kantai Seiribu (ed.), *Nihon Kaigun Chichukai Enseiki* (Dai 2 Tokumu Kantai, 1919), Also refer to Yoichi Hirama, 'Rising Sun in the Mediterranean: the Second Special Squadron, 1917–1918', in Ufficio Storico Della Marina Maritare (ed.), *The Mediterranean as an Element of Maritime Power* (Rome: Commissione Italiana di Storia Militare, 1998), pp. 39–54.
35. G.C. Dickson to K.G.B. Dewer, 9 May 1917, Paul G. Halpern (ed.), *The Royal Navy in the Mediterranean, 1915–1918* (London: Temple Smith, 1987), p. 469.
36. *Kaigun Senshi 4-9*, vol. 2, p. 314.
37. Ballard to Admiralty, 21 August 1917, Calthorpe to Admiralty, 28 October, 1917, op. cit., Halpern, pp. 282, 290.
38. *Enseiki*, pp. 239–40; The Times, *The Times History of the War* (London: Times Publishing Co., 1916), vol. XVIII, p. 458.
39. NGB, 6-3, p. 106, Greene to Grey, 17 January 1917, ADM116 Box 1702, FO371-2950, PRO.
40. Doc. (XC3347), *Japan at War 1914–1918* (British Embassy Tokyo, 21 February 1918), FO371-3233, PRO.
41. Doc No. 33087, British Embassy Tokyo 21 February 1918, FO371-3233.
42. Doc. 242, Memorandum on Anglo-Japanese Relations (Written for the Imperial Conference (March 1916), *BDFA II Part 2*, pp. 218–27.
43. Towa Kenkyusho (ed.), *Nihon no Taisi Toshi (Japanese Investment to China)* (Towa Kenkyusho, 1927), p. 32.
44. 'Nichiei Domei o Kaitei Subesi' (Revise Anglo-Japanese Alliance), *Dai Nihon*, vol. 3, no. 2, November 1914.
45. Refer to Soma Kuromitsu, 'Ras Bibar Bose' in Takeuchi Takashi (ed.), *Gendai Nihon Sisoshi Ajia Shugi (Modern Japanese History of Philosphy: Asianism)* (Chikuma Shobo, 1963).
46. *Yamato Shinbun*, 29 and 30 November 1915.
47. Indo-Jin Dasu ni Kansuru ken, Shinbun, Zatsushi, Torishimari Zatsuken Indo-Jin Torisimari no Ken (Control of Newspaper and Magazine: the Indian Activities), Japanese Diplomatic Archives.

48. Viscount Edward Grey, *Twenty-five Years, 1892–1916* (London: Hodder & Stoughton, 1925), vol. 3, pp. 33–4; Nish, *Alliance in Decline*, p. 262.
49. *Kaigun Senshi 3-4 Nen*, vol. 2, pp. 56–7, Yahagi Senji Nitsushi (Yahagi War Diary), NIDS.
50. Report of the Viscount Jellicoe of Scapa on Naval Mission of New Zealand, vol. III The Naval Situation in the Far Eastern Waters, N1-104, NZNA.
51. Memorandum prepared by the First Naval Member for the Acting Prime Minister (June 1919), A2219 vol. 10, ANA.
52. Ito Masanori, *Sotei Tekikoku* (Sasaki-Shutsupan, 1926), pp. 296–7.
53. IJN Intelligence Division, 'Why Anti-British Feeling Becomes Strong in Japan', in Okubo Tatsumasa (ed.), *Showa Shakai Keizaishi (History of Social-Economical: Showa Period)* (Daito Bunka Daigaku, 1989), vol. 5, p. 133.

For a more detailed exposition, please refer to my *Dai 1ji Sekaitaisen to Nihon Kaigun (World War I and the Japanese Navy)* (Keio University Press, 1998).

5

Britain, Japan and the 'Higher Realms of Intelligence', 1900–1918

John W.M. Chapman

A British military observer of the Russo-Japanese War argued that both sides 'owed their knowledge of each other far more to their secret service systems than to actual military reconnaissances' and derived much greater insight into each other's strategies from 'the higher realms of intelligence'.[1] These observations were made in 1909 when decisions on Britain's secret services and comparisons with other countries were made.[2] The intention was to create a clear hierarchy of intelligence with 'secret service' separated more clearly from the 'reconnaissances' of the Directorate of Military Operations (DMO) in the War Office, the Naval Intelligence Division (NID), consular and diplomatic services and relevant structures in the dominions, colonies and dependencies covered by the Cabinet's Committee of Imperial Defence (CID). Until then directors of military and naval intelligence had authority over foreign intelligence, mobilization and war operations and the Admiralty overseas trade protection. Service intelligence directors were given full responsibility for the negotiation of military and naval co-operation with Japan under the 1902 Anglo-Japanese Alliance, its later amendments and renewal. Representatives of both armed forces met in London in 1902 and 1907 and signed the military and naval agreements. In 1902, an agreement was signed by the British heads of service intelligence and the Japanese head of military intelligence, who signed on behalf of the Japanese Army. The role of military and naval intelligence was therefore clearly central to the implementation of the alliance.

Japan – 'attained perfection'

General Ewart (DMO) observed in 1909 that he had 'always understood that the Japanese owed a great deal to the perfection of their pre-arranged system of secret service' and the Chief of the Imperial General Staff, Sir William Nicholson, as head of military intelligence in 1902 indicated he had been fully briefed by Major-General Fukushima Yasumasa well in advance of the outbreak of war.[3] Colonel James Edmonds observed that 'in Intelligence work, as perhaps in everything pertaining to war, the Japanese have, in my humble opinion, attained perfection.'[4] At Yokohama in November 1905 Admiral Sir Gerard Noel reported how much was owed 'to the perfect system for wireless communication by wireless telegraphy organised between ships and along the coasts of Corea and Japan' and how the Japanese Fleet had dispensed with scouting, 'choosing rather to trust to a few scouts and wireless telegraph to inform them of the approach of the Baltic Fleet'. We now know that the foundation of Japanese strategy initiated in the night attack by torpedo boats at Port Arthur rested very substantially not just on the construction of most of their fleet by British shipyards, but also on the sharing of British tactical planning against Russian fleets, the provision of the most advanced wireless and range-finding equipment and the supply of intelligence by the Admiralty from 1902 onwards, with a most prominent role being played by Admiral Sir John Fisher as C-in-C of the Mediterranean Fleet and subsequently as Second and First Sea Lord.[5]

'Military adventurers'

In the 1890s concern over Russian imperialism was most keenly felt in North East Asia in relation to British interests in China. But at the same time, there was also European and American criticism of British policy in South Africa and fears of an anti-British coalition similar to Japan's experience with the Triple Alliance. There were also worries concerning the aggressive foreign policies adopted by France and the United States at this time. But secretly it was the foreign policy of Germany, in Europe and South Africa, which caused the greatest concern. The communications of Boer representatives in Europe were secretly monitored in London by censorship of the cables and intercepts sent from Aden by the Indian Army.[6] The German acquisition of Kiaochow in 1898 was viewed as opportunist. The speech by Wilhelm II about the 'Yellow Peril' and the alignment of Germany with Russia and France was regarded in Japan as a betrayal of the extensive co-operation with Germany since 1871. Germany's touting itself as an ally to both Britain and Japan was regarded suspiciously in London given Germany's pro-Russian tendencies. German efforts in London to promote an alliance also reflected the Kaiser's exasperation with the British Cabinet because they and the Japanese were unprepared to welcome his overtures.[7]

The belated arrival and arrogant attitude of the Germans at Peking during the Boxer Incident, after most of the dirty work had been done by the Japanese and British, was not appreciated even by their European allies. Colonel James Grierson, still theoretically British Military Attaché in Berlin, liaised with the Japanese and his knowledge of German was important, especially since so many Japanese army officers spoke German. Grierson's contacts with Fukushima were of no small significance. In conversations with Japanese officers in China and during a visit to Japan Grierson concluded that Germany would regret its patronizing handling of Japanese soldiers and diplomats.[8]

Close working relationships also developed between the IJN and China Fleet officers and a naval attaché, Captain Charles Ottley, was seconded from Washington in 1900–01. He produced considerable intelligence materials on Japanese developments. His statistics of fleet strengths for 1900 demonstrated the growing German naval presence after the Boxer Incident.[9] In November 1901 Sir Francis Bertie denounced Germany as an untrustworthy partner eager to see Britain and Japan embroiled in deadly quarrels with France and Russia. He nevertheless argued that Britain wished to see Russia stopped in its tracks in China, India and the Near East from encroaching on British interests, and for the alliance with Japan to provide the manpower and motivation to accomplish this in the Far East.[10]

Military versus naval co-operation 'in the event of war'

Britain had no experience of military alliances since the Crimean War.[11] The Army, however, recognized that Napoleon had remained at the zenith of his power for ten years after the decisive naval victory of Trafalgar and appreciated the Japanese Army position on early combined operations against the huge Russian land forces. The Admiralty, supported initially by the Japanese Navy, emphasized establishing prior command of the sea as a prerequisite for allied operations. But the secret naval agreement in January 1902 scarcely registered whole-hearted Admiralty commitment. The Senior Naval Lord, Lord Walter Kerr, immediately pointed out that Japanese interpretations of the first clause about acting in concert in peacetime could prove embarrassing. The Japanese had to be aware that orders to co-operate had nevertheless been issued immediately to Vice-Admiral Bridge in China but Kerr then observed that 'it may be hereafter necessary to give him additional secret instructions not known to the Japanese'.[12]

Although the War Office seemed happy that supreme command of land forces be given to the Japanese, it assumed it would be counterbalanced by appointing a British supreme naval commander. However, the preliminary discussions at Yokosuka in May 1902 made it clear that the two countries would take operational responsibility for separate command zones north and south of Amoy in the event of war. Bridge objected that enemy movements would not be dictated by an abstract line of latitude.[13]

The Japanese in fact dismissed the idea of operating jointly south of Amoy as 'rather academic' but the new DNI, Prince Louis of Battenberg, recognized that it was by no means certain that the IJN would accept a British supreme commander when Japan had six battleships and the China Fleet only four. He was unconvinced that the Japanese would support suggestions by Bridge that there should be a combined fleet offensive against the Russians. Bridge was also not convinced of Russian inferiority after visits to Port Arthur and

Vladivostok in 1903. Bridge believed the Russians could transfer substantial naval forces from Europe to the Far East before the capture of the Russian bases, but there is no indication that the Japanese were told this. Kerr and Battenberg rejected Bridge's analysis, suggesting planned additions to his squadron and joint strategy with the Japanese would ensure local supremacy in the Far East. They secretly made such arrangements in London with Sir Gerard Noel, who succeeded Bridge in March 1904. In addition to command issues, in London in 1902 General Fukushima asked Britain to send at least one Army corps to Manchuria. This was evaded by indicating that forces could not be diverted away from India. When Fukushima pushed harder on whether Britain intended to pursue an offensive strategy in India against Russia, it was again hedged as complicated by the Afghanistan problem.[14] Leaving Japan, Colonel Churchill argued for a general officer to confer with the Japanese Army direct in Tokyo but Earl Roberts suggested avoiding any step which might lead the Japanese into believing British thinking over reinforcement of Manchuria had changed and vetoed the suggestion.[15] The cautious War Office response led General Fukushima to visit India on his return home in autumn 1902. He had discussions with the Viceroy and the C-in-C, General Kitchener, stating that it had been agreed in London that a Japanese intelligence officer be sent to Simla. This proposal, like that permitting British and Japanese military attachés in third countries to exchange views and co-operate with each other, had not been acted on promptly and two months elapsed before the Winchester House Conference proceedings were approved by the Cabinet subcommittee.[16]

The Army's lack of enthusiasm for co-operation with Japan was reinforced by proposals circulating as early as 1902 about the need to establish an expanded British Intelligence Bureau with offices in Tientsin, Shanghai and Hong Kong. The proposal emerged from an initiative of the China Field Force, which discovered that intelligence about North China was hard to obtain and spread among seven different agencies. On arriving in Shanghai intending to travel on to Peking in 1900, officers discovered that they did not even have a proper map of the area. This prompted General O'Moore-Creagh at Tientsin to urge that Britain should follow the examples of the Russians, French and Japanese who had long-standing military agents in place.[17] The proposal was enthusiastically endorsed by the Admiralty, which had had a worldwide intelligence organization since 1893. It reviewed the regulations for the distribution and collection of intelligence in wartime in November 1904, seeking to incorporate liaison with military intelligence, and with colonial and dominions forces.[18] The proposed interdepartmental committee, however, took more than a year to deliver its report, and adopted a highly sceptical line. It argued that:

> Japan furnishes a valuable means of acquiring intelligence. The Japanese Government have many Agents in China, and would doubtless be ready

to make accessible to our Military Attachés in Peking and Tokyo and to our Intelligence Officers in China all important information their agents may obtain.

There was some distrust, but it was agreed it was the best they were likely to get and cheaper than 'spending money on the permanent maintenance of a large Intelligence Department'.[19] In practice, however, the temptation to accept was too great: Major Peach (MI2d) updated his March 1902 study on Japan's value as an ally by adding in May information about Russian forces east of Lake Baikal 'compiled by the British Intelligence Department in China, *from Japanese sources*'.[20]

But the British response to the Japanese Military Attaché's offer to Colonel Trotter (MI3) in May 1903 to organize secret intelligence-gathering co-operatively appears lukewarm and suggested 'we can only work with the Japanese by giving them some of our information in exchange for theirs, measuring the importance of the news we give to them by that of their communications to us . . . giving to the Japanese Military Attaché confidential, not secret, details'. Lord Lansdowne's view was to 'make use of Japanese agents freely in the Far East and perhaps employ them ourselves'. It remains to be fully discovered just how far the intelligence services of the two countries really collaborated in exchanging information about Russia, sabotage, subversion and counter-intelligence.[21] Excepting counter-intelligence, it is difficult to find any evidence that the two armies ever worked actively together: all the accessible data suggest the two countries collected data about Russia and exchanged them separately via attachés. The evidence in support of intimate naval co-operation, on the other hand, is positive.

'Avoid furnishing information to foreigners'

In May 1902 Admiral Yamamoto asked about access for Japan to 'all-British' cable networks so ensuring signals transmitted along non-British cables were reduced to a minimum. The IJN offered a cypher system for allied use at the same date and wanted Britain to suggest an alternative system so that the two could be compared and the more efficient be used for exchanges between allies. The Admiralty authorized meeting half the cost, but there is no surviving evidence that this code was actually handed over. On the other hand, texts of warning codewords for transmission in the case of the assembly of allied warships existed, but as early as 1903 the difficulty of making the Japanese *I-ro-ha* syllabary conform to the International Morse Code was reported by the British Naval Attaché in Japan. Provision was made in the 1907 military agreement for the naval cyphering arrangements to be copied by the two armies.[22]

In the course of the war, two valuable pieces of counter-intelligence were obtained via the IJN: first, a captured Russian courier, Eggard, was made available to the Admiralty for interrogation; he confirmed that relations between France and Russia had cooled of late.[23] Then the British Naval Attaché in Paris, Captain Morgan, reported a Russian contact, Bronard, prepared to provide military information, but Colonel Utsunomiya confirmed he had been dismissed from Japanese service because he was probably a Russian counter-intelligence agent.[24] Russian secret police were active in Paris and Berlin as well as at St Petersburg to gain entry and photograph documents and cypher tables wherever possible. Despite Eggard's information received in December 1904, for most of the war period Ambassador Hardinge was instructed that there were no grounds for suspicion, and no steps were taken to supply special cyphers until early 1906, after it had been claimed by the Russian Ambassador in London that his government had the text of a secret military agreement attached to the revised Anglo-Japanese Alliance signed in August. Hardinge had already indicated in April 1905 that foreign missions had been targeted and believed that some British cyphers had been obtained. This was accurate and there was close Russian scrutiny of Anglo-Japanese relations at this period. It was later reported that the Tsar presided at weekly meetings where foreign intercept findings were reviewed.[25]

The Russians scrutinized British diplomatic communications for evidence of support for revolutionaries, but there is no significant evidence of overt British assistance being given to the Japanese Army to support Polish and Finnish revolutionary groups. Japanese accounts of links with the Finns indicate that British ships were chartered to take Finnish revolutionaries and arms to the Baltic in 1905, but there is no suggestion anywhere that this was done with official British sanction. Recent evidence indicates that the text of orders to the Russian Black Sea Fleet was transmitted to Captain Kaburagi, the IJN attaché in London, and the source of British interception was the cable office manager at Syra, who received annual payments from Secret Service funds from 1900 to 1907 on the recommendation of Admiral Fisher.[26]

In peacetime Britain, covert activities brought unwelcome publicity at home, but there was involvement with censorship, interception and decryption and attempted sabotage in wartime before 1904. There were two main locations where such activities could be undertaken without breaching the law: one was India, where legislation existed earlier than in Britain on official secrets and 'defence of the realm'; the other was at sea, where it was just possible to obtain evidence of hostility. There are clear indications of the Indian Army intercepting Russian, Persian and Chinese telegraphic traffic, some of which was deciphered before 1914.[27]

In the case of naval interception, wireless telegraphy was an Admiralty responsibility from 1899 onwards, whereas censorship and monitoring of cables and the press was a War Office responsibility. There is evidence of interception of Japanese radio traffic from an early date, but the 1904 range of radio transmitters in naval operations was generally about 50 miles in daytime and 100 miles at night or in exceptionally good conditions. Good evidence has been discovered recently showing that the Japanese naval delegation to London in 1902 was given complete access to the latest British naval wireless system by Admiral Sir John Fisher while still C-in-C of the Mediterranean Fleet, and an overnight doubling in Japanese signalling capabilities was incorporated in the standard IJN wireless set introduced during 1903. A number of Japanese land stations were also erected across the Korea Straits, but experience in the Japanese naval manoeuvres of March-April 1903 'was not very successful'. This was reported to Bridge, unsuccessfully pressing for a wireless station at Hong Kong, when he visited Japan in April 1903 and reported he had 'already arranged for a beginning of mutual work in wireless telegraphy, which has to be carried out cautiously in order to avoid furnishing information to foreigners'.[28]

It is unclear, however, how far he went with his 'plan for Mutual Signalling practice' by the outbreak of the Russo-Japanese War. When it came, it is interesting that the Russians complained almost immediately about the use of a British ship, the *Haimun*, by Captain James, a *Times* correspondent, to observe naval operations in the Gulf of Chihli. The Russians threatened to seize such vessels and charge the journalists with espionage, arguing that radio reports could be intercepted and exploited by the Japanese, which would constitute a breach of neutrality. Although dutifully denounced by Admirals Bridge and Noel, what was withheld was that HMS Thetis at Weihaiwei helped to erect a tall radio mast there with the permission of the civil authorities to receive these signals from the *Haimun*, which had a retired Japanese naval officer on board allegedly acting as a censor. Tokyo denied official authorization, but it is likely he was a Japanese naval agent. An Admiralty letter to Sir Francis Campbell stated: 'On the assumption that the Japanese are sufficiently advanced in wireless telegraphy, it would be perfectly possible for them to intercept messages passing between the Times ship and the station at Weihaiwei.'[29]

British warships based at Weihaiwei were employed to maintain radio contact with the China Squadron during exercises and crossed frequently to Chemulpo to contact the British Legation in Korea. Although reports were received from British naval observers of Japanese naval operations on board the cruiser *Asahi*, it is also clear that there were independent sightings of Japanese vessels along the coasts of Korea and Japan. From early 1905, radio logbooks were issued to the China Squadron and warships encouraged to report exchanges with merchant and other ships. It is likely that intercepts of radio traffic from other warships were logged and HMS *Iphigenia* indeed recorded on 12 April 1905: 'very distinct Wireless Indications were received about 10 a.m. apparently from the Russians as the Code was unknown to us'.[30]

The Russian Fleet headed northwards, then eastwards from Formosa and disappeared until 18 May 1905, when its supply vessels were reported heading for Woosung. The Baltic Fleet continued northwards and was observed off Tsushima on 27 May by Japanese scouts who radioed for the Combined Fleet. News of its total defeat was relayed in two telegrams to Hong Kong and confirmed by the Japanese consul there before being relayed to the Admiralty, which had already instructed Admiral Noel to dispatch the battleships HMS *Centurion* and *Ocean* home as early as 7 May. These were followed by the battleships HMS *Albion* and HMS *Vengeance* on 10 May 1905. These instructions were not notified to the Japanese until after their victory at Tsushima.[31]

'The expression of permanent interests on both sides'

Either Admiralty intelligence about the low level of threat the Baltic Fleet presented was remarkably good or it represented a high degree of confidence in the ability of the Japanese Navy to intercept and deal with the Russian vessels. Britain reacted strategically to the impact of growing Russian debility following the Japanese capture of Mukden on 10 March 1905. Proposals had come from Admiral Sir John Fisher, the new First Sea Lord, in November 1904 to shift forces from the outlying naval stations back to Europe and in to abolish the Pacific Squadron in March 1905. The transfer of heavy units to Europe indicates an anticipation of the likelihood of German pressure on Russia and France, emerging over Morocco in early 1906.

The focus of international interest moved westwards but in April 1905, Captain Ottley (DNI) submitted a paper to Fisher on the future of the Alliance and recommended revision rather than rejection or renewal culminating in revision in August 1905.[32] Anticipating the impending Japanese victory, the Admiralty wrote to Noel on 19 June requesting him to revise operational orders for the combined Eastern Fleet in the event of war. His response of 30 September identified Japan and the USA as the only powers with battleships and seaboards in the Pacific, proposing that 'in the event of war becoming imminent with either of these Powers, the China Squadron will be concentrated at Hong Kong, and the Australian and East Indies Squadrons at Singapore'. As part of this shift, General Grierson (DMO since February 1904) discussed the need to increase surveillance of western Russia in February–March 1905 and agreed an increase in the number of agents employed in Berlin. It is important to remember that a good deal of the collection of secret intelligence about Russia was conducted in Berlin not only by the British network but also by the Japanese Military Attaché there through close contacts with the German military. Limited co-operation with Japan in secret service matters minimized British concern about information reaching the Germans via Japanese confidants. A War Office memorandum of June 1905 by Grierson on the Japanese Alliance discussions at the CID mentioned the possibility of Kiaochow as a potential target of interest to Japan in the future and of the IJN helping to clear these seas and protect the reinforcement of India.[33]

The most important development in British policy was the shift from the peacetime framework for the secret service in the event of a general European war submitted by Colonel Davies in May 1903. He ordered a fresh study resulting in a September 1905 paper 'Secret Service Arrangements in the Event of a War with Germany' which was circulated to ministers in the neutral states around Germany for their opinions.

Grierson had expressed the view in relation to Japan that 'for a treaty to be of real value it must be the expression of permanent interests on both sides'. He did not believe that Japan would co-operate with Britain in the direct defence of India, while Britain at most could only supply cavalry and horse artillery to assist in the Japanese defence of Manchuria and Korea against a renascent Russia. As an afterthought, Grierson stated: 'In the unlikely contingency of the United States being hostile, Japanese troops could be advantageously employed against the Philippines, and also against the United States themselves, thus indirectly assisting in the defence of Canada.'[34]

The defence of Canada and the possibility of war with the USA had been discussed intermittently since the mid-1890s. In 1902 Major Altham had observed (at the same time as consultations with the Admiralty on the Japanese Alliance) that war with the USA 'was the most difficult of all the contingencies to which this country is liable' and advised the War Office to consult the opinions of the Admiralty.[35] Lord Selborne, the First Lord of the Admiralty at this time, stressed in June 1903 'do not quarrel with the U.S. – do not put any more W.O. eggs into the Canadian basket'.[36] Therefore although the War Office and the Admiralty agreed on retaining the alliance with Japan, there was a point-blank refusal by the Admiralty to contemplate conflict with the USA. In addition to the abolition of the Pacific Squadron and the return home of five battleships from the China Station by the end of July 1905, the bases at Esquimalt and Halifax were handed over to Canada, the base at St Lucia was abandoned and those in Bermuda and Jamaica were reduced in scale.[37]

The military and naval discussions with Japan between 29 May and 4 June 1907 essentially suggested the retention of the existing levels of co-operation, especially intelligence exchange. Obligations were accepted to keep each other informed about future naval construction programmes in order to provide a basis for calculations about the need to maintain allied superiority over any hostile combination. Fisher argued that the Royal Navy would 'best guard the allied interests by destroying the ships of an enemy as they issued from their European bases, and thus prevent them from reaching any Eastern theatre of war at all'. The allied operations plan 'would depend on their strength relative to that of the enemy, and upon the varying circumstances of the war, it is not possible to lay down any hard and fast scheme, since such, if strictly adhered to, might lead to serious disadvantages'. The discussions, however, avoided any mention of the divergent British and Japanese strategies.

The renewed Anglo-Japanese alliance treaty of 1905 had been based on the assumption that it was unlikely that Japanese territory would be attacked by a single power – only some combination difficult to determine in advance. By 1908, when the War Office continued to express concern about US public opinion and theorized on conditions of war between the British Empire and the USA, the Anglo-Japanese Alliance itself was represented as a negative factor in Anglo-American relations. Since the alliance was due to last until 1915, the War Office argued that Britain could theoretically become involved in a war between Japan and the USA up to 1916. However, it was conceded that US–Japanese rivalry was of recent origin, racial and fundamental, but that both countries had good reasons to postpone any struggle.[38] Nevertheless, it was recognized that British naval superiority had declined from 3 : 1 in 1904 to only 2 : 1 in 1907 and that the reduction in British defence arrangements in Canada and the West Indies indicated that the USA need fear no complications in its relations with Britain in the event of any trouble with Japan. Since racial frictions existed in Japanese–Canadian and Japanese–Australian relations similar to those in California, these racial tensions alone were considered insufficient reason for going to war. But it was also noted that 'almost the entire United States fleet is now on its way from the Atlantic coast to the Pacific'.

'Their masters in the art of war, the Germans'

The British generally judged that the alliance represented a guarantee of Japanese territory and interests in the Far East. Any attack on British possessions in Asia was so improbable, especially after the Anglo-Russian and Russo-Japanese *rapprochements*, that no Japanese obligations to Britain existed. The close relations between the Japanese and German armies throughout the Meiji period never seem to have been forgotten. This was reinforced after 1905 by reports from British Army language officers seconded to Japanese Army units which pointed to the widespread adoption of German equipment and methods in training and staff work. Although there remained high praise for Japanese use of secret service preparations in peacetime, the summary prepared by Colonel Edmonds (MO5) in January 1909 prior to the decision to establish a distinct secret service organization at the end of April 1909 reflected the growing concern about German espionage in Britain. Colonel Edmonds' elaborate studies drew particular attention to the effective use of agents and disinformation by the Germans in France prior to 1870 and the unscrupulous nature of the German use of spies who did not hesitate to disguise themselves as French officers and men prior to battles. Edmonds added: 'The Japanese learnt the trick of using officers to perform menial duties as servants etc; in order to gain information, from their masters in the art of war, the Germans.' In March 1909 a lecture on the Japanese and Russian intelligence systems by Colonel Haldane (MO3) referred to the use of Japanese prostitutes in Port Arthur itself and concluded: 'In fact it has been truly said that the Japanese army is preceded by Geisha and spies, so if ever we hear of numbers of them landing in India or in any of our Colonies, we may be prepared for trouble.'

During 1909 Fisher and his DNI, Rear-Admiral Bethell, suggested that the Admiralty had been the object of 'embarrassing requests' for naval information from the Japanese, particularly from the Naval Attaché in London. A memorandum submitted in September 1909 reminded everyone that the existing alliance terminated in 1915 and might not be renewed. 'The nearer that date approaches the more important it becomes to be increasingly careful in giving information to a country which may after that date occupy only the position of a friendly foreign power.' It recommended that information provided to Japan in future be limited strictly to what was covered by the rather loose terms of the 1907 agreement. Though it was recognized that the Japanese side would probably reciprocate, it was stressed that 'while avoiding the appearance of any marked tendency to increased reserve, both in giving and asking information, care should be taken to give and ask for no more than is really important and cannot be obtained in some other manner entailing no obligations'.[39]

When the Foreign Office proposed early in 1911 to renew the alliance for another ten years, the view of the Admiralty was focused principally on the incorporation in Article 5 of arrangements for an Anglo-American arbitration treaty designed to reduce the chances of Britain being drawn into a US–Japanese conflict in the future. The view of the War Office was that the 1911 treaty continued to provide disproportionately large benefits to Japan, but the benefit to Britain of a reduction in naval forces and garrisons in the Far East and protection of Australia and New Zealand 'is certainly not less than it was in 1905'. Colonel Money (MO3) commented 'failing an alliance with Great Britain, Japan is quite likely to seek such assistance elsewhere, in a quarter least convenient for ourselves'. Brigadier Henry Wilson (DMO) was much more sceptical, suggesting that any sense of security for the Empire 'may be one of the worst features of the Alliance because it will tend to a feeling of false security leading to a relaxation of military and naval preparations for war' and referring to the 'enormous military and naval strength which is being developed with feverish haste by all the great Powers of Europe, Japan herself being in no wise behind hand'.[40]

Essentially, acceptance of the treaty was based on a compromise. Japan's financial position was seen as making it likely it would wish it to continue, while two alternatives were put forward by Admiral Bethell (DNI) in January 1910: either Britain would have to build up a Pacific Fleet, but would find it exceedingly difficult to match the known Japanese naval construction plans, or it would have to seek an Anglo-American alliance, which was impractical. The treaty was timed to coincide with the signing of an arbitration treaty with the USA in August 1911, but was signed in July. The US Senate refused to ratify the arbitration treaty.[41]

'The balance of advantage'

The British decision in 1909 to maintain a passive alliance relationship with Japan with neither going out of their way to provide more than minimal intelligence data existed for the next decade. At the end of the First World War, it was decided to review the amount and distribution of secret information available to Britain's allies, especially material of a technological nature, and how this should be handled in the future. Viewed from the perspective of 1918, Britain's ally Japan was summarized thus:

> Although in theory the Japanese were treated preferentially in regard to the exchange of secret information, in practice little or no confidential information as regards materiel was communicated to them, and we avoided taking advantage of their offers to communicate confidential information of any kind to us. It was felt that the acceptance of such offers laid us open to requests for information on their side, and that the balance of advantage was considerably in their favour.

During the war itself, Japan was grouped together with Italy 'and the lesser allies'. Whenever possible their requests for secret information were parried by excuses. However, it was recognized that it was 'impossible to prevent a large amount of confidential information from being given to them'. Secret information relevant to the prosecution of the war was shared but anything relevant to post-war developments withheld as far as possible. By comparison, France and the USA were given liaison officers attached to the Admiralty.[42] Most signal books and cyphers for communication with the Allies were shared during the war, with the exception of the General Signal Book and manual, which were supplied only to the USA. Preparations were made to introduce new cyphers and recognition signals as soon as possible.[43]

These conclusions on striking a balance between maximizing the security of one's own communications systems and testing foreign systems became increasingly acute between 1904 and 1919. Efforts were made in the Foreign Office to improve cypher security, particularly in relation to Russia during the war with Japan. However, in 1907, warnings had to be given to the Japanese Army over the use of Eastern Extension cable lines to Europe from China in peacetime since there were two known cases when a cypher was stolen and officials had sold information in the course of the Russo-Japanese War.[44]

The Admiralty's first edition of the Boats' Signal Book in 1903 was regarded as compromised since many of the copies issued went missing on the China Station. Reissued in 1904, it was re-worked by the Foreign Office and a dictionary supplied for telegraphic communication.[45] The previous situation prevailing on naval stations was that many intelligence reports were forwarded by the mails, but from 1903 such reports were forwarded by telegraph employing code and secret call-signs using 'all-British' cables. In 1913, there were further complaints about the revision of intelligence reporting on the China Station from the Bangkok Legation.[46] Changes in the reporting system on naval stations were considerable from 1904 to 1914 when the numbers of naval attaché posts were expanded and intelligence officers afloat were replaced by centres on land. The process was introduced to Hong Kong, Singapore and Colombo in December 1904 in relation to the movements of the Russian Baltic Fleet, and extended to Freemantle, Sydney and Cape Town in June 1911 and Shanghai in December 1913. No adequate organization had been put in place along the western seaboard of the Americas, which had been the province of the Pacific Squadron until 1905. The lack of a centre, such as that later set up at Callao, was blamed for the failure to achieve adequate communications with the squadron under Admiral Cradock, which was defeated off Coronel by the German Pacific Squadron. However, correspondence between Admiral Jerram at Hong Kong and the Admiralty before 1914 indicates that Japanese advice about the need for at least five British armoured cruisers on the China Station was ignored by Churchill despite the efforts of Sir Henry Jackson to alert him to the dangers posed by the strong German squadron in East Asia.[47]

Cable and wireless in wartime East Asia

An extremely important development lay in the establishment of radio stations with an adequate range, but the Admiralty sought to do this as economically as possible in conjunction with commercial firms rather than via a unified public service such as the Royal Australian Naval Radio Service. In many locations, such as Hong Kong, there were very lengthy delays and changes of mind before an effective mix of types of installation was established.[48] The German transmitters at Nauen and Norddeich, by contrast, were able to achieve an almost worldwide coverage from 1905 onwards. German cables were cut, thus forcing naval radio to fill the gap and consequently make it possible for interception and direction-finding of ships at sea to be accomplished. The heavy German dependence on radio before 1914 made it much easier to trace a larger number of signals compared to British use of cable, with the result that it was possible to obtain a more substantial basis for deciphering techniques. German warship traffic with merchantmen was extensively noted prior to 1914 and it was possible to notify the British port authorities to take action to recover German code materials overseas in ports such as Hong Kong, Fremantle and Sydney at the outbreak of war.[49] It was not possible to obtain solutions to other German code and cypher systems until the relevant codebooks were secured and rather later before solutions were produced by cryptanalytical techniques. The numbers of officers privy to any of these systems were kept exceedingly small and elaborate precautions were taken to avoid disclosing sources of decrypts, referred to as 'Japons' in wartime correspondence. A more systematic analysis of cable and radio became possible when the Foreign Office agreed to permit censorship of consular traffic and German use of Swedish circuits was discovered. This in turn revealed the extent to which German communications with the Far East via US cables had been taking place since 1914.[50]

After the seizure of Kiaochow and the Pacific islands, the Japanese expansion of trade with China and the rest of East and South East Asia plus the political demands of the Japanese military stimulated greater apprehension than either Russian adventurism or German opportunism. Japanese economic penetration of India and the interception of evidence of suspicious contacts between German diplomats and agents in neutral countries in Asia and Japanese supporters of Indian nationalism provoked an increasing mistrust of Japan not only in Britain and Russia, but especially in the USA, which had major repercussions for the conduct of war.

The alliance came under heavy attack in 1915 from spokesmen and propagandists, like the *Kokuryukai*, with ties with both Army and Navy, while peace feelers via Japan and Russia in Sweden and other neutral countries yielded interesting encounters. No significant change in the existing balance of power emerged until the February Revolution in Russia, which elicited Japanese talk of intervention prior to its actual involvement in summer 1918.[51] The Allied situation became more desperate because the effectiveness of the submarine counterblockade contributed to a crisis triggering US participation. Calls for the participation of Japanese battleships in European operations were rejected.[52] But, faced with the increasing likelihood of US involvement in the war, IJN did agree in February 1917 to supply ships to Malta and the Cape, provided that they were guaranteed the attachment of intelligence officers with access to cypher communication links with London and Tokyo.[53] Japanese flotillas were mainly employed as escorts for troop transports between the central and eastern Mediterranean rather than for minesweeping and anti-submarine warfare, although their work rate was phenomenal. They do not appear, however, to have been involved in the staff work at Malta, Otranto and Rome, where teams from Room 40 were involved in monitoring and deciphering enemy ship–shore communications with Pola and Constantinople directed toward sinking U-boats on passage to and from the main convoy routes. A rather belated Admiralty statement was handed over to the London Embassy on 14 May 1919 which referred to the flotillas' 'highest standard of efficiency' and observed that their 'zeal

... is beyond all praise'.[54] Nevertheless, there was a vague perception of the parting of the ways between the two navies, a feeling on the Japanese side of being in operations at sea but not fully involved. There is certainly no evidence, for example, that information or manuals about the fitting of Asdic direction-finding equipment first developed at the end of the war were ever passed on to the Japanese Navy. Being largely shut out of the close partnership that developed between Britain and the USA, the one way forward to acquiring knowledge of what had happened in the war to end all wars for the Japanese Army and Navy was through the eyes of the defeated.

Notes

1. Public Record Office, Kew (hereafter PRO), WO106/6150.
2. Memorandum of 4 October 1908: PRO: KV1/1 and CAB16/232.
3. Ewart to Nicholson, 12 January 1909 to Nicholson: PRO: KV1/2. More detailed background on contacts with IJA may be found in the Ewart Diary in the National Archives of Scotland (thanks to the permission of Lord Monro of Langholm) and the diary of General Aylmer Haldane in the National Library of Scotland.
4. 'Intelligence Methods in Peace Time': PRO: KV1/4.
5. Noel Report No. 966 of 15 December 1905 to Admiralty: ADM1/7804.
6. For Boer War codes see PRO: KV1/4, p. 69 and WO33/280.
7. Lansdowne Papers: PRO: FO800/115.
8. Grierson to Under-Secretary of State for War, 9 September 1901 in: ibid.
9. PRO: ADM1/7488 and Peach memorandum 25 March 1902, WO106/5549/Case 4.
10. As note 8 above.
11. Background papers by Captain Haldane (WO) and Rear-Admiral Custance Winchester House Conference in July 1902.
12. See Ian Nish, 'Naval Thinking and the Anglo-Japanese Alliance, 1900–1904', *Hogaku Kenkyu*, vol. 56, no. 3 (March 1983), pp. 5–14; PRO: ADM116/1231C.
13. Bridge Report of 15 May 1902: PRO: ADM116/1231B.
14. Minutes of Winchester House Conference, 8 July 1902: PRO: ADM116/1231C.
15. Churchill Report of 25 May 1903 to DMMI: PRO: WO106/48, G3/4.
16. Ibid., G3/3 and G3/4/1.
17. PRO: ADM1/7626B and ADM127/57.
18. See ADM1/8623/64; ADM116/1842.
19. ADM127/57.
20. Emphasis in the original supplement of 6 May 1902 to Peach (MI2d) memorandum of 25 March 1902 in: WO106/5549/4.
21. HD3/124.
22. See also John Ferris, 'Before "Room 40": The British Empire and Signals Intelligence, 1898–1914', *Journal of Strategic Studies*, vol. 12 (1989), pp. 431–57. For interest in India about the activities of nationalists in and visiting Japan before 1914: Grant K. Goodman, 'Dharmapala in Japan, 1913', *Japan Forum*, vol. 5, no. 2 (October 1993), pp. 195–202. NID 705 of January 1904, 'Japanese Naval

Manœuvres, 1903', in: PRO: ADM231/38; WO106/48, 'Secret Correspondence with the CID, 1907'.

23. ADM1/7775.
24. HD3/130.
25. See D.S. van der Oye, 'Tsarist Codebreaking: Some Background and Some Examples', *Cryptologia*, vol. XXII, no. 4 (October 1998), pp. 342–53 confirms that the Russians decyphered a message from Sir Thomas Sanderson to St Petersburg of 27 November 1901 authorizing the expenditure of Secret Service funds to discover the object of the mission by Ito Hirobumi to St Petersburg.
26. See the memoir of ex-Superintendent William Melville at: PRO: KV1/8. For an account of Japanese links with Finnish and Polish nationalists, see Inaba Chiharu, *Akashi kosaku: Boryaku no Nichi-Ro senso* (Tokyo: Maruzen, 1995) confirming that the Japanese Military Attaché in Berlin was a major source of military intelligence about Russia during the war. Some of Dr Inaba's findings on Anglo-Japanese exchanges of secret intelligence have been incorporated in the author's 'British Use of "Dirty Tricks" in External Policy prior to 1914', *War in History*, vol. 9 (2001), pp.
27. Ferris, 'Before "Room 40"'.
28. Bridge Report No. 283 of 20 April 1903 to Admiralty: PRO: ADM116/1231C; ADM231/38.
29. Ferris, 'Before "Room 40"' and PRO: FO46/589.
30. Noel Report No. 355 of 2 May 1905 to Admiralty: PRO: ADM1/7804.
31. It was concluded that supply arrangements had been made with Germany, which also employed vessels to break the Japanese blockade of Port Arthur in 1904. See PRO: ADM1/7730 and 7804 and K. Buckley and K. Klugman, *The History of Burns & Philp* (Sydney, 1981). Admiral Fisher wrote to Noel on 3 March 1905 of his intention to concentrate fleet units in home waters and asked that Noel 'must not please mind the raid we have made on your Fleet'. Orders for the departure of battleships from China were telegraphed notwithstanding Fisher's letter of 28 April 1905 to Lord Lansdowne claiming that table-top exercises indicated that the Japanese were viewed as inferior in strength to the Russians. NMM: NOE/20e and P.K. Kemp (ed.), *The Papers of Admiral Sir John Fisher* (London: Navy Records Society, 1960), vol. 1, p. 59.
32. 'Remarks as to the Future of the Anglo-Japanese Alliance', in: PRO: ADM116/1231C.
33. General Staff secret memorandum of 16 June 1905 to Foreign Office: PRO: WO106/5549/ 13.
34. WO106/5549.
35. Haldane (MO1) 'Memorandum on the Policy to be Adopted in the Event of War with the United States of America', 12 March 1902: WO106/40/ B1.
36. PRO: ADM1/8875. Admiral Fisher briefed R.B. Haldane and other Liberal politicians during 1905 on the risks of quarrels with France and the USA to vital British seaborne imports: NLS: Haldane Papers.
37. See PRO: ADM1/7730; WO106/40/Case B1/2.
38. PRO: WO106/40/ B1/2.
39. Admiralty to Foreign Office, 12 June 1911: ADM116/1231C.
40. PRO: WO106/5549/Case 18.
41. Foreign Office memorandum of 21 September 1914 to the Japanese Ambassador in London. WO106/5550.
42. ADM1/8541/280 and 8549/14.
43. Minute by the Director of Signals at the Admiralty of 31 March 1919 in: ibid. For

pre-war investigation of the idea of introducing machine enciphering systems, see ADM116/2101.

44. Colonel Shiba suggested at a meeting with General Ewart on 31 May 1907 that the British side should draw up a cypher and propose it for joint use and to consider the best arrangements for use of cables. WO106/5549; WO106/6150; ADM144/27, p. 128; ADM116/969.

45. After 1899, there was a considerable tightening up of British cyphers and the Army & Navy Signal Book used by military and naval attachés was replaced.

46. PRO: ADM1/8891; ADM1/8915.

47. For land-based centres see ADM116/1036–7 and ADM1/8623/64. The scheme for the China Station is at ADM1/7728. See also National Archives of Australia (NAA), CP78/16/1–2. The author is extremely grateful for the co-operation of Commander David Stevens and Mr Joe Straszek, Department of the Navy, Canberra. Admiral Jerram's papers are at: NMM: JRM/16/2.

48. For unsuccessful efforts by Bridge and Noel to persuade the Admiralty to establish a radio facility in Hong Kong: see PRO: ADM1/7869; ADM1/8473/262. Noel had the idea of long-range stations at Singapore, Hong Kong and Tokyo, but this was turned down. Russian naval wireless was first intercepted off Suez in January 1904 and subsequently by the China Fleet, but systematic research was only undertaken from the summer of 1906.

49. GOC, South China Report of 11 September 1914: WO106/28.

50. See HW3/1 and HW7 and ADM223 for monitoring and decryption between 1914 and 1919.

51. Russian representatives, apparently able to read Japanese signals, indicated that the Japanese were confident the German Army could not be defeated.

52. Major Somerville (MO3) of 15 December 1914 warned that the occupied islands could become a major naval base area for the Japanese domination of the Pacific, with just as much of a threat to US as to Australasian interests. PRO: WO32/4997.

53. A secret memorandum of 14 April 1917 recalled the visits of Japanese naval officers to Kedah and the carrying out of coastal surveys and provided evidence of the presence of 'Special Service' naval and military officers (*tokumu kyoku* and *tokumu kikan*) in both Singapore and Hong Kong'. WO106/869.

54. ADM116/1420.

Part II
From Allies to Antagonists

6
Double-Edged Estimates: Japan in the Eyes of the British Army and the Royal Air Force, 1900–1939

John Ferris

The British Army and the Royal Air Force (RAF) had mixed roles in Anglo-Japanese relations during the twentieth century. They had attitudes towards Japan ranging from racism to Japanophilism. Neither service shaped high policy before 1941, but both were central to war during the period 1941–45. More than any other British institution, the War Office tried to prevent that war and to prepare for it. The RAF and, more generally, British attitudes towards airpower were fundamental to Britain's disastrous experiences when that war began.

The War Office did not lead in the formulation of the first Anglo-Japanese Alliance, but since it helped to end strategic problems with Russia it became the great exponent of that alliance and of the quality of Japanese arms. Despite variations in views, Victorian military observers respected Japanese soldiers. In 1895, one military attaché assessed the IJA more favourably than British officers would have done any other non-western army – or indeed many western ones at that time, making observations that British analysts would continue to offer until cavalry and artillery were below the British standard. Infantrymen were 'bad shots, but otherwise . . . good soldiers', courageous, hardy, good marchers and intelligent, whose units moved with speed and discipline. IJA officers were well trained, if overly concerned with theory.[1] Such impressions were confirmed by the Russo-Japanese War, where the IJA was characterized by extraordinary self-sacrifice, bold commanders, aggressive operations and 'magnificent fighting spirit'. Still, British views of the IJA remained mixed. In 1907, one officer and later Military Attaché, Major Somerville, praised the efficiency and exoticism of the IJA:

> the ancient, fighting, feudal spirit still flourishes as yet practically untouched by the refinements and luxuries of our civilization; and to it is united a highly specialised knowledge of the science of modern war. A magnificent fighting spirit pervades all ranks, with a Spartan-like contempt for money and the luxuries of life.

Against this, officers had 'a total lack of imagination and of original thinking', and

> only seem capable of carrying out the obvious, without any consideration of the possibilities involved in a feint or stratagem. It is always safe to predict how any given situation will be dealt with; the end is almost always a frontal attack, carried out with the strict adherence to the rules of the drill book, and an almost entire disregard of the casualties that would be involved.

In 1914, the IJA was regarded as a formidable and modern army. Bypassed by the military revolution forced by fighting on the Western Front in the First World War, its reputation declined. During the inter-war years, the IJA differed fundamentally from western armies. It, rather than the German Army, was the opposite pole to the French style of operations. It preferred manoeuvre and disdained attrition more than any other army, favouring speed, mobility and daring far above firepower and set-piece battles. Until the costly battles around Shanghai in 1932, the IJA clung to the tactics pursued in the Russo-Japanese War; thereafter altering details while retaining their spirit. Battalions received additional machine guns, pack guns and mortars, and divisions further medium artillery and tanks, while its defensive systems began to rest on well-prepared fire positions. It made better use of firepower and was less reckless than before, but the IJA did not change its style of operations fundamentally. It still placed morale and speed over attrition. Firepower was intended to crack a crust of defence which otherwise would paralyse advance by infantry, and so restore the conditions for a war of movement. As one British officer wrote, 'the whole essence of Japanese tactics is to strike before the enemy has any opportunity of preparing his defence'. The IJA fought set-piece battles only when unavoidable. Its preferred mode of operations was a frontal pinning assault combined with the simultaneous envelopment of both flanks, the end being annihilation of the enemy, quick and complete. These operations were always daring and often reckless. The IJA misunderstood some fundamental aspects of modern war, but in confronting different problems than European armies required different solutions. It was designed for war in the vast and undeveloped mainland of Asia, against enemies with small force-to-space ratios and low standards of firepower, and command. It was rational to focus on manoeuvre rather than set-piece attacks. The IJA's mistake was to assume that every enemy would be as inferior as the Chinese. It failed to develop the mechanized firepower which dominated the Second World War in the West and it was outclassed hopelessly whenever an enemy transferred the force-to-space ratios and the materiel of Europe to Asia. Even so, the IJA's tactics and operations were effective. It was well suited to the military conditions of Asia and dangerous even to dedicated foes. Excluding only matériel, it matched the best armies on earth.

The IJA was a complex object to assess, but Britain had excellent sources on the topic in the Military Attaché's staff and some 35 language officers officially attached to the IJA for months at a time. Such officers were often denied access to certain matters, particularly after 1934, and they sought to determine through peacetime observations how the IJA would perform in war, which was no easy task. Assessment had perceptual and political dimensions, involving questions like: who reported on what? what information was ignored or emphasized at which institutional layer? Several groups were involved in this process: by far the largest body, the old China hands (officers at Shanghai, Tientsin and Hong Kong), along with military attachés, language officers and individuals visiting East Asia from elsewhere; and the members of the Military Intelligence Department (MID) of the War Office. The Army possessed few specialists on East Asia, but those they did have were intelligent men, surprisingly free from vulgar racism and ethnocentrism. One language officer, Malcolm Kennedy, was a noted authority on Japan during the 1930s; another, Charles Boxer, became an eminent international historian after 1945. Many of them fell in love with Japan. While serving at Hong Kong, Boxer frequented the *geisha* house at the Tokyo Hotel, imbibing intelligence and scotch in equal proportions. Unlike their predecessors before 1914, these men learned to eliminate their own ethnocentrism: they understood that even with dirty uniforms and unshaven officers, Japanese were good soldiers, and even more – that they despised British officers precisely because the latter cared so much about proper attire. All this information was assessed by the East Asian section of the MID. Its judgments were professional, nor did it emphasize negative and ignore positive reports about the IJA. It was largely staffed with Japanese specialists; after 1936, when British authorities turned against that country, this section became the final redoubt of the Japanophiles in Whitehall. Raw reports were rarely read by higher levels of command, who relied on the views of the MID. The War Office's official estimates of the IJA and its policy in East Asia faithfully reflected these views, but these did not circulate widely in the British and Indian armies, and their officers ignored the topic. In 1941–42, this weakness outweighed generations of assessment.

British analysts observed the IJA through preconceptions about war, Japan and its army. They assessed it by reference to two standards: against the actual adversaries and environment of East Asia and of a 'first-class' foe with the scales of equipment and the force-to-space ratios of Europe. The characteristics cited in these estimates were rated according to two scales – those of Europe and of Asia. Any army, of course, might be ideally suited to one set of conditions and for precisely that reason be unready to meet the other – no army could easily be well prepared for both. British observers agreed that the IJA was shaped solely for warfare against poorly-equipped and -trained enemies in Asia. Even after its occasional reverses during the 1930s, they rated the IJA far above every Chinese enemy and overestimated its quality relative to the Soviet Army. When comparing the IJA to themselves, conversely, British observers treated their own approach as the universal means to measure military value. They envisaged circumstances which centred on narrow fronts and dense quantities of men and material, where soldiers skilled in deliberate operations would eat alive enemies adopting the tactics of the IJA. Elsewhere the diner might become dinner. British observers judged the IJA by its ability to fight in Europe, not by their own in Asia and hence fell prey to two fallacies of a military ethnocentric nature: those of the 'paper standard' and the 'first-class power'. By 1941, they measured Japanese and British quality by the standard of Western Europe rather than eastern Asia; and assumed that this standard and these rankings would prevail in a third environment, that of South East Asia. Those British officers who were most experienced with the IJA, however, were fully aware of this problem. As one Military Attaché, Colonel L. R. Hill, wrote: 'In watching the tactics of a foreign army the tendency is to condemn out of hand where they fail to do what ought to be done according to our own ideas.'

These forms of military ethnocentrism, rather than broader bodies of thought like racism, were the single greatest cause for mistaken estimates of the IJA. During the 1920s, the IJA was conventionally – and correctly – criticized by observers who regarded firepower and controlled operations as the key to victory. After 1932, the IJA significantly improved its standing in these spheres, but then the ideas of the 'paper standard' and the 'first-class power', married to a contempt for Chinese armies, led many British observers to folly. They held that a first-class defender fighting from prepared positions in Europe would have smashed such Japanese attacks. This may have been true; these operations were not occurring in Europe. Nor could European conditions of war easily be transferred to Asia. During the Sino-Japanese War, the IJA achieved a high and effective synthesis of manoeuvre and firepower, but the old China hands thought this synthesis betrayed a degeneration of the Japanese – their first-rate spirit was in decay, replaced by third-rate firepower. And analysis focused as much on spirit as matter. Assessments of the IJA considered not merely its tactical characteristics but also the Japanese 'national character'. Empirical observation might illuminate the behaviour of Japanese individuals; generalizations alone could explain 'the Japanese', and the broader the question, the greater the degree of conceptualization required for an answer. Four different intellectual traditions affected these generalizations; classical racism espoused by writers such as Houston Stewart Chamberlain; scientific racism and its bastard child, social Darwinism; environmentalist thinking; and finally, the concept in which all of these tended to be merged, views of 'national character'. The qualities which Englishmen linked to Japanese stemmed from a mixture of all these. Although each concept sometimes worked independently, they generally hunted in a pack; and it is an error to assume that 'racism' always was top dog among them. This term must refer to the belief that notable traits occur, invariably or in some predictable fashion, among people of a given 'race' and for genetic reasons. Racism certainly was a component of the views at hand, perhaps dominant in certain minds and about some topics. Across the board, however, military and cultural ethnocentrism and views of national character were equally important components in this bundle of ideas. Neither form of racism distorted assessments of the IJA nearly so far as they did Japanese naval or air forces, and what is labelled 'racism' usually was cultural ethnocentrism tinged by racist terminology. For a combination of genetic and environmental factors, Japanese were regarded as lacking aptitude for machines and the capacity for innovation; but as having great endurance and organizational ability. Air and naval officers prized the first set of qualities far above the second; hence, these ideas led them to underrate Japanese pilots and sailors. Army officers respected the qualities in both categories; these concepts led them both to praise and to bury the IJA – to respect its infantry but to criticize its more technical combat arms, artillery and armour.

Between 1919 and 1932, British observers viewed the IJA's tactics as obsolete, though they also thought, as one officer wrote, 'the Japanese Army has, of course, got its difficulties, but there is no doubt whatever that it is a very fine fighting machine'. They regarded the Japanese as a conservative people who disliked change until it was forced on them, but who then could adapt with rare speed and efficiency. Thus, given time, the IJA could remedy its defects whenever it wished. British observers praised the physical and spiritual qualities of Japanese infantryman but questioned Japanese tactics. Still, they understood the logic underlying these tactics: that the IJA trained primarily for war in China and downplayed set-piece attacks and prepared firepower because these gave an enemy time to strengthen its defences and so to negate Japan's primary strengths: morale and speed of assault. They thought this approach could work against an inferior enemy, but not one which held its nerve and its fire. The setbacks of 1932 demonstrated the accuracy of these assessments, but British personnel in Japan calculated them judiciously. They held that the IJA was not 'fully ready for war' with any major power, including the USSR – a notable change in their views – but emphasized its fundamentally high quality and expected it quickly to overcome its weaknesses. During the 1930s, British observers in Japan offered a mixed verdict on these developments. The IJA practiced defensive exercises more frequently than before and emphasized prepared positions, firepower and counter-attack. On the assault, the IJA co-ordinated artillery, machine guns and infantry with greater effect. Yet battalions often charged enemy positions head-on from the march without even attempting to outflank them. Still, British observers in Japan did not change their opinions about the IJA. They criticized its tactics and attitudes toward firepower but believed that the IJA's quality was rising and might reach the western or 'paper' standard.

The War Office followed this lead. It relied on firepower and prepared positions for defence against the IJA, which it accurately viewed as a formidable foe with significant material limitations, dangerous on ground of its own choosing but vulnerable when forced to play its weaknesses against British strengths. After a thorough consideration of technical factors, throughout the 1920s British soldiers believed they could hold Hong Kong, their outpost most exposed to Japan, for three months until it was relieved, but by 1933, they concluded this would be impossible.[2] Again, in 1938 the Chiefs of Staff (COS) emphasized that 'artillery and machine guns in defence' were the key to defence in Malaya against the IJA; while the Army believed that a mechanized field force, deploying Britain's assumed advantages in that sphere, would be needed to defeat a Japanese invasion there. More generally, in 1934 the MID believed that Japanese equipment and tactics were below the European and even the Soviet standard. By 1935 it held that conditions were changing. After the Shanghai Incident, 'With characteristic vigour (for no people are quicker to act when mistakes are brought home to them, the Japanese at once started to put their military house in order'. While 'somewhat behind-hand' in equipment and tactics, the IJA's 'weaknesses are, to some extent, off-set by the excellent moral and physical qualities . . . (and) . . . fanatical patriotism and powers of endurance' of its soldiers. It 'can no longer be classed with the pre-war Armies of Europe' and its quality should improve quickly and rapidly. By 1936, the MID held that 'the war machine in Japan is functioning decently, if not admirably. Some of her 3rd line divisions may lack more modern armament but are, more or less, efficient'. By 1938, it adopted a formula which it retained until December 1941: 'The Japanese Army is a formidable fighting machine but probably has not yet reached the efficiency of the major western armies. It is, however, trained for and will probably only be required to fight in Eastern Asia where it will have inherent advantages over an opponent.' British views became more complex during the period 1937–41, as the Sino-Japanese War erupted and Japan and the USSR fought major border battles. IJA formations were smashed by the Red Army and sometimes fought to a standstill by Chinese forces. Although the IJA performed remarkably well in China, western observers credited these successes not to its skill but to Chinese incompetence. The IJA's success was taken to prove that it was a bad army not a good one. The more impressive its own performance, the worse seemed the Chinese, therefore the less impressive the Japanese. Thus, the IJA's reputation ebbed to its lowest level since 1904, precisely when its real accomplishments were surpassing those of that era. After a long assessment of the IJA's performance in the Sino-Japanese War, the British headquarters in China concluded that 'well trained and well led troops, thoroughly imbued with the offensive spirit, need not be afraid of encountering the Japanese Army in the field on anything approaching equal terms'. Though it underestimated the combat quality of the IJA, this assessment contained many accurate observations and some cautionary comments from the few Japanese experts in China. Everything indicates, however, that, unofficially, the old China hands had far less complimentary views. Angered at having to stand by as the IJA wrecked British prestige in China, insulting Britons and their womenfolk, they thought it a third-rate army, whose quality was so low that its characteristics were irrelevant – they could never be applied against a western force. As Noel Irwin, a senior officer at Hong Kong (and commander of the Eastern Army in Burma during 1942–43) wrote,

> One valuable fact seems to have come out of the Sino-Jap war, and that is the inferiority of the Jap soldier. On all sides I hear that he lacks courage, has little tactical knowledge, coordination in attack between arms and even between units or sub-units is absent and in the early stages technical training was of a very low standard. The war will, unhappily, have taught him much and if he were able to pass on to more ambitious heights of conquest now he might be a difficult customer but when all this is over it looks as if he will revert to a very third rate article. He seems a very different man to the Jap. of the Russo-Jap War. What he is, without a doubt, is a 'Bully' and against a European Power I don't believe you'd see him for dust except on the most unequal terms.

These observers fell prey to military ethnocentrism adulterated with vulgar racism. They mistook the IJA's appearance for its ability. Shocked by the dirty uniforms of Japanese soldiers, combined with sloppy military performance, they concluded that unshaven soldiers must be incompetent. Then they gauged Japanese tactics by European conditions and believed Anglo-Saxons must by necessity fight better than Chinese. These observers understood Japanese characteristics but misconstrued their quality, and their views poisoned the defence of Singapore. However, British observers actually based in Japan did not make the same errors. Their comments were phrased in defensive terms, because they knew that the IJA's performance did not impress others – it fell below their own expectation – but still they regarded the IJA with respect and accuracy. Major Wards, the Assistant Military Attaché, denounced the 'very dangerous' views expressed by westerners in China

> that the Japanese Army as a fighting force cannot be considered a first-class Army and that, in so far as land warfare is concerned, we need not really feel any anxiety in the event of war with Japan . . . In some respects the Japanese [sic] is clearly not up to the standard of a first-class power in Europe, but . . . the Japanese Army as it is to-day is a formidable force, well able to cope with any opposition likely to be met with at the present time in the Far East.

Such views mattered. They prevented the MID from accepting the mistaken assessments made in China, though it did alter its position. The MID held that the Sino-Japanese War had been tailor-made for the IJA. 'The easy victories which the Japanese have obtained may, however, have inculcated false ideas regarding the general ability of their army.' The MID emphasized the efficiency of the IJA, its 'admirable' staff work, bold operations, and its insistence upon rapid manoeuvre, envelopment and annihilation. Still, the IJA habitually took risks which were 'foolhardy judged by Western standards', its formations were always extremely vulnerable to counter-attack and its operations 'stereotyped'. Co-operation between artillery and infantry was mediocre, although improving. Japanese infantry relied excessively on armour to penetrate Chinese positions and underrated the effect of defensive firepower. Yet the MID heeded the Japanophiles and regarded the IJA with respect. The IJA had used its second-rate formations in China and its quality had not declined. Relying on firepower and declining to charge machine guns with bayonets fixed

> . . . are common sense principles of the Modern Battlefield which have been forced upon all infantry by the great fire effect of modern weapons. It would be a mistake therefore to assume that the Japanese are a contemptible enemy or that their morale of 1904–5, which was very high, has been seriously lowered.
>
> They cannot conduct a retreat and lack initiative when surprised or taken unexpectedly at a tactical disadvantage; but although apt to get panic stricken unexpectedly if taken at a disadvantage, they soon rally if not kept on the run . . . if convinced of the necessity for sacrifice there is no reason to suppose that they would not respond as in 1904, and there has [*sic*] been occasions during the present campaign when they have fought to the last man and last round and attacked repeatedly despite heavy losses.

During the four years before December 1941, the reputation of the IJA declined in British eyes – slightly in London and Tokyo, substantially in Shanghai and Singapore. Still, the overall record of assessment was respectable. British commentators in China seriously underestimated its quality. Observers in London generally placed the IJA in the second class of European armies – below the German and French, roughly equal to the Italian, and slightly worse than the Soviet military. This rating was low by European standards, but not dramatically so; and it was more accurate than the MID's assessment of many European armies. The MID accurately defined the IJA's ranking by Asian standards, although it overrated that of Britain. Observers in Japan provided extraordinarily accurate assessments of this issue. Their assessments and predictions are a model of military estimate conducted across cultural bounderies. All three groups placed a misleading emphasis on flaws in the 'national character' of Japan. The story of the assessment of the IJA's combat characteristics is a different matter. Members of all three groups understood the strong and weak points in the IJA's way of war, although they underestimated its ability to conduct retreats and to respond to unexpected circumstances. All offered a consistent and generally accurate picture of the IJA's style of operations, but with two important lacunae. None of these groups fully reported on the IJA's assimilation of fire-power into its style of war, and two of them misunderstood how it would be applied. While this problem was primarily conceptual, the product of military ethnocentrism, it was also affected by the limits to reporting. No observer ever warned in explicit detail of the power at the point of a Japanese attack, with its mixture of a razor edge of infiltration, a stranglehold of envelopment, a brutal smash of artillery and armour and ferocious infantry assault. These failures occurred because British opportunities to observe the IJA were limited at a time when the latter was experimenting with different operational styles. When the IJA did define its theory and refine its practice, it also prevented the language officers, those personnel most likely to under-stand these issues, from observing its exercises. Thus emerged an important gap in observation, at a moment when British officers in China believed that they could assess precisely those issues. The latter, in turn, only witnessed the IJA during the first months of the Sino-Japanese War, when its performance was mediocre and far worse than that of 1941.

No matter this failing, the General Staff appreciated the power of Japan and wished it to be friend rather than foe. In 1920–21 the War Office, more than any other department, wanted to renew the Anglo-Japanese Alliance (AJA). Until 1937 it continued to regard Japan as a potential ally. It thought the two countries had no conflicts of vital interests and one common threat, the USSR. It believed Japan would support stability in Asia, easing the two great problems which the British Army really feared – Russia or a resurgent Germany. The General Staff also held that Japanese enmity would cause embarrassment. It knew that war with Japan was possible, but alone among the fighting services, doubted that it could play a decisive role in one. Until 1938, the Army never conceived of large operations against the IJA, focus-ing on the defence of garrisoned bases, which seemed problem enough. The Army was small, its finances stretched by minor preparations against Japan. In case of war its tiny garrisons would face the initial attack alone; the RAF and the Royal Navy might never reach them in time. Even in the case of Singapore, General Milne, the Chief of the Imperial General Staff (CIGS), feared 'we were merely building a place which was liable to be raided at any time'. Some soldiers believed that rising population, lack of raw materials, and ambitions in China, ultimately might drive Japan to attack Britain but most thought that the threat was far away and doubted that Japan had reason to strike or to take great risks in doing so. Soon the view became bleaker. The Manchurian crisis showed that Japan might threaten Britain.

The General Staff knew that this meant British possessions in Asia were 'dangerously' vulnerable, but it also denied that a Japanese threat was imminent or inevitable. Britain could avoid that by recognizing Japanese expansion in Manchuria and restoring friendship with it, perhaps by renewing the AJA. Deverall was 'a strong advocate of an alliance with Japan or at least a friendly Japan', and emphasized the need not to embarrass the Japanese – 'they are a very sensitive race and they are orientals in all respects'.[3] The War Office trenchantly opposed Foreign Office policies towards Japan. Whether its line was feasible is uncertain, as is its supposition that British and Japanese interests could be reconciled, but its predictions were prescient.

By September 1935, the General Staff warned of change at hand. Britain must either renew the AJA or prepare against 'the possibility of Japanese aggression'. It used all its power in Whitehall to have Britain renew the AJA, but failed. Thereafter it became more pessimistic and passive. Japan was unlikely to attack the USSR, but probably would attack British territories if the latter joined a European war. Japan had plans to capture Singapore and an 'ultimate goal . . . the elimination of all opposition to her efforts to establish a dominant position in China; it follows, therefore, that Great Britain, by reason of her large interests in China, is regarded by Japan as the principal obstacle in her way.' In effect, the MID concluded, Britain headed Japan's enemy's list. Meanwhile, the IJA's attacks on British prestige in China drove the General Staff to see Japan as a foe, though it also believed 'Japan has bitten off about as much as she could chew and perhaps more than she could digest in China.' Until June 1940, it thought this would prevent a Japanese attack on the British Empire. It saw no choice but to give China enough support not to lose, which it knew must make Britain 'heartily disliked by both parties'.[4] The War Office had attitudes towards Japan unlike those conventional in Whitehall and it rated the IJA more highly than any other western army. But its labours were in vain. It failed to prevent Britain and Japan from becoming enemies or to gain the forces needed to meet that threat or to sell its estimate of the IJA to the old China hands, which came to dominate the Army in Asia. Meanwhile, the War Office contributed to errors about Japanese airpower and it lost control over defence in Asia to another fighting service, with different attitudes toward and experiences with Japan, the RAF. In 1920, the Imperial Japanese Navy (IJN) asked British help to develop airpower. Whitehall declined to assist the IJN officially, but it let aircraft manufacturers and an 'unofficial' mission of ex-Royal Navy Air Service (RNAS) personnel do so.[5] British firms and equipment shaped the birth of Japan's aircraft industry. Two-thirds of the 2000-odd naval aircraft built in Japan between 1922 and 1930 were British models produced under licence, or designed by Britons working for Japanese firms which followed British modes of organization.[6] Meanwhile, the Imperial Japanese Navy Air Force (IJNAF) was trained on the model of the RNAS; ironically, it became that service's only heir, because the RAF abandoned the RNAS's legacy. Even more, when Britain refused Japan information about aircraft carriers, the IJN secretly procured it by hiring John Rutland, an ex-RNAS and RAF officer with experience from the period when Britain solved the basic technical problems surrounding these warships.[7] The IJNAF received extraordinary access to the expertise of the best naval aviation force and industry of the day, in the most significant transfer of military technology and expertise of the inter-war era – a transfer that it exploited assiduously. By 1930 Japan matched Britain in naval aviation and its industry was better. Britain paid for this aid off Singapore.

The RAF doubted that this aid would cause danger. In 1921, it thought Japanese airpower 'in a very embryonic state, and the nation seems to have little "flair" for aerial work, possibly for the same reason that keeps them indifferent horsemen. It will therefore be a comparatively simple task to keep our lead over the Japanese in aerial matters.'[8] The RAF maintained few means to pursue that prediction, and usually ignored Japan, which it viewed through the prism of bureaucratic politics. One of its main arguments in inter-service battles at home was the idea of 'substitution', that airpower could handle jobs of the Army or Navy more economically than they, and that therefore the RAF should control such tasks and their finances. Though the RAF did not think Japan a threat, it saw the Singapore naval base as a chance. Control over its defence would feed several RAF squadrons, which could then sustain further substitution. By 1925, it formulated a remarkable theory, that the same squadrons in Asia could simultaneously replace infantry on the north-west frontier of India, cruisers for trade protection in the Indian Ocean, and 15-inch guns at Singapore, while the mere threat that Britain could deploy air forces to Singapore would deter Japan from war.[9] These were key roots for Britain's defence of Singapore in 1941.

The RAF thought Britain especially well-suited to use airpower and Japan uniquely susceptible to it. From 1920, it held that a few aircraft in Singapore 'would be of themselves the greatest possible deterrent' to Japan.[10] The IJN would not expose warships to the RAF near Singapore, and more; the RAF would frighten Japanese in peace and war. This idea stemmed from the RAF's general belief that strategic bombing could break the will of any nation, and the inchoate concept that Japanese were particularly vulnerable to it. British observers produced several generalizations about the Japanese 'national character', which shaped Whitehall's calculations about war with that country. They believed the Japanese soul was characterized by a mixture of repression, tension and unpredictability. The morale of Japanese, unused to setbacks or defeat, would snap if a sharp reverse occurred when war started; doubly so if an enemy struck the sacred land of Japan, views shaped by observation of Japanese behaviour during the Great Kanto earthquake of 1923. In 1921, one language officer speculated that 'the destruction by aerial bombing' of shrines central to state Shintoism could shatter Japanese nerve.[11] In 1941, the MID held that Japanese, while tough fatalists, had no experience of defeat, and were apt 'to panic in an unforeseen emergency. Air bombing on an intensive basis of Japanese towns might well cause such panic, as incendiaries would be particularly effective against native Japanese houses'; 'the best way to attack their morale would be to shake their faith in their own invincibility, and the immunity of their shores from attack' through bombing.[12] Such views were widespread. In 1940, the British Naval Attaché in Tokyo, argued that in the event of war, British carrier-borne aircraft should immediately bomb Japanese cities. This

> would create such havoc and despair, which might well knock Japan out at once. The cities would be a sheet of flames which no fire brigade could cope with. Machinery would be destroyed which could never be replaced in Japan. The moral effect would be so great, when one considers that it would be the first time that war had been brought to their sacred country, that anything internal might happen.

The Foreign Office thought that the despatch of just one aircraft carrier to the Pacific would deter Japan or destroy it – at a time when the IJN had the most dangerous carrier force in the world![13] Naturally, RAF officers shared such ideas.

RAF views of Japan rested on assumptions more than evidence. The Air Staff paid little attention to Japan. An Air Attaché was first appointed there in 1934, and perhaps five RAF personnel served as language officers with the Imperial Japanese Army Air Force (IJAAF) between 1918 and 1939. The RAF really had just one Japanese expert, R.W. Chappell, who served as language officer in the 1920s, Air Attaché during the 1930s and the senior air intelligence officer at Singapore in 1941. He and other RAF observers in Japan were hampered by cultural and institutional ethnocentrism. They believed that where the IJAAF differed from the RAF it must be inferior. Thus, RAF enlisted men served for 12 years, the IJAAF had short-term conscripts: this explained why equipment was badly maintained in IJAAF units, and indicated that failing must continue so long as the IJAAF relied on conscripts. RAF officers distorted the significance of individualism for air combat, and held that since Japanese culture emphasized the group above the individual, they must make poor fighter pilots – not so. Even worse, when RAF observers saw specific weaknesses, they looked for general causes to explain them. Once formulated, these took on a life of their own, predicting problems which *must* emerge in the future. Because Japanese made poor horsemen, they must lack the social classes which alone produced good pilots, because industry was rare in Japan, Japanese must be bad with machines, and unable to make good aircraft or maintain them: therefore, aircrew and equipment must continue to be bad. Ideas of national character mixed with racism lay at the root of these explanations. RAF officers doubted that any non-western people could develop good pilots and air forces and used national stereo-typing to assess every country. These problems were doubled because Japanese air forces and industries were in their infancy, and redoubled because the RAF focused on the worst of the two air forces of Japan, the IJAAF, a poor service struggling to achieve mediocrity. There were many weaknesses to observe. This made strengths easy to overlook.

Though no British naval aviation personnel were seconded to the IJNAF, they respected that service, more than any western observers did the IJAAF, largely because it had been trained on the RNAS model. RAF observers were more negative about the IJAAF. Units were well organized but maintenance shoddy. Pilots were poor to mediocre, marked by energy, courage and dis-cipline, but an Air Force . . . 'cannot fly by discipline alone'.[14] 'Immersed in theory to the exclusion of practical work', officers were 'almost entirely lacking in initiative and although he has had no opportunity of proving otherwise would not appear to make a good fighting pilot'.[15] Whatever force these assessments had before 1930, then Japanese air forces rose sharply in quality – the IJNAF surged past the Fleet Air Arm and ran the RAF a race, though the IJAAF remained inferior – while Japan's aircraft industry and designers produced some excellent models. By 1936, Japan entered the first rank of airpowers, if it never quite matched Britain, Germany or the United States, and its relative standing slowly slipped. Foreign observers miscalcu-lated its achievements. In 1932, the last year in which foreigners could freely observe Japan's air forces and industry, they were mediocre. Then, as a revolution in airpower occurred in Japan and throughout the world, observers tried to gauge developments which Japanese tried to disguise. Forced into guesswork, foreigners doubted that air forces once moving at a sluggish pace could suddenly have picked it up as the Japanese were doing. They retained images true of infancy but not adolescence, while generalizations coined to explain old weaknesses now predicted future ones. The guesses of RAF observers were slightly worse than usual, especially about aircraft design. Chappell noted that Japanese wished to improve the quality of their aircraft, but 'one does not need to be a Sherlock Holmes' to discover that almost every model was copied from western designs. 'At present there appears to be no likelihood of Japan producing anything original'.[16] British observers assumed that Japan could not produce first-rate aircraft in large numbers or match the leading edge of development, precisely when such stereotypes ceased to be true. Given the technological revolution of the period, this led to exactly the wrong prediction, that the relative quality of Japanese air equipment would slide instead of rise. In fact, between 1935 and 1941 Japanese and British aircraft were roughly equal in quality, though ultimately the British industry had far more breadth and depth.

All this was reinforced by observation of the Sino-Japanese War where, until 1939, the IJNAF and IJAAF generally deployed older equipment. Their performance was mediocre – but no more so than that of the French, Russian and Italian air forces or of RAF bombers before 1942. British observers thought this performance incompetent because they compared it to what they imagined airpower and the RAF could do; unfortunately, imagination outstripped reality. In 1937, the senior RAF officer in Hong Kong thought IJNAF operations in South China dismal failures, because pilots, poorly trained and equipped, could not bomb effectively in perfect conditions, concentrate forces, assess vulnerabilities or strike them. 'Whether they are learning by experience remains to be seen.' His successor answered this question in the negative. Though 'very nearly unbelievable' to report, the Japanese had overcome none of their elementary problems.[17] As with the British Army, though to a lesser degree, RAF observers in Japan and China had different views. In 1937, Chappell thought IJAAF training 'probably varies considerably, excellent in some units and in other cases may be dangerously poor'. The IJNAF and the IJAAF could handle Chinese and possibly Soviet air forces, 'but cannot be considered a major hazard to any first class Power fighting under equal conditions'.[18] By 1939, his judgment rose considerably. Japanese air forces had fought well in China, because their training and organization were sound. The 'spirit of readiness to die for the Emperor proved invaluable in maintaining the morale of pilots at the highest pitch'. Its aircraft industry was efficient and should soon match 'the lesser of the 1st class Powers'.[19] These views, however, had no effect.

British estimates of the IJAAF rose between 1920 and 1941, but then they began from a low level. In 1920, the RAF pledged to defend Hong Kong with four squadrons against 12 IJAAF (which probably was possible at that time). In 1922, it noted that Japanese pilots were slow to train and 'the statement has arisen that the Japanese are not, and never will make good pilots'.[20] The RAF maintained this confidence for 15 years. Though it recognized a rise in Japanese airpower, it believed that Japan had barely budged the ratio of quality against the RAF, which could still match at least twice its weight in Japanese aircraft. By 1937–40, official British estimates of Japanese airpower were unfavourable, but not entirely so. The COS noted that British and Japanese equipment in Asia were roughly equal, and the RAF 'greatly inferior' in strength but far better in quality, especially regarding maintenance. Japanese pilots were 'fairly good' and their morale 'very high'; their 'main weakness . . . is lack of initiative: a plan once made is rigidly adhered to, even when circumstances make an alternative imperative. There is no lack of courage – volunteers would be forthcoming for desperate adventures of any kind.'[21] The RAF's *Handbook on the Air Services of Japan*, its only official compendium on the topic, stated

> The Japanese are, and always have been, a race with strong military traditions. They possess fully the virtues of loyalty, physical courage, endurance, and determination. They are very inquisitive, and conscien-

tious and indefatigable imitators, displaying much discrimination in the use they make of the inventions and methods of others. Their facility in co-operation is also remarkable, as opposed to the strong individualism of the Anglo-Saxon. They possess an infinite capacity for taking pains, great powers of organisation even down to the most minute detail, and a very definite gift of careful planning. Intensely suspicious and naturally secretive, they are able to put their plans into action at the chosen moment with suddenness, speed and efficiency, but with all their qualities they have a definite lack of imagination. The unexpected and the illogical embarrass them more than other races and when their plans break down they lack the capacity to improvise hurriedly, to grasp a new situation quickly or intuitively to rearrange their minds . . . Their fighting qualities, the legacy of a mighty warrior caste, are to be respected; they are systematically inculcated by education, precept and example with the traditions of personal honour and self-sacrifice. These together with a distinct touch of fanaticism, combine to make the individual no mean adversary.

The Japanese 'as a race are accustomed to discipline and to regimentation' and had a 'latent streak of savagery and cruelty which war brings to the surface – a phenomenon not confined to the Japanese'. Their pilots were brave and disciplined, good at set pieces but, with some 'brilliant exceptions', they were 'slower witted' than Europeans: 'the national tendency to slow thinking and consequent dependence on routine must prove a handicap in turning out young pilots as good as those of the leading European Air Powers'. The 'standard of flying' had improved and 'can now be classed as good'. The RAF assessed Japanese operational characteristics well, noting that against China, it had first acquired air superiority by attacking enemy airbases, and then emphasized close air support. 'Japan can hold her own in the air against the U.S.S.R., but she cannot yet be considered the equal, in essential respects, of the leading air powers of Europe.' Its aviation industry was mediocre, though improving. Its aircraft were efficient, but not 'of performance equal to that of the first class European powers or of the U.S.A.'.

Japanese designers have not yet reached a standard equal to that of the designers of the leading European countries. Hence for aircraft of the highest military performance they have to depend on purchase . . . As yet the Japanese have shown no national inventive genius in the whole wide realm of mechanics. Their undoubtedly efficient machines derive entirely from Western models, copied or modified. It is not to be supposed, therefore, that in the highly specialised and ever advancing technique of aircraft design they will do more than follow western ideas for a considerable period. Thus in this particular, their efficiency vis a vis Western Power [*sic*] is limited.[22]

These estimates were wrong; and unofficially most British observers had worse ones, fed by ethnocentrism and vulgar racism about Japan, and over-confidence about themselves. Japanese airpower was believed to have five weaknesses – mediocrity in maintenance, industry, aircrew and air combat, and a psychological inability to withstand strategic bombing. Commanders at Singapore noted

> Experience in CHINA goes to show that in all cases when determined A.A. fire, even in small volume, was encountered it has had the effect of driving the Japanese aircraft to high altitudes with consequent deterioration in their bomb aiming. We consider it probable that severe casualties inflicted on the Japanese both by fighters and by A.A. defences would cause a serious drop in their morale. It is further doubtful if their maintenance and supply organisation could withstand serious losses operating at such a distance from their factories.[23]

The Air Attaché at Chungking thought most Japanese air equipment second-rate. The IJAAF was bad: 'a determined defence and the initial infliction of even the smallest loss' would wreck it. IJNAF pilots were better. They would fight to the death, 'if he is outclassed, he will ram rather than run.'[24] There were 'cracks . . . in this imposing façade' of Japanese airpower. Its staffs could not handle 'prolonged or efficient air opposition', it was unused to opposition and 'Japanese do not take their defeats very well.'

> If the opening Japanese air effort can be thrown back with considerable loss, it will place the Japanese Air Services in a dilemma from which they will take a long time to recover; a well-organised defence which can inflict initial losses disproportionate to the weight of the attack will receive its reward in the form of breathing space, for the Japanese are most religiously 'text-book'; they take time to ponder counter-measures; and they are most careful not to venture again into what has proved to be a dangerous area before they are satisfied that they can escape more or less unscathed.[25]

These comments reflect the confidence about airpower which underlay the defence of the British Empire in Asia against Japan. As one leading British air journal, *The Aeroplane*, wrote during the Tientsin crisis, 'judging by what one hears, the Japanese Air Force would not be much of a menace to a first-class European Air Force . . . Sooner or later we shall have to settle who is the boss of the Pacific . . . we may yet see our Air Force deciding whether the white man or the yellow man is to rule the East.'[26] That estimate was prophecy, but double-edged.

Notes

1. Captain N.W.H. Du Boulay, 'Report on the Japanese Army', 5 December 1895, PRO: WO 33/56. P.A. Towle, 'British Estimates of Japanese Military Power, 1900–1914', in Philip Towle (ed.), *Estimating Foreign Military Power* (London: Croom Helm, 1982). Unless otherwise indicated, all quotations in the text are taken from John Ferris, 'Worthy of Some Better Enemy?: The British Estimate of the Imperial Japanese Army, 1919–1941, and the Fall of Singapore', *The Canadian Journal of History*, vol. XXVIII, pp. 224–56.
2. 64th meeting of the COS, 23 January 1928, CAB 53/2; 96th meeting of the COS, 9 December 1930, CAB 53/3; 107th meeting of the COS, 28 February 1933, CAB 53/4; COS 233, 'Defence of Hong Kong', CAB 53/21; 234th meeting of the COS, 4 April 1938, CAB 53/9; COS 579 (J.P.), CAB 53/31; COS 725, CAB 53/38; COS No. 117, 146, CAB 53/14; Ong Chit-Chung, *Operation Matador: Britain's War Plans Against the Japanese, 1918–1941* (Singapore: Times Academic Press, 1997), pp. 72–6.
3. Minute by Cavan, 8 December 1925, PRO: WO 32/5916; Minute by Deverall, 2 February 1937, WO 106/130.
4. DDMI to DMOI, 25 June 1938, WO 106/5469; Memo by MI2, 9 May 1938, WO 2106/5541.
5. John Ferris, 'A British "Unofficial" Aviation Mission and Japanese Naval Developments, 1919–1929', *The Journal of Strategic Studies*, vol. V (1982), pp. 416–39.
6. These figures are derived from those on the production of aircraft scattered through the pages of Robert C. Mikesh and Shorzoe Abe, *Japanese Aircraft, 1910–1941* (Annapolis: Naval Institute Press, 1990).
7. GC&CS No. 012144: PRO: HW 12/41; No. 12246, HW 12/42; No. 12469, HW 12/43. These messages are Japanese telegrams which British codebreakers deciphered: cf. Chapters 4 and 10.
8. CID Paper 120-C, CAB 5/3; Draft CID paper, 'The Future Military Menace to the Empire and the Means by Which it May Be Met', undated but early 1921 by internal evidence, RAFM: Trenchard Papers, C.11/1, issued in a variant form as CID 156-C: PRO: CAB 5/4.
9. 'Precis of lecture by C.A.S.', January 1925: AIR 8/45.
10. Ibid., note 10.
11. Memorandum by K.S. Morgan, undated but ca. spring 1921: FO 371/6681.
12. 'Japanese Morale', memorandum by MI2c, 31 March 1941: FO 371/27890.
13. Minutes by Ashley Clarke, 19 November 1940 and R.A.B. Butler, 21 November 1940, F 5308: FO 371/24711.
14. Memorandum No. 2, 9 February 1937, by Air Attaché: FO 371/21037.
15. Tokyo Embassy despatch, No. 23, 18 January 1924: FO 371/10309; Military Attaché Tokyo, report No. 16, 27 May 1926, Tokyo embassy despatch, No. 443, 13 August 1927: AIR 5/756; Tokyo embassy despatch, No. 639, 20 December 1927.
16. Memorandum by Chappell, 28 January 1937: AIR 2/2008.
17. Memoranda by Bishop, 16 November 1937 and 24 March 1938, memorandum by Walser, 23 August 1938: DNDO: D. Hist.
18. Memorandum by Chappell, 28 January 1937: PRO: AIR 2/2008.
19. Air Attaché, Tokyo, January 1939, 'Annual Report on Aviation in Japan': FO 371/23570.

20. CID Paper 120-C: CAB 5/3; RAF Monthly Intelligence Report, No. XIII, 5.22: AIR 5/810.
21. COS 596, 14 June 1937: CAB 53/32.
22. SD 130, 'Handbook on the Air Services of Japan', 2085–956/2: NAW: RG 165.
23. Report of Singapore Defence Conference, 1940, 31 October 1940, App F: AWM 113/MH/1/95.
24. Hong Kong Naval, Military and Air Force Intelligence Report No. 4/41, 1 May 1941: PRO: WO 208/722.
25. Ibid.
26. *The Aeroplane*, 19 July 1939, p. 78.

7
The Royal Navy and Japan, 1921–1941

Ian T.M. Gow

The years 1920/21 marked a major shift in Admiralty perspectives on the IJN. Pressures to retrench plus the possible non-renewal of the Anglo-Japanese Alliance compromised Britain's ability to constrain an expansionist Japan. In 1919 RN planners felt Japan could be disregarded as a threat 'whether as an individual power or as a partner in any combination' and the USN was the only navy that concerned them.[1] However, in 1920 a shift occurred with the appointment of Beatty as First Sea Lord. He highlighted the enormous disparity in naval spending between the USA and Japan and later told the Prime Minister: 'Japan's naval power is almost as great a menace as that of the United States'.[2] He then pointed out that Japan and the USA, having established a construction lead, would 'thus relegate Great Britain to the third Naval Power'.[3] This growing concern was underlined by the Admiralty's refusal in 1920 to allow an IJN visit to the carrier *Eagle* or to provide a naval aviation mission.[4] In January 1921, war plans drawn up against Japan suggested that long-range operations against Australia were unlikely, but that they might take Hong Kong either to keep or to bargain with and that seizing Singapore was possible but unlikely. The plans recommended a fleet larger than the Japanese main fleet to move to Singapore, provided fuelling arrangements were in place. The British Fleet was then to seek out and defeat it at the first opportunity and then, from Hong Kong or further north if captured, to implement a blockade and anti-submarine warfare strategy in order to bring Japan to its knees.[5] In July, Beatty addressed the Imperial Conference on the need to plan for a war with Japan. He stated Japan would strike quickly once hostilities were declared, hitting Hong Kong first and then possibly Singapore and Borneo. Everything depended on the speed with which the British Fleet could reach the Far East, engage in a decisive battle, destroy the main Japanese Fleet, gain control of sea communications and then blockade Japan. Beatty stated that holding Singapore would eliminate all danger to Australia and New Zealand, noting Singapore was an important base for offensive operations against the IJN.[6] Beatty felt a Singapore-based fleet merely to contain the IJN too risky, it had to destroy their fleet.[7] Beatty courted the Dominions, using Singapore as a means of easing their fears whilst attempting to obtain a greater contribution to Imperial naval defence. The official decision in 1921 to establish a major naval base at Singapore was costly, made necessary by the revolutionary shift from coal- to oil-burning ships, and required an expensive supply route. The bulging of ships also made existing docking facilities in the Far East obsolete. There were debates about where to site an appropriate harbour and fuel and repair base for the Fleet. Hong Kong was unsuitable and Sydney too distant to support offensive strategies. The Singapore concept emerged whilst the Alliance was still extant and renewal still possible. A Penang conference of the C-in-C of the China, East Indies and Australian Squadrons even suggested that a higher command be located at Singapore.[8] The Singapore threat was not lost on Japanese policymakers and attaché reports from Japan suggested an orchestrated campaign against the base.[9]

Before the Imperial Conference could agree on this, a call for a naval limitation conference came from Washington, necessitating a rethink in terms of the USN, the IJN and the Alliance. There seems to have been little naval preparation for Washington and preliminary meetings were discouraged by the Americans. With specific regard to Japan, they were to press for a ratio of 3:2 for GB (and the USA) and Japan based on equality of fleet plus a percentage to guarantee victory, a percentage because of the long distances involved and a percentage to leave some ships in European waters. They recommended the abolition of submarines, something Japan would not accept. The RN was prepared to give up Weihaiwei but needed to secure Hong Kong. They also hoped that Japan would accept no naval base further south than Formosa.[10] Naturally the most important objective was to exclude Singapore from any discussion on fortifications. Chatfield feared upsetting either US or Japanese colleagues commenting 'the Japs at any rate will try & claim us as their ally and friend'.[11] The most important issue of all was, of course, the capital ship ratio. The RN required a ratio of 15:15:9:5:5, believing that by limiting Japan to nine and slowing her replacement rate would require a much smaller British naval force in the Pacific in the event of war, 'cripple her [Japan's] power of building navies in time of war' and make the Singapore problem easier.[12] Britain went along with American pressure to limit Japan to a 5:5:3 ratio whilst suggesting this ratio made Japan impregnable given the vast distances involved. Admiral Chatfield added that he would offer not to place a force in the Pacific equal to Japan, with this ratio. The British were sympathetic to Japan retaining the *Mutsu*.[13] Britain also disagreed with Japan over armed merchantmen. Britain did manage to keep Singapore and dominion bases out of the fortification agreement, but the American agreement to non-fortification effectively eliminated their power in the Western Pacific thus contributing further to British concerns over Japanese naval power in the Pacific. The abrogation of the Alliance limited the British ability to constrain Japanese ambitions. The

Japanese always felt that the British colluded with the Americans and it is true that the British and American civilian and naval delegations did meet and discuss strategy vis-à-vis Japan.

The Washington Conference limited capital ships, diverting the naval race on to auxiliary vessels. The naval attaché in Tokyo stated that Japan would build to the limits of her financial strength, to the limits of the spirit of the Washington Treaty 'and perhaps a little beyond it'.[14] Japan immediately launched into constructing so-called Treaty Cruisers and, since they outgunned all other cruisers, this caused Beatty to press for larger expenditures to combat the Japanese. Only the Navy, he insisted, could restrain Japanese aggressive tendencies. The Empire, he stated ominously, 'rested on Japanese sufferance'.[15] Here we see the RN using Japan to browbeat Cabinet as Beatty's concerns with the Japanese threat intensified. Ignoring the fact that IJN cruisers were aimed against the US Pacific Fleet, Beatty argued cogently that Britain needed 70 cruisers – a 25 per cent increase over the Japanese for fleet duties plus nine for trade duties – to be able to cope with Japanese cruisers in fleet action and in trade protection.[16] The RN double-counted the Japanese cruisers and wanted 25 per cent of both and then added obsolete 8-inch-gun coastal cruisers to raise the figure even higher. There is thus substance to Churchill's accusations of exaggerated Admiralty claims. There was also a panic within the Admiralty that secrets had been passed between the civilian aviation mission to the IJN and the mission did pass on valuable information allowing IJN aviation to catch and then overtake the RN.[17] There was also an unfounded rumour of a Japanese takeover of the Paracels.[18] In 1923, the Admiralty decided to redeploy the main fleet to the Mediterranean ready to dispatch it to Singapore and carried out Operation MU to test the problems of getting to Singapore. Interestingly the Blue Fleet (Japan) scored direct hits with aircraft but only slowed the ships by one knot.[19] After the Kanto earthquake, the China Squadron offered help 'to their old and faithful ally' including medical supplies and food. The First Lord of the Admiralty at the Imperial Conference of 1923 warned of the dangers of a war against Britain by Japan 'if there were a European combination against us at the same moment'.[20] In 1924, the Combined Staff College examined the possibility of an attack on Singapore by the Japanese but deemed it impracticable. This analysis assumed that the Singapore base had been fully reinforced in the very year construction was halted![21] Meanwhile the DCNS, Keyes, repeatedly asserted the continuing threat from Japan.[22] This perhaps was the high point of the government uncritically accepting the Japanese threat as Beatty neared the end of his office. Churchill's correspondence with Keyes, to be C-in-C Mediterranean, the key post for Fleet passage to Singapore, indicates a division of naval views. Churchill was highly dismissive of Beatty always 'accusing them [IJN] of going mad and attacking us' and the Admiralty always exaggerating every danger from that quarter.[23] Keyes, reflecting perhaps a balanced view of

Japan, agreed that Japan had no intention of attacking the British Empire but 'will turn Europeans out of China and in time Asia unless we are sufficiently strong to make it not worth her while to attempt it. Something must be done to check her naval expansion or keep pace with it.'[24] He added Japan would 'oust us from the Pacific altogether unless she knows we are in a position to resist her'. Churchill's Treasury now summarily dismissed Beatty's demands stating 'with the four cruisers "Britannia rules the waves"' – without them, 'we are at the mercy of Japan'.[25] The CID were told Japan was prepared to take the gravest risks to secure to all their battleships in an air bombardment of Singapore and Beatty concurred saying that the Japanese would take such risks to gain control of the China Seas and the Indian Ocean.[26] Churchill, however, persuaded the Cabinet to take a more realistic view of Japan and the ten-year rule was extended, ruling out war with Japan until after 1935. Churchill ominously suggested that if war did break out, the fleet 'would not be sent out to the Far East in the first years of the war'.[27] Economic austerity and a continuing ideological disposition towards naval arms limitation either amongst the big three or through the League combined with the weakening of Beatty's influence over CID and the Cabinet ensured that the Admiralty's fears of Japan gradually lost their effectiveness. Nevertheless, in 1926 debates continued within CID and this was exacerbated by the time elapsing before British naval intelligence picked up Japanese mobilization efforts, ranging from 24 hours to 8 days.[28] The RN did reinforce the China Fleet that year. Fleet exercises and research continued but the tide had turned and Austen Chamberlain, like Churchill, suggested the Admiralty were obsessed with an imaginary war with Japan and had persuaded themselves such a conflict was imminent.[29] The Admiralty did try to limit IJN surveillance in Britain. Already lacking good access in Japan and with Britain flooded with IJN personnel visiting armaments firms, Chatfield now refused IJN officers entry to the naval constructors' course when IJN withheld information about the cruiser *Furutaka*.[30]

The League's disarmament initiative achieved little and in 1927 the Admiralty again prepared for naval limitation talks. The conference foundered on Anglo-American differences, but improved Anglo-Japanese naval relations as they worked out compromise solutions only to be rejected by the Americans. Beatty had had preliminary soundings with Admiral Jones (USN) and apparently agreed to parity in cruisers with the USA and to reject a 5:3 ratio with Japan.[31] At the conference, Balfour decided to come to an agreement with the Americans and then confront the Japanese, thus confirming Japanese fears of Anglo-American coercion. There were numerous instances of Anglo-American collusion, although some IJN officers in the delegation planned to work with the British to get a united front against the Americans, but were overruled.[32] The Japanese were still concerned over the Singapore base and the impact of the loss of the Alliance on their naval strategy. The Admiralty position prior to the conference, anticipated clashes with the Japanese in a number of areas such as the scrapping of capital ships, reduction in their size, abolition or limiting of submarines that never emerged. The deadlock with the United States led Gibson, the chief US delegate, to suggest that the British and the Japanese provide a compromise and the Americans would agree. Over two days an Anglo-Japanese agreement was thrashed out with the Japanese conceding to Britain over light cruisers to match a concession on overall tonnage. The result, 12 : 12 : 8 (a figure that had been discussed between the USA and GB earlier in the conference) in heavy cruisers and 500000 : 500000 : 325000 tons for USA, GB and Japan plus retention of 25000 tons of overage vessels seemed a sensible compromise, but it was promptly rejected by the US delegation, the British Cabinet and also Tokyo, who wanted a 10 : 10 : 7 ratio. The inability of the three powers to design a suitable formula ultimately destroyed the conference and damaged Anglo-American relations, but it possibly improved Anglo-Japanese naval relations. Indeed, at one point a Japanese naval representative at the conference apparently suggested that, if the conference failed, the Anglo-Japanese Alliance should be revived. The RN now turned to battling the Treasury over restoring the Singapore programme and getting the needed cruisers. Churchill, having read the Geneva reports, wrote exultantly 'Beatty's Japanese bogey has completely collapsed. The poor creatures do not intend as you will see, to build any more cruisers until after December 1936'.[33] That same year, the C-in-C China reported that the King had told him 'whatever you do be nice to the Japanese'. The Mediterranean Fleet, meanwhile, exercised again getting the fleet to Singapore against Japanese resistance. That same year, the Admiralty decided to defer sending three battlecruisers and possibly an aircraft carrier to strengthen the China Fleet. In April 1929, the CID told the Admiralty that 'aggressive action on the part of Japan within the next ten years is not a contingency seriously to be apprehended'. Churchill added that it was not now necessary to make preparations for additional expenditure at Singapore, for a decisive battle in the Pacific or send a British battlefleet superior to, or at least equal in strength to the seagoing navy of Japan.[34] However in May, the Admiralty again stated 'war in the Far East must be the basis on which preparations are made' and remarked that the need for reinforcing Singapore was even greater.[35]

Admiralty documentation of the 1920s always assumed that with a reinforced Singapore and a fleet of equal or slightly superior size to the Japanese, they would defeat them in a decisive battle. If Singapore was not reinforced, they would do it over a period of three or four years. Admiralty views carried far less weight in the second half of the decade, but the IJN threat ensured some strengthening of the naval position in the region. Intelligence on the IJN after the abrogation of the Alliance, with few important IJN naval engagements IJN to observe, was poor. Access to key personnel and establishments was now reduced to the level of other European powers.[36] Replies were now in Japanese rather than English. Whether this cooling of relations was solely due to alliance abrogation or whether it also indicated injured IJN feelings over Anglo-American collusion at Washington is unclear. Newspaper monitoring was increased, but inside information, not only on the emerging Japanese naval air service but also on the IJN in general required better access. The British Aviation Mission, comprising many former RNAS officers, did provide information which the attachés used to extrapolate to the Navy as a whole. Naval aviation developments occupied considerable attaché attention, in part because this was improved, albeit limited, access. It was also possibly because the RN was locked in a battle with the RAF over the future of the Fleet Air Arm. On many occasions in the 1920s, officers such as Beatty used the fact that the IJN and the USN had their own naval air services in inter-service manoeuvring. The view from Tokyo indicated that the Japanese continued to provide evidence of bravery and superb fighting spirit, but reinforced the view that they lacked creativity and initiative. The tone of attaché reports on the Japanese naval air service gradually shifted from being dismissive to including grudging respect. Attachés also predicted that the Japanese would suffer greatly from the ending of the alliance in that they were still highly dependent on foreign technological knowledge and this would slow their rate of development. Consequently, reports regarding German naval technological support increased in frequency.[37] Clearly the intelligence from Tokyo was now more speculative and the lack of access itself was probably a major contributor to the Admiralty's increasing concern with the Japanese 'threat'. The C-in-C China's intelligence was even more disappointing, apart from confirming that whilst the Japanese naval officers were polite and welcomed straight talking they did not reciprocate. Australian naval intelligence was also reduced severely after Washington. The Japanese cruiser programme and a growing suspicion that even the Treaty cruiser limits were being exceeded were the only intelligence the Admiralty really needed. This ensured that the possibility of war with Japan, even if not imminent, remained central to naval planning for a containment strategy or a decisive battle with the IJN throughout the 1920s. The fact that the Japanese had technologically advanced ships, good men to man them and leaders with recent combat experience (even if the younger officers had inadequate seagoing experience, according to the attachés) never shook the RN confidence. Either the Japanese would back down in the face of an obviously superior navy or if a decisive battle was to be fought there would only be one winner, the RN, which would then blockade Japan and bring her to her knees.

This all rested on assumptions of superiority, but also on there being no naval threat in European waters. The re-emergence of the feared German Navy and its possible alliance with a Mediterranean power, Italy, seriously undermined the ability of the RN to commit a force to meet the IJN in a decisive battle. Given also the fact that American naval support was uncertain, the RN at the end of the decade looked woefully unprepared for problems in the Far East against a formidable foe.

By the end of the 1920s, the Admiralty faced an increasingly difficult political environment. Internationally the Kellogg–Briand Pact, the League of Nations Preparatory Commission on Disarmament and the proposed London Naval Conference all militated against increased naval expenditure. Domestically, the new Labour government was committed to disarmament and social and economic reform funded partly by reductions in military expenditure, plus the annually confirmed ten-year rule. The improved international situation offered no immediate naval threat within Europe. The 'Summary of Naval Policy' now made clear that despite the difficulties with the Americans at Geneva, 'war with the United States was not a possibility'. Moreover, since Japan was the next strongest naval power 'war in the Far East must be the general basis on which preparations are made'.[38] This would mean continued progress on the Singapore base and on cruiser construction. The outgoing First Lord, presenting his budget, cancelled three cruisers from the 1927–28 programme and the 1929 programme was drastically affected by the financial situation. The decade ended with the call to yet another naval conference at London and another possibility of containing Japan through naval limitation agreements. The upcoming naval conference, with the possible abolition of the submarine, offered the Treasury reductions in military budgets. The 1930 estimates contained no building programme, postponing it until after the London Conference. The submarine programme was suspended, although the naval attaché in Tokyo drew attention to the remarkable development of Japanese submarines but was now unable to provide accurate figures on naval aviation in Japan.[39] Thus, whilst Japan had made tremendous progress in auxiliary ship developments to offset the 5:5:3 ratio, Britain was falling behind. The Singapore base had made slow progress but the floating dock was now in place. However, by October 1929, all major work was postponed for five years. Hong Kong remained weak and the Admiralty had to look to the London Naval Conference to contain the IJN.

The Admiralty's main focus of attention was the USN and the IJN and especially their 8″-cruiser construction. British naval planners had to revisit old ground with the Americans and then, if they managed to reach an accord, to confront the Japanese. For Britain the problem was that they needed a large number of small cruisers whereas the Americans needed a small number of large cruisers for their Pacific strategy vis-à-vis Japan. The split in cruiser sizes – 10000-ton 8-inch-gun Washington treaty cruisers versus smaller 7–8000 ton 6-inch-gun cruisers, which the British needed for trade protection – was the key problem, especially since the Americans were demanding parity in cruisers in terms of global tonnage with Britain and numbers. However, Anglo-American discussions directly involved Japan because of the ratio which Japan needed with regard to the United States.

Britain sought the abolition of battleships, the reduction in maximum size of battleships to 25000 tons and 12-inch guns and the abolition of submarines, knowing that the Japanese would oppose submarine abolition. The preparatory discussions provided agreement between the British and the Americans to force Japan to concede or give up her positions on the overall ratio. This compromise by Japan caused major political problems at home from its Naval General Staff. Attempts to abolish the submarine failed. Britain had however compromised heavily on cruisers reducing the number to 50 from their absolute minimum of 70 but only until 1936. The three powers all agreed to extend the capital ship holiday for a further five years.

RN planners spent the remainder of 1930 preparing for the forthcoming Geneva Disarmament Conference of the League in 1932 which achieved little. Its only benefit was that it forced the Japanese to report to the Disarmament Commission naval figures which the British naval attaché in Tokyo had been unable to obtain. The increasingly secretive approach of the Japanese plus the withdrawal of British naval and air personnel from the IJN created great difficulties for information-gathering. The section of the naval reports from Tokyo devoted to 'IJN Future Policy' ceased, presumably because of the scarcity of reliable data. The London Treaty did restrain Japan in capital ship and cruiser construction, albeit temporarily. However, RN planners were well aware that their entire naval strategy in the Far East depended on sending the main part of the British Fleet to Singapore if war broke out. But they now needed to take into account a European threat and retaining units in Home and Mediterranean waters to cope with Italy or a rearmed Germany.

1930 was a relatively quiet year in the Far East. The conditions necessary to persuade a cash-strapped British government to fund a fleet for Europe and the Far East and to complete the Singapore base were the emergence of an aggressive European power either in the Atlantic (Germany) or in the Mediterranean (France or more likely Italy) or an open threat to British interests in the Far East or Pacific by Japan. Delays on the Singapore base, postponed building programmes and the further ageing of Britain's capital ship fleet by the naval holiday agreed at the London Conference, plus a Cabinet refusal to consider further building plans until the League Disarmament Commission met, produced a steady deterioration in the RN's position.

The Manchurian Incident in 1931 and the Shanghai Incident the following year showed the weakness of League collective action. More importantly they indicated the weakness of the RN to deal with an aggressive Japan, especially during the Shanghai and Jehol conflicts of 1932–33. The Admiralty Board in 1931 gave scant attention to the Manchurian Incident, partially because it was not seen as navally significant but also because the Navy was dealing with the Invergordon Mutiny. The mutiny had one important spinoff for naval involvement in the Far East in that Admiral Dreyer, the DCNS, a highly talented officer, was a political casualty. He was sent to the second-rank China Fleet as C-in-C rather than to more prestigious commands. He spoke up about the imminent Japanese naval threat to British interests in the Far East throughout his period of office. The China Fleet, occupied with flood rescues and its own HMS *Petersfield* scandal, virtually ignored it. But the Shanghai Incident, erupting with breathtaking suddenness in January 1932, shook the RN. Unlike Manchuria, there were numerous European and American observers witnessing ruthless carrier-borne aircraft bombing civilians and ill-disciplined and ill-trained landing forces. The main units of the China Fleet were all ordered to Shanghai and tensions began to run high as Admiral Kelly, C-in-C China, warned the Japanese C-in-C, Admiral Shiozawa, that if Japanese aircraft continued to fly low over his ship he would open fire.[40] This caused serious concerns within Whitehall and at the British embassies since the incident might lead to war with Japan. The China Fleet was actually bottled up in the Whampoo river and thus an easy target for the superior IJN forces present. However, the Shanghai and Jehol Incidents did allow the Admiralty to take budgetary offensives. The Naval Plans Division's stark report, designed for maximum effect, stated that:

> a) our forces at Shanghai and Tientsin were surrounded by superior forces, our 3″-gun cruisers were surrounded by overwhelmingly superior force in the Yangtse river, our 6″-gun cruisers, 2 sloops and 12 gunboats were exposed to attack by superior forces and d) defence was non-existent at Singapore, Trincomalee completely undefended etc.[41]

One can see here the China Fleet pressuring for increased forces and the Admiralty battling for overall increases in budget to cope with a volatile Far East situation. The Admiralty attacked the ten-year rule, signalling its imminent demise. Resisting pressure to adopt either a collaborative approach to Japan or to take economic sanctions which might actually exacerbate the situation, the RN now sought to reopen the Singapore defences issue and to re-examine Trincomalee and Hong Kong. Views of Japanese inefficiency were severely challenged by a report from HMS *Suffolk* attesting to the speed and effectiveness of the Japanese landing operations at the Woosung Forts. The Japanese landed 10 000 men, six guns, 15 tanks, equipment, motor vehicles, anti-aircraft guns and 12 crated aircraft using only 66 000 tons of shipping. The RN, the *Suffolk* captain observed, would need 215 000 tons for a similar venture.[42] The COS now evaluated the Japanese as capable of destroying facilities there quickly as well as oil supplies. The First Lord suggested there was a report of Japanese preparations to invade Singapore at this time, although there is no evidence of this in either British or Japanese archives.[43] The Admiralty also knew that Japan's supplementary naval plans after London indicated Japan was continuing to build up to Treaty limits. Moreover, the Japanese position at the Geneva Disarmament Conference (1932) and for the forthcoming London Conference that only parity with the USN was acceptable, indicated that Japan was unlikely to remain constrained by limitation agreements. In early 1933, Japan withdrew from the League, but by the end of that year had signed an armistice over Shanghai and Anglo-Japanese tensions were noticeably reduced. Germany now gave notice of withdrawal from both the League Disarmament Commission and the League itself and Italy's imperial ambitions caused RN planners great concern. The COS were optimistic that, with the help of France, Germany could be contained and that, with the re-commencement of steady progress at Singapore, the Admiralty could deal with Japan. The Admiralty hoped the new Defence Requirements Committee would release funding to deal with Japan. It did recognize Far East as a major priority but named Germany as the immediate potential enemy and increased air expenditure far more than naval expenditure.[44] The Admiralty indicated the German threat was still potential whilst the Japanese was real but the DRC reflected a growing consensus on accommodation with Japan and even a non-aggression pact as the most effective means of containment. The Exchequer, supported by the First Lord of the Admiralty, argued that a non-aggression pact would be helpful in negotiating a successful naval limitation agreement. The British Ambassador in Tokyo suggested instead that it might be used by the Japanese to compensate for the failure of a naval limitation conference. The First Sea Lord, Chatfield, whilst accepting an accommodation strategy, argued repeatedly that it was tantamount to placing the fate of Britain's Far Eastern and Pacific Empire in the hands of the Japanese.[45] The C-in-C China argued for accommodation whilst at the same time preparing for a sudden IJN strike at Hong Kong. The Admiralty, realizing that it would not get the funds to rebuild the fleet fast enough, switched to an accommodation with Germany. The Anglo-German Treaty was designed to enable the Admiralty to deal with the emerging German and Italian threat whilst retaining a measure of superiority to send a fleet in order to Japan. By the end of 1934, however, despite numerous meetings prior to the forthcoming naval conference, with diplomatic and IJN representatives in London, and despite Japanese reassurances that Japan was not seeking parity with Britain, it was clear that naval limitation agreements would no longer be able to contain the IJN. Italy's campaign against Abysinnia provided the RN with the nightmare of a toothless League and Britain facing a triple threat from Germany in home waters, Italy in the Middle East and a Japan free to build the navy she wanted. The weakness of the RN was shown clearly by the decision to denude the Home Fleet in order to send units to the Mediterranean leaving Britain exposed to a German threat. In addition, the withdrawal of major units from the China Station to the East Indies Station and the Home front and the subsequent withdrawal of East Indies units to Europe indicated the priority of Europe over the Far East. Japan's announcement in late 1934 that she was abrogating the Washington Treaty and her subsequent withdrawal from the 2nd London Conference now created a real dilemma. The 2nd London treaty provided an escalator clause allowing Britain to build if nations outside the agreement breached agreed naval limitation limits. The British and the Americans did threaten to use this to get Japan to agree to limits in capital ships only to be curtly rebuffed, Japan denying the IJN was building larger ships. Containment and accommodation seemed the only available measure for ameliorating Japanese behaviour in the Far East.

The following year saw all pretence of sending a main fleet to the Far East abandoned. It was 'not possible' and, even if it were despatched, there were now doubts it could actually arrive unmolested by the Italians. The situation was eased by the Anglo-Italian Accord in June but again the Admiralty received a setback when within weeks the Spanish Civil War erupted. The key factor in developing a strategy against Japan seemed increasingly to be not what the IJN did but what happened in budgetary battles in London and the naval situation in the Mediterranean and the Atlantic. The 2nd London Naval Conference resulted in improved Anglo-American relations, including closer policies towards Japan. Agreements on an improved exchange of technical information and even intelligence sounded promising, although the Americans' far greater efforts yielded little. Hopes were raised of the Americans making up for deficiencies in British naval power in the Far East and Pacific but little resulted. In July 1935, the Joint Planning Committee was again asked to do a Far Eastern Appreciation, but surprisingly assumed war with Japan and benevolent neutrality in Europe. The increasingly tense situation in China had led to a serious incident in which RN personnel had been arrested, beaten and their officers insulted by Japanese police. The failure to provide an apology caused the British to suspend the forthcoming visit by the China Fleet to Japan and subsequently all future naval visits to Japan. This might have reduced intelligence-gathering, but visits seldom produced anything important. The year end brought rumours of a Japanese Anti-Comintern Pact with Germany that worried the Admiralty. The First Sea Lord again suggested accommodation with Japan, albeit temporarily, and now calculated 70 days to Singapore (which might be delayed by events in Europe) for the Fleet.[46] The JPC criticized the narrow remit, stating it was folly to try and plan for a war with Japan alone. It suggested economic restrictions as the only sure method of defeating the Japanese, stating that an earlier result would only be possible if they could get a fleet together of the correct size, get it to the Far East and then, under circumstances favourable to the RN, get the IJN to engage and indicating that the Japanese could avoid this situation by refusing to engage.[47] From September, the Admiralty, seeking to avoid antagonizing the Japanese, agreed that Japanese ships could stop and search ships flying a British flag if no British ship was available to do this. The worsening situation resulted in an urgent request to send two ships immediately to Singapore. The Admiralty refused, stating that such an action would be more of a temptation to the Japanese than a deterrent.[48] They returned to their main fleet orthodoxy stating that only a fleet capable of taking on and defeating the Japanese was viable. However, although there was an agreement that the main fleet would be sent even if Singapore were not ready, the Admiralty felt unable to reinforce the China Squadron. Eden had told the Americans confidentially, but misleadingly, that Singapore was fully ready.[49] The year ended with the sinking of the *Panay* and the bombing and damaging of four British gunboats and casualties and damage to HMS *Ladybird*. The *Panay* Incident raised Admiralty hopes of America coming in against Japan. It was now suggested to the Americans that the British could send eight capital ships if they would also agree to send a fleet and this 'demonstration approach' might avert war with Japan. However, the Americans were still unwilling to commit. Admiral Chatfield also rejected the idea stating that 'the fleet we would send would not be equal to the Japanese'.[50] Roosevelt felt the USA might send a cruiser squadron, but nothing happened.

By the beginning of 1938, Chatfield wrote that if they were to send a fleet at this time Britain would be left so weak that 'we should be subject to blackmail or worse'.[51] In February, the Singapore base was opened. However, by April the Admiralty gravely doubted they could send an 'adequate fleet' at all since it was impossible for them to fight a war on three fronts. British diplomats in Bangkok, China and Japan urged a visiting squadron to be sent as a 'demonstration', but the Admiralty rejected this. The Konoye statement on the 'New Order' and the seizure of Amoy, 300 miles north-east of Hong Kong and seizure of Bias Bay 50 miles along the coast from Hong Kong caused the Ambassador in Tokyo to request a squadron be sent and remain at Singapore. By early 1939, Admiralty planners were sceptical of being able to send a fleet 'of the requisite strength' even to neutralize the Japanese Fleet. The IJN now had modernized all of its 10 capital ships, 12 eight-inch cruisers, eight aircraft carriers, five seaplane-carriers, 83 modern destroyers and 61 submarines according to DNI. The British China Fleet, comprising four cruisers, five destroyers, five escort vessels, one aircraft carrier and 17 submarines and needed massive reinforcement to 'neutralize' this modernized Japanese fleet. Because of the European situation, the Admiralty had begun withdrawing the best Far Eastern units to the East Indies, the Mediterranean and even to home waters. Replacements were 1915 D-Class capital ships – slow, unprotected and totally unsuited for Eastern waters. Later it would move all slower vessels from the East Indies and China Stations to the Mediterranean. The best the Admiralty could promise for the Far East in peacetime was one cruiser by 1942. Again, accommodation with Japan re-emerged within the Admiralty. First Sea Lord Backhouse succinctly commented: 'a reduction in the number of our enemies is as definite an accretion to our strength as is the increase in the number of our battleships.'[52] Admiral Chatfield, now Minister for Co-ordination for Defence still felt that when the RN were able to send a fleet of seven or eight capital ships to the Far East despite its inferiority it could defeat the IJN because of its greater efficiency and effectiveness.[53] But splits in the Naval camp were emerging. Backhouse had, by appointing his own think-tank under Admiral Drax, begun to break away from the main fleet to Singapore orthodoxy. The conclusion Drax reached was a small but balanced fleet of fast ships, prioritizing defence of communications lines in the Indian Ocean and the territorial integrity of the Pacific Dominions. This resembles somewhat Churchill's' flying squadron proposal in 1940. Backhouse argued for a quick and decisive knockout of Italy, then sending a fleet to the Far East to 'cover' against the IJN. This fleet would secure Singapore, secure communications in the Indian Ocean, secure Australian and New Zealand and launch economic warfare against Japan.[54] There were some in the Admiralty who believed that economic restrictions would make Japan more rather than less aggressive. The Admiralty also began to try and persuade the Pacific Dominions to pay for or even build capital ships and initiated discussions with the French and the Dutch in the Far East on naval co-operation. The best solution remained co-operation with the USN. The RN now, in desperation, withdrew their gunboats from Japanese sections of the Yangtse. Ominously, the DCNS Admiral Cunningham suggested it was impossible to state how soon and what size of fleet they could send and that it was for the government of the day to decide whether to abandon the Eastern Mediterranean or the Far East.[55] The Plans Division still held to the orthodox main fleet approach and thought the absolute minimum was to send a force capable of defeating 75 per cent of the IJN, the maximum force they thought Japan would throw against them. Naval Planning was now, of course, complicated by having first Admiral Chatfield as Minister for Co-ordination of Defence pushing the 'main fleet, decisive battle' thesis. In addition, there was the return first as First Lord and then Prime Minister of Winston Churchill, arch-proponent of the view that Japan would not wage war on Britain.

The RN caused a diplomatic incident with Japan in early 1940 when, contrary to orders not to intercept within sight of the Japanese mainland, they stopped and removed German sailors from the *Asama Maru* in sight of Mount Fuji. The Japanese retaliated by boarding the SS *Wing Sang*, but the RN refused to hand back all the German sailors.[56] When France fell in 1940 followed by Italian entry into the war, the British government stated no pretext at all was to be offered to Japan which might result in incidents or war. With France no longer available to neutralize Italy and hold the Western Mediterranean, with bases available to Japan in Indochina and with Japan in total possession of almost all the China coastline, the situation was desperate. The COS now stated that they could not send a fleet to the Far East *and* cope with the threats from the German and Italian Fleets. In July, the COS asked that a general settlement be sought with Japan for peace in the Far East. In October, the Japanese landed forces at Weihaiwei forcing Britain to give up its lease and evacuate its RN personnel. However, the COS were agreed that even the emergence of Japanese bases within air range of Malaya and Singapore, plus an overland threat to Malaya and the hopeless situation of Hong Kong, could not justify the despatch of an adequate fleet and declaring war.[57] They did debate whether an invasion of the Netherlands East Indies might be a *casus belli*. The First Sea Lord was opposed and this resulted in a major inter-service dispute.[58] The signing of the Tripartite Pact indicated Japan had taken sides but might still not enter the fray.

The impact on German–Japanese relations of the Russo-Japanese Non-Aggression pact in April 1941 was the only positive development in that year. There were numerous conferences at Singapore to co-ordinate mainly naval and other matters with the Dutch, the Dominions and the China Fleet and local units but perhaps the most important developments were the secret discussions with the Americans in London and Washington.[59]

The massive problems in Europe and the unwillingness of the Americans to commit in the Pacific left the Admiralty by 1941 with very limited options. Avoiding conflict was one option but negotiations with the Americans was pushed since defeating Japan required combined Anglo-American naval forces. The various discussions with the Dominions, the Dutch, the Malayan authorities and the Americans continued. The Americans remained convinced the British wanted American support for Imperial defence rather than prioritizing joint efforts to halt the Japanese, especially in the Pacific.

The Admiralty was heavily involved in two major political disputes prior to the outbreak of the war. The first with the other service chiefs related to the Netherlands East Indies (NEI). The Admiralty doggedly refused to agree to declare war on Japan if she invaded the NEI unless the Americans were committed and the Dutch defended themselves and refused it as a *casus belli* if the Americans were not involved even if the Dutch did fight.

The second dispute was over the despatch of a fast force to Singapore involving the *Prince of Wales* and the *Repulse*. The Admiralty had always rejected as pointless and dangerous the view that a small force be sent. By the end of the decade they began to question whether they could send a fleet at all, whether it could be sent immediately if they could and even how big it was. In 1941, the First Sea Lord began to envisage a 'fleet in being' comprising two units in the Indian Ocean which in the event of war would protect trade routes and convoys. Backhouse also considered a flying squadron capable of protecting trade routes, raiding and ensuring the territorial integrity of the Dominions but unable to relieve Hong Kong.[60] This fleet could not take on the IJN main battlefleet even with support from Dominion navies. Admiralty options were: (a) the whole fleet to defeat Japan in its home waters; (b) a major fleet (seven or eight capital ships) which under favourable conditions to the RN (the seven–eight fleet) could defeat the IJN Main Fleet or a limited defensive operation (the small balanced fast capital ship fleet). Churchill was under pressure from the Foreign Office, the Dominions, the C-in-C China and C-in-C Far East to deter the Japanese actively. There were suggestions to despatch one or two capital ships to

Singapore in peacetime or to persuade the Americans to put on a display of force at Singapore. But the Admiralty resisted thinking this might encourage the Japanese rather than deter them. The Admiralty insisted the only real deterrent was commitment of significant naval forces that the IJN would perceive as capable of meeting them in a decisive battle.

There was in early 1941 a suggestion by the COS, responding to pleas from the Australian premier that a battlecruiser and an aircraft carrier would be sent into the Indian Ocean *if war broke out*, followed later (March 1942 at the earliest) by five more capital ships. By June, the COS were hinting that the need for a deterrent against the Japanese was now more urgent than hitherto. On 25 August, Churchill sent an 'action this day' communication for a deterrent squadron in the Indian Ocean comprising the smallest number of the best ships.[61] The suggestion was for the *Duke of York* with the *Renown* initially and a fast aircraft carrier. It was to operate in the Aden–Simonstown–Singapore triangle and the *Duke of York* was to work up en route. This force was to be despatched *prior* to war breaking out. Pound, the First Sea Lord, stating that with only eight of his 15 capital ships available he needed his best *KGV* ships to hunt down the *Tirpitz*. The Admiralty plan was based on a gradual build-up rather than a fast squadron. The suggestion was one capital ship by early 1942, the *Nelson*, *Rodney* and a small carrier, *Hermes*, with the *Ark Royal* by April 1942 and in an emergency the *Indomitable* plus four old First World War R-class ships for troop convoy duty in the Indian Ocean. These two squadrons would await further reinforcements before taking on the main Japanese fleet. Churchill strongly opposed this, questioning the speed and capability of older battleships referring to them as 'floating coffins'[62] to the small fast squadron providing a show of strength to deter the Japanese. The Admiralty preferred building for main fleet action with its two units either on their own or with the Americans to take on the main Japanese fleet eventually whilst securing Indian Ocean communication lines. The Admiralty tried to counter Churchill's pressure by pointing out that the *Tirpitz* analogy did not fit the Far East situation. The DCNS pointed out that the older battleships were more capable than Churchill suggested. On 20 October, the First Sea Lord clashed openly with the Prime Minister, stating one fast battleship would not deter the Japanese but six would. The *KGVs* were all needed in the Atlantic, but he would assign the four R-class to Singapore not, as previously, to the Indian Ocean. Seeing Churchill undeterred, Pound suggested a compromise. The *Prince of Wales* could go to Simonstown and see if it had an impact in deterring the Japanese. Churchill agreed and they agreed that they would decide what further action should be taken later. However, the next day the Admiralty signalled to the fleet that the *Prince of Wales* was bound for Singapore, on the 23rd told the Americans it was sailing for Singapore and on the 25th Admiral Phillips, its commanding officer, knew he was bound for Singapore. The main interpretation of this is that Pound and Churchill had already agreed formally, that the committee had agreed and Simonstown was a face-saver for a defeated First Sea Lord. Marder has suggested that Churchill had agreed to Pound sending the fast squadron on to Australia after refitting at Singapore but there is no documentary evidence of this.[63] The most intriguing new theory is that far from being defeated, Pound had manoeuvred Churchill into agreeing to send the four older ships to the Indian Ocean and had agreed the fast squadron as part of a secret plan the Admiralty had worked out with the Americans but not discussed with Churchill.[64] This was based on the fleet having its forward base at Manila, not Hong Kong, and thus by the time Churchill knew what was going on he was faced with a fait accompli, having told the Americans he had despatched the force and could not retreat. Since earlier that year he had overruled a decision to send the four older ships or a larger fleet to the Far East, this has some plausibility. One could argue that the Admiralty motivation for committing significant forces was to impress the Americans rather than the Dominions or civilian or military authorities in the Far East. The decision to send such a squadron, with crews still working up and without an adequate destroyer screen, was risky but to allow it to proceed without the aircraft carrier which had ran aground is even more surprising. However, we should bear in mind that it was peacetime and so a demonstration had some merit. Field-Marshal Smuts put it best when he stated after the *Prince of Wales* had left Capetown: 'If the Japanese are really nippy there is here the opening for a first-class disaster.'[65] The loss of these two major units, the fall of Singapore and Hong Kong plus the retreat of all naval units to the Indian Ocean were a traumatic shock to the reputation of the RN.

In conclusion, British naval intelligence throughout the period, even with the meagre additional information from the Americans, added little on strategic and operational plans, the technological power and even the actual size of IJN super-battleships. The RN seemed limited to the 'Fortress Singapore' strategy and a main fleet and a decisive action. There were suggestions that the Japanese would be well-prepared, would act very quickly and would attack on a number of fronts, but these were all subordinated to a more traditional view. Namely, the Japanese were not efficient, were slow and ponderous and would be ultra-cautious. Whilst not being quite as naïve as Churchill about such matters, the Admiralty did seriously underrate the capacities of the Japanese. It has been suggested that our naval authorities failed to obtain the information or perhaps failed to read the signs when they were presented to them. Certainly, the 1930s data from Japan was poor and the Japanese were extremely effective at keeping secrets. For most of the period, the Admiralty wrestled with the problem that their strategy on Japan was always contingent on what European navies might do and what the Americans were willing to do in the Pacific as well as in the Atlantic. The RN remained wedded to a decisive battle in the Far East without American support, but only under the most favourable conditions. However, the 1930s had shown that the Japanese could not be contained by League, naval limitation agreements or even accommodation and appeasement. For the RN, it remained confident that it could fight and win but it would do so when it was ready and under favourable conditions. The IJN was not to oblige them; the former pupil was to now have the opportunity to teach its former master a number of significant lessons.

Notes

1. 'Post-War Naval Policy', 12 August 1919 in *The Beatty Papers, Vol. 2, 1916–1927* (Aldershot: Navy Records Society, 1993), p. 52.
2. Beatty to Long, 15 December 1920: ibid., p. 126.
3. Ibid., p. 127.
4. See J. Ferris, 'A British "Unofficial" Mission and Japanese Naval Developments, 1919–1929', *The Journal of Strategic Studies*, vol. 5, no. 3, pp. 416–39.
5. Plans Division Naval Staff memorandum in: *Beatty Papers*, pp. 139–40.
6. Ibid., pp. 176–80.
7. Ibid., p. 178.
8. Nicholas Tracy (ed.), *The Collective Naval Defence of the Empire, 1900–1940* (Aldershot: Navy Records Society, 1997), p. xiv.
9. 1924 Tokyo RN Attaché Report, p. 40: PRO: FO371/ F1871.
10. 'The Evolution of British Diplomatic Strategy for the Washington Conference', in Goldstein and Maurer (eds), *The Washington Conference 1921–22* (Ilford: Frank Cass, 1994), p. 23.
11. Chatfield to Keyes, 28 October 1921: *The Keyes Papers, Vol. 2 1919–38* (London: Navy Records Society, 1980), p. 56.
12. Chatfield to Keyes, 29 November 1921: ibid., p. 62.
13. Ibid., p. 63.
14. 1923 RN Attaché report, p. 38: PRO: FO371 F1699/1699/23.
15. Memorandum by Secretary of CID, 19 February 1923: *Beatty Papers*, p. 366.
16. J. Ferris, *Men, Money and Diplomacy: the Evolution of British Strategic Policy 1919–26* (Ithaca: Cornell University Press, 1989), p. 164.
17. Ibid., p. 82.
18. Dennis Smith, 'The Royal Navy and Japan: In the Aftermath of the Washington Conference' (unpublished paper), pp. 7–8.
19. 'Exercise MU', *Keyes Papers*, pp. 152–5.
20. B.A. Gordon, 'The Admiralty and Imperial Overstretch, 1902–41', in G. Till (ed.), *Seapower: Theory and Practice* (London: Frank Cass, 1994).
21. Keyes to Richmond, 19 May 1924: *Keyes Papers*, p. 96.
22. Ibid., p. 97.
23. Churchill to Keyes, 22 March 1925: ibid., p. 111.
24. Keyes to Churchill, 24 March 1925: ibid., p. 112.
25. Ferris, *Men, Money and Diplomacy*, p. 161.
26. 'Collective Naval Defence', Minutes of COS Sub-Committee, 24 February 1925: Tracy (ed.), *Collective Naval Defence*, p. 391.
27. Ferris, *Men, Money and Diplomacy*, p. 164.
28. S. Roskill, *Naval Policy between the Wars, Vol. 1, 1919–1929* (New York: Walker, 1968), p. 463.

29. Ferris, 'The Last Decade of British Maritime Supremacy, 1919–1929', in G. Kennedy, K. Neilson, D. Schurman (eds), *Far Flung Lines: Essays on Imperial Defense in Honour of Donald Mackenzie Schurman* (London: Frank Cass, 1996), p. 148.
30. A. Marder, *Old Friends, New Enemies: the Royal Navy and the Japanese Navy 1936–41* (London: Oxford University Press, 1981), p. 8.
31. J.C. McKercher (ed.), *Arms Limitation and Disarmament: Restraints on War, 1899–1939* (Westport, CT: Praeger, 1992), p. 111.
32. Churchill to Keyes, 6 January 1928: *Keyes Papers*, p. 237.
33. Tyrrwhit to Keyes, 10 February 1928: 'Collective Naval Defence', ibid., p. 438.
34. Ibid.
35. S. Roskill, *Naval Policy between the Wars, Vol. 2, 1930–1939* (New York: Walker, 1976), p. 21.
36. See especially correspondence contained in *Kaku Taishikan-zuki Bukan Oofuku Bunsho Meiji 33 – Showa 11, NIDS.*
37. RN Naval Attaché report 1925, p. 66: PRO: FO371/FO11707 F1678/949.
38. Roskill, *Naval Policy*, vol. 2, pp. 21–2.
39. RN Attaché Report for 1929, p. 42: PRO: FO 371/FO14756.
40. P. Haggie, 'The Royal Navy and the Far Eastern Problem 1931–41', PhD Thesis, University of Manchester 1974, p. 61.
41. Ibid., p. 67.
42. *HMS Suffolk* Report, 10 March 1932: PRO: ADM/1/9551.
43. Tracy, *Collective Naval Defence*, p. 476.
44. W. Wark, 'In Search of a Suitable Japan: British Naval Intelligence in the Pacific before the Second World War', *Intelligence and National Security*, vol. 1, no. 2 (1986), p. 191.
45. Haggie, 'The Royal Navy and the Far Eastern Problem', p. 137.
46. Roskill, *Naval Policy*, vol. 2, p. 352.
47. Ibid., p. 352.
48. Haggie, 'The Royal Navy and the Far Eastern Problem', p. 243.
49. Ibid., pp. 246 and 255.
50. Ibid., p. 248.
51. Ibid., p. 256.
52. Ibid., p. 284.
53. Marder, *Old Friends, New Enemies*, p. 342.
54. For Drax's theories, see Haggie, 'The Royal Navy and the Far Eastern Problem', pp. 299–302.
55. Ibid., p. 305.
56. Ibid., pp. 359–60.
57. *War with Japan*, vols 1 and 2: *Background to the War* and *Defensive Phase* (London: HMSO, 1995), p. 17.
58. Ibid., p. 18.
59. See I. Cowman, *Dominion in Decline: Anglo-American Relations in the Pacific 1937–41* (Oxford: Berg Publishers, 1996).
60. Haggie, 'The Royal Navy and the Far Eastern Problem', p. 302.
61. Marder, *Old Friends, New Enemies*, p. 220.
62. Ibid., p. 222.
63. Ibid., p. 229.
64. Cowman, *Dominion in Decline*, pp. 231–62.
65. Marder, *Old Friends, New Enemies*, p. 391.

8
Britain, Japan and Inter-War Naval Limitation, 1921–1936

Tadashi Kuramatsu

Naval questions were one of the major issues at the heart of Anglo-Japanese relations in the inter-war period. Between 1921 and 1936, from Washington to London, naval limitation conferences, which Admiral Togo reportedly described as 'wars without actually exchanging shells', were focal points of this issue. They were one of the most important and time-consuming concerns for the Royal Navy and the Imperial Japanese Navy (IJN).

For Japanese foreign policy during the inter-war years the naval limitation question had a particular importance since it served as a barometer of the enthusiasm of the Japanese government for international co-operation and its commitment to 'internationalism', as opposed to the 'unilateralism' which came to characterize its policy in the 1930s. It was also a barometer to gauge the degree of civilian control over the military, which became increasingly difficult as the inter-war years progressed. For the Admiralty, naval limitation conferences were a sort of double-edged sword and, while they had to fight off the pressure from their civilian masters to reduce their strengths for financial or diplomatic reasons, they also saw and tried to use these conferences and international agreements on naval limitation as a means to achieve their objectives: the introduction of advantageous qualitative limitation and leverage to make the British government commit itself to certain building programmes. This essay examines the issues of naval limitation from 1921 to 1936 in the context of Anglo-Japanese relations, though some references will also be made to the Americans, since the issues were rarely bilateral and usually had a tripartite dimension. In the limited space available, it will not be possible to describe the proceedings of the naval limitation conferences nor present a comprehensive overview. It is an essay, focusing on selective aspects of the topic. Finally, there will be a brief analysis of the influence of intercept intelligence on naval conferences.

In 1920, prompted by Article 8 of the League of Nations Covenant (the so-called disarmament clause), the IJN set up a body called 'The Study Group on the issues concerning the League of Nations' (*Kokusai-renmei kankei jiko kenkyu-kai)*, which examined the issues of naval limitation. Its first report stated that the maximum strength for the IJN should be 24 capital ships (8–8–8 fleet) and the minimum 16 (8–8 fleet).

One of the objectives of the IJN was to make the difference with the Anglo-Americans as small as possible by insisting on the principle of equality among sovereign countries. As for the actual measures of limitation, they expected that it would be unlikely that all countries would agree to a particular principle and that it would be a compromise between each country's proposals. As the least objectionable means, they recommended fixing the number of capital ships and leaving other ships unlimited.[1] The group produced another report in expectation of an imminent naval limitation conference proposed by the United States.[2] The following two points were added: firstly, there would be no insistence on the 8–8 fleet as long as the balance with Britain and the United States was maintained; and secondly, there was an absolute necessity of having a naval strength greater than 70 per cent of the United States Navy.

In Britain, a strategic review had been going on in the post-First World War world. In June 1921, the decision was made in Cabinet to build a naval base in Singapore.[3] In October, prior to the Washington Conference, a memorandum by the Admiralty was considered at the Committee of Imperial Defence (CID), which generally accepted its argument.[4] The memorandum stated that the main concern was 'to ensure that Japan cannot develop a naval base any further to the southward than Formosa, thereby threatening the communications with Hong Kong, our most advanced naval base in the East, and generally bringing Japan nearer our vital interests in India and the Pacific.' The safeguards for this purpose would be 'an international guarantee of the territorial status quo in the Pacific and the reaffirmation of the terms of the Mandates for the ex-German Pacific Islands, whereby Japan is precluded from establishing a naval base in those islands for which she has accepted the Mandate.' As for naval bases in Asia, Weihaiwei may be returned but Hong Kong is 'a different matter' and 'without it, the whole Chinese coast would be at the mercy of Japan, and we should have no base whence to operate in the event of war with Japan'.[5] As for the possible means of naval limitation, it concluded that limitation on the numbers of capital ships would be the only practical measure. In other words, they reached the same conclusion as their Japanese counterparts. Regarding the question of ratios,

> To discount the great Navy which Japan is developing in the Far East we need a total naval strength equal to that of Japan, plus the percentage necessary to give reasonable certainty of success in battle, plus the percentage necessary to compensate us for the disadvantage of operating at a great distance from our main bases with the inadequate docking and repair facilities available in the Far East, plus the percentage necessary to

enable us to retain in Home Waters a force capable of dealing with any European Powers which might be drawn into the conflict, or to deter them from being so drawn.

In their consideration 'the total percentage of superiority to meet these requirements amounts to 50 per cent, *i.e.*, a ratio of two Japanese ships to three British'.[6]

It is beyond the scope of this essay to examine what actually happened in Washington and what was agreed there. Suffice to say that it was an unprecedented success but failed nonetheless to limit the number of auxiliary vessels and, as soon as the Conference ended, there was general expectation that another conference would be called in the future.[7] How seriously the belief of Anglo-American collusion in Washington was held in Japan is not certain, but the very fact that the Navy Minister, Admiral Kato Tomosaburo, the Japanese delegate, had to write to his home government that 'Anglo-American coercion is a fantasy which has never occurred to us delegates in Washington' may be taken as a good indication.[8]

The experience of the Washington Conference offered different lessons for the Navy of each Power. For the United States, the Washington Naval Treaty became a sacred monument of successful American diplomacy, showing to the world that they could contribute to a substantial advance towards world peace, free from the entanglement of the League of Nations. Therefore, the simple extension of the 5:5:3 ratio to those vessels not covered by the treaty between Britain, Japan and the United States, which embodied two essential principles of the US Navy, parity with Britain and sufficient superiority over Japan, was their main agenda for a second conference.[9]

The Japanese, on the other hand, (perhaps naïvely) believing that the existing strengths of each Power would be a basis for the ratio to be determined at a second conference, just as the ratio for capital ships was fixed at the Washington Conference (or so it was explained to them), concentrated on building as many auxiliary vessels as possible before the next conference.[10] Their objective at a forthcoming conference was to improve their allocation of 60 per cent of the strengths of the Royal and US Navies, fixed by the Washington Naval Treaty, and to increase it to around 70 per cent in the category of auxiliary vessels against particularly the United States, identified as the potential enemy No. 1 in the new *Teikoku kokubo hoshin* (Imperial Defence Policy), which was revised in 1923 in the light of the Washington Conference.[11]

The British, although quietly accepting parity with the United States in the categories of capital ships and aircraft carriers at the Washington Conference (the Admiralty objected more to the idea of a 'building holiday', concerned with the upkeep of their armament industry, though the Treaty allowed construction of two capital ships, *Nelson* and *Rodney*), were determined to claim more cruisers than any other country.[12] For this purpose, the Admiralty devised a 'ton-mileage' formula, under which the more trade routes a country had to protect, the more cruisers it would be allowed to have.[13]

In contrast to Japanese naval planning, which did not at this time regard Britain as a potential enemy, in the mind of the Royal Navy Japan was the prime enemy in their war plans. As 'a basis of preparation for war', the Admiralty policy stated, 'The United States is not considered in this respect. Japan being the next strongest naval power, requirements in the event of war in the Far East form the general basis on which preparations are made.'[14] Furthermore, since the strategic position in the Western Pacific had been adversely affected because 'the United States have agreed not to develop their Naval Bases to the westward of Hawaii ... this rules them out, so far as effective interference with Japan in the Western Basin of the Pacific Ocean is concerned, *and leaves the British Empire the sole Power to counter, with Naval Forces, any aggressive tendencies on the part of Japan.*'[15]

The improving situation in Europe provided scope for a second conference. In February 1925, after the successful settlement of the Dawes Plan and the re-election of Calvin Coolidge as US President, the possibility of an American invitation to such a conference was raised in conversation between Austen Chamberlain, the British Foreign Secretary, and Frank B. Kellogg, the departing US Ambassador to Britain and Secretary of State-designate.[16] Interestingly, each side subsequently blamed the other for raising such a sensitive issue. Although the Americans were keen on the idea, the British were cautious, especially because they were sure that the French, who had dragged their feet over ratifying the Washington Naval Treaty, would refuse to participate and the Admiralty made it clear that the participation of France and Italy was a *sine qua non* in any naval limitation conference. In any case, the rumour of another conference prompted the navy of each Power to undertake the task of making preparatory studies for a second conference, which culminated in the abovementioned policies to be pursued in any future conference. Interestingly, the Japanese study also concluded that the participation of France and Italy was most desirable, albeit for different reasons from the British. The Japanese felt that the Franco-Italian presence would counter the Anglo-American pressure. Their study for a second conference stated as one of the lessons learned from the Washington Conference that 'it is necessary to co-operate with France and Italy', especially the former.

At the Preparatory Commission for general disarmament, which opened in May 1926 under the auspices of the League of Nations, the limitation of naval, land and air armaments was considered simultaneously. Japan co-operated with Britain and the United States and they agreed that a separate conference on naval disarmament would be more productive. The main obstacle to such a scheme was the Admiralty's insistence on French and

Italian participation. This change in the attitude of the Admiralty occurred towards the end of 1926.[17] Realizing the futility of the Geneva meetings and worried about the economic burden of naval expansion, the Admiralty moved to initiate the London Conference, at which they would state their case to the world. However, the Americans forestalled the British. Satisfied with the co-operative attitudes of Britain and Japan at the Preparatory Commission, President Coolidge invited Britain, France, Italy and Japan to a negotiation for the limitation of naval armaments, which became known as the Coolidge (or Geneva) Naval Conference of 1927. It may have been an 'afterglow of the Alliance': there was still a pro-British feeling among the Japanese naval officers. A memorandum drafted by naval members of the Japanese delegation to the Geneva Conference advocated close co-operation with the British, which met with strong objections from Viscount Ishii of the Foreign Ministry and one of the chief delegates, and instead a principle of strict neutrality was adopted.[18] It was, however, a logical tactic for the Japanese to align themselves with the British since their main aim was to achieve a better ratio against the US Navy.[19] At any rate, if there were any people who believed in the existence of Anglo-American collusion at the Washington Conference they could not believe what had happened at Geneva only six years later. The dominant feature of the Conference, discord between Britain and America and each of these two Powers trying to win over the Japanese to their side, came to the fore from the outset. The Japanese delegation was keen to exploit the situation as the Chief Naval Adviser sent a telegram to the Navy Ministry that 'both Britain and the United States are trying to win over Japan to their positions. Since this could be one of the means to achieve our claim, our delegates are for the moment keeping an attitude of "not too close, not too distant" (*fusokufuri*)'.[20]

At Geneva, the American insistence on maintaining parity with the British made the matter complicated for the Japanese. Although on the surface this had nothing to do with Japan's main concern regarding the ratio against the United States, they were interconnected in a strange way. For the Japanese, the main purpose of the Conference was clear: to achieve a better ratio against the United States than the 60 per cent set at Washington five years earlier, preferably a ratio of 70 per cent. The problem for the Japanese was that, because the Americans insisted on parity with the British, Tokyo had to assume that the ratio against the United States would be the same as that against Britain. Therefore even though it would have been acceptable for the Japanese to settle for a lower ratio against the Royal Navy, they could not publicly admit it. One of the fundamental dilemmas for the Japanese delegates at Geneva was: 'We should not assume that the ratio against Britain would not be that against the United States.'[21] In the end, the Anglo-American dispute over cruiser questions sank the Conference. The Americans insisted on their right to arm all cruisers with 8-inch guns, which was exactly what the Admiralty wanted to avoid and for that reason they had earlier considered calling a conference themselves. During the Geneva Conference, the Japanese believed all along that the British would eventually give in to the American demand and then the Anglo-American united front would force the Japanese to accept the ratio which was less than they claimed.[22] They certainly underestimated and could not understand the quarrel between two English-speaking countries. In the aftermath of the breakdown it was even rumoured that the next war would be fought among the Anglo-Saxons.

In the following year, the British risked further alienating the Americans by the so-called Anglo-French Naval Compromise, which was a sort of compromise between these countries: no limitation on small cruisers which the Royal Navy wanted while keeping army reserves out of the limitation as the French wanted. Actually, the Japanese supported the compromise because they were keen to limit heavy cruisers which they thought would be valuable for the Americans in a Pacific war. In drafting a reply to the British, however, the Japanese dampened their enthusiasm for the Compromise after learning that the Americans and Italians were against it.[23] Any dream of revival of the Anglo-Japanese Alliance was dashed since the British had dropped it in the face of American objections. The IJN's Committee for the Study of Naval Limitation was set up in October 1927, following the collapse of the Geneva Conference. Its report foresaw the difficulty at any future conference that the Americans would 'absolutely oppose' the Japanese demand for the 70 per cent ratio and acknowledged the fact that they would have to choose between accepting unsatisfactory terms and refusing to conclude an agreement.[24] In the IJN, especially among the Naval Staff, the 70 per cent principle became more rigid and was even more strongly advocated after the appointment of Admiral Kato Kanji and Vice-Admiral Suetsugu Nobumasa, Chief and Vice-Chief of Naval Staff respectively.[25] As a result, the so-called 'three principles' were adopted in the instructions prepared for the delegates to the London Naval Conference: 70 per cent overall, 70 per cent for heavy cruisers and 78 500 tons for submarines.[26]

In recent years there have been several studies arguing that the concession made by the British at the London Conference of 1930 was not such a disastrous decision as has been suggested and that, on the contrary, it was rather a clever ploy by the Admiralty to achieve a more realistic level of cruiser building. This is actually not a new argument and has been previously put forward by those people accused of this 'betrayal'.[27] Less controversially perhaps, one of the 'deadly blows' the London Naval Treaty dealt the Royal Navy was the five-year extension of the ten-year naval holiday originally agreed at Washington in 1922. This not only reduced her capital ship strength further but also, and more critically perhaps, inflicted serious damage on the British naval armament industries, which had already been weakened by the Washington Treaty but managed to survive on a fairly steady level of cruiser building in the 1920s and a promise of capital ship building after 1931, which was now further postponed.[28] Probably the officers of the US Navy were the better judge of the Royal Navy's demise, since after London they more or less abandoned 'Plan Red', a hypothetical war plan against Britain, being convinced of the inability of the Royal Navy to engage in such an encounter.[29]

After London, the IJN seemed to have decided that, unless their terms were accepted, they were not going to agree to any further naval limitation agreements and made strenuous efforts to abrogate the Washington Naval Treaty. At the World Disarmament Conference which opened in 1932, the Japanese for the first time put forward proposals for severely limiting so-called 'offensive' vessels, advocating the abolition of aircraft carriers and the limitation of the size of battleships and the number of 10 000-ton 'treaty' cruisers. Furthermore, at the preliminary negotiations, which started in 1934, the Japanese advocated the 'common upper limit' as the only accept-able principle for naval limitation on the ground of equality between sov-ereign countries.[30] On 7 September the same year, it was decided to abrogate the Washington Naval Treaty.[31] On 29 December, the Japanese government publicly gave the notice of termination of the Treaty, which would cease to be in force after 31 December 1936. The new *kokubo hoshin* adopted in 1936 included Britain as its potential enemy for the first time.

Thoughts on inter-war naval limitation and British codebreaking

Until recently it was impossible to know the true extent of the success of British intelligence in reading Japanese communications in the 1920s. Evi-dence was confined to odd references and A.G. Denniston's statement that

> the cryptographic task was for the first ten years almost non-existent so far as diplomatic work was concerned . . . Probably not more than 20 per cent of the traffic received was circulated, but throughout the period down to 1931 no big conference was held in Washington, London or Geneva in which he did not contribute all the views of the Japanese government and of their too verbose representatives.[32]

The declassification at the Public Record Office in recent years of the files of intercepted telegrams sheds new light on this subject.

Before looking at the actual telegrams, some general observations have to be made. First, it is difficult to assess the usefulness of intelligence at international conferences. For example, one scholar states that because the Americans were reading Japanese telegrams at the time of the Washington Conference they were able to 'force the Japanese to accept a smaller naval ratio'.[33] It was never as simple as that and it could equally be argued that because the Americans were reading these communications they allowed the Japanese to retain *Mutsu* and also agreed to Article 19 of the non-fortification clause. Secondly, the location of the conference was very important in relation to the 'listening posts', where the 'intercepts' were made. For example, it was easier for the Americans to obtain the materials if the conference was held in Washington. Thirdly, the time taken in deciphering was also important and to benefit fully from the intelligence, it had to be done in a short space of time.

Turning to the actual deciphered telegrams, the translations were, as far as the author has seen and compared them with the original Japanese, generally of high quality. Thanks to Denniston, the translators' names are known to be Hobart-Hampden, who spent 30 years in the East, and Sir Harold Parlett, formerly a counsellor at the Tokyo Embassy.[34]

For the duration of the Washington Conference, there are only a few telegrams and these are from the delegates in Washington to the London Embassy. Also it took two weeks or more to decipher. Denniston suggests, however, that 'some assistance during the Washington Conference' was provided by reading the American diplomatic code.[35]

For the Geneva Conference, which lasted six weeks, there are over 30 telegrams in the file. Judging from these the telegrams sent from Geneva to Tokyo did not seem to go through London and probably all of them in the file were actually those repeated to London. It took on average ten days to decipher Japanese telegrams. Because it was a relatively short conference, and given the deciphering time, it was unlikely that the information came in particularly useful.[36]

If the Washington Conference was a great success for 'the American Black Chamber', certainly the London Naval Conference was a similar triumph for GC&CS. There are 397 deciphered intercepts in the file, which is the special file for the Conference, and 239 of them are of Japanese origin.[37] At London they took only about three days to decipher, so the information could have been really useful but the real negotiations as far as the Japanese were concerned were conducted with the Americans. It may, however, have spurred Prime Minister Ramsay MacDonald to send the personal message to his Japanese counterpart Hamaguchi Osachi in late March 1930 to urge him to accept the so-called 'Matsudaira–Reed Compromise'.[38]

Interestingly, some telegrams, especially those sent in a cypher reserved for the sole use of the Japanese Head of Missions, give us an insight into what was happening in Japanese government at this time. For example, one such telegram tells the story leading to the decision to abrogate the Washington Naval Treaty in 1934. The decision was taken at a Cabinet meeting on 7 September and communicated to Matsudaira Tsuneo, the Ambassador to London, in two telegrams.[39] These were accompanied by another, more personal message from Foreign Minister Hirota Koki to Matsudaira.[40] This latter message describes the Navy Ministry's policy as 'unreasonable', since the reasons given 'did not merit endorsement'. The views of the Foreign and Navy Ministries were 'absolutely opposed to one another'. Following a conference of five ministers on 24 July, the Foreign Ministry proposed to set 'the time limit' for achieving parity with the United States at 'a fairly distant date ahead' and, by dividing it into two periods, to avoid any violent change and to reduce the shock to the Powers concerned. Although even these proposals proved unlikely to be acceptable to Britain or the United States, Japan would be in a better 'position to show that her attitude had been just and reasonable'. Above all, this was 'the solitary and only scheme which fitted in with the views put forward at the Conference of the Five Ministers'. The Navy Ministry, however, maintained 'that it was absolutely necessary for reasons of national defence to secure equality of armaments as soon as possible by means of a single Treaty'. At the Cabinet meeting on 28 August Admiral Osumi Mineo, the Navy Minister, declared that, if the line suggested by the Navy Ministry was not followed, 'he would not be able to keep his service under control'. Hirota countered by saying that if such proposals were adopted, the preliminary negotiations 'must inevitably end in a rupture' and 'as the person responsible for the conduct of the country's foreign policy, I could not accept such a responsibility.' At this juncture the Prime Minister, Admiral Okada Keisuke, intervened and said that for the moment they should proceed with the proposals put forward by the Navy Minister.

It is perhaps an irony that this information is now only available to historians thanks to the British who were so adept at reading 'gentlemen's mail'.

Notes

1. 'Gunbi seigen mondai ni kansuru kenkyu narabini ketsugi', 25 August 1920, Kaigunsho, *Gunbi seigen taisaku kenkyu* [hereafter *Taisaku kenkyu*] (*Hei*), August 1928, vol. 10, National Institute for Defence Studies (NIDS), Tokyo, pp. 23–49.
2. 'Kafu kaigi gunbi seigen mondai ni kansuru kenkyu', 21 July 1921: ibid., vol. 11, pp. 8–57.
3. Cabinet Conclusions, 50(21)3 of 16 June 1921: PRO: CAB 23/26. It can be argued, however, that the decision was more of a 'declaration' of intent than actually 'initiating a programme of action'. J. Neidpath, *The Singapore Naval Base and the Defence of Britain's Eastern Empire, 1919–1941* (Oxford: Clarendon Press, 1981), pp. 55–7.
4. Memorandum by the Naval Staff, n.d., 277-B: PRO: CAB 4/7; CID Minutes, 145th Meeting, 14 October 1921, CAB 2/3. Also see Memorandum by the Standing Sub-Committee, 24 October 1921, 280-B, CAB 4/7.
5. Cf. C.M. Bell, ' "Our Most Exposed Outpost": Hong Kong and British Far Eastern Strategy, 1921–1941', *Journal of Military History*, vol. 60, no. 1 (January 1996), pp. 61–88.
6. The 2:3 ratio of 66.6 per cent or thereabouts was the dividing line, equilibrium

of offensive and defensive naval forces in a battle fought close to the defending country, commonly accepted as a result of historical studies as well as mathematical equation and the reason behind Japan's insistence on 70 per cent and the United States' 60 per cent in subsequent naval conferences.

7. Recent studies on the Conference are to be found in, E. Goldstein and J. Maurer (eds), *The Washington Conference, 1921–22: Naval Rivalry, East Asian Stability and the Road to Pearl Harbor* (London: Frank Cass, 1994).

8. Navy Minister to Navy Vice-Minister, 16 January 1922, *Taisaku kenkyu (Hei)*, vol. 11, pp. 106–9.

9. Memorandum by the General Board, 26 June 1925, Box 8, Disarmament Series, Records of the General Board, Record Group 80, National Archives, Washington DC.

10. In this connection, although there is no doubt that some of the Japanese vessels, especially cruisers, exceeded the treaty limits, 'it is hard to believe, as was and sometimes is still stated in Western maritime literature, that the full overweight condition of these ships was a deliberate transgression of the treaty's limits.' E. Lacroix and L. Wells, *Japanese Cruisers of the Pacific War* (Annapolis, MD: Naval Institute Press, 1997), pp. 91 and 83 note 6.

11. Gunbi seigen kenkyu iinkai, *Gunbi seigen ni kansuru kenkyu*, May 1925: Enomoto collection, NIDS.

12. Reviewing its policy in the light of the Washington Treaty the Royal Navy felt that 'in view of the world-wide commitments of the Empire, the provision of this class of vessel [cruiser]' is 'a matter of the first importance'. Memorandum by the Naval Staff, Aug. 1922, 176-C: PRO: CAB 5/4.

13. PRO: ADM 1/8683/131: Naval Disarmament Conference: Admiralty Views on Question of Further Limitation of Naval Armaments, Memorandum on Limitation of Naval Armament Prepared by Admiralty at the request of the Cabinet.

14. Minutes of the Meetings of the Board of Admiralty, 2589: Summary of Admiralty Policy, 1925–29, 3 June 1929: ADM 167/79. The original memorandum was prepared by Vice-Admiral W.W. Fisher, the Deputy Chief of Naval Staff, and in ADM 167/80. Captain Egerton, the Director of Plans Division, 1925–28, was reported to say that he 'has three safes in his room, which contain the plans for naval action in the case of Eastern (Far East), Western (American) and European wars . . . [and] the Eastern safe is full, the European safe half full, and the Western empty. Under no circumstances do they [the Admiralty] consider a war with America possible.' Doc. 31, 27 August 1925, in W.J. Hudson and J. North (eds), *My Dear P.M.: R.G. Casey's Letters to S.M. Bruce 1924–1929* (Canberra: Australian Government Publishing Service, 1980), p. 78.

15. Memorandum by the Naval Staff, Aug. 1922, 176-C: PRO: CAB 5/4; original emphasis.

16. *Foreign Relations of the United States 1925*, vol. 1, pp. 3–11; Cabinet Conclusions 7(25)20 of 11 February 1925: PRO: CAB 23/49.

17. For the British initiative for the Conference see T. Kuramatsu, 'The Geneva Conference of 1927: the British Preparation for the Conference, December 1926 to June 1927', *Journal of Strategic Studies*, vol. 19, no. 1 (March 1996), pp. 104–21.

18. 'Tai kaigisaku koyo', n.d. [23 May 1927], *Nihon Gaiko Bunsho* [hereafter *NGB*], *Junevu kaigun gunbi seigen kaigi* (Tokyo, 1982), pp. 54–5; diary of Commander Sato Ichiro [a member of the Japanese delegation to the Geneva Conference; hereafter *Sato Diary*], 23 May 1927 [in the possession of Shintaro Sato, Ichiro's son]; Ishii Kikujiro, *Gaiko zuiso* (Tokyo, 1967), pp. 42–3.

19. In Britain, Captain Egerton 'regretted the fact that our policy of appeasing the United States led us to break with Japan.' Hudson and North, *My Dear P.M.*, Doc. 87, 12 January 1928, pp. 241–2.

20. Kobayashi to Vice-Minister & Vice-Chief of Naval Staff, 23 June 1927: *Taisaku kenkyu (Hei)*, vol. 11, pp. 202–3.

21. Kobayashi to Vice-Minister, 18 July 1927: *Taisaku kenkyu (Hei)*, pp. 228–30. As Commander Sato put it: 'It is simply beyond our power to prevent Anglo-American parity, therefore we should assume that the ratio against Britain is the ratio against the United States.' *Sato Diary*, 12 July 1927.

22. Japanese delegates to Foreign Minister [Tanaka Giichi], 24? July [received on 25 July] 1927, *NGB, Junevu kaigun gunbi seigen kaigi*, pp. 201–4.

23. *Taisaku kenkyu*, addenda, Part 1, pp. 2–6; *NGB, 1930-nen rondon kaigun kaigi*, vol. 1 (Tokyo, 1983), pp. 16–34.

24. *Taisaku kenkyu (ko)*, vol. 3, p. 7.

25. Kato became CNS in January 1929 and Suetsugu VCNS in December 1928. In contrast, Vice-Admiral Nomura Kichisaburo, the predecessor of Suetsugu, held an opinion that 'in view of the general situation, a 5:5:3 ratio could be accepted in order to stop the unlimited expansion of the American and British fleets'. *Sato Diary*, 25 March 1927. Furthermore, Kato's predecessor Admiral Suzuki Kantaro, who had been a hero of the Sino- and Russo-Japanese wars commanding torpedo boats, did not share Suetsugu's enthusiasm for submarines. Okada Keisuke [Okada Sadahiro, ed.], *Okada Keisuke Kaikoroku* (Tokyo, 1987), pp. 82 and 283.

26. *NGB, 1930-nen rondon kaigun kaigi*, vol. 1, pp. 304–10. It should be noted that throughout the instructions, the ratio of 70 per cent referred strictly to as against the US Navy and the Royal Navy was not mentioned.

27. For example, see F.C. Dreyer, *The Sea Heritage: a Study of Maritime Warfare* (London: Museum Press, 1955), pp. 273–4. Dreyer became the Deputy Chief of Naval Staff in June 1930 just after the London Naval Conference.

28. John Ferris, ' "It is our business in the Navy to command the Seas": the Last Decade of British Maritime Supremacy, 1919–1929', in K. Neilson and G. Kennedy (eds), *Far Flung Lines* (London: Frank Cass, 1996), pp. 124–70.

29. W.R. Braisted, 'On the American Red and Red–Orange Plans, 1919–1939', in Gerald Jordan (ed.), *Naval Warfare in the Twentieth Century 1900–1945: Essays in Honour of Arthur Marder* (London: Croom Helm, 1977), p. 180.

30. In the context of Anglo-Japanese relations the negotiations coincided with the so-called '1934 Anglo-Japanese rapprochement' initiative. See Hosoya Chihiro, '1934-nen no Nichi-Ei fukashin-kyotei mondai', in Hosoya Chihiro, *Ryo-taisenkan no Nihon gaiko, 1914–1945* (Tokyo, 1988), pp. 115–40.

31. *NGB, 1935-nen Rondon kaigun kaigi* (Tokyo, 1986), pp. 112–13.

32. A.G. Denniston, 'The Government Code and Cypher School between the Wars', in C. Andrew (ed.), *Codebreaking and Signals Intelligence* (London: Frank Cass, 1986), pp. 55–6.

33. C. Boyd, *Hitler's Japanese Confidant: General Oshima Hiroshi and MAGIC Intelligence, 1941–1945* (Lawrence, KS: University Press of Kansas, 1993), pp. 6–7.

34. Denniston, 'The Government Code and Cypher School between the Wars', pp. 55–6.

35. Ibid., p. 54.

36. Drea claims that the Japanese had 'some success' around the time of the Geneva Conference in reading foreign diplomatic codes, but his sources are so weak it is difficult to accept at face value. E.J. Drea, 'Reading Each Other's Mail: Japanese Communication Intelligence, 1920–1941', *Journal of Military History*, no. 55 (April

1991), p. 190. His source, which he lists as Military History Department's research documents, is an internal report produced by an associate member of the department, Ariga Tsutao, who himself says 'it is difficult to substantiate the fact'. It has since been published as Ariga Tsutao, *Nihon rikukaigun-no johokiko to sono katsudo* (Tokyo, 1994). Incidentally, it says that (in 1929) unlike the American codes, the Navy did not get to work specially on the British codes due to lack of manpower: ibid., p. 309.

37. The file is at PRO: HW12/126.
38. See Nish's essay in vol. 1 of this series, p. 273, note 50. For example, as early as 14 March, Wakatsuki Reijiro, the Japanese chief delegate, sent a special despatch to Foreign Minister Shidehara Kijuro writing that 'the moment has now arrived when a final determination is essential . . . [and] the above-mentioned telegram represents our final request to the Government for instructions.' Matsudaira to Shidehara, 14 March 1930 [decyphered on 18 March], N.C. 213: PRO: HW 12/126; Asada Sadao, *Ryotaisenkan no Nichi-Bei gaiko* (Tokyo, 1993), p. 185. The 'above-mentioned telegram' which was sent on the same day is in *NGB, 1930-nen rondon kaigun kaigi*, vol. 2 (Tokyo, 1984), pp. 131–2; N.C. 220: HW 12/126.
39. See note 31.
40. Hirota to Matsudaira, 7 September 1934 [27 September], No. 058036, PRO: HW12/183; Gaimusho hyakunen-shi hensan iinkai (ed.), *Gaimusho no hyakunen*, vol. 2 (Tokyo, 1969), pp. 515–19.

9
The Path Towards an 'Anti-British' Strategy by the Japanese Navy between the Wars

Yoshio Aizawa

The end of the Anglo-Japanese Alliance

On 13 December 1921, as the first result of the Washington Conference, the Four-Power Treaty was signed between Japan, Britain, the United States and France, thereby bringing to an end the Anglo-Japanese Alliance, which had lasted since 1902. Neither the Imperial Japanese Army (IJA) nor the Imperial Japanese Navy (IJN), responsible for Japan's national defence, raised strong objections to this loss of an ally. This may be taken as evidence of the reduced military significance of the Anglo-Japanese Alliance since the end of its important mission in the Russo-Japanese War. At the time of the outbreak of the First World War, this alliance was undoubtedly the basis for Japan's entry into the war. However, the Japanese entry into the war and the wartime co-operation between Japan and Britain as allies was characterized as much by mutual suspicions as by mutual co-operation. Therefore, it was natural that the Anglo-Japanese Alliance was replaced at the Washington Conference by the Four-Power Treaty, which called for a loose co-operative relationship among its parties, and which included a United States that was strongly opposed to the continuation of the Anglo-Japanese Alliance. The Washington Conference thus defined new Anglo-Japanese and Anglo-Japanese-American relationships in East Asia for the post-First World War period.

However, by September 1940, twenty years after the end of that alliance, Japan had formed an alliance with Germany, which was already at war with Britain. Thus when it is recalled that in December of the following year Japan herself entered into a war against Britain, the break-up of the Anglo-Japanese Alliance can be viewed from a different perspective. In twenty years, Japan and Britain went from being allies to becoming opponents in a war. Of course, the end of the alliance did not immediately result in Britain being recognized as the hypothetical enemy. With respect to China policy in the late 1920s, there was a renewed awareness in the IJA of Britain's value as an ally, and there was some talk of resurrecting the Anglo-Japanese

Alliance. However, the breaking up of the alliance was originally more important in that it was the decisive action in the breaking away from the British by the IJN, which had seen the Royal Navy hitherto as both model and mentor. The IJN, on the one hand, accepted throughout the 1920s the arms limitations of the Washington Treaty signed with Anglo-Americans, even though they were dissatisfied about their inferior ratio. On the other hand, they acquired the naval technology no longer available from Britain, due to the break-up of the Anglo-Japanese Alliance, through increased interchange with Germany.[1] The resentment felt by the IJN over the shoddy treatment by the British of the Japanese units sent to the Mediterranean during the First World War also helped to push it away from the British. This anti-Anglo-American, pro-German trend in the IJN, which deepened in the inter-war period, fused with the resentment in the Navy over the limitations imposed by the Washington Treaty in order to strongly influence Navy policy in the 1930s. Furthermore, the IJN was an organization for which the strategy of expansion out towards the South Seas (*Nanshin ron*, or 'Southern Advance Policy') was a fundamental and crucial concept. Because of the direction of the policy, the southern advance was inevitably expected to bring the IJN into conflict with the British, who had the largest proportion of colonies in South East Asia.

The IJN's Southern Advance policy (*Nanshin ron*)

The IJN's plan to expand southwards, known as the southern advance policy, was first formally developed after the Russo-Japanese War. At this time, whilst the IJA continued to see Russia as hypothetical enemy No. 1 and to prepare itself for war against it, the IJN adopted a strategy of naval expansion based on the US Navy as the new hypothetical enemy. Then, to provide a logical justification for this naval expansion, the IJN put forward the southern advance policy. In March 1913, an official pamphlet of the IJN called *Kokubomondai no Kenkyu* (Study of National Defense Issues)[2] was published, carrying the joint signatures of the Navy Ministry and the Naval General Staff. Its principal author was Sato Tetsutaro, the leading naval strategy theorist of the time, who had also written such papers as *Teikoku Kokuboshi ron* (Study of National Defense Strategy). In it, it was strongly argued that Japan should seek to be a maritime power – that is, Japan should make it her national policy to expand overseas rather than on the Asian mainland, and that naval power should be the centrepiece of Japanese military strength. Then, as the goal for this seaward expansion, a southern advance was proposed as follows: 'Our Empire should direct careful attention to the regions in the South Seas from the political, commercial and colonial standpoints . . . One region which should be seriously considered for the expansion of our empire is the Dutch East Indies.' Furthermore, in this study, the argument which viewed the United States as a hypothetical enemy and called for increasing the IJN to 70 per cent of the US Navy was advanced, and even though it had the character of a document which outlined an all-inclusive justification for naval expansion, it certainly formed the basic conceptual framework for the naval military preparations which took place after its publication.

The 8–8 fleet naval expansion plans (8-battleship, 8-battlecruiser fleet plan) were abandoned as a result of the conclusion of the Washington Naval Treaty that occurred amid moves towards arms reduction following the First World War. However, despite the Japanese request at this conference for a naval ratio of 70 per cent of that of the United States or Britain, this did not materialize, and so as a result strong resentment towards the United States and Britain remained. In particular, the view that the United States was the hypothetical enemy gained credibility. Furthermore, the fact that the German possessions in the Central Pacific, which had been occupied by Japan during the First World War under the leadership of the IJN, were entrusted to Japan as the Mandated Islands after the war provided the IJN with a concrete 'place' from which to develop their southern advance policy. The United States was named as the principal hypothetical enemy in the Imperial National Defense Policy (*Kokubo hoshin*) of 1923, and the southern islands were recognized as an indispensable, strategically important position for operational strategies against the United States. Thereby, the IJN's southern advance policy of southward expansion as a lifeline to the Mandates took the form of a theory of strategy that designated the United States as the hypothetical enemy. As a strategy aimed at the United States, the southern advance policy could be said to have been a 'southern defence' policy rather than a 'southern advance' policy if its characteristic as a tactical move to defend against the advance of the US fleet towards the Western Pacific is emphasized. However, it can be said that there was no change whatsoever in the role of the policy of the IJN in 'turning heads towards the South Seas' in order to justify the establishment of a large navy. In the 1920s, the IJN tried to make up for the inferior ratio of 60 per cent ratio in capital ships vis-à-vis the United States or Britain by greatly increasing the number of auxiliary ships, such as heavy cruisers and submarines, which were not included in the Washington Naval Treaty. Then in 1930, while the capital ship limits as set at the Washington Conference continued, negotiations were held in London to limit auxiliary ships and the IJN again threw down the gauntlet in demanding a 70 per cent ratio with respect to the United States and Britain.

Therefore, it was natural that renewed enthusiasm was shown within the IJN for the southern advance policy in the 1930s following the conclusion of the London Naval Treaty. At this time, the IJN became very dissatisfied at not being able to achieve the 70 per cent ratio in the London Naval Treaty, albeit by a very small margin, and the IJN subsequently forced a withdrawal from the naval arms limitation agreements with the Anglo-Americans, and thus embarked on a new naval expansion plan. From this time onward the southern advance policy, whilst intensifying its expansionist trend as a reaction against the Washington Treaty System, also caused open ill-feelings towards Britain over and above those felt towards the United States, the principal hypothetical enemy.

Britain as a hypothetical enemy

In July 1935, the IJN formed the South Seas Plan Committee with the aim of contributing to the establishment of a South Seas plan under IJN authority. This included conducting 'various surveys and studies of everything related to the Outer South Seas from the point of view of national defense and the national policy relating to it'. They first investigated a possible advance towards the outer southern islands (such as British Malaya and Borneo, Dutch Indies, and French Indochina) and methods of developing such an advance and thus specifically started to study a possible southern advance. In this committee's study, the IJN did not necessarily play a primary role as regards an advance on the outer southern islands, rather, peaceful methods such as economic expansion or immigration were the basic methods studied.[3] In a continuation of this, in March of the following year (1936), a body to investigate the naval system was established. This 'aimed to conduct studies of how to improve and enrich the content of naval policies'. In particular, in the following month the Committee No. 1, whose mission was to 'study concrete proposals about naval policy which are needed to realise imperial national policy', drew up a proposal for the Navy's future foreign policy, *Kokusaku yoko* (National Policy Guidelines).[4] In these guidelines, the IJN proposed a 'Hold in the North, Advance in the South' strategy, by stating: 'The basic policy of imperial national policy guidelines should be to reinforce various policies domestically while securing a foothold for the empire on the continent and simultaneously expanding southwards.' Regarding policy towards the 'various southern countries', the IJN believed:

> Domestically, a method which will permit unification (of policy making and execution) should be discussed and determined and the necessary organizations established, while the administration of Taiwan and the Mandated Islands should be strengthened. Internationally, a gradual expansion should be attempted, through the use of immigration and economic expansion or the time being, while careful preparations shall constantly be made against pressure and interference from Britain, the United States and the Netherlands, which is naturally to be expected, and the completion of preparations of forces, for an emergency, is necessary.

This emphasis on peaceful methods, such as economic expansion in the southern policy, is the same as can be seen in the deliberations of the South

Seas Plan Committee. However, it was somewhat more extreme than such deliberations in the sense that it did mention the possibility of a resolution by force (completion of preparations of forces), albeit with the caveat 'just in case', against Britain, the United States and the Netherlands. The order in which the countries expected to interfere with Japan were listed – that is, 'Britain, the United States . . .' – also indicated the relative degrees to which the Navy believed them to be potential enemies. The IJN's policies for Britain and the United States which were outlined in the National Policy Guidelines were as follows:

Policy towards Britain
Careful caution must be paid to possible action by Britain to use another foreign power, in particular the United States, the Soviet Union or China, to apply pressure on Japan, and we must take advantage, whenever possible, of the delicate political situation in Europe and the political situation in the British colonies in order to expand our national power into the cracks among British interests in East Asia. Furthermore, economic and cultural ties with British possessions shall be intensified, in order to check their anti-Japanese policies.

Policy towards America
In order to oppose the traditional Far Eastern policy of the United States, armaments shall be held at a satisfactory level, the United States' approval of the Japanese Empire's status in East Asia shall be sought, and the establishment of a friendly relationship, based on economic interdependence, shall be also sought.

It is clear from this that the stance towards Britain was more confrontational and challenging than the stance adopted towards the United States.

The trend in which Britain was increasingly seen as a hypothetical enemy by the IJN resulted in the listing of Britain, for the first time, as one of the hypothetical enemies in the Imperial National Defense Policy of 1936. This was undertaken on the IJN's initiative. The principal instigator, Fukutome Shigeru, Chief of the No. 1 (Operations) Section of the Naval General Staff, said the Imperial National Defense Policy of 1923 needed to be revised because 'it has become impossible to leave Britain and the Netherlands out of our calculations as hypothetical enemies, aside from the United States, the Soviet Union and China, which have heretofore been our hypothetical enemies'.[5] Nakazawa Tasuku, a member of the Naval General Staff's Operations Section and the Navy's representative in the group that actually drafted the revisions to the Policy, said Britain must be treated as a hypothetical enemy because 'when Japan adopts a southern advance policy and carries out an economic expansion into the Dutch East Indies, it is to be expected that the Dutch will depend on Britain and harden their anti-Japanese attitude'.[6] This indicates that the identifying of Britain and the Netherlands as hypothetical enemies was a method of writing into the Imperial National Defense Policy the programme for an advance southwards into the South East Asia region.

Furthermore, the IJN's view of Britain as a hypothetical enemy also showed itself in the actual political relations with China. In September 1936, in the aftermath of the Pakhoi Incident (an anti-Japanese terrorist incident which occurred in the Canton region), Nakahara Yoshimasa, Chief of the Policy Section, Naval General Staff who had the nickname, 'South Seas King of the Navy', had the perception that 'Britain fundamentally does not like the expansion of the Japanese Empire into China, and has attempted to block this at every opportunity', and went on to determine that 'the problem ultimately lies in our relations with Britain. Therefore, no words are needed, just action; Britain's throat should be cut in her sleep, *i.e.* by advancing on Hainan Island', and thus very nearly set into motion the occupation of Hainan at that time.[7]

In the first half of the 1930s, the IJN increased the tension in Japan's foreign relations by breaking out from the naval arms reduction treaties. In particular, such tensions attained an urgency vis-à-vis the United States, which was Japan's hypothetical enemy No. 1 throughout the period in which Japan abided by the naval treaties. In fact, the various naval armaments expansion plans, which the IJN undertook after abrogating the naval treaties, were aimed almost exclusively at the United States. In the southern advance policies which the IJN actually considered in the so-called 'Period of Crisis' after the abrogation of the naval treaties, however, the degree to which Britain was seen as a potential threat increased rapidly relative to the United States. In June 1936 Paul Wenneker, the German Naval Attaché in Tokyo, described the changes in the IJN in the mid-1930s as follows:

> I was able to confirm, to my surprise, that by contrast with the period of more than six months before, when the whole Japanese Navy had still, as much as ever, seemed to be fixed intently and unflinchingly on America as the only future opponent, of late a fundamental change in this attitude has come about even among front-line units. In the front line, they actually advocate an even tougher line than the Navy Ministry itself, from which the influence in this direction undoubtedly stem and where I have for some time past been observing the phenomenon. America is no longer regarded exclusively as the future enemy, but now it is primarily England. It is practically certain that operational investigations are being conducted against a fleet attacking from the south-west – Singapore.[8]

In the latter half of the 1930s, the IJN's southern advance strategy changed in character from a 'defensive' strategy against the United States to an 'offensive' strategy aimed at Britain.[9]

Britain and the strengthening of the German–Italian–Japanese Anti-Comintern Pact

On 25 November 1936, just after Britain formally became a hypothetical enemy of Japan in the text of the Imperial National Defence Policy of 1936, the Anti-Comintern Pact between Japan and Germany was signed. One year later, Italy joined this pact, and the treaty relationship among Germany, Japan and Italy was born. However, the Japanese proponent for the German–Japanese Anti–Comintern Pact, Oshima Hiroshi, the Japanese Army Attaché in Berlin, continued to advocate strongly 'the strengthening of military ties with Germany, in preparation for the conflict with the Soviet Union', which continued to be the IJA's hypothetical enemy No. 1 after the signing of the Anti-Comintern Pact. The movement to strengthen the Anti-Comintern Pact, which began around the summer of 1938, also had as its beginnings the actions of Oshima which were aimed at strengthening strategy in preparation for a war with the Soviet Union. The principal objective of the IJA regarding the Anti-Comintern Pact basically did not change until the negotiations aimed at strengthening the pact failed due to the signing of the Russo-German Non-Aggression Treaty on 23 August 1939. In other words, the IJA at this time was seeking a Japanese–German Alliance in order to fight a war with the Soviet Union – that is, to 'advance north'.

In contrast to such movements within the IJA, the IJN, whose basic strategy was traditionally to advance south, opposed the Anti-Comintern Pact from the time it was signed. Even Nagano Osami, the pro-German Navy Minister at the time the Pact was signed, showed a negative reaction to the Pact because he was 'absolutely opposed to a war with the Soviet Union, which means a northern advance'.[10] Yonai Mitsumasa, C-in-C Yokosuka Naval District at the time of the Pact's signing, was also dismayed when he heard that the Pact had been signed, saying, 'why doesn't Japan join hands with the Soviet Union?' This was a natural reaction for Yonai, who had been assigned to posts within the Soviet Union for many years, and who had previously been advocating friendly relations between Japan and the Soviet Union.[11] It was therefore natural that the IJN itself opposed the IJA's efforts to strengthen the Anti-Comintern Pact, which would thereby increase animosity towards the Soviet Union, from the summer of 1938 onwards. It is clear from the comments and recollections of the Navy Ministry's staff in the discussions on the strengthening of the Pact that the IJN viewed it with alarm, interpreting it as a means of the IJA of 'advancing north'.[12] For Yonai, who was the Navy Minister at the time, any strengthening of the Pact, which would also strengthen the hostility towards the Soviet Union, was problematic from the beginning. Furthermore, since this was also the 'proper' position to take from the standpoint of the IJN's traditional southward strategy, the advantage within the Navy clearly lay with Yonai and the other leaders of the Navy Ministry. They adamantly opposed the strengthening of the Pact, regardless of how strongly the middle-ranking, pro-German officers in the Navy called for the strengthening of German–Japanese relations.[13]

The common interpretation today of the issue of strengthening the Anti-Comintern Pact is that the point of contention between the IJA and the IJN was whether to include Britain as an object of the Pact or not. In other words, it is said that the IJA, which was extremely eager to form a Japanese–German alliance in order to prepare for the war with the Soviet Union, wanted to acquiesce to German desires to include Britain as a target in the Pact, whereas Yonai and the other Navy leaders, 'fearing the worsening of Anglo-Japanese relations', followed the pro-British tradition advocated by the IJN since its creation and opposed any strengthening of the Pact, which was tantamount to forming a Japanese–German Alliance.[14] In reality, however, in the first half of the period in which the negotiations concerning the strengthening of the Pact were held, the attitude of the Yonai administration was anything but pro-British. This can be seen from the IJN's involvement in the negotiations concerning an Italo-Japanese Pact, which was part of the strengthening of the Anti-Comintern Pact. The negotiations with the Italians took place between the summer of 1938 and early 1939, and were eventually merged into the negotiations concerning the strengthening of the Anti-Comintern Pact. According to a report by the Italian Naval Attaché in Japan, while the IJN showed no interest in an anti-Soviet, anti-Communist tripartite agreement, they were very much in favour of an anti-British agreement – '[Japan and Italy] guaranteed to take action, regardless of the circumstances, against the British if Japan or Italy found itself in direct confrontation with the British'.[15] The leaders of the Yonai administration also were very hopeful of securing such an anti-British agreement.[16] Furthermore, the Yonai administration chose this time, when anti-British feeling within the IJN – which had been rising since the outbreak of the Sino-Japanese War of 1937 – was reaching new heights, to carry out the occupation of Hainan Island (in February 1939). This made clear the Yonai administration's willingness to oppose Britain. Yonai's predecessor, Nagano, had actually refused to carry out the occupation of Hainan in the aftermath of the Pakhoi Incident, because it would strongly aggravate the Anglo-Americans.[17]

Ultimately, the negotiations aimed at strengthening the German–Italian–Japanese Anti-Comintern Pact lost all meaning for a possible alliance against the Soviet Union with the sudden signing of the Russo-German Non-Aggression Pact on 23 August 1939 and all Anti-Comintern Pact negotiations were terminated. Within the IJN, however, this agreement between Germany and the Soviet Union acted as a catalyst for further attempts to strengthen relations between Germany and Japan, and Germany, Italy and Japan. This can be seen in the document entitled *Taigaishoseisaku no rigaitokushitsu* (Benefits and Losses of Various Foreign Policies),[18] which was drafted by the Chief of the Navy Ministry's Research Section, Takagi Sokichi, on 24 August, the day after the signing of the Russo-German Non-Aggression Pact. In this document, various proposals concerning the overall policy that Japan might follow in order to deal with the new international situation created by the non-aggression treaty were listed by Takagi, as follows: (i) a completely independent, 'go-it-alone' policy; (ii) an alliance with Britain and France (and the United States); or (iii) an alliance with Germany and Italy. Takagi compared these possible policies with each other, and concluded that the alliance with Germany and Italy would be the most beneficial to the Japanese Empire, because this would enable the war against the Soviet Union – that is, the 'Northern Advance' policy advocated by the IJA – to be avoided, and would be most convenient for unifying the direction of national policy (towards the south). In this paper, Takagi also expressed a low opinion about Anglo-Japanese co-operation as follows:

> Although the IJN would provide extensive guarantees which would include British India, French Indochina, Australia, New Zealand, [and] the Dutch East Indies, as well as British interests in China, Japan would only receive in return benefits which are relatively minor in scope, such as mediation of the Sino-Japanese War and economic assistance.

Thereafter, Vice-Admiral Nomura Naokuni, who was the central figure among the pro-German forces in the IJN, and others worked through Captain Lietzmann, the German Naval Attaché in Tokyo, in order to explore, in Germany, the possibilities of a Japanese–German–Soviet agreement which would be aimed at the British.[19] The IJN's concept of a four-nation alliance which included the Soviet Union led directly to the creation one year later, in September 1940, of the Tripartite Pact between Japan, Germany and Italy.

Signing of the Tripartite Pact

At first glance, the failure of the efforts to create a Japanese–German alliance, which was brought about by the termination of the negotiations to strengthen the Anti-Comintern Pact, seemed to mean a victory for the IJN in general and for advocates of Anglo-Japanese co-operation in particular. This victory, however, was the result of the sudden German–Soviet *rapprochement* and the consequent self-destruction of the position of those advocating an anti-Soviet alliance. It was by no means the result of wide acceptance of the idea of Anglo-Japanese co-operation. Support for such co-operation became even more of a minority viewpoint within the IJA and the IJN after the Russo-German treaty. Anti-British feelings within the IJA were nearing flash point as a result of the Tientsin Incident in the summer of 1939. Furthermore, hostile feelings towards the British led to a violent anti-British movement within Japan at this time. This coincided with the final efforts by Yonai and the other Navy leaders to oppose the strengthening of the German–Japanese Anti-Comintern Pact, which is why the IJN was seen as the ringleader of the pro-British forces. As mentioned earlier, however, the degree to which the IJN was pro-British was questionable: the hostile sentiment towards the British did not change in either the IJN or the IJA after the summer of 1939. It was in such circumstances that war broke out in Europe on 1 September 1939, and two days later led to a state of war between Germany and Britain.

The triple alliance between Japan, Germany and Italy (the Tripartite Pact) was signed on 27 September 1940, approximately one year after the outbreak of fighting in Europe. This alliance between Germany and Japan was formed at the height of the 'Battle of Britain'. The character of this alliance, however, was completely different from that of the German–Japanese alliance which had been proposed earlier in the negotiations for the strengthening of the Anti-Comintern Pact. Whereas the purpose of the former alliance proposal was to strengthen strategy against the Soviet Union, and therefore was looking to the north, the 1940 alliance was seen by Japan as a necessary step to drawing the Soviet Union into a four-nation alliance in order to strengthen strategy towards the south – that is, against Britain and the United States. In other words, Japan's strategy concerning the Tripartite Pact matched perfectly with the IJN's southern advance strategy and four-nation alliance concept. It was therefore natural that at this point the IJN suddenly and completely reversed its position, held until the previous year, of opposing any German–Japanese alliance. This is also indicated by the fact that the IJN confirmed that the alliance would have a southwards orientation, from the condition that Germany would mediate Soviet–Japanese relations, when it agreed to the signing of the treaty.[20] The IJA too, as of the summer of 1940, put aside momentarily its own basic, northward-looking strategy of 'Soviet Union first', and changed over to a policy of strengthening the so-called Southern Measures against Britain and France, such as cutting off the supply routes to Chiang Kai-Shek, as a means of resolving the Sino-Japanese War.[21] The difficulties the IJA had faced in the Nomonhan border conflicts with the Red Army in the summer of 1939 had led many within the IJA to advocate caution against the Soviets. In these circumstances, serious negotiations began between Germany and Japan in September 1940, and an agreement was reached and the alliance treaty signed in short order.

Unlike the formerly proposed Japan–German alliance, however, the Tripartite Pact which emerged had a much greater potential for damaging Japanese relations not only with Britain, but also with the United States. The United States was already supporting Britain, which was fighting for its life in Europe. This meant that any conflict between Japan and Britain in South East Asia had the potential to become a conflict between Japan and the United States. This concept of the inseparability of Britain and the

United States made itself strongly felt in the decision-making process of the IJN, which for so many years had seen the United States as the hypothetical enemy No. 1, and which was thoroughly familiar with the threat posed by it. It was this linkage of Britain and the United States which led to the IJN's reluctance in 1941 to expand further southwards, because the IJN, while confident of its ability to win a war against Britain alone, had to be cautions about a war involving the United States.[22] Unfortunately, however, reluctance to engage in a war with the United States could not become the majority viewpoint within the IJN, because, after all, the Navy had spent years requesting huge budgets, the justification for which was this very need to prepare for a war with the United States! Ultimately, the listing of Britain as a hypothetical enemy in the Far East, which took place in the mid-1930s with the IJN in the lead, linked the conflicts in Europe and Asia, and meant a selection had been made which would turn any Anglo-Japanese conflict into a direct conflict between Japan and the United States.

Notes

1. Aizawa Kiyoshi, 'Japanese–German Naval Relations', *The Journal of International Studies*, no. 37 (Sophia University, Tokyo, January 1996), pp. 55–74.
2. Tsunoda Jun, *Manshu mondai to Kokubo hoshin* (Hara Shobo, 1967), p. 726.
3. Hatano Sumio, 'Nihon kaigun to "Nanshin": Sono seisaku to riron no shiteki tenkai', in Shimizu Hajime (ed.), *Ryo-taisen kan ki Nihon-Tonan ajia kankei no shoso* (Ajia keizai kenkyujo, 1986), pp. 217–23.
4. Shimada Toshihiko and Inaba Masao (eds), *Gendaishi-shiryo 8: Nitchu senso 1* (Misuzu Shobo, 1964), pp. 354–5.
5. Fukutome Shigeru, 'Hogo ni kishita "Kokubo hoshin" ', *Bessatsu Chisei: Himerareta Showa-Shi* (December 1956), p. 176.
6. Nakazawa Tasuku Kankokai (ed.), *Kaigun chujo Nakazawa Tasuku: Sakusen bucho/Jinji kyokucho no kaiso* (Hara Shobo, 1979), p. 14.
7. Shimada Toshihiko, 'Kawagoe/Zhang Oun kaidan no urabutai' (1), *Ajia kenkyu*, vol. 10, no. 1 (April 1963), p. 64.
8. John W.M. Chapman (ed. and trans.), *The Price of Admiralty: the War Diary of the German Naval Attaché in Japan 1939–41*, vol. 1 (Sussex: Saltire Press, 1982), pp. xiii–xiv.
9. Boei Kenkyujo Senshibu, *Shiryo-shu: Kaigun nendo sakusen keikaku* (Asagumo Shinbunsha, 1986), p. 37.
10. Boei Kenshujo Senshishitsu, *Senshi-sosho: Daihonei-kaigunbu/Rengo Kantai*, vol. 1 (Asagumo Shinbunsha, 1975), p. 337. Sakai Tetsuya, *Taisho demokurashi taisei no hokai* (Tokyo Daigaku Shuppankai, 1992), p. 202.
11. Niina Masuo (ed.), *Kaigun senso kento kaigi kiroku* (Mainichi Shinbunsha, 1976), pp. 64–5.
12. Harada Kumao, *Saionji-ko to seikyoku*, vol. 7 (Iwanami Shoten, 1952), p. 268. Sanematsu Yuzuru, *Yonai Mitsumasa hishokan no kaiso* (Kojin-Sha, 1989), p. 62.
13. Kiyoshi Aizawa, 'The Tripartite Pact and the Japanese Navy's Strategy', *The Navy in Interwar Japan*, IS/96/311 (LSE/STICERD, July 1996), pp. 1–10.

14. Nomura Minoru, *Taiheiyo senso to Nihon gunbu* (Yamakawa Shuppansha, 1983), p. 194; Asada Sadao, *Ryo-taisen kan ki no Nichi-Bei kankei: Kaigun to seisaku kettei* (Tokyo Daigaku Shuppankai, 1993), p. 233.
15. Vardo Ferreti, 'Kaigun wo tsujite-mita Nichi-I kankei, 1935–1940', *Nihon rekishi*, no. 472 (September 1987), p. 83.
16. Tsunoda Jun (ed.), *Gendaishi-shiryo 10: Nitchu senso 3* (Misuzu Shobo, 1963), pp. 186, 227.
17. Doi Akira (ed.), *Showa shakai keizai shiryo shusei: Kaigunsho shiryo*, vol. 2 (Daito Bunka Daigaku Toyo Kenkyujo, 1980), pp. 466–7.
18. Ito Takashi (ed.), *Takagi Sokichi: Nikki to joho*, vol. 1 (Misuzu Shobo, 2000), pp. 333–5.
19. Chapman, *The Price of Admiralty*, pp. 18–19.
20. Nihon kokusai seiji gakkai Taiheiyo senso gen'in kenkyubu (ed.), *Taiheiyo senso e no michi 5: Sangoku domei/Nisso churitsu joyaku* (Asahi Shinbunsha, 1987), p. 202; Yoshii Hiroshi, *Nichi-Doku-I sangoku domei to Nichi-Bei kankei* (Nanso-Sha, 1977), p. 64.
21. Hatano Sumio, *Bakuryotachi no Shinjuwan* (Asahi Shinbunsha, 1991), pp. 36–9.
22. Gunjishi Gakkai (ed.), *Daihonei-rikugunnbu sensoshidohan/Kimitsu sensou nisshi*, vol. 1 (Kinsei Sha, 1998), p. 75.

10
Britain, Japan and the 'Higher Realms of Intelligence', 1918–1945

John W.M. Chapman

By 1918, the Anglo-American combination in cryptanalysis ensured that there was no hiding place for those sympathetic to the enemy, Germany. There were powerful groups in Japan with such sympathies already evident to London in 1915. Claims were advanced in the press that the alliance with Britain impeded Japanese demands for the abandonment of racial prejudice and for greater influence in the world, while the performance of British troops at Tsingtao was criticized.[1] In the spring of 1916, a further media assault was launched in the wake of the boarding of the steamer *Tenyo Maru* by HMS *Laurentic*, in Japanese-controlled waters.[2] The arbitration treaty with the USA in the 1911 version of the Anglo-Japanese Alliance was criticized and comments advanced about the small thanks received for Japanese help in suppressing the Singapore Rising, recent assaults on Japanese sailors in Singapore and the murder of a Japanese engineer.

These incidents sparked off concern in India about alleged Japanese espionage in India, Tibet, Nepal and China and Japanese commercial competition and encouragement, with German funding, of exiled Indian seditionists. The Singapore mutiny of Rajput Muslims had led directly to the establishment of security organizations in the whole region implementing directives from the Overseas Special Intelligence Bureau of MI5 engaging in postal and cable censorship, passport control and the employment of under-cover agents from the Indian CID in East and South East Asia to keep Indian dissidents under surveillance.[3] An Indian network was identified as operating in Britain, Switzerland, Germany and the USA and obtaining funds from German officials in Shanghai, Washington and New York for seditious literature and the export of arms to raise rebellion in India via US and Japanese middlemen. Until the USA joined the war, steps to put pressure on Indian and other dissidents were potentially hazardous and efforts to persuade the Japanese police to expel Indian residents such as Rash Behari Bose encountered resistance as a result of protection from prominent and influential Japanese nationalists. David Petrie, a subsequent director of MI5, was sent first to Bangkok and then to Tokyo to establish 'a consolidated agency' and the Indian authorities pressed in May 1916 for a 'better organised Intelligence Agency so far as Indian interests are concerned'.[4]

Secret memoranda from India had been entrusted to Beilby Alston, newly appointed Minister at Peking, to hand over in person to Ambassador Greene in Tokyo, who responded with a conference of British diplomatic and consular officers in the Embassy. Both Colonel Somerville and Captain Brand had already reported at length to Ambassador Greene and London the revelations which had been exposed during the Siemens–Schückert scandal about large bribes being demanded from suppliers to IJN at least since 1910 and 'if these infernal scoundrels will sell their own country like this, how much more gladly they will sell ours, and any information we may be foolish enough to give them'.

In addition to being looked at by Commercial Attaché Crowe, the material was submitted to Ernest Hobart-Hampden, who had served in the Japanese Consular Service for 28 years, and C.J. Davidson, vice-consul at Yokohama for 12 years, who had specialized in Indian affairs. Greene reported that the Japanese had a penchant for spying and that he had already discussed the problem of the harbouring of 'revolutionaries and undesirables' in Japan in June 1915. When efforts had been made to get the Japanese authorities to expel the two most prominent Indian agitators in Japan, they had been protected by Pan-Asianist lobby groups that were able to exert strong pressure on the Cabinet and the political parties. They also had the funds to procure arms supplies for Indian groups. Greene felt that Britain needed to stand firm with Japan over China, but hoped that the British dominions would adopt a more tolerant attitude to immigration. He had been pleased about the recent Russo-Japanese accord and hoped that something similar could be achieved in US–Japanese relations. He argued for a revision of the Anglo-Japanese Alliance, with greater support for Japan against the USA and the elimination of India altogether from the Alliance text. Greene's report finished with an expression of hope about the failure of German militarism as a good exemplar of future Japanese behaviour.[5]

Shortly after this appraisal, 'very secret' information was passed to Tokyo about an approach from a member of the Mitsui family to Emil Helfferich, the most prominent German agent in the Netherlands East Indies. This expressed dissatisfaction with the foreign policy of Kato Takaaki, claimed the support of Yamagata and Okuma and requested Helfferich to contact influential Germans about 'the possibility of an agreement between Russia, Germany and Japan, the British Empire to be partitioned, Australia, India and the Malay states being reserved for Japan'. With such evidence, which had also been relayed to MI5, it is hardly surprising that 'Indian Sedition in Japan' was brought to Cabinet level in February 1917 and the finger squarely pointed at the sinister influence of Japan. But when official pressure had been brought on Japan to have the Indian ringleaders arrested and deported, one was smuggled to the USA and the other spirited into hiding. It was concluded that 'the seditionists are everywhere in close relations with German agents, and draw most of their funds from the same source'.[6]

With US support, it was possible to isolate the German community in China and remove officials involved in undercover activities across the Pacific, leaving the Japanese isolated from middlemen who had been linking them to German agencies. US Army counter-intelligence agencies were able to deal openly and co-operatively with representatives of MI1c and MI5 in Washington and New York, where surveillance of Indian and Irish activities had been a significant undercover task. Military control officers were appointed in Tokyo in 1918 to regulate movements. In Britain, controls over the activities of Japanese personnel seconded to examine various aspects of the war production and management system were enforced more rigorously by MI5 officers in the course of 1917. There were objections, for example, to the granting of any further concessions to Japanese officers allowed as observers on the Western Front except in return for reciprocity in the treatment of the British personnel in Japan. The demands of the war had reduced the pre-war system of language officers being seconded to Japanese units and proposals were put forward in February 1917 for a further four appointments. The War Office considered it necessary 'should we ever find ourselves at war with Japan'. Complaints were raised in turn by Major-General Inagaki and Colonel Kono, recently expelled from Petrograd, discontented at being kept sitting round doing nothing urging that they be treated more satisfactorily 'as the best preparation for a future close co-operation between our two Armies'.

Meanwhile, the crisis over Russia which emerged alongside increasing US involvement in the war produced the most complicated relations with Japan during 1918. Proposals had been made as far back as February 1917 to Foreign Secretary Balfour to persuade the Japanese to intervene on the Eastern Front. In January 1918, Sir F.T. Piggott, a friend of Ito Hirobumi, had approached Lloyd George and suggested the despatch of the Connaught Mission to Japan and presenting the Emperor Taisho with a field-marshal's baton to influence the Japanese Army to match the gesture of the Japanese Navy by agreeing to the despatch of forces to the Western Front. However, by the time they arrived in June 1918, priorities had switched to the need for Japanese intervention in Siberia in response to the Allied intervention at Murmansk soon after the peace of Brest-Litovsk.[7] This was complicated by the fact that there remained much sympathy for the German Army. While many senior Japanese Army leaders welcomed the idea of resuming the struggle with Russia, the Japanese Navy reacted against being pressured by the USA to act in ways which could well be counterproductive to Japanese commercial interests that had greatly expanded in Russia since 1907. Whereas suspicions about Japanese intentions and motives had been stimulated in Europe as well as the USA since the end of 1914, the greater

Japanese interest in intervening in Siberia was welcomed in Britain and France, but much less so in the USA.

Intelligence 'entailing no obligation'

The Russian dilemma had added to British uncertainty and intensified interest in the reading of Russian and Scandinavian cypher traffic, particularly by Section MI1b, which was responsible for the decryption of foreign military and diplomatic codes. The section may have been one of several employing J.H. Gubbins, who had been head of the Japan Consular Service in Tokyo until 1914, and was used as a Japanese interpreter to scrutinize press and correspondence to and from London.[8] There is no clear evidence of successful decryption of Japanese cypher traffic in London before August 1918, although Japanese traffic on British-controlled lines from Hong Kong to Singapore and India may well have been monitored from 1915 or 1916. The first indication of such a CX message refers to Japanese military intervention in Russia.[9] In Australia, concern was being expressed to MI5 about the impossibility of preventing the Japanese from secretly organizing submarine anchorages. Anxiety existed that Japan wanted to acquire control of northern Australia, capture Australian trade and overthrow the White Australia policy. MI5 responded: 'while refusing to give advice or definite opinion on so controversial a subject [it] quite approved the work of testing the nature of the Japanese "peaceful penetration" of Australia'.[10]

However, US public opinion was drawn to the fissures between the USA and the Europeans over the concessions already made to Japanese demands. The fundamental US opposition to acceptance of reparations from Germany came within an ace of a US departure from the Versailles Conference.[11] Japanese representatives in Europe denounced the USA as exceedingly greedy, warning Britain that if the alliance with Japan were sacrificed on the assumption that the USA would relent on British debts, then the British leadership was sadly mistaken.

There was little sympathy for the Japanese position over Shantung or the Pacific islands mandate, and a compromise emerged from the Versailles conference.[12] The continuing unwillingness of the Allies to share advanced technologies with the Japanese, tempered by a desire to try to claw back lost markets after the war, was undercut by the seizure and distribution of German technology among the Allied states and then by the German sale of naval technology to the Japanese Navy. Britain became aware of the expansion of Japanese trade in arms with Germany initially as a result of the decryption of Polish diplomatic traffic between Warsaw and Stockholm in November 1919 and subsequently learned of the supply of U-boat designs to Japan as part of the expansion of British efforts to read Japanese diplomatic and attaché traffic from 1919 onwards.[13]

Procedure 'Y' – 'they may not credit us with an equal degree of intelligence'

No significant efforts appear to have been made in Britain, however, to intercept and analyse Japanese Navy wireless transmissions despite the fact that Japan was a potential opponent in a future war. The US Navy, however, established monitoring stations in China and at Guam and Cavite and arranged for the photographing of the principal IJN codebook, the so-called 'Red Book', by means of a break-in at the Japanese Consulate-General in New York in 1921.[14] Evidence from Australian archives, on the other hand, indicates that the Navy Radio Service had been compiling quarterly logs about Japanese cable and radio traffic home from the Pacific islands from sometime during the war. IJN had supplied information about their naval wireless stations in the Pacific islands from early 1915 and complaints were regularly being made by the China Fleet and Australian Navy about radio interference from the Funabashi and Truk transmitters during the early 1920s.[15] Japanese Morse was known in London before 1919.[16]

There was little understanding, however, of what was being intercepted, due probably to the unsatisfactory state of training of the personnel involved. It was not until 1924 that automatic recorders came into use and it became more practical to retrieve intercepted texts and GC&CS in London could issue instructions to those vessels in the China Fleet which could come within closest range of Japanese warships to send recordings to London.[17]

This technological improvement coincided with the appointment of Eric Nave to HMAS *Sydney* after serving as a language officer in Tokyo from 1921 to 1923.[18] It was not until late 1925 that the Admiralty issued copies of the W/T Red Form for recording intercepted signals and instructed that 'they must never be forwarded other than by all-British route'. Although intended mainly for the China Fleet, copies were supplied to two Australian vessels in Pacific waters north of Australia. But by this stage, Nave had been appointed to the China Fleet to supervise the interception of Japanese signals, call signs and wavelengths and to operate a dictaphone. The Australian Navy Office participated eagerly in the scheme by sending intercepts from HMAS *Sydney* to the Admiralty. In reply, it was indicated that Japanese warships were only likely to be intercepted when visiting Australian waters and suggested that they wait until the China Fleet had overcome the greater than anticipated difficulties of interception.[19] Nave, however, succeeded in establishing a basic framework for intercepting Japanese signals, but in early 1926 the Admiralty rejected his recommendation for the establishment of a special organization on financial grounds. It was decided that the most economical step was for interception by ships at sea rather than from shore stations because of the rarity of Japanese naval cyphers being intercepted: 'Their Lordships attach great importance to secrecy in this matter, for although the Japanese, like the Germans in the late war, may be doing the same thing, they may not credit us with an equal degree of intelligence.'[20] It was proposed that the best prospects of interception were on the China Station, but that Melbourne should be asked to provide suggestions to the DNI at the Admiralty. In January 1924 the Admiralty had had intimated in passing the importance in war of a powerful naval radio station to be erected in Australia 'if Singapore and Hong Kong have been lost'.[21] But in 1926 the Admiralty commented:

> With regard to the question of War organisation, Their Lordships are of opinion that the difficulty of passing intercepts from such places as Shanghai to Singapore rule out the latter as a deciphering centre. Consider, for example, an intercepting station at Shanghai. The chances are that the cable to Hong Kong, or from Hong Kong to Shanghai, would be cut. But if it were left intact, would it be able to deal with the traffic and would the cable company, who would probably be under Japanese supervision, be allowed to accept it? Nor can W/T be used, for the fact that intercepts are being passed must be kept secret. Nor does Hong Kong appear to be suitable for this purpose, for owing to its distance from Japan, it would have to be supplied from other areas and its liability to attack is an additional objection.

It was suggested that it would be best to station an intercept vessel in the seas close to Japan during strained relations and when war came to despatch a merchant ship with portable wireless interception equipment to a nearby neutral country. But it was felt best to wait until more was discovered about Japanese codes and cyphers, preferably while still at peace, and then to proceed to establish suitable radio intercept stations.[22] Thanks to the 'great progress' subsequently made as a result of the work done on the China Station, Nave was congratulated in June 1926 on his 'great zeal and ability', then went on to make further advances with the Japanese reporting code and the recypher tables for the Japanese Naval Code and his transfer from Hong Kong to GC&CS was requested.[23] Before leaving for London, Nave went home on leave to Melbourne in November 1927 and had discussions with the Australian Navy Office and took to London material collected by Australian vessels sent to the area around the Mandated Islands.[24]

At GC&CS from January 1928, Nave was reported to have done 'exceptionally good work' on the nine-letter Japanese Naval Code, with the result that some 800 deciphered signals were sent out to the China Fleet that year. The recypher tables were changed in August 1928, but his progress was actually more hindered by the loss of Commander Shaw, his Japanese interpreter. Nave's solution was passed on to Hong Kong for the local command to make independent decrypts, while Nave himself went on to make progress with the code used by Japanese naval attachés during 1929. Although Nave was given replacements, none remained on the job for long and Nave was also pressed to work on cryptograms generated by the naval disarmament talks in London. The work of interception was constrained by a lack of sufficient trained ratings in the China Fleet. Moreover, the delays in intercepts received from Hong Kong at GC&CS meant that the delays in sending decrypts to the Far East caused 'a serious lapse in the passing of intelligence to China'. The response from the few genuine cypher signals intercepted in India and Australia brought suggestions to concentrate on traffic analysis rather than decryption. On the other hand, the introduction of short-wave and high frequency transmitters meant that radio emissions previously handled by medium-wave receivers at shorter ranges had to a great extent been superseded. From 1932, 'the Admiralty authorities were unable to cope with the volume of Japanese cryptographic matter received from sources other than the Nore'.[25]

The lack of rapid feedback from interception services was discussed by the Chiefs of Staff in 1928. One reason for delay and indecision lay in the attitude of the Air Staff, which had been agitating for a more significant role in the defence system. A scheme for the creation of a Far Eastern Intelligence Bureau at Hong Kong was rejected.[26] The situation in the Far East was transformed by the events in Manchuria in 1931 and the Shanghai Incident and following a conference at Singapore in January 1934, the Far East Combined Bureau (FECB) was inaugurated at Stonecutters Island off Hong Kong. This stemmed from a report by Captain W.E.C. Tait who argued that there might be a 'sudden declaration of war by Japan against the British Empire' with 'swift and powerful attacks on Hong Kong and Singapore'. He had been sent out by the Admiralty to make recommendations about improving the deficiencies of the peacetime PNIO to cope with Japan. It was argued that the FECB should be a non-executive agency, and include intelligence officers from all three services, co-ordinated by a naval director, to bring together all kinds of intelligence from across the Pacific, including Colombo and Ottawa. Warning of Japanese hostile intentions could, it was argued, be obtained from close surveillance of the pattern of Japanese merchant shipping returning home.[27] In the 1930s, interception and decryption by Army units overseas tended to focus on Russian traffic from the station at Sarafand in Palestine but work was also done by the Indian Army at Simla and Abbottabad. There was some interception of Japanese material in India but it was limited and out of date by the time it reached London. FECB had a small number of Army and Air Force personnel drawn from formations in China and the Army had tried throughout the inter-war period to monitor Japanese Army traffic which was expanding considerably after September 1931.[28] However, the bulk of the personnel in Hong Kong, remained the traditional teams of service intelligence officers directly responsible to local service chiefs, while small groups covered matters of security intelligence and there was a single MI6 officer at Shanghai from 1923 to 1941, Harold

N. Steptoe (1892–1949). This network was later supplemented by groups at Hong Kong and Singapore. Progress on Japanese naval and diplomatic decrypts in the 1930s at GC&CS was markedly superior to those on the Italian and German groups in the Naval Section and progress was sustained from 1936 when Commander Nave was at Hong Kong and from September 1939 to May 1940 at Singapore.[29]

Procedure 'W' – 'large errors frequently occur'

Nave's transfer to the Far East coincided with the supply of new high-frequency direction-finding (H/F–D/F) equipment to Hong Kong and Singapore and on 14 August 1936 the Admiralty informed Melbourne that it considered 'the first objective of the organisation should be the interception, identification and location of potential enemy ships and shore stations' in co-operation with the China Fleet. It also considered it highly desirable to establish three new D/F stations in Australia to form the Far East Direction-Finding Organisation (FEDO).[30] By April 1938, the Admiralty reported that Hong Kong and Singapore were the only stations equipped with H/F–D/F and that the equipment now due to be installed at Darwin could not be brought into commission until the middle of 1939. Concern was expressed 'in view of the situation in the Far East and the difficulty that is experienced in obtaining fixes of Japanese ships' about the need to erect the equipment without delay.[31]

In November 1938, Admiral Noble reported that tests had been undertaken on the China Station to check the accuracy of D/F bearings of Japanese warships by placing equipment on British warships whose positions were known. This had revealed that 'large errors frequently occur' but the situation was further complicated by the fact that the high-grade cypher normally employed to relay D/F bearings to other stations could not be employed because suitable equipment was not available on the China Station. A conference at Hong Kong suggested that there was a need to check the calibration of the equipment and concluded that 'D/F has not been of a great deal of use except in one case where the Combined Fleet was located while returning to Japan'.[32] The Admiralty replied on 3 February 1939, referring to the problem of 'scattering' on all H/F–D/F stations, where the error could range from 50 to 300 miles, but suggesting that the 'extremely unfavourable site conditions' at Stonecutters might show up in large errors there and expressing confidence that a high degree of accuracy should be achievable at Kranji.[33] On 17 April 1939, the Admiralty pressed for an early opening of the H/F–D/F station at Darwin so that a third station could work alongside Hong Kong and Singapore as soon as possible, following completion of an extended test involving Stonecutters, Kranji and Bombay Fort in March and April 1939.[34] Each station sought to pinpoint the location of the China Fleet flagship, HMS *Kent*, and detect the variations of each station in relation to the true position of the warship. Initial conclusions were that Kranji, which had obtained bearings of the Combined Fleet to and from Tsingtao in March 1939, was unreliable when targets were in the Gulf of Tonkin. Stonecutters could be relied on for bearings south of the Pescadores and had in fact followed Japanese warships from Hainan northwards. Bombay, because of the distances involved, provided no useful bearings, but would be tried again when the China Fleet sailed from Hong Kong to Weihaiwei. This could usefully be checked by the new station proposed for Darwin, especially as this was better sited for obtaining bearings for the area round Japan and the Philippines.[35] Gaps in coverage might best be filled by planned stations at Penang, Trincomalee, and Fremantle.

The outbreak of war in Europe enabled the testing of the H/F–D/F system under wartime conditions and made it much less likely that the movements of German vessels in the Indo-Pacific region would escape Allied scrutiny to the same extent as in the First World War. An early success recorded by FEDO was the interception of the German cruiser *Graf Spee* in the Mozambique Channel and evidence that the ship had returned to the South Atlantic rather than heading on into the Indian Ocean. The detection of German armed raiders and supply vessels in the Central Pacific provided excellent targets for D/F analysis, but little could normally be done in the case of movements between Japan and the Mandated Islands.

'Certain most secret material . . .'

British and Australian co-operation in intelligence was matched by co-operation between Germany, Italy and Japan. German–Italian co-operation on French signals and coding systems dated from 1933 and was expanded to cover Britain in 1935 during the Abyssinian crisis.[36] The concentration of Home Fleet units in the Mediterranean and of China and East Indies fleet units off Italian East Africa provided unusually active exchanges of cypher traffic by wireless and because these were accompanied by visual sightings made it possible to reconstruct the Administrative Code.[37]

One of the most important leakages in British security lay in the Italian knowledge of the relay of intercepted Italian cypher signals being sent to London from Malta and Gibraltar.[38] There is clear evidence also that the Italians were using agents to break into the office of the Governor of Hong Kong and into British and other naval premises in China in order to obtain copies of secret correspondence of the C-in-C of the China Fleet in the late 1930s and passing these discoveries on to the German Navy and Foreign Ministry.[39] It has also been established that in 1935 a copy of a study by Captain Vivian, the British Naval Attaché in Tokyo, on Anglo-Japanese relations since 1922 was shown to Captain Paul Wenneker, the German Naval Attaché, who photographed it. A copy was relayed to Berlin in the summer of 1935 and statements that the Japanese Navy and Air Force were 'second-rate' were passed on to the Japanese Navy in the course of discussions leading up to the London Naval Talks of 1935–36. From the time of German discussions with Admiral Nagano Osami, relations between the Japanese and German navies became increasingly intimate, but their significance was very much driven into the background by the prominence given to accounts of secret service and anti-Comintern co-operation with the Japanese Military Attaché in Berlin, Major-General Oshima Hiroshi. Information on this was relayed to the *GRU* station chief in Amsterdam, Walter Krivitsky, who defected to Britain.[40]

As a result of Italian acquisition of intelligence about Britain, it was argued with both German and Japanese naval attachés in Rome that Britain would have to make a strategic choice between defending the Middle or the Far East and that it was likely that Japan would have the capacity to occupy Hong Kong, the Philippines, the Dutch East Indies, French Indochina and even Malaya.[41] In Tokyo, Admiral Wenneker was already encouraging the Japanese Naval Staff on 1 August 1940 to believe that 'if Japan went into action against Hong Kong or Singapore, this step would undoubtedly be very much welcomed on the German side'.[42] However, it was already clear to the German side that the principal concern of the Japanese Navy was with the threat from the USA. Events in Europe were nonetheless seen as having produced a 'sea change' in the Japanese Navy's appraisal of the USA.

It is important to note that the outcome of the Norwegian campaign had a much greater impact on the IJN than that in the Low Countries and France. A special feature was made of the German conduct of operations in Norway in briefings given to the Italian and Japanese navies. Whereas the Italian Navy was well aware of the degree to which British naval cyphers had been penetrated as a result of the intimate collaboration between the German and Italian decrypt agencies, there is no evidence that the Japanese Navy was properly briefed on this subject until the end of 1943. The Japanese Naval Mission to Europe was given some broad indications of the importance of radio location techniques in operations at sea in March 1941, but the German Naval Staff refused to provide Japanese representatives in Europe with any briefing.[43] The IJN was not told that the successes of German operations in Norway, Greece and elsewhere depended to a crucial degree on the German ability to decipher up to half of all British naval signals so that the Japanese Navy's perception about the capacity to overcome US superiority in the Pacific was directly based on incomplete information about Anglo-German relations in the early stages of the Second World War.

Nevertheless, the perceived weakness of the British position in East Asia was confirmed at the end of 1940 through the seizure by the raider *Atlantis* from the *Automedon* off Penang of:

> material that exceeded our highest expectations: the whole top secret mail for the Far East Command, new cipher instructions for the fleet,

secret information for seafarers, net and mine clearance manuals, a comprehensive report of the War Cabinet concerning the defence of the Far East, Secret Intelligence Service material and much else besides.[44]

Most attention has been paid to the copy of COS (40) 592 of 15 August 1940 which was passed to the Japanese Naval Staff by Admiral Wenneker on 12 December 1940 with a copy being supplied to Captain Yokoi in Berlin in the guise of a secret agent report.[45] The COS report was used on the German side to press the Japanese to attack Singapore and the German Foreign Ministry was authorized by Hitler by the end of 1940 to embody this as a major initiative, but it actually formed only part of the scheme for strategic deception accompanying Operation Barbarossa.[46]

What is less clearly understood, however, is that the huge losses of code and cypher material from the *Automedon* contributed decisively to major operational damage in the Mediterranean from mid-January 1941 onwards. Losses included the whole of the mail for the SIS station at Singapore which made it much easier to exclude all such materials from public scrutiny as security-sensitive.[47] It is clear, however, that an Inter-Service Cypher Committee was established early in 1941 under the chairmanship of the DNI, Admiral Godfrey, which traced the losses of 'certain most secret material' to Singapore, creating great confusion there and in Australian military intelligence during this period.[48] The investigation of British cypher insecurity was not concluded until September 1941, when Admiral Godfrey informed the Joint Intelligence Sub-Committee (JIC) in London of the replacement of recypher tables by one-time Naval and War Office cypher pads, but it took time for new tables to be issued worldwide and some British attaché communications were still being read as late as October 1941. On 5 December 1941, a British MTB was sunk off Crete, and a copy of the Small Ships' Code was retrieved and relayed to Rome and Berlin, making possible knowledge of Royal Navy positions worldwide from 6 December. This was relayed to the Japanese Naval Attaché in Berlin and by radio to Tokyo via Admiral Wenneker.

'The United States diplomatic cypher is not sufficiently secure'

The signature of the Three Powers' Pact in September 1940 did more to convince US opinion than anything in the previous decade that Japan was conspiring with the European Axis. Until then, the possibility of Anglo-American co-operation against Japan had fluctuated alarmingly. American strategic materials and technology were critical for the Japanese economy in the inter-war period, whereas it was possible to function without British economic co-operation. For example, the Japanese economy obtained co-operation from US independent oil refiners and escaped dependence on Esso or Shell supplies, but still required to import 80 per cent of crude oil requirements. It was possible to discriminate against importing from Britain so long as access to the US economy and to US-owned businesses abroad was assured. Access to the Russian economy in 1939 provided ways of escaping the worst effects of the Anglo-French blockade, but in the same year the US denunciation of the 1911 trade agreement with Japan was a great blow.[49] Anglo-American thinking was dominated until November 1941 by the perception that Japan and Italy were simply riding on German coat tails and if the German priority were tackled square-on, the other issues would be resolved.[50]

These perceptions were strongly influenced by separate Anglo-American insights into individual policies of the Axis States derived from decrypted communications. The major breakthrough was the US Army success in reading the machine cypher employed for communications between the *Gaimushô* and Japanese embassies abroad. Nothing appeared from monitored diplomatic signals of the fact that the Japanese Army and Navy were intent on war until the final stage of US–Japanese negotiations in the latter half of November 1941. This was because both Churchill and Roosevelt were convinced that Japan could not rationally decide to attack the USA, especially once Germany became embroiled in the Soviet–German conflict. The recommendation of the JIC on 7 February 1941 was that 'financial and commercial measures against the Japanese should be taken in concert with the United States and other friendly nations'.[51] At the same time, Captain Wylie was on a tour of the Netherlands East Indies, Australia and New Zealand prior to handing over FECB and was arguing that 'the basic difficulty is that the Dutch (and U.S.A.) and British Intelligence Services have not yet been brought together'.[52] This began to be resolved when the British delegation visiting Washington in February 1941 agreed to pool intelligence gained by both sides about the Japanese threat. Access was provided by the US to the necessary equipment for the reading of Japanese diplomatic communications, while Britain provided information about 'W' and 'Y' procedures in the Far East.[53]

Captain Harkness convened a meeting of British, Australian, Dutch and US signals specialists at Singapore on 27 February 1941, including Lieutenant Jefferson R. Dennis USN, Officer in Charge of Station CAST in the Asiatic Fleet as an observer. The meeting set out proposals for a Far East Inter-Allied Communications Board with fixed communications linking Cavite, Singapore, Canberra and Batavia, shared secret call-signs (ANDUSCAL) and recognition signals (ANDUSREC). A special flag cypher linking the British, Dutch, Australian and US commands was worked out at Singapore.[54] It was agreed that any hint of compromise of cyphers or codes would be notified to the other parties. There were objections from Admiral Hart in Manila who 'did not consider that he should take an active part in an organisation obviously directed against Japan whilst U.S.A. is neutral'. The Japanese Navy's JN25 system had been changed in October 1940, but by this date the FECB had experienced 'more success with cryptography than for some time past and that Consular, Diplomatic, four-figure Naval and Merchant Ship broadcast codes and cyphers have now been made available from friendly sources'.[55]

There was evidence of progress in Anglo-American staff talks in Washington where a formula of 'the closest co-operation between British and American officials in the Far East' had been adopted and included the appointment of a US liaison officer to FECB at Singapore. The JIC in London had reservations in turn about the scope of information to be handed on to US contacts so long as the USA did not join in hostilities and had not taken adequate security precautions: 'in this connection it is to be noted that the United States diplomatic cypher is not sufficiently secure'. This exclusion included the sharing of any information about SOE and SIS activities and all matters connected with operational planning.[56] What was also omitted even from the list of exclusions as late as March 1942 was that British progress with the resolution of some of the German Enigma machine cypher systems which, along with high-frequency direction-finding and known losses of Italian cypher books in the Mediterranean, ironically helped to convince the German cypher security authorities that their system was safe.

The Japanese Naval and Military Missions to Berlin and Rome from March to June 1941 prompted the Germans to insist that any discussions about Japan joining the war be conducted in Berlin and that whatever was done to assist the Japanese should be directly determined by its utility for a Japanese entry into the war. Nothing was permitted to be said about the attack on the USSR until 3 June 1941 and then only in conversations between Hitler and Ambassador Oshima. The telegrams from meetings between Oshima and the German leadership were monitored and deciphered in Washington and London. However, Oshima's statements to the Army, like those of Admiral Nomura Kichisaburo to the Navy from Washington, could not be read.[57] Clear efforts were made by Britain at this time to circulate rumours of an Anglo-German peace in Turkey (whose communications were being read by everyone) and for 'Japan to be made to think that the US and the Soviet Union are ready to work on air attacks on Japan if they move south'.[58]

Diplomatic enquiries in Moscow and Kuibyshev reassuring the Japanese that the Soviet strategy was to defend their own territory independently in Europe and Asia were reinforced by the reading of parts of the State Department's radiograms between Moscow and Washington by 15 October 1941.[59] German-Italian co-operation in the reading of US communications appears to have been extended to Japan in the course of 1941 and an important Italian contribution came in the form of the reading of the Cairo–Washington circuit, which provided valuable information on the conduct of British military operations in North Africa.[60] The Japanese Navy indicated that there was every sign of Soviet reinforcement of the front opposite

Manchuria in July 1941 and on 22 August Admiral Wenneker was assured that decisions had been taken in Tokyo not to become involved in the German–Soviet War. These statements were relayed to the Soviet Union by Dr Richard Sorge, who was on good terms with Wenneker. The Japanese Navy made it clear to naval attachés abroad that the war in Russia was likely to develop in ways similar to those of the Japanese in the vast Chinese hinterland. On 17 October 1941, the arrest of Dr Sorge, together with his radio operator, Max Clausen, confirmed the likelihood that the USSR would stay out of any clash between Japan and the Western Powers; the Japanese Navy in turn put forward a proposal to act as mediator between Germany and the USSR in order that both allies could concentrate on the defeat of Britain, as advocated by Japanese representatives in Berlin and Rome – either through a landing in the British Isles or through the destruction of the British fleet.[61] This development highlighted the fundamental divergence in German and Japanese strategic interests.

Ambassador Shigemitsu's view in London in June 1941 was that people in Britain were confidently expecting an American entry into the war and he was astonished that British morale remained high and even anticipated a final victory after spring 1942. Captain Mitsunobu's belief remained that the massive deployment of torpedo bombers and the assistance of the French Mediterranean Fleet would achieve the defeat of British forces in the eastern Mediterranean. This view received a great deal of encouragement from the statements of the British Naval Attaché in Tokyo, Rear-Admiral Boyce.[62]

In October 1941, shortly before returning home, the Japanese Naval Attaché in London confirmed that anti-Japanese feelings in Britain were worse than ever and that a political grouping around Foreign Secretary Eden claimed that a Japanese attack would produce an immediate US entry into the war.[63] A rendezvous was established in Lisbon between Admiral Kondo and Captain Mitsunobu, who visited Captain Löwisch on 9 October and handed over items of information from Bombay, Istanbul and Tokyo. They complained that the British authorities were delaying the despatch of Japanese signals, thereby ensuring information that would be out of date. He also mentioned his planned meeting in Lisbon and invited him to contact Berlin to ascertain which particular questions they would like Mitsunobu to put to Kondo.[64] The Japanese Combined Fleet was convinced it was now capable of taking on all-comers and that it was likely that US material superiority would be absorbed substantially by the demands of the two wars in the European theatre. The timing of major offensive operations in the Pacific was confirmed by the discovery that the threat of US–Soviet military co-operation in the Far East was a bluff and all last-minute British efforts to sow further doubt about an Anglo-German deal and to provide accurate figures of the German–Italian oil supply crisis in November 1941 were contemptuously dismissed by the Japanese Naval Staff.[65]

So long as preparations could be made in peacetime for war, accurate intelligence about British and US dispositions in the Indo-Pacific area could be gathered and forwarded to Tokyo.[66] Tight restrictions had long been imposed by the Japanese armed forces since 1931 on foreign and even allied observers, leaving surveillance of communications as the sole effective mode of appraisal even for allies. However, despite the steps taken in the development of signals intelligence and cryptanalysis by the end of 1941 the superiority of Axis over Allied intelligence remained marked. The seriousness of the Japanese threat was already appreciated by the War Office by the spring of 1941 and additional forces were being drafted into the region as perceptions of the Japanese threat intensified. Much material and equipment from Britain and the USA was diverted to the defence of the USSR. British requests to the USA to transfer naval forces to Singapore had long been seen as a more feasible proposition than diverting units from the Mediterranean. A decision was taken to install a small number of RAF D/F stations in Malaya in the course of 1941 between Changi on Singapore Island and Mersing, only 70 miles to the north, with a further three being installed in the vicinity of Singapore shortly before the Japanese attack. These units could detect incoming aircraft at about 75 miles distance, but no low-flying aircraft nor surface vessels, and the three stations with this capacity could not provide a plot beyond the optical horizon. Consequently, almost the whole of Malaya north of Mersing was devoid of air defence radar and the sole naval H/F–D/F station was at Seletar. Admiral Phillips of Force Z is reported to have ordered radio and radar silence on sailing into the Gulf of Siam in order to avoid being located by enemy D/F, but was detected optically by the chain of enemy submarines and unable to use the radar to spot attacking aircraft and to radio for air support from the mainland.[67]

Intelligence management and deadly quarrels

By the end of 1941, an extensive naval H/F–D/F network had been established across the Indian and Pacific Oceans and steps taken to expand and improve co-operation among the national networks. Following a proposal in December 1939 by the Australian Chief of Naval Staff, Admiral Colvin, to establish separate cryptanalytical facilities, the Australian Army began to employ academics at Sydney University in January 1940 to examine Japanese diplomatic traffic.[68] This facility was expanded from August 1940, with the new staff including Commander Nave, who was recovering from ill-health. A small parallel unit was established in New Zealand in the summer of 1941, linked to FECB and GC&CS.[69] But it was not until the Japanese attack that rapid reorganization and expansion of these capabilities were undertaken. The expansion of Japanese capabilities in Britain concentrated on the role of SOAS in producing translators, interpreters and codebreakers in a multi-service operation, unlike that at the University of

Colorado for the US Navy, which may well have exacerbated wartime rivalries between the American services.[70]

After reorganization in September 1941, the Indian Signals Intelligence Service was forced to turn to coping with the war against Japan as part of an actual war zone and reconstituted from 17 April 1942 as the Interservice Wireless Intelligence Staff (IWIS). The support given by Japan to the Indian nationalist movement since before 1914 was revived in the 1930s and a conference held in Tokyo in 1937 was attended by Rash Behari Bose. Propaganda targeted Indian communities in South East Asia, with special attention paid to Indian troops. This focus was extended after 1940 to Germany and Italy, where captured Indian troops from North Africa were organized as special units, particularly following the arrival via the USSR of Subhas Chandra Bose. He was subsequently transported by U-boat to the Far East in January 1943 to participate in the activities of the Indian National Army (INA) in Rangoon and Bangkok under the auspices of the *Hikari Kikan*. Agents were recruited to return to India on board Japanese and German submarines and supplied with radio equipment to report back intelligence, but most surrendered or were picked up by the Indian branch of the Radio Security Service.[71]

Discussions were held in 1941 about the integration of British, US, Australian and Dutch communications in the event of a Japanese attack. The United States, still neutral at this stage, urged caution and proposals were put forward via the Australian mission in Washington for the preparation of more direct naval communications between Hawaii and Australia. This at first suggested that it lay outside the existing US–British naval communications plan discussed in Batavia in June 1941. When this was put down to differences of opinion within the US Navy, test transmissions were conducted via Cavite. These indicated that the circuit was slow and could constitute 'a bottle neck, and if it is put out of action Australia will have no communication with U.S. ships or stations in waters in which we are vitally interested'.[72] In December 1941, Admiral Layton at Singapore cabled Admiralty and Melbourne saying that in view of the anticipated scale of air attack, he proposed withdrawing naval 'Y' and special intelligence from Singapore 'by first opportunity' and transferring to Australia. On Christmas Eve, Layton altered his request to temporary accommodation for part of FECB in Australia 'with a view to eventual permanent installation in Ceylon'. Following an offer from Admiral Sommerville to accommodate FECB with effect from 5 January 1942 at Colombo, it was moved to Colombo to serve with the East Indies Fleet, which it followed to Kilindini and then back to Ceylon as HMS *Anderson*.[73]

The most testing period came during spring 1942 with the IJN's two-pronged incursion into the Bay of Bengal and the Indian Ocean. FECB in its new home is credited with early warning of the approach of the Japanese assault group off Ceylon on 5 April 1942. However, the enemy failed to locate the main units of the Eastern Fleet in the Maldives despite a break in operations to obtain intelligence from the German *B-Dienst* (a major provider of intelligence to Japanese submarine operations) and came away without any decisive gains. Appeals by the Admiralty to Admirals King and Ghormley for pressure on the IJN to distract its attention from the Indian Ocean were met by the despatch of bomber aircraft from the USS *Hornet* on the Japanese capital on 18 April 1942. This demonstration of Allied solidarity contrasted directly with the refusal of Hitler to modify attacks on southern Russia and the Caucasus in favour of striking at Suez and seeking to effect a junction with Japanese forces.[74]

The Australian Special Intelligence Unit, headed by Commander Nave, remained at Melbourne, working primarily on Japanese diplomatic and consular material. Army and RAAF units, some withdrawn from the Middle East, provided personnel for a joint venture with the US Army Signals Service Agency from March 1942 in the form of the Central Bureau, with special wireless units in the front line in New Guinea and the islands north of Australia.[75] The Australian contribution in the South-West Pacific to the provision of intelligence was substantial in combination with the efforts of the British Pacific Fleet operating from Australian bases and of the Australian-led British XIVth Army in Burma which in 1944–45 undertook the largest-scale and most effective land battles against the Japanese Army in the whole of the Pacific campaign.

Conclusion

The history of the Anglo-Japanese relationship in the first half of the twentieth century was dominated by their relations with third parties, Germany and the USA. In order to negotiate the perils of international relations, Britain opted for intelligence 'entailing no obligation', yet it was obliged to resort to methods and technologies which were morally distasteful in frustrating the objectives of rival nations through preparation for conflict in times of peace. At first British policy towards Japan successfully sought to frustrate Russian ambition while covertly wishing to frustrate a wider German ambition to dominate the international system, but in the process frustrating the ambitions of IJA against Russia and those of IJN against the USA. It was a characteristic of both the Anglo-Japanese and the Axis Alliances for Japanese policymakers to insist on a very narrow commitment to its allies beyond a fixed geographical zone within which Japanese forces sought to impose monopolistic armed control. Allies outside this zone were expected to impose monopolistic control over it without any overt Japanese assistance and to avoid crossing over the latitudinal boundary in the case of Britain or the longitudinal boundary in the case of Germany and Italy. This inflexibility stemmed as much from the domestic politics of the Japanese military and naval bureaucracies and the struggle for strategic priority between Army and Navy as from a determination to minimize obligations to their allies and foreign influence over Japanese strategy. It led to a policy stance that was not conducive to trust between allies. The contrast between the Anglo-American Alliance and the Axis Alliance was summed up in April 1942 by the refusal of the Axis partners to evolve a combined strategy in relations with Britain and the Soviet Union. For Britain, repeating the task of frustrating Soviet ambitions after 1918 without alienating the Soviet Union was part of an equation that was frankly unsustainable without the willing co-operation of the USA, whose support was essential in 1917 and 1941 to implement the 'higher realms of intelligence', an absolute prerequisite to the management of the international system during the twentieth century.

Notes

1. PRO: WO106/5552.
2. Tokyo Embassy secret report No. 155 of 10 April 1916 in PRO: WO106/869.
3. Singapore was the regional centre of security operations, see PRO: KV1/15, p. 133.
4. For Japan and Indian intrigues, see PRO: KV1/16. India Office secret memorandum of 13 May 1916 in WO106/869.
5. Greene secret and confidential Report No. 485 of 26 September 1916 in ibid. See the private papers of Major E.L. Piesse (1880–1947), DMI in Australia for most of World War I. National Library of Australia (NLA): Piesse Papers, MSS882, vol. 5/5–7 and 9–20.
6. PRO: WO106/5550 and 5553.
7. WO106/869 and ADM116/1812.
8. Gubbins was involved in setting up the programme for Army language officers in Japan after 1905 and also on the establishment of the less successful naval scheme: ADM1/7728, Case S275/04. See I.H. Nish, *Britain and Japan: Biographical Portraits* (Richmond: Japan Library, 1997), vol. II, pp. 115–16 for information on Gubbins' wartime career.
9. CX 045416 with MI1c minute on Tokyo Tel. No. 1002 of 15 August 1918: PRO: WO106/869. Attempts were made to discover if there were any evidence of wireless transmissions by Germans in China in 1917: WO106/28; KV1/16, p. 124. See also HW3/92 on Army links with the Government Code & Cypher School established in 1919 under Admiralty control and transferred to the Foreign Office in 1922.
10. See PRO: KV1/15, pp. 35–6 and KV1/16, p. 38.
11. For Premier Hughes' cables on Allied Council and British and Dominions representatives in Paris: National Archives of Australia (NAA): CP290/3 – Bundles 1–2 (January–May 1919).
12. President Wilson argued in favour of mandates instead of outright annexation against opposition from Hughes: ibid.
13. PRO: HW12/1, p. 70. For acquisition by IJN of German U-cruiser designs, see Fitzmaurice (DNI) secret memorandum No. 082/23 of 14 July 1923 in ADM1/8636/40. See also the author's 'The Transfer of German Underwater Weapons

Technology to Japan, 1919–1976', in C.J. Dunn and I.H. Nish (eds), *European Studies on Japan* (Tenterden: Norbury Press, 1979). Asdic sets were supplied to Australian light cruisers in the immediate post-war period: NAA: MP472 – 1/20/11703.

14. See J.W.M. Chapman, 'Japanese Intelligence, 1918–1945', in C. Andrew and J. Noakes (eds), *Intelligence and International University Press Relations, 1900–1945* (Exeter: Exeter University Press, 1987), p. 175 note 12, his 'No Final Solution', *Intelligence and National Security* vol. 1, no. 1 (January 1986), pp. 13–47 and his 'Japan and German Naval Policy, 1919–1945', in J. Kreiner (ed.), *Deutschland–Japan Historische Kontakte* (Bonn: Bouvier, 1984), p. 240.

15. Spooner (Navy Office) to Major Piesse, 21 December 1920: NLA, MSS882 – Series 5/139. See Rear-Admiral Ley, British Naval Attaché in Tokyo, to Captain Kobayashi, 24 March 1920 and reply by Captain Nomura Kichisaburo of 12 April 1920, and Vice-Admiral Duff, C-in-C China, to Admiralty, 17 August 1920, referring to reports from Stonecutters (Hong Kong) and Seletar (Singapore) radio stations and HMS *Hawkins* in NAA: MP981 – 622/202/440.

16. MacCandie to Commodore RAN, 21 October 1919 refers to CB1023, 'Wireless Telegraphy, British and Foreign' in ibid. Appendices E and J Penang Naval Conference, March 1921: NAA: MP1989. Admiralty letter M01227 of 5 October 1921 predicated the training of wireless operators in Japanese Morse 'if the Japanese are enemies' and in International Morse 'if the Japanese are friends'.

17. Lambert (GC&CS) minute of 22 August 1924 to Admiralty: PRO: HW3/1–15. History of the Naval Section confirms interception of foreign naval signals was resumed in 1924. The most comprehensive account of the interception and decryption of Japanese signals in Britain is Michael Smith, *The Emperor's Codes* (London: Bantam, 2000).

18. Nave to Commodore RAN, 14 October 1924, NAA: MP1049 – 1997/5/196.

19. Admiralty M0349 of 19 November 1925 to Australian Navy Office: ibid.

20. Admiralty M00408 most secret of 13 January 1926 to Hong Kong and 13 April 1926 to Melbourne confirmed the term 'W/T Procedure Y' be used in future to denote interception of foreign cypher signals.

21. Admiralty M01464 of 16 January 1924 to Chief of Naval Staff, Melbourne.

22. As note 20 above.

23. Admiralty M0749 of 16 June 1926 to Melbourne encloses report by Nave of 30 March 1926 on Procedure 'Y': NAA: MP1049 – 1997/5/196.

24. Baillie-Grohman (ACNS, Melbourne) minute of 7 October 1926.

25. See reports of the Naval Section of GC&CS in Naval Section History, Doct. Nos 22, & 28 covering 1928–1930: PRO: HW3/1; NAA: MP1185 – 1997/5/305.

26. Discussed at Singapore in 1927: NAA: A1420 – 6/71. For Pacific Naval Intelligence Organisation (PNIO) see PRO: ADM1/8623/64; ADM116/1842 & 1420. Blaker's proposals of 16 January 1928 were regarded as too radical and found no support: WO106/5393.

27. NAA: MP1049/9 – 1990/2/275. PRO: ADM116/3121. For interception of Japanese radio traffic in the Marshall and Caroline Islands: NAA: MP1049 – 1997/5/196; MP1185 – 1997/5/305; PRO: WO106/6143.

28. PRO: HW3/92.

29. HW3/1, Clarke Papers, 41 and 59.

30. Admiralty M03752 to Australian Navy, 14 August 1936: NAA: MP1185 – 1997/5/305.

31. Admiralty M02134 most secret of 25 April 1938: ibid.

32. Noble circular of 2 November 1938, 11 October 1938 at: NAA: MP1185 – 1997/5/329.
33. Admiralty M07754 of 3 February 1939 to C-in-C, China: ibid.
34. Admiralty M04126 of 17 April 1939.
35. For German comparison see: *OKM/3.Abt.Skl.B-Leitstelle* secret, 'Englische Bewegungen in ostasiatischen Gewässern vom 1.–16.6.1939'.
36. Initial contact made by Captain Patzig, Chief of the Secret Military Intelligence Section in the German Ministry of Defence (*Abwehr-Abteilung*).
37. See Donald MacLachlan, *Room 39* (London: Weidenfeld & Nicolson, 1969), pp. 77–8 and 82.
38. *OKM/3.Abt.Skl.3584/39 g.Kdos.Chefsache* of 28 April 1939.
39. J.W.M. Chapman, 'Japan, Germany and the International Political Economy of Intelligence', in J. Kreiner and R. Mathias (eds), *Deutschland–Japan in der Zwischenkriegszeit* (Bonn: Bouvier, 1990), p. 57, note 54.
40. See the author's 'The Imperial Japanese Navy and the North–South Dilemma', in J. Erickson and D. Dilks (eds), *Barbarossa: the Axis and the Allies* (Edinburgh: Edinburgh University Press, 1997), p. 192, note 42; statements by the late Lord Gladwyn Jebb, NHK TV.
41. Captain Löwisch, German Naval Attaché in Italy, *B.Nr.Gkdos 1419/39* of 7 July 1939 on a discussion with Admiral Sansonetti in *OKM:M Att Rom:'Italien – Land,' Bd.1 (1939–1940)*.
42. *The Price of Admiralty*, vol. 1, p. 171.
43. Ibid., vol. 4, p. 935. The Japanese Naval Attaché in Berlin was supplied with information from the *Abwehr* but information based on decryption limited to content and the fact of decryption omitted.
44. Ibid., vol. 2, pp. 513 and 582–3, note 4.
45. Ibid., p. 338.
46. *Barbarossa*, p. 192, note 42.
47. Non-disclosure of information in Britain has been assisted by the fact that the war against Japan has not been included in the official history of British intelligence by Harry Hinsley, but recently many GC&CS files have been released to the PRO.
48. PRO: CAB81/88, 99 and 100. The issue of security in Singapore was opened up in the spring of 1940: see Wylie circular No. 8/033/3 of 1 December 1939 and his No. 184/069 of 9 March 1940: NAA: MP1185/8 – 1937/2/159. See also NAA: A432/15 – 1955/4432.
49. See the author's 'The "Have-Nots" Go to War', in Ian Nish (ed.), 'The Tripartite Pact of 1940', *International Studies*, vol. III (1984) (London: STICERD/LSE, September 1984).
50. Kennedy Diary, University of Sheffield Library, entry for 5 November 1941.
51. Löwisch (Rome) *B.Nr.Gkdos 12/41* of 4 January 1941 to Navy: *OKM: M Att: 'Italien – Land,' Bd.2, 1940–41*.
52. Captain Wylie discussions with the Australian Navy Office on 1–4 January 1941: NAA: MP1185 – 2021/5/529.
53. A copy of an FECB manual of 10 August 1940 was handed to Commander Wenger of the US Navy (Op-20-G): see National Archives, Washington DC, RG 457, Box 1383.
54. The Enigma system was constructed by a Dutch engineer, Otto Scherbius.
55. Newman (Director of Australian Navy Signals), memorandum of 19 March 1941: NAA: MP1185 – 1937/2/415.
56. Confirmed on 8 May 1941 by report from Admiral Bellairs: PRO: CAB81/88.

57. PRO: HW1 selection of intercepted materials relayed by Brigadier Menzies to Churchill from September 1940. Japanese military attaché reports began to be read from the spring of 1943, those of naval attachés from 1944. April 1941: National Archives, Washington DC, RG 457, SRNA 058 and 035-6. The Japanese were perceived to believe that their cypher systems were 'completely unbreakable'.

58. National Archives, Washington DC, RG457, SRNA 0118. JIC 21st Meeting, 15 July 1941, JIC (41) 284 of 14 July 41 and JIC (41) 288 of 28 July 1941 in PRO: CAB81/88 and 103.

59. *The Price of Admiralty*, vol. 4, pp. 675–6. For mediation proposal on 21 August 1941: National Archives, Washington DC: RG457, SRNA 0135. For statements of Mrs Evdokia Petrov to the ASIO on 15 May 1954 on her work for the Japanese Sub-Section and handling of materials derived from acquired Japanese code materials: NAA: A6283/1–4.

60. This was the so-called Black Code: National Archives, Washington DC, RG 457, RH-373 and 375.

61. *The Price of Admiralty*, vol. 3, p. 487.

62. Wenneker (Tokyo) *Tel.Nr.457/41 gKdos* of 5 June 1941 to German Navy High Command: *OKM: M Att: 'Japan – Mobilmachung,' Bd.4, (1941)*, p. 95.

63. On 14 October 1941 the Combined Fleet reported to Tokyo a signal from the British C-in-C, China at Singapore to Admiral Boyce in Tokyo complaining about the presence of Japanese patrol vessels and submarines in the vicinity of Hong Kong and arguing that any incident that might arise would be the responsibility of Japan. National Archives, Washington DC, RG457, SRNA 0152 and 0156. Movements of military members of the Japanese Embassy in London curtailed in line with Japanese restrictions on foreign missions in Japan: JIC, 24th Meeting, 8 August 1941: PRO: CAB81/88.

64. Löwisch (Rome) *B.Nr.Gkdos 1604/41* and *1606/41* of 9 October 1941 to Berlin and letter *B.Nr.Gkdos 1616/41* to Mitsunobu.

65. *The Price of Admiralty*, vol. 4, pp. 735 and 738.

66. See special intelligence and naval attaché reports for the latter part of 1941, mostly recovered after 1945 from J25, J4, J5 and J6 intercepts in National Archives, Washington DC, RG457: SRH-406.

67. For the impact of changes in the Japanese Navy's cypher system from November 1941 National Archives, Washington DC, SRH-406, Appendix II.

68. Australian inter-service conference held in May 1941 in Melbourne on feasibility of breaking of Japanese diplomatic codes and report that 'valuable "A.1" intelligence has already been obtained from our Procedure Y organisation as it stands' and 'it is strongly recommended that it should be built up to a satisfactory size as quickly as possible'. NAA: MP1049 – 2037/3/102; A816 – 43/302/18; – 37/401/425; PRO: ADM223/496.

69. Suva radio station with 24-hour intercept capabilities seen as 'a really valuable contribution to the F.E.C.B. and New Zealand's war effort in general'. New Zealand National Archives, N Series 1 – 030/33/18; PRO: ADM223/496.

70. See Ôba Sadao, *The 'Japanese' War* (Folkestone: Paul Norbury, 1995); Komatsu Keiichiro, *Origins of the Pacific War and the Importance of 'Magic'* (Richmond: Japan Library, 1999) seeks to attribute significance to US mistranslation of intercepts for the worsening of US–Japanese relations in 1941. A US 'Purple' machine was received in London in February 1941 and independent translations supplied to Churchill, see PRO: HW1.

71. For 'Japanese Conspiracy against India' by Lieut. Col. Stratton, see NAA: A6923/3

– SI/3. *Hikari Kikan* report 2 September 1945, see NAA: A6923/3 – SI/1. History of 'The Signal Intelligence Service in India and South East Asia Commands, 1939–1945' submitted to GCHQ.

72. Newman to Admiral Royle, 4 July 1941: NAA: MP1185/8 – 2037/2/929.
73. NAA: MP1185/8 – 1937/2/159. Most of FECB's files were lost on evacuation from Singapore. Material on HMS *Anderson* at Kandy in PRO: HW4. History of signals intelligence against Japan see at HW3/102; diplomatic materials at HW10 (cf. Kennedy Diary) and Japanese Military Section at HW3/156.
74. See Löwisch *B.Nr.Gkdos 2004/41* of 31 December 1941 in *OKM: M Att: 'Italien – Land,' Bd.3, (1941–42)*, pp. 178–80.
75. NAA: A6923/3: SI/1, SI/2 SI/3 file 16/6/502 SI/8. Thanks to staff of the National Archives, Canberra and to Lieutenant-Colonel David Horner and Dr Coral Bell (ANU).

Part III
From Foes to Friends

11

The Imperial Army Turns South: the IJA's Preparation for War against Britain, 1940–1941

Haruo Tohmatsu

Introduction

In the 18 months between the early summer of 1940 and the winter of 1941 the Imperial Japanese Army (hereinafter the IJA) spent time in close observation of new developments. The power vacuum generated in the British, French, and Dutch colonies of South East Asia by the German conquest of Western Europe in the spring of 1940 suddenly gave rise to the possibility of a war against the British, French, and Dutch as a way of seizing control over the rich natural resources under their dominion. Since its formation, the IJA's organization and planning had continued, with its principal focus being upon Siberia and China. However, spurred on by these new developments, in 1940–41 the IJA's focus suddenly switched southwards. In pursuing the ultimate objective of the Dutch East Indies, the advancing IJA had two obstacles to break through: In the east, the defeat of US military forces in the Philippines and the Western Pacific and the support offered thereto by the US Pacific Fleet stationed in Pearl Harbor. In the west, the Japanese forces aimed at the subjugation of the British forces stationed in Hong Kong, the Malay Peninsula, Singapore, and Burma. While the Imperial Japanese Navy (IJN) was to be principally responsible for winning the war against the Americans in the Pacific, it was to be the land battles against the British in South East Asia which the IJA troops were chiefly to deal with. According to Japanese strategic planning, the order of the invasion was to be as follows: (1) the occupation of Hong Kong, (2) the seizure of the Malay Peninsula and Singapore, (3) the exclusion of the British forces from Burma, with the Malay Peninsula and Singapore being the most important targets. Whilst leaving the overall discussion on the overall strategic planning for the IJN and IJA to Professor Kiyoshi Ikeda's chapter in the second volume of the present series,[1] this essay outlines the IJA's war preparations against Britain on a tactical and operational level, focusing on its invasion plan for the Malay Peninsula and Singapore.

The IJA's perception of the British Army prior to the war

The IJA began seriously considering the possibility of a war against the British forces in South East Asia around the end of 1940, barely a year before the outbreak of the Anglo-Japanese war. Ever since the Meiji period (1868–1912), while both the Japanese military and the general public respected Britain as a great sea power, the British Army had been viewed rather less favourably. With the dissolution of the Anglo-Japanese Alliance in 1922, the formerly-held pro-British sentiments gradually declined. This was clearly evidenced in later years by the inclusion of Britain in the list of potential enemies, in the third revision of the Imperial Defence Policy (*teikoku kokubo hoshin*) in 1936. Nevertheless, Britain was still number four in the list behind the arch foe the Soviet Union, with the US and China occupying the second and third places respectively.

In strategic planning, military equipment, education and training, the IJA assumed that a war would be fought with the Red Army in northern Manchuria and the Siberian tundra. Indeed, there was a period when all the training and education of the IJA was based on the 'Anti-Soviet Infantry Combat' (*tai-sogun hohei sento*) and the 'Outline of Anti-Soviet Combat Techniques' (*tai-sosen yoko*) issued by the Inspectorate General of Military Training (*kyoiku sokanbu*) in 1932–33.[2] Despite worsening relations with the Americans and the British concurrent with an intensification of the Sino-Japanese War, there was essentially no change in the policy of IJA's preparations that were in effect against the Soviet Union. This was because of the view that if military preparations were formulated to defeat the Red Army – which the IJA considered to be the strongest army in the world – then a weaker force must surely capitulate with ease. Furthermore, even if a war with Britain did eventuate, it would not consist of battles fought on open fields of Europe or the deserts of the Middle East; rather, it would be fought in the streets of the British-held territories of China such as Hong Kong, Tientsin, or Shanghai, or in the jungles of the British colonies in South East Asia. This was the background behind the fact that anti-British strategic planning had not been carefully thought out by the IJA.

War preparations against Britain, 1940–1941

In the summer of 1940 the IJA started seriously to consider the possibility of war with Britain. It was an interesting coincidence that at around the same time Germany proposed that Japan should seize Singapore. Germany had failed in its twin objectives to obliterate the Royal Air Force in the Battle of Britain in the summer of 1940 and to secure a landing on the British Isles. In the wake of the German–Italian–Japanese Tripartite Pact concluded in September of the same year, Germany attempted to regain some ground and to further increase its blockade on Britain by trying to convince the

Japanese government and the pro-Nazi factions in the Japanese military to capture Singapore. According to Richard Sorge, the Soviet spy who gained the confidence of Eugen Ott, the German Ambassador to Japan, in January 1941 meetings were held over a week in the German Embassy in Tokyo. In these meetings Ott and his Army, Navy, and Air Force Attachés discussed the feasibility of an IJA seizure of Singapore. They concluded that the best chance of success lay in an invasion army advancing south from Thailand into the Malay Peninsula towards Singapore. With this blueprint, Ott tried to persuade Japanese Army and Navy General Staffs to attack Singapore. Furthermore in Germany, during February and March 1941, Hitler and the German Foreign Minister Von Ribbentrop attempted to persuade Lieutenant General Oshima Hiroshi, the Japanese Ambassador to Berlin, and the visiting Japanese Foreign Minister Matsuoka Yosuke to invade Singapore.[3] In addition the German Army General Staff tried to persuade Lieutenant General Yamashita Tomoyuki, the Japanese Army Air Force Inspector General (*rikugun koku sokan*) who was visiting Berlin in the capacity of the head of the military observer mission. Later, at the start of the war, Yamashita was to be appointed C-in-C of the 25th Army (hereinafter the 25A) which was responsible for the invasion of the Malay Peninsula and Singapore.[4]

As it turned out, Germany need not have gone to all the trouble because from the end of 1940, the IJA was independently carrying out its own investigation for the invasion of South East Asia. Firstly, in December 1940, under the orders of the Imperial General Headquarters (*Daihonei*, hereinafter the IGHQ), in Taipei a research unit was set up in the Headquarters of the Taiwan Army, which was responsible for planning military operations in tropical conditions.[5] At that time Taiwan hosted a high concentration of organizations and institutes relevant to tropical studies. Among them were the Government General of Taiwan, the Taihoku Imperial University, the Taiwan Bank, the Taipei Branch of the South Seas Association (*nan'yo kyokai*), the Taiwan agencies for the South Seas Bureau (*nan'yo-cho*) and Foreign Ministry's Chamber of Commerce (*gaimusho tsushokyoku*), and private companies such as the Ishihara Mining Company (*Ishihara kogyo*), to name but a few. Indeed, it was a place where the IJA could obtain a great deal of information about South East Asia. The highly secret 82nd or Taiwan Army Intelligence Unit (*Taiwan-gun kenkyubu*, hereinafter the TAIU) was composed of five sections – namely, planning, medical, veterinary, accountancy, and construction – and was headed by Major General Uemura Mikio, the Taiwan Army Chief of Staff. He was assisted by Colonel Hayashi Hideyoshi, Lieutenant Colonel Tsuji Masanobu (later Chief Operations Staff of the 25A), Major Asaeda Shigeharu of the Taiwan Army Headquarters, and about thirty other officers and men. They worked on the following five subjects:

(1) With respect to formation and equipment, what allowances have to be made for combat in the extreme conditions of the freezing cold of north

Manchuria and Siberia, and the tropical jungles immediately south of the Equator?

(2) Compare the formation, equipment, and tactics of the Red Army with the British and Americans. Then remodel and improve the tactics that were employed against the Red Army with a view to being used against the British and Americans.

(3) What measures would need to be adopted for health and hygiene, nutrition, and in particular, anti-malaria treatment in the tropics?

(4) Formulate the policies to be used in the occupied territories, giving consideration to the lifestyles and traditions of the indigenous population.

(5) Gathering information on the topography of the Malay Peninsula, the Philippines, Burma, and the Dutch East Indies.[6]

In April 1941 the TAIU submitted to the Army General Staff the first report consisting of some twenty to thirty studies detailing the result of investigations on the above five topics. Based on these studies, landing drills and tropical zone military manoeuvres were carried out on Hainan Island in mid to late June (referred to later). Taking the results of these manoeuvres into consideration, in August the TAIU submitted to the Army General Staff its second and final report before ceasing its operations. While it is indeed unfortunate that these two reports have not survived, their essence can be found in the small booklet entitled '*Koredake yomeba ikusani kateru*' ('The war can be won just by reading this'), put together and issued by the Army Section of the IGHQ in October 1941 (referred to later). Furthermore, the training regulations issued from August 1941 and thereafter by the Army Section of the IGHQ concerning the Malay operations strongly reflected the results of the research carried out by the TAIU. Even though the research was hastily completed in less than six months, it had achieved, according to the words of Lieutenant Colonel Tsuji, almost all of its operational and tactical objectives.

Another essential part of the war preparations was the topographical study of many of the possible battlefields. In the summer of 1940 the South East Asia Unit (*nanpo-han*) was formed within the Section Six of the Second Division of the Army General Staff. Some of its members were smuggled into South East Asia for the purpose of gathering the latest information.[7] The investigation of the Malay Peninsula was conducted by such personnel as Lieutenant Colonel Tanigawa Kazuo and Captain (later Major) Kunitake Teruto of the General Staff, and Lieutenant. Colonel Yahara Hiromichi of the Intelligence Section of the IGHQ (at the end of the war he was the Deputy Chief of Staff of the 32nd Army in the defence of Okinawa). At that time, it was extremely difficult for Japanese nationals to enter British-held South East Asia. However, between January and March 1941 Captain Kunitake, disguised as a member of the Japanese Consulate, successfully completed his investigation of the landmass of the Malay Peninsula. The parts of the investigation that the IJA appreciated most were those illustrating the sheer size of the peninsula, the amount of rivers and bridges, and the width (or to be accurate the narrowness) of the roads that criss-crossed the jungle. From a beach landing at Kota Bharu on the east coast, then a march longitudinally down the peninsula to Singapore a distance of about 1000 kilometres would be covered. The distance was equivalent to that between Tokyo and northern Kyushu, or between London and Inverness. As the retreating enemy would certainly destroy the 250 bridges that crossed the rivers of varying sizes on the route down, it was essential to have the capacity to rebuild them quickly. Furthermore, the topographical conditions, in which dense jungle grew on both sides of the road to a maximum width of approximately ten metres, an attack on both flanks would be at best difficult. Therefore, a sudden and overwhelming display of firepower and motorized superiority to break through the enemy line was critical for success. The results of this reconnaissance were reflected in the training, formation, and equipment of the IJA units engaged in operations on the Malay Peninsula.

Concurrent with the intelligence investigations were the processes of selection, transportation, and assignment of men to the actual combat units; reorganization of troop formations and material in accordance with the proposed operation; exercises and training, and accumulation of the necessary munitions.[8] The IGHQ chose the 5th and the 18th Divisions and the Imperial Guard Division to be the mainstay of the 25A, which was to take charge of the operations for Malaya. The 5D garrisoned in southern China was ordered to assemble in the Shanghai vicinity and on orders from the IGHQ commenced landing drill on 12 October 1940 on the Choshan Islands. On 6 December 1940 the Imperial Guards, 18D and 48D under the command of the South China Area Army (*minami-shina homengun*) were ordered to conduct tropical combat training as well as landing exercises. The 5D had been trained since the mid-1920s specifically to be an expert unit in landing and its skill has been fully proved in a number of landing operations in coastal China. As the three divisions were currently engaged in operations in the semi-tropical areas of southern China, they were thought to have little trouble in adapting to the tropical climate of the Malay Peninsula.

The Imperial Guards and the 5D together with the 48D were collectively referred to as 'Order 16' (*juroku-rei*) type divisions, and in November 1940 were converted from pack horse units to fully motorized units, a feat which was a remarkable effort for the IJA as the progress of its mechanization was comparatively slow. The Imperial Guards consisted of 12 594 men, 816 trucks, 41 sidecars, 16 light armoured vehicles, and 36 pieces of 75 mm to 150 mm field artillery; the 5D had of 15 261 men, 914 trucks, 46 sidecars, 16 light armoured vehicles, and 36 pieces of 75 mm through 150 mm field artillery. Contrastingly, the 18D was equipped with pack horses referred to as 'Army Order' (*riku-rei*) type division and consisted of 21 775 men, 50 trucks, 7 sidecars, five light armoured vehicles, 5709 horses and thirty pieces of 75 mm through 150 mm field artillery.[9] From around 1938, the IJA modified the structure of the infantry divisions from two brigades comprising four regiments (a four-unit system) to three regiments (a three-unit system). However, in the case of the Imperial Guards and the 18D, the old system of the two brigades comprising four regiments was retained. This was in accordance with the planning of the Malay operations that called for the formation of a number of independently acting detachments. For example, on the first day of hostilities, when an advance party made a forced landing in the face of the British garrison at Kota Bharu, it was commanded by Major General Takumi Hiroshi, the Commander of the 23rd Brigade of the 18D.

The typical British army division had 72 pieces of field artillery, approximately double that held by its Japanese counterpart. To counter this, the 25A was reinforced with two heavy field artillery regiments and a few independent mortar battalions, thus increasing their firepower. Later, for example, in the battles on Buki Thema Hill in Singapore, the mortar battalions particularly showed their devastating effectiveness, armed, as they were, with gigantic 330 mm-calibre Type 98 rockets (*kyuho*). In addition, as a result of the Ro-go Special Exercise (mentioned later) two independent engineering regiments were attached to the 25 A. They were well equipped with bridge-constructing equipment, and amply demonstrated their ability to rebuild the bridges destroyed by the retreating British forces. The armoured firepower assigned to the 25 A consisted of one tank corps (three tank regiments), a total of 228 medium and light tanks. In 1941 the IJA's main tanks were the Type 97 medium tank (15 tonnes, maximum speed 38 km/hr, armed with one 57 mm gun and two 7.7 mm machine guns) and the Type 95 light tank (7 tonnes, 40 km/hr, armed with one 37 mm gun and two 7.7 mm machine guns). Although their performance was judged to be slightly inferior to western tanks of a similar vintage, they worked against an enemy that lacked tanks and had few effective anti-tank guns.[10] The scout regiments (*sosaku rentai*) of the Imperial Guards, the 5D, and the 18D had a combined total of 37 Type 97 light armoured vehicles (a *tankette* in all but name, its performance was approximately that of the Type 95 light tank). These tanks and armoured vehicles were collectively used combined with the motorized infantry, artillery, and engineer units. While of a small scale, they demonstrated in the Malay operations a degree of breakthrough power similar to that of the German Panzer divisions in the Blitzkrieg of spring 1940. The breakthrough of the Gittra Line by the Saeki Detachment formed around the scout regiment of the 5D (December 1941) and the Battle of Srim River in which a Japanese mixed unit of the 6th Tank Regiment and approximately one hundred infantry and engineers crushed a superior British force by surprise (January 1942) were only a few of such cases.[11]

Although difficult to find supporting documentation, it is entirely feasible that the Yamashita Mission which had returned to Japan from Germany in June 1941 made clear the necessity for the IJA to urgently apply the methods of German motorized armour units, and that this was put to practical use by the fighting units, at least at a tactical level.[12]

This Lieutenant General Yamashita was soon to be appointed the C-in-C of the 25 A (Yamashita later took the command of the First Area Army of the Kwantung Army in Manchuria, then went on to command the 14th Area Army in the defence of the Philippines). The 25 A (including support units) consisted of 125 408 men, 7320 vehicles, 11 516 horses, 183 pieces of 75 mm through 150mm field artillery, and 60 anti-aircraft guns. In contrast, the estimated British deployment in Malaya and Singapore was 60 000–70 000 forces and 320 fighting aircraft.[13]

What kind of training and exercise, then, did the fighting units of the 25 A go through? For a year and a half prior to the outbreak of war with Britain, the IJA underwent ten large-scale manoeuvres that were both directly and indirectly related to the Malay campaign. In December 1940 the Inspectorate General for Military Training conducted an infantry mobility exercise in which bicycles were used to transport troops for approximately 400 km from Toyohashi in Aichi Prefecture to Kanemarugahara in Tochigi Prefecture. This was the origin of the success of the Silver Wheel Unit (*ginrin butai*) that swiftly advanced on the Malay Peninsula towards Singapore.[14] Far more important were the large-scale cross-sea landing manoeuvres carried out between 27 March and 4 April 1941 and the tropical jungle warfare exercises held in June of the same year on Hainan Island, off the coast of southern China. The former was called the *Ro-go* Special Exercise and was presided over by General Yamada Otozo, the Inspector General (C-in-C of the Kwantung Army at the end of the war). The exercise was conducted in the following order: Lieutenant General Imamura Hitoshi (later C-in-C of the 14 A in charge of the seizure of the Dutch East Indies) commanded approximately two regiments of the 5D. After grouping in Shanghai, the regiments boarded transports at the Choshan Islands at the mouth of the Yangtze River, and crossed the East China Sea towards Kyushu Island. A detachment of the Navy Second Fleet escorted the convoy throughout the crossing, and the Army 5th Air Corps provided the air cover. While escort forces destroyed any resistance offered by the coastal defence forces, the main units landed at Karatsu Bay, with smaller units at Hakata, Tachibana Bay and Kagoshima Bay. After securing airfields they pressed forward and attacked the main base at Sasebo.[15] It was obvious that this was a dry run for the landing on the Malay Peninsula and the advance to Singapore. Lieutenant General Suzuki Sosaku, the Senior Aide to Inspector General Yamada, became the Chief of Staff of the 25 A. Imamura's key staff officers included Colonel Ikeya Hanjiro, Major Fujiwara Iwaichi (the mastermind behind the organizing of the anti-British Indian National Army), and the aforementioned Captain Kunitake and many commissioned officers from the 25 A. The exercise revealed the necessity of speeding up the landing operations, strengthening the measures to thwart air attacks during landing, and improving shipping efficiency. As a result, the following were redesigned and attached to the transport convoy: the landing command headquarters in charge of conducting landing operations, on-board anti-aircraft regiments, signal units, and engineer units.[16]

In late June a jungle warfare exercise was conducted in Hainan Island under the supervision of the TAIU. In this exercise, an infantry battalion spent a week at sea under strictly limited water rations on an overcrowded transport in a tropical climate. After the landing the battalion was joined by an artillery company and an engineer company and they surveyed the island on bicycles.[17] The geography, climate, and vegetation of Hainan Island very closely resembled that of the Malay Peninsula, and the circumference of the island was about 1000 kilometres, which was approximately the distance between the planned point of landing of Kota Bharu and Singapore. At the same time, the Chiba Tank Training School (*Chiba sensha gakko*) was carrying out landing and mobility drill for the Type 97 medium tank in the thick rainforest on the same island. This drill included research on heat insulation using coconut leaves, clearing the woods, negotiating paddy fields, and mechanical maintenance under the trying conditions of the extreme heat and humidity.[18] After the completion of these exercises, on 12 August 1941 the IGHQ issued command number 924 to the 25 A assembled in the Southern French Indochina which signalled the start of jungle training, drills for penetrating units (teishintai), and mechanized coordination exercises. Essentially, these exercises were to be the final polish applied to the troops' combat skills.[19]

Conclusion: 'The war can be won just by reading this'

This chapter has given an overview of the IJA's preparations for war against Britain on operational and tactical levels. To conclude the present essay, we will briefly consider the experiences of average front-line officers and soldiers.

Based on the research carried out by the TAIU, in October 1941 the Army Section of the IGHQ issued the booklet 'The war can be won just by reading this'. More than 400 000 copies were printed and they were distributed to virtually all of the officers and men who were to take part in the invasion of South East Asia.[20] Comprising seventy pages (and divided into 18 sections), this booklet was small enough to fit into the breast pocket of the uniform, and was written in simple language. The headings read: (1) Where is South East Asia? (2) Why and how do we fight? (3) In what way will the war progress? (4) How should one behave on board ship? (5) Landing operations (6) Advancing in tropical conditions (7) Camping in the tropics

(8) Scout precautions (9) Combat (10) Precautions against gas attack (11) Precautions for signal soldiers (12) Precautions for motorised troops (13) Love your weapons (14) Rations (15) Hygiene (16) Equestrian hygiene (17) Manoeuvres (18) Conclusion.

This booklet was thoroughly practical and was used by all troops as reference material prior to operations. For example, the progress made by the 5D was as follows: in the second half of November 1941 it grouped at Hainan Island, embarked, sailed south, and finally on 8 December landed on the Malay Peninsula. According to the diary kept by the 3rd Company of the 1st Battalion of the 11th Infantry Regiment of this division, during the above period nine days were set aside for 'preparatory study' (two days exclusively for reading materials). The main activity of this 'preparatory study' was a thorough reading of everything contained in 'The war can be won just by reading this'.[21] The most important section was that which dealt with landing. There are two quotations which were strongly emphasized: contained in the section entitled 'Landing operation after a long voyage' was the phrase 'landing operation has conventionally been thought of as being difficult, however, the highly efficient crack troops of the Imperial Army have never lost a landing operation yet.'[22] 'Failure is inexcusable so once we touch the shore, it will be held. Battles are won. The enemy is weak, even beneath Chinese soldiers, and their tanks and warplanes are a rattling collection of misfit odds and ends', read a line in the section 'Once a landing is made, victory is assured'.[23] A typical scene on board transport cargo would probably has been that of a soldier in one of the shelf bunks or on deck maintaining or caring for his rifle leafing through the booklet.

For the Japanese who were at war with China subsequent to the Manchurian Incident, the war with Britain was the first general war against a white, European power for a quarter of a century since the First World War, or for 36 years since the Russo-Japanese War. While the officers and men of the 25A had gained considerable fighting experience against the Chinese in central and southern China, one may wonder what additional intelligence was given to them as regards fighting the new enemy, the British in South East Asia. In the aforementioned booklet, 'The war can be won just by reading this', there was a section entitled 'Are the British more powerful than the Chinese?' This contained some of the following phrases: section: 'While the [British] commissioned officers are by and large white gentlemen, the majority of non-commissioned officers and rank soldiers are of indigenous race, as such, there is no spirit of solidarity in the army.' 'Some measure of caution should be exercised due to the fact that the British possess many more warplanes, tanks, vehicles, and heavy artillery than the Chinese. However, they won't be of much use since not only are a great number of them obsolete but also the soldiers using them are weak.'[24] Similar observations can also be seen in the words of General Yamashita, the C-in-C of the 25 A, when he gave an address to his troops on 20 November 1941: 'The weakest points of the British forces is that they are of mixed races, have no *esprit de corps*, and are weak and frail. If one good blow is directed at the centre of command and the main white fighting units, the rest will automatically crumble.'[25] The Japanese, who had undergone extensive training with a view to fighting the Red Army, which they saw as the strongest in the world, thought it would be simple to defeat the British. The British, according to the Japanese perception, lacked solidarity between the white officers and the coloured NCOs and men. It was furthermore argued that white soldiers not only had an overreliance on their weapons, but were also lacking in fighting spirit. In the aforementioned 'Outline of Anti-Soviet Combat Techniques', formulated for fighting the Red Army, the Soviets were seen as being cowardly and uncoordinated, lax, unscientific and unsystematic, and as such, it was estimated that their forces would collapse once besieged or outflanked.[26] Despite their enormous defeat in the Nomonhan Incident in September 1939, the IJA did not appreciably modify its anti-Soviet combat techniques, for which the IJA was to later learn costly lessons. However, what was not effective against the Soviets at Nomonhan in 1939 did work out in Malay in 1941–42, and annihilated the British Army.

Notes

1. See Professor Ikeda Kiyoshi's essay in the second volume of the present series.
2. Senshi-sosho, *Kanto-gun*, vol. 1 (Asagumo shimbunsha, 1969), pp. 177–80.
3. *Misuzu Gendaishi-shiryo, Zoruge jiken*, vol. 1 (Misuzu Shobo, 1962), pp. 271–2; Sugita Ichiji, *Johonaki senso shido* (Hara Shobo, 1987), p. 165. For the simulation held at the German Embassy, see edited and translated by John Chapman, *The Price of Admiralty: the War Diary of the German Naval Attaché in Japan 1939–1943*, vols 2 and 3 (Sussex: Saltire Press, 1984), pp. 526–32.
4. Kojima Noboru, *Shisetu Yamashita Tomoyuki* (Bungeishunju, 1969), p. 178.
5. Senshi-sosho, *Marei shinko sakusen* (Asagumo shimbunsha, 1966), p. 52.
6. Tsuji Masanobu, *Singaporu: unmei no tenki* (Tozainambokusha, 1952), p. 7.
7. Sugita, *Johonaki senso shido*, pp. 144–7.
8. *Marei shinko sakusen*, chapter 1.
9. Yamashita Yoshiyuki, *Shinajihen daitoasenso niokeru shidan no hensei*, NIDS.
10. W.S. Kirby, *The War against Japan*, vol. 1 (London: HMSO, 1957), pp. 163 and 168.
11. For the achievement of tank regiments in the Malay campaign, see Katogawa Kotaro, *Teikoku rikugun kiko butai* (Shirogane shobo, 1974), pp. 5–21.
12. *Yamashita shisatsudan hokoku* (record by Ayabe Kitsuju), NIDS.
13. Estimate on 4 November 1941, in Sambohombu (ed.), *Sugiyama memo* (Hara shobo, 1967), p. 392.
14. Okamura Seishi, 'Tosuibu no konran', *Gunji kenkyu* (January 1969), pp. 148–9.
15. *Marei shinko sakusen*, p. 53; Ho nijuichi kai (ed.), *Hamada rentaishi* (1973), pp. 358–60.
16. Sempaku zanmu seribu, *Shinajihen iko shusen madeniokeru sempakubutai narabi sempaku kankeno kenkyurekishishiryo*, NIDS.

17. *Marei shinko sakusen*, pp. 52–3; Tsuji, *Shingaporu,* pp. 11–12.
18. Chiba rikugun sensha gakko, *Kainanto niokeru enshu kiji,* NIDS.
19. *Marei shinko sakusen*, p. 54.
20. Tsuji, *Shingaporu*, p. 13.
21. *Hohei dai juichi rentai daisan chutai jinchu nissi,* vol. 3, NIDS.
22. Koredake yomeba ikusani kateru, NIDS, pp. 16–17.
23. Ibid., p. 33.
24. Ibid., p. 15. For the racist aspects of this pamphlet see John W. Dower, *War without Mercy: Race and Power in the Pacific War* (New York: Pantheon Books, 1986), pp. 23 and 207–8.
25. *Hohei dai juichi rentai daisan chutai jinchu nissi,* vol. 3, 20 November 1941.
26. *Kanto-gun,* vol. 1, p. 183.

12
'Ground of Our Own Choosing': the Anglo-Japanese War in Asia, 1941–1945

John Ferris

The Malayan campaign was the most humiliating and significant defeat in British military history. Between December 1941 and February 1942 the outnumbered IJA killed or captured 139 000 Commonwealth troops. Just 3500 soldiers of *Nippon* were slain. This debacle had many roots. For Britain, menace in Europe produced weakness in Asia, miscalculations of Japanese intentions and of British airpower led to underestimating the danger, pursuing policies which led Japan to attack with Britain unable to defend. Britain had greater military resources than Japan but, fighting a major war in Europe, could not be strong in Asia. Sending enough forces to Singapore to support a cautious policy of deterrence against Japan was possible but, instead, Britain remained weaker and more provocative in Asia than necessary. It thought that cautious Japanese statesmen, unlikely to risk attacks on both Britain and the USA, could easily be deterred from war. These attitudes involved mistaken views about British and Japanese airpower. British leaders believed Japan's air forces were mediocre, and could throw little power against Malaya because they lacked forward bases and required most of their strength to match Soviet air forces; thus, even outnumbered two or three to one, it was felt that a few second-class British aircraft could defeat Japanese air forces and any amphibious assault on Malaya. Whitehall did not even send out the air force it thought necessary, assuming enough warning of danger to provide reinforcements. When Japan attacked Malaya, however, it was with surprise, a four-to-one superiority in air strength and better equipment than the RAF possessed there. Conversely, the Commonwealth army in Malaya roughly matched the invaders in strength and equipment, but was badly prepared for war. By December 1941, only 23 per cent of its units had received adequate training even to battalion level. Divisions were filled with the dregs of two armies, the Indian and Australian, which were rapidly expanding. Commanders did not know how to train conscript masses for operations, and neglected this under a massive burden of administrative duties. Disastrously, Commonwealth armies pursued a Western Front 1918-type war focusing on set-piece battles of high intensity, complexity and precision, with tightly controlled firepower. When it worked it was effective, wrecking the IJA in Burma during 1944. In order to function, however, it needed well-trained personnel plus rapid recalibration to fit South East Asia and the IJA. Little of this was done, largely because generals ignored accurate official assessments of the IJA, relying on the unfavourable views of old China hands.

Commonwealth forces were low in quality, unready for Japanese infiltration tactics, its ferocious assaults or bold use of poor armoured equipment. They were scattered across the country, unable to move or concentrate quickly or respond to the unexpected. They thought they would win easily, but they deserved to lose and they did.[1]

On 8 December 1941, the IJNAF wrecked Britain's chances to check Japan through airpower. The RAF failed to stop invasion or sink transports at sea and began to abandon the fight, noting that its forces must withdraw 'beyond the reach of enemy fighters, otherwise they will be destroyed in the next few days', though given their inferior equipment and strength, aircrew fought bravely.[2] Then, the IJA routed Commonwealth troops. The Australian General Gordon Bennett wrote, 'this retreat seems fantastic. Fancy 500 miles in 50 days – chased by a Jap army on stolen bikes without artillery'.[3] After landing in the Thai port of Singora, the IJA crashed through the 11th Indian Division, disorganized from a half-hearted attempt to seize that port, and drove rapidly down roads, its vanguard mixed with the wreck of British units. Commonwealth forces never had time to recover from defeat or retreat – the IJA always struck, one officer wrote, before they had 'any opportunity of preparing [their] defense'. The senior British commander on the battlefield, General Heath, described the IJA as 'very insidious and penetrating . . . not an enemy we can bring to battle on ground of our own choosing'.[4] Superior concentration gave the IJA numerical superiority on every field, its units being superior to 90 per cent of Commonwealth forces. They infiltrated through or round all defences. If units bunched on a road, it outflanked them and badly trained men, finding their communications cut, withdrew or ran, losing all heavy weapons in the first encounter. When confronting good bushfighters like the 12th Indian Brigade or the 8th Australian Division, the IJA smashed through with armour or sidestepped overall flanking formation. If divisions developed a long thin line perpendicular to the road system, the IJA concentrated men and firepower and broke it, isolating units on either flank, which often disintegrated. Excellent firepower within battalions and effective use of armour allowed the IJA to fillet British positions by driving down the roads. These experiences broke the nerve of units and commanders and multiplied the mistrust between British, Indian and Australian components. Each blamed the other for letting them down; each was right. Men cut and ran and Singapore fell without a real fight.

The Malayan campaign and Japan's drive through Burma to the Indian frontier during early 1942 demonstrated the inferiority of Commonwealth forces but not that of their system of warfare. Their trained units fought well against Japanese who had been specially prepared to fight in Malaya. The IJA also won when it avoided fighting on ground of British choosing. It was different where it engaged forces with high firepower and narrow fronts, most notably during the struggle for Hong Kong Island. Here British forces blocked the IJA on the coasts, funnelling it into the interior where it faced its toughest fighting of the first nine months of the war. Hong Kong Volunteers, half-trained Canadians and remnants of Scottish regulars, their command wrecked, held superior numbers of Japanese from a conventionally trained division for four days. They fought until half of their own men were casualties and took as many of the enemy with them, partly because British artillery received its only opportunity before 1944 to blast exposed Japanese targets. These 2500 combat soldiers killed and wounded almost as many Japanese as the 35 000 on Singapore Island. This showed that the British estimate of the military balance was not wrong – if appropriate force-to-space ratios were established and brave men found, even at the worst of the war, Commonwealth forces performed well against the standard Japanese tactics. Had they fought this well further south, Singapore would have held several weeks longer, its garrison defeated but not humiliated. The IJA ignored every proof that Commonwealth forces could fight and their style of operations could work.

British generals found these lessons difficult to learn or apply. Veteran generals grasped the key points, that troops 'must be *trained*. They DO NOT know their jobs as well as the Japanese and there's the end of it', that 'we must try to establish our principal object as the killing of the enemy rather than the holding of ground. This has yet to become an obsession.'[5] These ideas were not turned into practice, and in April 1943 the Malayan debacle was repeated in the Arakan peninsula on the Indo-Burma frontier. Generals had vague ideas for war and did not ensure these could work. The Eastern Army, which commanded the Indo-Burma frontier, emphasized that brigades must hold defended areas dominating communications and the country, all self-supporting, backed by reserves capable of 'rapid offensive action once the target is presented'. None of this was achieved. Defences were long lines with holes but no reserves, each formation isolated. The War Office gave India a low priority among theatres. Archibald Wavell, the commander of the Indian Army, did not even know the holes existed. Visiting the front during April 1943 his response to a brigadier's complaint that men were raw recruits was that 'Every sepoy who leaves India is a trained soldier'.[6] The great Indian Army failure was actually training. GHQ India took two initiatives in the area, having 17th Indian Division develop a 'light' structure for operations in rough country and a brigade, the 'Chindits', train for deep penetration operations, but did little with the rest of their Army. Staff officers drew useful conclusions on how to fight the IJA, but lessons were not stamped upon soldiers. Only in December 1942 did its Directorate of Military Training (DMT) begin to create 'uniformity in doctrine and procedure' even in manuals. Until April 1943, training in Japanese methods 'was largely theoretical and on training exercises the enemy was frequently assumed to behave in every respect as would British troops' – the same fatal errors as in Malaya.[7] Disorganization hampered training, as did malaria, civil disobedience and natural disaster.

Divisions were left to train as they chose. By combining 'theory and intensive experiment', 17th Indian Division developed new systems of organization and tactics suited to central Burma.[8] The units involved in the 1943 Arakan campaign, however, had little training. Raw recruits manned some companies. These were low in physique and morale, inexperienced with their weapons or with any operation beyond the platoon. 26th Indian Division complained that its reinforcements were 'most distressingly' low in quality and this was typical.[9] In the Arakan, three divisions failed to take positions manned by companies, or to withstand attacks from regiments. Japanese assaults were launched exactly as in Malaya and succeeded because Indian forces had not learned old lessons and they also failed a new test. Japanese defences were well camouflaged, holding all of the highest ground in forest or swamp, even if this stretched forces very thinly. These positions were dotted with foxholes and earth and wood bunkers, vulnerable only to direct hits, and supporting each other by gunfire, with a few snipers also placed outside. Fire held and killed, while the strongest possible reserves were maintained for counter-attacks. Hidden machine guns covered positions far away, or threw murderous enfilade fire at point-blank range. British firepower failed to scratch these defences. Indian forces, slowed by slope and undergrowth, stalled as defensive fire struck front, flank or rear, took heavy losses and withdrew or else entered a position, only to be thrown out by grenades, mortar shells and counter-attacks at bayonet point – often an IJA section broke an Indian battalion.

Generals did not appreciate these weaknesses until the enemy exposed them. Wavell thought 'we may find Japanese opposition very much lower than we expect in Burma if we can only act with boldness and determination . . . The Jap has never fought defensively and may not be much good at it.' He hoped to drive the enemy from Burma, but settled for a limited attack on a long front, 'to bring Japanese to battle with purpose of using up their strength particularly in the air'. This aim turned to dust. British forces played into all the IJA's strengths. They attacked at the head of a long and narrow corridor, their flank exposed to raids, fighting not as an Army but as brigades, throwing unconnected battalions head-on at IJA positions. Failure began at the bottom and rose to the top. Contrary to custom, Corps and Army commanders had to tell divisions how to deploy battalions. The commander of the Eastern Army, Noel Irwin, thought this a 'monstrous' necessity, produced by the weakness of senior commanders, lack of training and the lack of determination of many of the troops. Yet Irwin's ideas of how to handle the battle were flawed. He was a conventional soldier, whose instinctive response was unsuited to these particular circumstances. He favoured 'highly concentrated effort(s) by air' to destroy enemy defences, the deployment of 'sufficient waves of t(roo)ps not only to capture each objective, but to swamp anything which might be encountered en route', the use of 'deceptive simulative attacks to confuse the JAP of our intentions and also to make him disclose beforehand, his countermeasures against our attack; and thirdly; very detailed planning and preparation even down to the role of very nearly every man'. He aimed to move just 1000 yards through an 'exceedingly slow rate of advance', learning lessons which would allow more impressive operations. When this failed, he blamed his subordinates and conceded failure. Britain could win only by becoming 'immeasurably superior to the Jap in numerical strength', which would take a year. He was right. Soon William Slim, the head of XV Corps, commanding the thick of the fight, reported that his forces could not even launch major raids. Indian units abandoned the Arakan, some collapsing during the withdrawal. Wavell's chief of staff claimed that the Indian Army over-expanded to meet Imperial needs, resulting in a second-class army.[10] Wavell informed Whitehall 'main cause of failure has been inferiority of our tactics both in attack and defence to really skilful and enterprising opponents', and a 'lack of offensive spirit or proper grip'. These comments were self-criticism. 'When will they be trained?', noted Lord Alanbrooke, the CIGS.[11]

The Arakan marked the turn in the Anglo-Japanese war in Asia. By May 1943, that war finally mattered and Britain devoted more resources to it. Churchill insisted that Whitehall 'keep the heat steadily turned on'. He sought solutions in firepower and the deployment of Chindits while, more appropriately, Alanbrooke pursued improvements in conventional forces. Burma remained a secondary theatre and in its aim to balance power and commitments, Britain could not supply all the resources needed for victory. In particular, the air supply which delivered victory at Imphal was available only because Americans provided it in order to support China; without this, Britain might never have beaten the IJA. Meanwhile, many resources went to the unsuccessful operations of Chindits and Sino-American forces in Burma, costing more to mount than the IJA spent to stall, or to preparations for vast amphibious assaults that never quite succeeded. Still, for the first time in this war British forces had a significant edge in firepower and the chance to fight as they wished. Britain hoped to win through seapower, strategic bombing, Chindits or combined operations, but none of them worked: success rested with the 14th Army in Burma. That campaign remained a sideshow to both sides. British authorities even feared that Britons did not want to fight Japan and established committees to strengthen 'The Nation's Will to Continue the War Against Japan After the Defeat of Germany and Italy'.[12] Despite this concern over morale, British forces remained a minority in the 14th Army, no larger than African troops, and the Indian Army dominated the campaign.

Ironically, British infantry battalions were also made to fight with less fire-power and received more casualties than other Commonwealth forces, because one-third of them served with the Chindits, units drawn primarily from white soldiers and thrown into ferocious operations against Japanese forces. Burma was the last of Britain's great Imperial campaigns and a costly one, fought by armies which had placed little emphasis on Japan from before December 1941, in a theatre where they had not expected to fight, against major problems of sickness and supply. In order to deploy the material power fundamental to its style of war, Britain had to create an elaborate new supply system. It never had more military power in India than between 1943 and 1945, but the maintenance of this eroded British administrative power, contributed to the great Bengal famine and the collapse of the Raj, along-side victory against Japan and the restoration of British power in South East Asia for a last generation.

The Arakan taught all British commanders the need to train and to kill. Before he took over the 14th Army, Slim appreciated the need for a 'total change in our strategical ideas', insisting the need to change from holding lines to striking forces tasked to defeat Japanese from strong pivots of manoeuvre (not hold or gain territory) forcing the Japanese to attack them direct if they wished to open up a line of communication for large-scale advance:

> sufficiently stocked and garrisoned to enable them to hold out even if surrounded. The essential is that the area *must* have garrisons large enough, not only to make quite sure they are secure, but to provide ade-quate striking forces. Brigade group posts are too small. We always plan too small. Battalion posts are just sacrifices. Further, whatever we do we must secure to ourselves the main essential airfields . . .[13]

Britain should forget frontal assaults on small positions and not 'try to take him on in the hill jungles, where he has every advantage, but lure him down into the plains where we can hit him', fighting from strong positions sup-plied by aircraft. These were not the words of a prophet; they were con-ventional, like those of Eastern Army the year before. Every British general wished to fight the IJA on open ground where force-to-space ratios were good, firepower effective, and Japanese tendencies to launch unceasing frontal attacks could be exploited. Slim differed from the generals because he had a better idea of how to achieve these aims and wished his Army to fight as an army, rather than as a bunch of battalions. Moreover, he had solved only the problem of IJA attacks – not surprisingly, since defence was the role of his forces in British strategy. Slim had no answer to Japanese defensive systems and knew the IJA 'won't be lured easily into the open lowlands'. Luckily, in 1944 the enemy did attack where the British were strong. Japanese strategy, combined with the first Chindit operations and the forward deployment of the 14th Army so as to support bigger things planned elsewhere, led IJA commanders to believe that operations in central Burma would forestall a British thrust and offer the chance to destroy the Raj. Had the IJA stayed on the defensive in Burma, it might have survived that war undefeated.

Other problems were solved through osmosis. The Arakan produced humiliation, not annihilation. Units were whipped but lived to learn. No formation had worse experiences there than 26th Division, which criticized its 'creaking machinery of command' and thought the proficiency of its men 'very much too low'. It appreciated the need for good training and tactics designed against the IJA: 'The objective in every attack must be the extermination of the Jap in a given area rather than its territorial occupation. Frontal attacks against Jap prepared positions should never be undertaken.' Every attack must be ready against certain counter-attack; defences must be like Japanese ones, small in size with large reserves and integrated fire posts. Similarly, General Messervy drove the green soldiers of 7th Division towards tactics suited to a return match in the Arakan. 'It is NOT defeatist to recognise that our usual method of supporting infantry does NOT work in the circumstances here. They must outwit him, out-think him, out-fight him and lick him . . .'.[14] All Indian divisions put such ideas into practice, following the path the best had blazed six months before. By November 1943, the best formations were good and average ones were competent. Physical fitness, morale and acclimatization rose and the quality of commanders improved, as the Indian Army's best generals turned from the desert to the jungle. It also ensured an effective level of basic and unit training establishing advanced centres to spread 'a common tactical doctrine throughout the Army'. Officers and men routinely received courses in 'jungle warfare'. 'G.H.Q. Jungle Warfare School' at Shimoga outlined Japanese tactics drilling in effective responses. The Indian DMT produced a good jungle warfare manual, *The Jungle Book*, while circulating widely accurate accounts of the IJA's quality and tactics. These documents derived clear lessons from British failures and Japanese characteristics, such as that the speed of a Japanese advance 'cannot be over-emphasised; to underestimate it is disastrous' recommending overestimation.[15] Lessons were incorporated into the 'battle drill' institutionalized across the 14th Army. Many officers were dubious about the mystique of jungle warfare and uniform training. The commander of 5th Indian Division felt battle drill 'is tending nowadays to become "a blind order of obedience" . . . what must be taught . . . is principles and NOT drill, which can only lead to our tactics becoming stereotyped and hidebound'.[16] But stereotyped training was better than none at all, and the debate on theory and practice helped create a tactical style derived from 1918 fit the Burmese jungles.

Recalibration was not easy. British tactics were designed to smash formations by blasting wide areas with firepower, advancing over the wreck, and forcing soldiers to run or surrender. An enemy holding a series of small and hard positions until every man was dead would survive any unfocused bombardment and then wreck every advance. The British could defeat such a foe only by learning to kill every Japanese they fought. It is sometimes thought that Commonwealth forces did so eagerly and from hatred; not so. They had no wish to take this action at all, because it was inconvenient – it required a fundamental change in organisation, in a direction officers did not wish to go. The tactics of extermination were adopted from necessity rather than racism – Commonwealth soldiers hated the Japanese no more than they did the most nazified elements of the *Wehrmacht* and little more than most Germans – but this did produce a callous attitude toward the enemy. IV Corps held. 'All plans must be regarded from the aspect of their potential for killing Japs rather than from the angle of attaining tactical objectives. The former precedes the latter and is the shortest way to attaining the objective.'[17]

Nothing was more difficult to recalibrate than firepower. In order to be effective in Burma, the sophistication, centralization and weight of fire had to decline precisely when these characteristics were rising in Europe, while officers were tempted by those peddling the biggest firepower available, such as mass bombardment by rockets. All of this was inappropriate to the situation in Burma, where Japanese forces were dispersed, the terrain was broken, and the deployment of massive firepower might splinter logistical systems. Officers had to learn that one accurate gun offered better results than barrage by four, and that fire was needed as much to clear undergrowth as to blast bunkers, because concealment was central to Japanese positions. Ultimately, firepower provided the razors which bled the IJA dry, but old-fashioned blades were the most useful. In 1946, senior IJA officers regarded artillery as the best British weapon – it inflicted 50 per cent of casualties, although it was 'extremely wasteful' of ammunition – closely followed by tanks, and then by barbed wire, mortars and light automatic weapons.[18] In autumn 1943, the War Office and the Indian General Staff began taking the right steps to develop that power, realizing better logistics by air were the key to deploying firepower in rough country. They converted one-third of divisional artillery into 'Jungle Field Regiments', replacing heavy equipment by lighter, including mortars for guns. Training in these ends had barely started by February 1944, and had not overcome the effects of standard practices – officers focused on precise fire plans and lengthy ranging 'instead of getting on with the job'.[19] Divisions went into Imphal-Kohima with their artillery at an experimental stage, and learned to make it work through trial and error.

All arms had far to go. On 26 January 1944, at Razabil in the Arakan, for the first time an infantry brigade of the 14th Army attacked with the full range of fire support, artillery and aircraft to soften the enemy, and a moving barrage and 25 tanks to shepherd infantry through the killing ground. Despite overwhelming superiority, it failed. Bombs and guns inflicted no damage; tanks demolished bunkers, but had no accompanying infantry to exploit the opportunity. When the bombardment began, troops fell back 1000 yards and they did not return to their forward positions until long after it had halted. Then they fell behind their barrage and tanks, while 'there was usually complete silence from all our supporting arms during the vital last lap of the assault'. This failure taught important if elementary lessons. In order to clear undergrowth, neutralize weapons and support an assault by a battalion, divisional headquarters had to co-ordinate sophisticated fire support while also being able to respond immediately and flexibly to a company officer, since 'an error of a minute might ruin all'. Tanks could provide 'decisive' support – given the IJA's poor anti-tank power, they 'can dominate any battlefield in which [they] can move freely'. Similarly, staff officers at XXXIII Corps concluded that all recent Commonwealth attacks in Burma had failed to apply 'several old principles. Each one emphasises the need for very careful preparation leading up to a deliberate common sense drill.' These lessons included, 'Blitz tactics never pay. They are a gross waste of valuable life and material and evidence that the plan of attack has never been studied in detail. We must attack with brains not brawn.' Reconnaissance was 'pathetic', artillery and air barrages universal and useless.

> The surest means of destroying a position was by careful drill and the principle 'hasten slowly'. So long as we possess a strong offensive power and force the Jap to stand, by riveting his attention, he will retain his static role and such tactics , although not dashing, will steadily and surely succeed.[20]

In 1944, the learning curve was steep, rising as practical experience linked to research in the rear. The British came to know their enemy and how to defeat it.

The difficulties involved in fighting the IJA, its skill and its unique tendency to fight to the death, produced complex attitudes towards the Japanese. Wavell, exasperated by an enemy which defied 'all rules, both at strategy and tactics' and constantly whipped him, used harsh terms, saying they combined 'the fanaticism and mobility of the savage with modern weapons and training'. Shimoga insisted that men learn to 'hate the Jap', and Japanese officers as 'generally found wearing glasses, the result of much book study, and V.D. endemic . . . '. Slim described them as

> a fanatical enemy unsurpassed in his insect-like qualities of persistence and vicious ruthlessness, as 'man-sized soldier ants'. They would follow

their orders without deviation until they were killed, and nothing but killing would stop them. It was this, above all, which made them so formidable. Otherwise they did not constitute a first-class army.

Still, he praised their military ability. 'None was a tougher or more formidable adversary than the Japanese . . . The Japanese are a well trained enemy and in my experience they always fight to the last. All armies talk about fighting to the last man and the last cartridge but the Japanese are the only people who put it into practice.' This sort of professional respect for the IJA was widespread, and nor were attitudes marked solely by hatred or racism. Even Shimoga explained Japanese behaviour in cultural terms, rather than racial ones. Japanese soldiers were 'trained in German methods, therefore stereotyped' and 'owing to Shintoism, will hold the pos[itio]n to the bitter end, and will die at his post'.[21]

Military attitudes were functional, and dominated by one aim: how to smash the IJA. Some, especially psychiatric specialists, held that by race and culture Japanese soldiers were 'very susceptible to noise and shock tactics', and suggested the development of special weapons or tactics to achieve that end. Commanders rejected such ideas. 'The characteristics of the Japanese soldier under fire do not differ materially from those of troops of other nations. It was, however, generally agreed that taken unawares the Japanese soldier experienced a sort of mental paralysis which is probably more prolonged than would be the case with Western races.' Japanese were frequently compared to Germans and attitudes towards the two were similar. No doubt many Commonwealth soldiers hated their foe, but they did so without particular encouragement from their superiors. Contrary to conventional views, official assessments of the IJA did not aim to dehumanize the enemy: instead, they stressed how human Japanese were – how much like British or Indian soldiers. Intelligence summaries with wide distribution discussed topics like marriage customs and religion in Japan.[22] IV Corps informed officers that 'the first and most notable point to remember is that the Japanese are great natural fighters' with 'guts', high morale and a 'peculiar mixture of idealism and animalism'. 'The Japanese is a first-class fighter . . . but he is subject to the same human failings as the rest of us, and he can be beaten and must be.'[23] Officers had to shake the inferiority complex which had emerged among their men, and to describe Japanese as subhuman or inhuman could reinforce the idea that they were superhuman. Meanwhile, soldiers needed some explanation as to why the IJA fought in the unprecedented fashion that it did. Precisely as Commonwealth forces developed tactics designed to kill every Japanese soldier they met, they received an education in Japanese culture; the better they understood the enemy, the better they could destroy them.

By April 1944, Britain had achieved only part of this aim. Anglo-Indian units were finally competent. They could withstand major attacks, so long as units remained supplied, but their defensive tactics were imperfect and they still had no means to attack effectively. The IJA solved these problems because it despised its enemy and their style of war. An IJA staff assessment of the Arakan offensive thought Anglo-Indian generals 'poor', British soldiers mediocre and Indian troops 'bad':

Commonwealth forces attacked in a slow and stereotypical fashion. On the defence, fronts were strong but flanks weak, while positions in rough country were flimsy. From this the IJA drew lessons, identical to those issued on Taiwan in 1941 – attack and crush white troops, hit flanks, drive deep, take risks, and assume 'the tactical standard of the ANGLO-INDIAN Army is on the whole very low'.[24] This critique of the Arakan was accurate, but the IJA drew false lessons – that Commonwealth forces were worse than Chinese ones, could not improve and would be beaten by the same old tactics. British artillery, for example, was used poorly in the Arakan while tanks failed dismally. The IJA assumed they could not overcome these problems and misunderstood the power these arms would have: midway through the battle of Imphal-Kohima, IJA officers were stunned to learn that the British tanks could fight in rough country, wrecking any position penetrated. Japanese commanders attacked Commonwealth forces precisely where they were strong and wished to fight, because they believed their enemy must be weak wherever it stood; and they did so through an extraordinarily deep and logistically fragile lunge which must produce either immediate victory or disaster. Japanese commanders were so overconfident that they did not realize this decision was a gamble. They lost the battle, the British did not win it.

In August 1942, British commanders had selected the Imphal area as the best place to defend India, advance into Burma and engage the IJA. In 1943 and 1944, in order to defend India, they deployed most of their forces in Burma to that region, where they received months of experience with the terrain. The Imphal plain met all of Slim's prerequisites, providing several airheads, being well supplied, and capable of being garrisoned by brigades or divisions with ample firepower, which could fight as an army on rational principles:

(a) The minimum of troops will be tied to the ground for static defence. Such static defences will be carefully organised to serve as bases for the action of mobile reserve.
(b) In every defended locality the maximum number of troops will be held as reserves in a counter-attack role.
(c) The principle of concentration will be observed to the full, even though this may necessitate allowing the enemy temporary access to important areas until our counter-attacks are launched.
(d) Immediate and deliberate counter attacks will be organised, reconnoitered and rehearsed without delay.[25]

British commanders aimed to answer the Japanese onslaught by withdrawing to defended airheads. Events did not progress as either side hoped. 120 000 Commonwealth combat soldiers stood around Imphal and in the Arakan. 75 000 Japanese, at the top of their form, struck as planned and with greater speed than the British expected. Slim's first attempts to control this battle were wrecked and several Commonwealth formations caught out as badly as the 11th Indian Division in Malaya. British commanders had ample warning of Japanese intentions, but the thrust took them everywhere by surprise.

In the Arakan on 4 February, the headquarters of 7th Indian Division was overrun and its personnel forced to flee through wild country to a tiny and tactically poor position held mostly by support personnel and penetrated during the first nights. Around Imphal on 14–18 March, the IJA attack forced 17th Indian Division, the area reserve, to fight 100 miles backwards, while far to the north Commonwealth forces stood at an unplanned position, Kohima, for weeks barely able to deploy a gun or tank at key points. Slim's rational plans were reversed – his reserves were tied down in combat, his men scattered in static defences, his army fighting in fragments, counterattacks hard to organize. Still, the IJA's assault failed. It had the initiative but used it to do what Slim wanted, to fight on ground of his choosing. Slim's operations miscarried, but not his strategy. The IJA could not smash his garrisoned airheads and destroyed itself in the attempt. By engaging all of his units at once, the IJA made them fight as an army. Defeat and the need to retreat exacerbated splits between Japanese generals and paralysed action until it was too late, while Slim found new reserves and fresh options, which his men executed. Some of the formations most badly overrun – for example, 7th and 17th Indian Divisions – were among the best Commonwealth forces in Burma, with able commanders and determined soldiers, while just enough supply aircraft were available to support 120 000 men surrounded far from their railheads. Above all, the Indian Army finally matched the IJA in a soldier's battle, won by infantry rather than firepower, though British superiority here was significant. When the IJA came closest to success at the start of the battle, its attacks were hammered by mortars, guns and tanks. Later, armour led all attacks – the movement of just one tank to key positions cracked Japanese defences at Kohima and elsewhere. Both sides fought with skill and courage and heavy casualties, but 16 Japanese died for every Commonwealth soldier – 65 000 to 4000 – because the IJA could not treat so many wounded so far forward. They died in droves, killed by their commanders, the survivors wrecked as soldiers.

This bloody Japanese disaster led to more disasters. The IJA could not replace its losses in quantity and quality while Commonwealth forces mastered their style of war and the IJA. Japanese veterans fought well – in north Burma they checked larger forces of Chindits, Americans and Chinese, and inflicted heavier losses on them, in the IJA's best defensive battle of the

Pacific War, while in the Arakan six Japanese battalions stalled four Commonwealth divisions and withdrew at their own pace. As the 14th Army moved from Imphal to Mandalay, however, its main front, led by an infantry brigade, its spearhead a mechanized battalion with 50 armoured fighting vehicles, working closely with aircraft and artillery, could smash any defence the IJA could muster. The Japanese, no longer able to hold a front while striking at flank and rear, could merely mount a fighting withdrawal, hustled by British mechanized forces. Attacks on IJA defences remained difficult, but British techniques improved, guided by their increased knowledge of Japanese habits. The IJA established a killing ground, for example, by holding fire until attackers were deep into its positions. The British used this, infiltrating deep into positions, identifying where the enemy stood, with prearranged support from guns, tanks and machine guns ready at a moment's notice, then fighting a set-piece battle on a small scale with a tiny cost – to them: in contrast, every battle killed every Japanese.[26] Catastrophic losses forced the IJA to rely on units, often of support personnel, that were inexperienced with the tactics developed to exploit British weaknesses. They fought desperately but clumsily, their attacks degenerating into human waves against barbed wire and machine guns – precisely what the British were trying to lure them into doing. 36th Indian Division held that stereotyped IJA tactics could be manipulated into suicide, but cautioned that 'the Japanese must be rated as a courageous hardy fighter . . . Whatever the shortcomings of his higher commanders – the Japanese junior leader must be classed with the best in the world when it comes to minor tactics or fighting in thick jungle.' 17th Division noted that captured orders show 'an astonishing degree of conceit among JAP commanders', who ordered their men to do the impossible and so destroyed them.[27]

This British system became increasingly sophisticated and superior, and was again recalibrated, so as to use mechanized firepower for quick breakthrough and deep exploitation in the open territory of southern Burma. Divisional transport switched from mules to trucks and aircraft. Generals looked for means to 'entice the Jap out' to 'fight on ground of our own choosing', providing juicy targets and concealing their strength so as to exploit the IJA's 'conceit' and aggressiveness.[28] Imphal-Kohima was the kind of battle British soldiers of the inter-war years expected to fight against the IJA, especially in 1945. British operations combined deception and surprise to daze the enemy, and manoeuvre and firepower to dice it. When Slim's initial hopes to trap and smash the IJA in south-central Burma failed, he formulated new ones which his men executed, in one of the most impressive manoeuvres on land in the Pacific War. While half his army, in XXXIII Corps, attracted the IJA's attention and lured its reserves into bloody and futile counter-attacks on a northern axis, 50 000 combat soldiers in IV Corps formed a new one to the southwest by crossing 300 miles of rough terrain, undetected by the enemy. Then both halves of a trap slammed shut. XXXIII

Corps crossed the Irrawaddy River on 12 February 1945 south towards Mandalay behind an 'earthquake' of bombs and petrol and a barrage of 80 guns on a 2000-square-yard area, containing most Japanese artillery in the region – perhaps 5 per cent of the strength which would have supported such an operation in Europe, but effective all the same. The last Japanese reserves in Burma were thrown into intense attacks and thrown away. Then British armour and mechanized infantry under IV Corps whipsawed east across the Irrawaddy, and 100 000 men struck sharp and heavy blows over a hundred-mile front. Japanese units broke into fragments and were destroyed by their commanders and the enemy. In the last great battle of the campaign, in April-May 1945, when all remaining IJA units broke out across the Sittang River, 97 Commonwealth soldiers died for 15 000 Japanese. In the last 18 months of the war, Japan lost Burma and perhaps 100 000 men killed, for 7000 of their enemy.[29]

During the period 1941–45, war became the relationship between Britain and Japan. Armies developed to fight in Europe and Manchuria clashed in South East Asia, where neither proved absolutely better than the other. These armies were in a state of balance for a remarkably short period of time; their struggle produced some of the most one-sided battles of the Second World War. Each side won triumphs or suffered disasters depending on how far circumstances favoured them, or how successfully they adjusted to them. Initially, training was the IJA's trump card, as material later was for Britain. These battles cost Britain and Japan similar levels of casualties, though most 'British' losses came from other Commonwealth forces. They produced examples of courage (both sides in Burma), incompetence (Japanese generals at Imphal) and shame (British commanders in Malaya). Despite this, British and Japanese military opinions of each other did not change. By 1945, British soldiers assessed their enemy as the War Office had done during the inter-war era, confident that they would win on ground of their choosing, because they were doing so; at the same time, IJA officers despised the British 'because they avoid close combat, never attack by night, and are afraid to die', even though Britain was winning precisely because of some of these characteristics. One staff officer, Lieutenant Colonel Fujiwara, appreciated the key points better than most. The British fought through 'a scientific computation of the forces and supplies required to ensure success', the Japanese 'prepare only one-half or two-thirds of the forces required and try to achieve quick results by the skillful handling of small forces in surprise attacks'. Perhaps British forces had relied too much on firepower and deliberate operations for Japanese taste, but still their approach had been reasonable, given the 'century's difference' between British and Japanese weapons, and it had worked.[30] Indeed, Britain could not have won without material superiority, but that was also its way of war; it defeated an enemy designed to win despite the handicap of inferior weapons, and it did so only because Commonwealth forces became as brave and skillful as Japanese.

These battles are forgotten in Japan and Britain, not surprisingly, for they did not matter much then or now. Slim wrote that in Burma the IJA suffered the 'greatest defeat' in its history, a statement often repeated but wrong.[31] In August 1945, the Red Army annihilated the Kwantung Army of 1 200 000 men, for perhaps 5000 Soviet soldiers killed. The defeat in Burma ranks high among Japanese disasters, alongside those in New Guinea and the Philippines, but Japan would have lost the Pacific War no matter what happened at Imphal. The fall of Singapore inflicted heavier damage on Britain, but the significance of this event should not be overrated: it merely hastened British decline in Asia. Before the Anglo-Japanese war, each side believed that the stake was mastery over Asia; in this sense, both of them lost the Pacific War.

Notes

1. For a more thorough discussion, cf. John Ferris, 'The Singapore Grip: Preparing Defeat in Malaya, 1939–41', prepared for Anglo-Japanese conference at Hayama, September 2000.
2. GHQ/FE 9/12/41, 'Employment of Aircraft, Malaya, 9.12.41': PRO: AIR 23/3575.
3. Gordon Bennett Diary, entry 31 January 1942; AWM 67/3/25 Pt 1.
4. 'Note on Interview with Captain W.G. Grindell, 2nd Bn E. Surreys, 14/5/42 [*sic*]': PRO: WO 106/2550A; 'Notes on G.O.C.'s Tour', 20 December 1941: WO 172/15; Heath to Barstow, 29 December 1941: WO 172/38.
5. Alexander to Wavell, 29 April 1942, Hutton Papers, 3/1/5; Note by Hutton, 3/4: BLHCMA.
6. Eastern Army Operation Instruction No. 3, 13 April 1942, No. 7, 11 July 1942: PRO: WO 172/377; minute by Grigg, 4 May 1942, WO 106/2853A; John Calff, 'Memorandum on the Campaign in Burma, 1942–43', undated but *circa* November 1957, Basil Liddell-Hart Papers: BLHCMA 4/34.
7. Monthly Training Report of the DMT, December 1942 and April 1943: L/WS 1/764.
8. '17 Ind Div Training Instruction No. 1', 4 June 1942, passim.
9. 'Sequence of Lessons Arakan', Twenty-sixth Division, 12 June 1943: PRO: WO 172/2008.
10. Joint Staff Mission, Washington to Armindia, 16 May 1943, passim, CAB 106/164.
11. Alanbrooke to Churchill, 30 March 1943, Churchill to Alanbrooke, 24 March 1943: WO 216/34.
12. 'The Nation's Will to Continue the War Against Japan After the Defeat of Germany and Italy', draft minutes of meeting, 20 May 1943, passim: WO 193/156; cf. AIR 20/4659.
13. 'Appreciation . . . of the Situation in the Arakan', by William Slim, 24 March 1943: WO 172/1888.
14. 'Sequence of Lessons Arakan', GOC 26 Indian Division, 12 June 1943: WO 172/2008; '7 Ind Div Comd's Operational Notes', No. 3, 14 January 1944; No. 8, 3 January 1944, passim: Messervy Papers, 5/3, 5/8, BLCMA.

15. *The Jungle Book*, Military Training Pamphlet No. 9 (India), September 1943: L/MIL 17/5/2250.

16. GOC Fifth Indian Division to Advanced Headquarters ALF SEA, 19 January 1945: PRO: WO 203/2475.

17. 'Appreciation of the Situation on 4 Corps Front by G.O.C. 4 Corps, 20 Sep. 1943 [*sic*]', Gracey Papers, BLHCMA, 1/5; 'Ambushes, The Jungle Alphabet for Patrols', GHQ Jungle School. Shimoga, NAM 7304–1-2, National Army Museum, London.

18. SEATIC Bulletins Nos 243, 244, 245: Gracey Papers, BLHCMA, 7/3.

19. 'School of Artillery (India), Report on 3" Mortar Course Serial No. 2', 4 February 1944: PRO: WO 203/544.

20. 'Report on Assaults by Infantry Supported by Tanks, Artillery and Air Against Japanese Positions', 1 March 1944, Major Howell, Research Directorate, WO 232/39; 'Minutes of the Conference on the Methods to be Employed in Dealing with Japanese Defended Positions', XXXIII Corps, 18 March 1944: WO 203/715.

21. XV Indian Corps Weekly Intelligence Summaries, Nos 8, 24 July 1942, No. 11, 14 August 1942: WO 172/421.

22. Precis, undated, for lecture at GHQ Jungle School, 'The Jap is not a Superman', NAM 7304-1–2; Wavell to Liddell Hart, 14 March 1943: Basil Liddell-Hart Papers, LH 1/733, BLHCMA.

23. IV Corps Intelligence Summary, No. 4, 13 June 1942: PRO: WO 203/407; for further examples, cf. WO 208/3853, 3854, 'Notes on the Japanese Army, A Guide to Training', WO 231/31.

24. Wartime Translations of Seized Japanese Documents: ATIS Reports, 1942–1946, University Press of America: 10-EP-187, 'Imperial General Headquarters Army Department, Lessons from experiences in the Akyab Area, 25.7.43'.

25. 14th Army, 'Directive for Major-General R.P.L. Ranking', 30 March 1944: PRO: WO 172/4163.

26. C-in-C, 11th Army Group to DMT, War Office, No. 12037/GT, November 1944: WO 203/1090.

27. HQ Seventeenth Indian Division Div. to I Corps, 26 March 1945: WO 203/2524; Thirty-sixth Division, 6 March 1945, 'Japanese Tactics in the Withdrawal', WO 203/2524; 'Battle Instructions for Jungle Fighting', undated, but late 1944 by internal evidence, from Thirty-third Division: WO 203/2475; cf. WO 203/2607.

28. 'WASP Exercise, Discussions re Equipment etc. Plans, Reports and Appreciation, Oct 1944', WO 203/1987; cf. WO 203/1988.

29. SEATIC Bulletins No. 243, No. 245, Gracey Papers, BLHCMA, 7/3.

30. SEATIC Bulletins No. 243, No. 244, No. 245, Gracey Papers, BLHCMA, 7/3.

31. Slim, *Defeat into Victory* (London, 1962), p. 307.

13
The Anglo-Japanese War and Japan's Plan to 'Liberate' Asia, 1941–1945

Sumio Hatano

The invasion of South East Asia and the plans for the end of the war

In July 1940, with a commitment being made for a southward push, the Japanese Army (IJA) and Navy (IJN) put all their efforts into producing a battle plan for war in South East Asia against the Americans, British and Dutch territories, and they produced a plan for this by the summer of 1941. However, there was a key difference in the plans put forward by the Japanese Army and Navy regarding the invasion of South East Asia. After the Russo-Japanese War, the IJN had based their strategy on a Pacific-centred anti-Anglo-America strategy, their main plan being a 'clockwise strategy' moving from the Philippines, to Java, Sumatra and Malaya. This stressed the importance of removing the danger of an attack by the USA by invading the Philippines. However, the IJA favoured an anti-clockwise movement, landing first in Malaya, and moving in an opposite direction to that proposed by the IJN. It was thought that if the Far Eastern British Empire was invaded, Japan could avoid the involvement of the USA in the war. The movement of the IJA into South East Asia also limited its enemies to British and Dutch territories, and meant that an attack on the Philippines could be avoided or delayed. In the end, there was a lack of information about each route's advantages and disadvantages making any decision difficult, and on 5 November 1941, the Emperor issued a decree, 'The Army and Navy's Southern Strategy Agreement', which stated that both the Philippines and Malaya would be swiftly attacked, with a left and right southerly movement crossing into the Dutch East Indies.

The objective of this southern movement was to destroy and occupy American, British and Dutch bases, their main areas of operation being the Philippines, Guam, Hong Kong, Malaya, Burma, and Indonesia. The agreement indicated those areas that were to be invaded at the beginning of the operation, but after that changes in strategy meant that this soon became obsolete.[1] In addition to the South East Asia invasion plan the IJN, under the control of Admiral Yamamoto Isoroku, planned a separate attack on Pearl Harbor. This was part of a plan which aimed at destroying the American Fleet based at Pearl Harbor thus bringing the war to a swifter end, although many military leaders believed that Japan would be more successful in a war against Britain rather than one against the USA.

In early September 1941, three months before they opened hostilities, the IJA and IJN drew up their plan ('The guidelines for operations against America, Britain and the Dutch').[2] At the centre of this was the idea of ending the war, its main points being: 'Force the surrender of the Chiang Kai-shek government, force the surrender of the British and Australian forces and this will cause the Americans to lose the need to continue the war'.

In other words, it was believed that the defeat of the Chiang government and the British would bring about a rapid end to the war. According to this plan, there was no choice but to take over Hong Kong and Shanghai in order to bring about the surrender of the Chiang government. After the attack on Pearl Harbor, any operations against China would 'if possible avoid waste' and no active military action would be carried out.[3] On the other hand, in order to bring about a British surrender, Japan would have to rely on German military force. There were three ways in which the Japanese could help in the German war against Britain in Europe:

(1) Japan could co-operate with Germany's push into the Caucasus, the Middle East and North Africa, by opening a new front in Western Asia and India, and thereby threatening the power of the British Empire in Asia.
(2) To relieve the German burden of fighting against the Soviet Russians, thus freeing resources to be used against the British. This would be achieved through Japan acting as an intermediary and negotiating peace between the Germans and Russians.
(3) To respond to a request from the Germans by attacking the Soviet Far East.

The third of these was Germany's most consistently requested option. Some Japanese military leaders agreed that they should co-operate with this plan. However, the maintenance of good relations with the Soviets was necessary for the success of the war in South East Asia, and so the option preferred by Germany was never carried out.[4] The Army, Navy and Foreign Ministry actively pursued the second option, but the Germans did not want to give up the possibility of an IJA attack on the Soviets and also there was little response from the Soviet side to the possibility of a peace with the Germans. The best way to end the war was to defeat the British, and this required the establishment of German supremacy and the invasion of the British mainland, a very ambitious project. Although an agreement on co-operation between Japan and Germany was made in January 1942, it was limited to within 70° East longitude. Moreover the agreement did not concretely define the way in which the two armies would co-operate.[5] Thus of all the options outlined above, only the first was carried out – Japan relied on the belief that the push south would be a success.

The push south and its areas of operation

The invasion of South East Asia

The strategy of southern incursion depended very much on the 'first strike' capability of Japan's air force, and it started with the surprise attack and landing on Kota Bharu in Malaya. This happened exactly one hour before the attack on Pearl Harbor. The air attacks on Hong Kong, Guam and the Philippines continued according to plan, and after the first day of military operations, Japan had almost established control of the air in South East Asia. The torpedoing and sinking of the new battleship, *Prince of Wales*, and the fast battlecruiser, *Repulse*, on 10 December meant that the British Far Eastern Fleet lost much of its power. Shortly afterwards, the invasion of Hong Kong was completed on Christmas Day despite considerable British resistance. The destruction of the American air force based in the Philippines was also completed in around ten days, and on 2 January 1942, the 14th Army occupied Manila. The American main force withdrew to the Bataan Peninsula and continued to resist until April when MacArthur fled to Australia.

On the Malay Peninsula, the 25th Army, now at its southern tip, moved on to Kuala Lumpur. The main force, using the Johore causeway, started its attack on Singapore and the British surrendered on 15 February. The largest oil refinery in the Far East, at Palembang in Sumatra, was also seized by the IJA, after a surprise parachute attack on 14 February. Since the invasion of Malaya and the Philippines finished ahead of schedule, the campaign schedule for the Dutch East Indies was stepped up, and on 20 January, it was agreed that the IJA should invade Java. After conquering the islands of Sumatra, Timor, Celebes and Borneo, the main force of the 16th Army landed in Java. The Javan army surrendered with little resistance on 9 March. In this way, the Southern Incursion Strategy was quickly achieved. The main reasons for this were quick decision-making on the part of the commanders, the continued destruction of Allied oilfields, and the inability of the Allies to send reinforcements. The IJA had first conceived of and studied the idea of a war based in South East Asia in December 1940.[6] Despite its comparatively late development, this strategy was a success because the Japanese did not confront a major force dispatched from Britain, America and the Netherlands – instead they met an ill-equipped and demoralized colonial army.

The strategy of cutting off India and Australia from the British Empire

The planning for the aftermath of the Southern Incursion Strategy was discussed at the beginning of 1942 by the IJA and IJN and finalized at the Imperial Headquarters-Cabinet Liaison Conference on 7 March. The wording of the central clause of this new strategy was far from clear, generating one of the most fiercely debated discussions around the strategy of the military. After the successful completion of the southern incursion, the IJA devoted themselves to the strengthening of their defence and the exploitation of the resources of the occupied territories. The movement of troops in Manchuria (now considered to be part of Japan) to prepare for an attack against the Soviets was also borne in mind.

However, the IJN disliked this defensive strategy. It believed that Japanese forces could be overwhelmed by a reinforced Allied army, and stressed the importance of continuing the incursion into the Pacific. Therefore, the discussions between the Army and Navy ended without agreement and it was generally accepted that any plan would require both a defensive and an offensive strategy. The IJN and the IJA both still felt that joining with the Germans to defeat the British was the only way to bring a favourable end to the war. This is why a policy of cutting off India and Australia from the British Empire was pursued.[7]

The Imperial decree of 15 April 1942, 'The IJN Operation Plan for the Second Stage', reflected the Navy's wish for an offensive strategy, and outlined three fields of operation:

1. The invasion of Port Moresby, followed by the invasion of Fiji, Samoa and New Caledonia, the so-called FS strategy.
2. The interception of British and Indian forces by invading Ceylon.
3. The invasion of Midway and the Aleutians.[8]

The first option would stop the use of Australia by the Americans as a base for operations, thus isolating it from use as a place of retreat for US forces. However, the Japanese Fleet, under the control of Admiral Yamamoto, chose the third option of attacking and driving out the American Fleet from Midway and the Aleutians, because naval power would play a decisive role in this policy.

The Army proceeded in their preparations for the FS strategy, but at the beginning of April, as a result of the IJN decision to push ahead with the battle for Midway rather than adopting the FS strategy, the Army could do nothing but go along with the IJN plans. However, this resulted in the loss of four Japanese aircraft carriers, largely as a result of the breaking of Japanese codes by American intelligence.

The FS strategy was subsequently abandoned, and while the Japanese Fleet was undergoing reconstruction at the beginning of August, the Americans commenced landings at Guadalcanal. After this Japanese aircraft carriers only participated in two other sea battles – at the Solomon Islands and in the South Pacific. In order for Japan to be successful in cutting off the Allies, an invasion of Ceylon and the incursion of the Germans into the Middle East were necessary. However, the IJA, who had been told by the German military attaché that any such incursion was not possible in the near future, did not agree with the plan of a naval incursion into the Indian Ocean. At the end of June 1942, when the Germans had started their incursion into Russia and started heading towards the Caucasus and seeing the Germans' superior strength, Japanese military commanders anticipated that the Caucasus would be seized by the end of 1942. The Germans were then expected to enter the area between Suez and western Asia in the spring of 1943.[9] In response to the entrance into Africa of the German army at the end of June 1942, plans were drawn up for the reassembling of the IJN Fleet and an attack on targets in the Indian Ocean. With regard to German entry into North Africa, Admiral Nagano Osami, who had pressed for the ending of the FS strategy, remarked: 'We must prepare for the possibility that the Axis Powers will remain undefeated'. He also said that it would be advantageous to co-operate with Germans in a strategy against the western Indian Ocean. This combined forces' strategy was to use submarines and naval force to seize a huge area from Ceylon to Chagos, almost as far as Madagascar. However, because of the American attack on Guadalcanal, the opportunity to implement this plan was lost.[10]

The construction of an independent India and Burma

The southern sphere of influence and construction in Burma

The invasion of Burma had a strong significance for the IJA. It not only cut off the supply route between Rangoon and Kunming for the Chiang government in China, but also advanced the effort to separate India from British control. The initial intention was for this operation to cease when the IJA had taken control of the air bases in the south of the country, the focus of the Japanese attack being centred on Malaya and the Philippines. However, the IJA continued to put the Burma Operation before all others, believing that this would hasten India's separation from the rest of the British Empire. Before the start of the operation, the IJN had been most enthusiastic accumulators of intelligence about Burma. Central to this intelligence operation was Mr Kokubu Shozo, who had lived for some considerable time in Burma. At the request of the IJN, Kokubu had contacted members of the independence movement, proposing that young Burmese should start military training and start a revolt under the banner of freedom and independence. This was proposed to the government in the form of 'The Burma Independence Plan'.[11]

In the second half of 1940 the Army, which had no information about

Burma, sent Lieutenant Suzuki Keishi as part of their intelligence operation. And in January 1941, due to the work of Kokubu, the Army and Navy worked jointly to establish an operational unit, the *Minami Kikan* in Bangkok. Members of the *Minami Kikan* were assisted in entering Burma by Burmese patriots, who were a section of the Thakin Party, and they began to incite revolt in many different places throughout the country. At the beginning of the war, the 15th Army had occupied Bangkok and had created the Burmese Independence Army, which was one of the basic elements in the plan of establishing independent government in the south.

Once the 15th Army had completed its preparations in Bangkok, it entered and seized Moulmein in southern Burma, which was the main area of support for the independence movement. However, this strategy was soon to change to that of occupying the whole of Burma. The Army General Staff wanted to see supplies to China (the Chiang government) cut off and the removal of British influence by, at the earliest, the end of 1941. It proposed invading the main part of Burma, from central Mandalay to the western town of Akyab, using intelligence gathered from the southern control post.[12] The Southern and 15th Army were puzzled by this instruction, but started operations on 17 February, and captured Rangoon on 8 March. Even though the area of this Southern Strategy had increased, there was to be no change in the policy towards independence, and some efforts to further this policy continued. However, the military commanders became increasingly passive about the promotion of Burmese independence, and much more active in the direction of a continuance of military occupation.[13]

The occupation of Rangoon thus had to advance in two possible ways: the installation of a military government (that is the IJA) or the promotion of independence. Lieutenant Suzuki pushed for this independence, but it was rejected by the Southern Army. Then Lieutenant Suzuki, under his Burmese name of Bo Mojo, proclaimed the establishment of the *Baho*, or central government. However, on 15 March, the 15th Army announced that there would be no independent government in Burma until after the war.[14] On 3 June, the military government and the Southern command announced the dissolution of the Independence Army, and Lt. Suzuki left Burma, with the patriot troops being absorbed into Burma's national army.

Fujiwara and the India strategy

After the surrender of Singapore, Hong Kong, Malaya, Java, Shanghai and the Philippines, the independence movement amongst Indians living in Asia gathered strength. There were even some sympathizers amongst those who had been taken prisoner by the Japanese. The person responsible for focusing this movement was Lt. Col. Fujiwara Iwaichi. In addition, from the summer of 1941, Japanese military intelligence had started working with the India Independence League, a secret society that was aimed at Indians living in Asia, and co-operation commenced in operations against the British.

Under the orders of Gen. Sugiyama Hajime, the Chief of the Army General Staff, Fujiwara entered Thailand, and using a base in Bangkok that had been created by the military attaché Colonel Tamura Hiroshi, the anti-British movement among Indians living in Asia was organized.

At that time it was deemed necessary to win over Indians involved in the fighting in Malaya, and guide them towards co-operating in the anti-British movement.[15] Mohan Singh, the leader of the anti-British movement among surrendering soldiers, used this co-operation to boost the Indian independence movement.

Singh established the Indian National Army, which took part, as a lightly armed special operations force, in the battle for Singapore. After the surrender of Singapore, the number of soldiers in the Indian National Army quickly increased, reaching 42 000 by the end of August 1942.[16] Following this progress, Fujiwara was ordered to expand his area of operation and with this in mind Colonel Iwakuro Hideo was based in Saigon from the end of April 1943. Iwakuro was in charge of more than 250 people who were involved in producing propaganda for Indians, and he was also responsible for the infiltration of 'patriots' into India, and the strengthening of the Indian National Army. Iwakuro held an independence movement conference in Bangkok in the middle of June 1942, attended by the leaders of the movement and of the Indian National Army, some 110 people. This conference recognized the formation of a formal independence movement, and chose Bihari Bose as its supreme commander.[17]

Bihari Bose, also appointed as the Japanese representative of the Indian Independence League, and who worked as an intermediary with the IJA, was someone who the Japanese heavily relied upon. The main decision reached at the conference in Bangkok was the acceptance of the Indian National Army as part of the Axis Powers, but it also included some statements which were not so readily accepted by the Japanese. These called for the liberation of Indian territory and the drawing up in future of a new constitution. However, the meeting also made clear its anti-British stance, making the political factions at the conference 'the sole political entity which represents the real Indian People' with Japan pressing for these groups to recognize the Japanese-backed independence movement. The conference also pushed for the return of Chandra Bose, who was now in Germany, and asked Japan for assistance in this.[18] Chandra Bose, who had become increasingly disillusioned by Hitler's passive attitude to Indian independence, also felt that he wanted to return to Asia and take part in the fight against the British.[19] However, the Japanese government also adopted a passive approach to the question of Indian independence. The main reason for this was that there was still uncertainty about the path the Indian Independence League and the National Congress would take in the future.

This failure to respond on the part of the Japanese only heightened Indian doubts about Japanese plans for the future of their country. Chandra Bose had petitioned the Axis Powers for aid with Indian independence before the start of the Pacific War. He had proposed the formation of a joint Axis/Indian army which would enter India, and had also formulated proposals regarding the formation of a provisional government.[20]

In Japan, military leaders and the Foreign Ministry put forward their proposals for a joint declaration of the Axis Powers regarding Arabia. However, the Germans were far from enthusiastic about these policies. Hitler felt that this would make the any future compromise with the British quite impossible. What Germany wanted from Japan was not help with the situation in the Middle East but for them to attack the Soviets. On 25 July the Japanese government decided to refuse this request.[21]

The 21st Operation and the setback in India

The anti-British movement and Burma strategy that were reaching their peak in summer 1942 revived interest in the idea of an invasion of eastern India. At the beginning of August, the Southern Army submitted a proposal for an invasion of eastern Assam to military headquarters. The objective of this was to cut off the air supply route to China, to nip any British counter-offensive in the bud, and to cut India off from Britain.

The military commanders then ordered the Southern Army to prepare for what they called 'the 21st Operation'. In August 1942, in response to this move Iwakuro indicated that in order to remove the British from India, more work was needed on creating an anti-British movement which would work in tandem with any invasion. Fujiwara also tried to avoid the use of military force by allowing the Indian National Army to take part in the invasion.[22] Iwakuro's efforts to help India now became subordinated to the overall strategy against India. Eventually the whole 21st strategy was abandoned due to the needs of the operations in the Solomon Islands (South Pacific) at the beginning of August. This was the genesis of the Imphal strategy. Now that Japan was committed to a policy of Indian invasion, military intelligence observed that an armed invasion might actually turn the National Congress in India against the Japanese.[23] Despite this, Iwakuro tried to control the independence movement by military force. Mohan Singh stated that he had been given little encouragement at the Bangkok conference when he had asked for a guarantee of Japanese support.[24] After this, Singh was relieved of his position, pushing the Independence movement and the Indian National Army to the verge of collapse. The only way forward now seemed to be to wait for the return of Chandra Bose from Germany.

Allied retaliation and the CBI (China–Burma–India) theatre

Withdrawal from Guadalcanal

MacArthur, when he was in Australia after the Battle of Midway, proposed that the Allies take advantage of the success at Midway by means of a surprise attack on the Bismark Islands and Rabaul. The US Navy, however, preferred a slower stepwise operation and the result of the disagreement was the formulation of an attack plan in which Rabaul was to be taken via a slow, stepped northern advance. Nimitz regarded the recently commenced Japanese efforts to build an aerodrome on Guadalcanal in the Solomon Islands as a serious threat to Australian–US communication lines. He thus decided to take the initiative and to launch an offensive by landing on Guadalcanal. He eventually succeeded in occupying the island in August 1942. Although the Japanese repeatedly tried to retake the island, severe degradation and losses in shipping combined with an inability to replace ships lost ensured their ultimate failure. Furthermore, the Japanese loss of mastery of the air to the USA meant that refueling transports could not operate effectively. The 30 000 Army troops stationed on Guadalcanal were forced to endure near-starvation conditions and the IJN lost many ships, aircraft and trained personnel. After six months of fighting, at the end of December 1942, the Japanese High Command decided to withdraw. After the outbreak of fighting on Guadalcanal, an Indian Ocean Strategy was put into effect but it had fewer than ten submarines and a number of German U-boats which were active in the destruction of Allied transport shipping.

After withdrawal from Guadalcanal in February 1943, the Japanese High Command formulated and completed a new strategy in March that then received the Emperor's approval.[25] While the IJA was to be primarily engaged in the war effort in Burma, the main combat arena for joint Army–Navy forces was to be that of the Southeast Pacific, focusing notably on the securing and preservation of the central and northern areas of the Solomon Islands, Lae in New Guinea, and the Samoan Islands and westward. Accordingly, the first half of 1943 saw the emergence of heavy fighting in northern New Guinea and the Solomon Islands. In the Northeast Pacific region, the US Army landed on Attu Island and until the summer, the defence line fell back to the Kurile Islands. In both of these combat areas (the Southeast Pacific and the Northeast Pacific), the preservation and maintenance of strong sea transport lines was essential for the Japanese. However, due to the many demands for shipping reinforcements, the supply thereof critically deteriorated. Although the Japanese military command had issued requests to reduce the size and concentrate the area of the war zones, the Army General Staff had been engaging in redesigning the overall war strategy. In July 1943, as a result, with an amendment to national defence policy designed to secure long-term invincibility against the US forces. The amendment stated that even if the worst came to the worst, a distinction between those regions which must be defended at all costs and those which could be sacrificed must be established.

At an Imperial Conference convened in September in the presence of the Emperor to decide the 'General Outlines of the War Guidance' as a new national defence policy, it was decided that the Kuriles, Ogasawara,

Micronesia, Western New Guinea, Sunda and Burma were to be classified as territories that must be held at all costs. One of the reasons why establishment of these territories was considered essential was that the Imperial Headquarters (the Army and Navy General Staffs) had determined that the Allied counter-offensive was to begin in the second half of 1943. However, they were not sure whether the offensive was to take place in the Pacific or in the Indian Ocean areas. Furthermore, after the surrender of Italy in September, the following were considered as being possibilities: diversion of the British Fleet in the Mediterranean to Asia; landing and offensive advance of British forces in India and Burma and a joint British–US attack on Sumatra, Andaman and Nicobar Islands. The Combined Fleet Command of the IJN gave warning on 15 August of the strategies that the Japanese could carry out in the Pacific (Plan Z) and on 15 September, those in the Indian Ocean (Plan Y). The Japanese Navy had never given any thought to the idea of creating a defence line composed of aligned strongholds and, accordingly, could not adjust to the new directive concerning territories that must be defended at all costs. In particular, despite the existence of this directive, Commander Koga Mineichi obstinately clung to the notion of an all-ensuing naval battle as envisaged by Plan Z.

By October, the Combined Fleet Command thought that due to the location of the US aircraft carriers and to various pieces of intelligence that they had received, the likelihood of Plan Z being put into operation was quite high. They therefore deployed the major part of the fleet into the Wake Island area, reduced Japanese potential fighting ability by moving air force troops into the Rabaul area and engaged the enemy in the Bougainville Island naval battle with the result that when the Americans came to attack the Gilbert and Marshall Islands, the Japanese could not be put Plan Z into operation.[26]

At the Quebec Conference held in August 1943, the heads of the Allied governments approved the war strategy formulated by the Allied High Command. This strategy sought to liberate the Philippines and included two routes of attack: (i) the northward route from northern New Guinea, under Macarthur's control; and (ii) the westward route from the central Pacific via Saipan and Palau, under Nimitz's control. Essential to the successful operation of the latter route was the manufacture of the long-range B-29 bombers and, the air force having to provision the Mariana Islands so as to allow bombing raids on China, eastern India and the main islands of Japan. The Americans pushed west from the Marshall and other islands and in February 1944, made a surprise attack on the largest Japanese naval base, Truk, which paralysed its operations. In New Guinea, MacArthur pushed west up along the north coastline, isolated the Japanese bases and by the end of May, had made a landing on Biak Island, one of the territories that the Japanese military decided had to be held at all costs.

After occupying the Marshalls, the US Joint Chiefs of Staff decided to abandon the Truk Islands strategy and to directly attack the Marianas. Admiral Spruance of the 5th Fleet devised the Marianas Plan which called for a large fleet including seven aircraft carriers to be mobilized, air corridors between Japan and the Caroline Islands and New Guinea to be cut off, a submarine base to cut off transport shipping lanes between Japan and the Dutch East Indies and, finally, acquisition of a B-29 air base.

After the raid on Truk Island, the Imperial Headquarters decided to increase the Army–Navy forces designated to defend Saipan in the Marianas, the most important of the territories which had to be defended and, in early May 1944, it ordered the execution of Plan A which involved annihilating the main fighting potential of the attacking US Navy, most of which would be concentrated in the fleet. After heavy offshore bombardment, the Americans commenced the landing on Saipan on 15 June, and finally occupied it on 7 July after a battle that claimed 39 000 lives. The fall of Saipan meant that the policy of territories that must be defended was now rendered inoperable and also that the Japanese mainland was now within reach of B-29 bombers. In Japan, the loss of Saipan resulted in the collapse of the Tojo Cabinet.

The CBI theatre and Burmese independence

At the Casablanca Conference in January 1943, the Allied Powers decided to take back Burma and to resume ground communications with China. In the Quebec Conference held in August of the same year, it was decided that Chinese forces would advance into Burma from Yunnan, and that the British would attack from Karewa from the Ledo road and head to Mandalay. Around the end of 1943 a landing would be effected on the southwest coast and Rangoon itself would be directly attacked. The USA favoured an attack from the north of Burma, a policy particularly advanced by General Stillwell who was stationed in China and who had been engaging in transporting Chinese troops to India and carrying out their equipping and training in Assam in accordance with US methods. The British countered by demanding that the Americans should head towards Singapore and effect its relief rather than attacking Burma. In the resulting British–US strategy stalemate, Stilwell took the initiative, attacking the north of Burma in October 1943. Meanwhile British and Indian forces were concentrating troops in Imphal and Akyab and the Chinese-controlled Burma Invasion Force attacked North-east Burma from Yunnan.

The Japanese Imperial Headquarters decided that it was mainly the job of the Imperial Army to repel these Allied counter-offensive attacks on Burma. In March 1943, the Japanese Army was reorganized so as to tighten its defence of Burma. Immediately prior to taking up the post of commander of the Japanese occupying army, Lieutenant-General Kawabe Shozo had an interview with Tojo. In the course of this, in addition to being told to prepare for Burmese independence, he was also instructed that 'the foreign policy for Burma is no more than the precursor of that for India and all the important objectives could be left to India'.[27] The 5th Army Commander Mutaguchi Renya, under the control of Kawabe, determined that it would be impossible to defend Burma in a war on many fronts against the powerful Allied offensives and that a surprise attack on the resistance movement centred on Imphal should take precedence. He thought that, in view of their limited equipment and firepower, rather than fighting on the flat plains of the central region, it would be better to remain in the hilly and thickly forested areas. Due to the difficulty in maintaining supplies, the Southern and Burmese District armies' efforts were initially sporadic. However, because Kawabe did not have any specific strategy for defending Burma, he slowly conceded the virtue of his subordinate's way of thinking. In August 1943, the Imperial Headquarters ordered the Burmese District Army to make preparations for the Imphal strategy which was to start early in the new year. At the same time, the Tojo Cabinet declared Burma independent under Prime Minister Ba Maw. One of the objectives of adopting the policy of an independent Burma was to promote the destabilization of the Indian subcontinent.

Imphal strategy and Indian independence

In May 1943, Chandra Bose, who had come to Asia from Germany by submarine, advocated an anti-British war effort by reorganizing the Indian National Army. To that end he requested Japanese assistance. Immediately prior to the Great East Asian Conference in November 1943, the Japanese government officially recognized the Provisional Government of Free India under Bose and granted them two island chains occupied by Japan: the Andamans and the Nicobars. The Japanese General Staff devised the *Hikari Kikan* to be under the control of the Southern District Army and to be used against British India. However, the purpose was not to assist the independence movement but rather as a means to further their own Indian campaign. The enthusiasm of the Japanese Army for an independent India as envisaged by the *Fujiwara Kikan* at the beginning of the war had largely evaporated and had now been replaced by the view that the removal of the British could only be achieved by military occupation of the subcontinent.[28]

After the Great East Asian Conference, Bose informed the Japanese government and military that the Hikari Plan was a severe hindrance to the operation of his provisional government and the Indian National Army and was, furthermore, an obstruction to the independence movement. He therefore demanded of the Japanese government that the *Hikari Kikan* be abolished or be radically reformed as a diplomatic organization under the Foreign Ministry, but the military rejected his requests. In January 1944, the Imphal strategy was set in motion. The 31st Division crossed the Chindwin River in March, crossed the mountainous border into India and in early March it occupied Kohima, the vital crossing to India. This occupation stirred the Japanese nation and the 31st Division received high praise from the Emperor. The 33rd and 15th Divisions, on the left flank and centre respectively, had made preparations by 10 April to surround Imphal and the implementation of the strategy was expected to be highly successful. The British-Indian Army, however, had urgently airlifted troop reinforcements and supplies and had accordingly created solid defences on the outskirts of Imphal. With very powerful forces at their disposal they commenced an attack to retake the Kohima crossing.

The lightly provisioned 15th Division, lacking food and ammunition, could not defeat the British who won due to the linked support and communications between the army and air force units. Brigadier Wingate was a supporter of the Chindit strategy, which maintained that infantry units would win battles in India provided that they had sufficient air support. This was put into practice in this case and Wingate was proved correct. It could certainly be said that the Japanese strategies were poorly reorganized until plans incorporating airlifting of large armies to reinforce ground troops were instigated. On 17 August, Commander Mutaguchi ordered Sato Yukinori, the leader of the 31st Division, into a general attack on Imphal. However, based solely on his own judgment Yukinori, at the end of May, ordered a withdrawal in order to avoid total annihilation of his division. When the strategy was originally formulated, it had been the intention to reinforce the 31st with five motorized companies, but only 20–30 jeeps and some ammunition had actually been delivered between the end of April and the end of May. The Burmese District Army, by reinforcing the 33rd Division and by appointing a new commander, expected it to be successful in its attack on Imphal. But the troops were thoroughly exhausted by this stage and only managed to reach the Tollbon area. On 22 June, the Kohima–Imphal road was taken by the Allies and on 1 July, the Imperial Headquarters ordered the Imphal Strategy to be suspended. A total of 7000 Indian National Army troops were engaged in the Imphal battle and although the Provisional Government of Free India had been promised control of British India, defeat in the battle ensured that this was never realised.

In north Burma, the Allied forces under Stilwell fought against the Japanese 33rd Army (18th and 56th Divisions) and the Chinese Army made sporadic advances in an effort to open ground communications from Ledo to China. The 18th fell back from Namhkan to Kamain and, at the end of June, the supreme commander of the Burmese District Army decided to pull out of north Burma. Leaving behind units to defend Myitkyina, the 18th withdrew back to the region bordering India. At the strategic crossroads of Myitkyina, these defence units and the Allied forces engaged in particularly severe fighting before the former capitulated in early August. In early May, the Chinese Army, which had been trained by the Americans and was therefore quite different to and much stronger than conventional Chinese forces, commenced a full repulsion of Japanese forces in the Yunnan region.

Fighting against the Japanese 56th Division, there was a continual series of 'one step forward, one step backward' encounters. By November 1944, the Allies had liberated all south of the line from Myitkyina to Yunnan. However the 33rd Division continued to fight in the Namhkan region to block off the road linking China and India, but fell back to Senui in February 1945, thus liberating the road that had been under Japanese blockade since May 1942.

In September 1944, the Southern District Army in Burma ordered that the primary objective of the 15th Division (that had now withdrawn from Imphal) was to hold southern Burma (south of Lashio on the banks of the Irrawaddy River, Mandalay and Enanjon). However, with the British-Indian Army crossing the Irrawaddy in January 1945, the Japanese urgently revised their strategy which involved tanks and heavy artillery. The 28th Army, assisted by the Indian People's Army, threw all their effort into the fight which took place on the banks of the Irrawaddy. At the end of February, the British seized the Meiktila airfield thus bringing the 15th Division to its knees. In addition, riots erupted in the district under control of the 28th Army led by the Burmese People's Army. In May, British tanks and the British–Indian Army which had landed from Akyab, seized and occupied Rangoon. Finally, Bose renounced his intention to march on India from Burma, and he attempted to flee and join the Russian-backed freedom movement active in the north of India, ignoring demands from Japanese Headquarters to concentrate his forces for an all-out push against the Indian mainland. From 1942 until total withdrawal, a total of 160300 Japanese troops lost their lives in Burma.[29]

The final battle for the Philippines and Okinawa

Defeat at Leyte and its impact

After the loss of Saipan, the Japanese Imperial Headquarters withdrew the defence line to the Kuriles, the mainland of Japan, Okinawa and the Philippines and its essential function (referred to as the Sho-go Strategies) became to repel any US forces which encroached thereupon. The defence of the Philippines, Okinawa and Taiwan, the mainland of Japan (including Hokkaido) and the Kuriles were given names of Sho-1, Sho-2, Sho-3 and Sho-4 respectively but it was Sho-1 (Philippines) that was particularly seen as being the most critical. The government and the military both agreed that the best course of action was to quickly overcome the Americans in the Philippines. Then, under these favourable conditions, they would attempt to conclude a peace treaty.

On 7 October, the Americans landed on Suluwan Island in the mouth of Leyte Bay and, on the same day, Imperial Headquarters ordered the V1 strategy to be put into operation. As a result, part of the Fleet that was damaged in the Taiwan fiasco was sent into the attack. The conditions that met MacArthur on Leyte were excellent. General Yamashita, who was chosen to be commander in charge of the 14th District Army, decided to have the decisive land battle on Luzon Island but Imperial Headquarters changed this to Leyte. On 20 October, the Americans commenced their landing on Leyte Island and the Allied Fleet estimated that they could storm Leyte Bay quickly, but they were hindered by the presence of motorized divisions and submarines. The IJN lost a total of 30 ships in the battle of Leyte, including aircraft carriers and battleships, and were almost annihilated. The landing was greatly assisted by guerrilla informants and guerrilla attacks against the Japanese. After the landing, the guerrillas came under the command of the Americans and were invaluable in blocking Japanese supply routes and communication networks and also in taking part in reconnaissance missions.

When the Americans landed at Lingayen Bay on Luzon Island, Imperial Headquarters, wishing to avoid a decisive battle, opted for a long-drawn-out war. However, due to the overwhelming firepower of the Americans plus resistance by the Philippine guerrilla activities, 300 000 Japanese troops were dispersed in the hills.

In the autumn of 1944, comprehensive studies carried out in the War Ministry determined that the war in the Philippines had been lost and it predicted that if Japan was to surrender to the Allies, the Americans would advance into Japan, the armed forces would lay down their arms, the Emperor system would be abolished, a democratic style of government would be enforced, and Japanese nationals would be shipped out to foreign countries to work as slaves.[30] Rather than submit to such an ignominious fate, they reasoned that there was no choice but to resist all Allied efforts on the mainland. In January 1945, the Japanese Army and Navy decided to launch the 'Imperial Army–Navy Operation Plan for Defence of the Empire' which called for the destruction of the Allies in Japan and its neighbouring islands, Manchuria and China. With the power of the IJN largely crushed, the IJA decided to leave 60 divisions on the mainland for its defence and the mainland was seen as being the final war zone, with Okinawa being the curtain-raiser.

Political impact of the Okinawa battle

The US Army determined that the next objective after the Philippines was to be the islands of Iwojima and Okinawa. Iwojima was particularly valued as a base for American fighter aircraft to escort their B-29 bombers. The battle at Iwojima began in the middle of March and fighting was particularly fierce, resulting in 24 000 American deaths and casualties. At the end of March, the US forces had advanced as far as the Iwo aerodrome and the Japanese mainland was now within the range of the P-51 fighters. On 1 April, the US Fleet appeared off the west coast of Okinawa with a total power of 1400 warships and 180 000 troops. 77 000 people defended Okinawa, including

25 000 boys who had been conscripted into volunteer armies. The IJN, which had lost so many of its warships, was now largely reduced to the use of air squadrons. A special offensive strategy named *Kikusui* was launched. All aviation fuel was to be used for the special offensive, in which 2400 fighters in the *Kamikaze* squadrons were to be sent against the US forces. However, at the end of May, the Americans' use of the radar network allowed the detection and shooting down of Japanese aircraft and thus, damage to air-craft carriers and battleships was kept to a minimum. By June, the war had claimed the lives of 100 000 Japanese enlisted men (including those who had been recruited as volunteers), and a further 20 000 non-enlisted people had died as a result of the war. Following the defeat at Okinawa the policy of the Emperor, government and military changed from one of 'strike hard then surrender conditionally' to a request to 'end hostilities' which was conveyed to the Allies by the Russians.[31] However, the commissioned officers in the War Ministry still fervently believed in the peace plan after an all-out direct strike against the Allies on the mainland. This resistance movement was the greatest hindrance to the acceptances of the Potsdam Declaration of 26 July.

In the hope of ending hostilities which was conveyed by the Russians, the government had not made any comment officially regarding the Potsdam Declaration, which was still unsigned by the Russians. But it was the drop-ping of the atomic bomb on Hiroshima on 6 August and the entry of Soviet Russia into the war on 9 August that caused it to break its silence and change its allegiance from resistance and the peace followed by the Emperor's deci-sion to surrender.[32]

The surrender of Japan and the Japanese Army in South East Asia

Resistance by local armies and the Southern District Army

The Japanese armies in China and South East Asia knew the conditions attached to the Japanese acceptance of the Potsdam Declaration on 10 August. The Foreign Ministry sent an unedited announcement by Morse code which arrived faster than that sent to Allied governments by standard telegraphic message. The message was received by Japanese units abroad. However, those units which were particularly patriotic (especially those in China) did not accept the contents of the message, believing it to be an Allied ploy. In addition, in quick succession, the Southern Army in Burma, the 8th Area Army in Bangkok and the 7th Area Army in Singapore sent telegrams to the Imperial Headquarters demanding that they be allowed to continue the war.[33] These demands served to encourage retaliation against the Allies on the mainland and to encourage many of those army officers who had advocated a decisive battle on the homeland.

After the surrender, Lord Mountbatten sent a telegraphic message to the

Allied occupying forces giving list of requirements that would facilitate the ease of the surrender of the Southern Army. He called on Field-Marshal Terauchi Hisaichi to sign a formal declaration of surrender in Rangoon. Because of ill-health, Terauchi deputized a proxy with full signatory powers who requested the following conditions with respect to the Southern Army: the existing command system to remain in force until all soldiers were repatriated back to Japan; all arms to be laid down; all rights of POWs to be strictly observed and, within two years, all civilian and military Japanese nationals to leave all areas of South East Asia and be returned to Japan. The Chief of General Staff at Rangoon, General Browning, flatly refused, stating Allied demands that the Japanese surrender be unconditional. The Japanese Army had clearly shown that they would not capitulate to unacceptable demands: however, Browning made it a condition that the Japanese acceptance or rejection of demands placed upon them would not depend upon their decisions; rather, it would depend upon the will of the Allied command. With respect to the first request, the British military insisted that the Japanese command system be dismantled and that a declaration of surrender be signed in each district. However, upon strong petition by the Southern District Army that the Japanese troops would be mistreated if this demand were to be realized, the British relented. The British military accepted the other three requests and on 28 August, the Rangoon surrender was enacted (the official surrender ceremony was enacted on 12 September).

The 1 600 000 Japanese civilians and military who remained in China (not including Taiwan and Manchuria) at the time of the Japanese surrender were repatriated back to Japan by June 1946. However, this was against a background of growing strife in the various areas within China. Because the Japanese government decided to support for the reconstruction of China by the Chinese Nationalists, 30 000 Japanese remained in China after the surrender.[34] Around 10 000 remnants of the 1st Army and civilians remaining in Shanxi Province repeatedly requested to be repatriated, but were turned down by the Nationalists, under whose jurisdiction they found themselves. It is said that around 2600 former Japanese Army soldiers fought against the Communists until 1949.[35]

In South East Asia also, many former Japanese soldiers remained due to the complex regional politics. In September 1945, the British planned to advance to the west coast of the Malay Peninsula: however, this advance was opposed by the Americans who intended to directly attack the Japanese mainland. The attack was never carried out as Japan surrendered prior to this. The Allied Forces under the command of Mountbatten accepted the grounding of arms and repatriation of 740 000 troops, freed 120 000 POWs of the Japanese and internees and reinstated public order.[36] The British placed priority on the release of the POWs and internees and by May 1946, they had returned 96 000 people. Due, however, to lack of space on the transports, the repatriation of demobilized soldiers proceeded much more slowly and by the same time, only 45 000 had gone home. With US assistance, 59 000 had been returned by June that year.

The Japanese Army in post-surrender South East Asia

In accordance with the British demands, some of the Japanese troops who had laid down their arms served in security roles throughout the region. This was criticized by the Americans, who favoured their speedy return to Japan. However, after the Japanese surrender, it was deemed necessary to have small numbers of former Japanese army troops serve in policing public security in the South East Asia region. Mountbatten made maximum use of these soldiers in jobs that were ostensibly for the demands of military necessity although actually, it was for the purpose of rebuilding the colonies.[37] In addition to engineering and agricultural works, they were useful in preventing strikes in times of labour disputes. In Indochina, the French military used armed former Japanese soldiers to keep civil peace during France's conflict with the Republic of Vietnam.[38] The Vietnamese who were trying to establish the Republic of Vietnam had good relations with officials from the Japanese government as a reasonable number of Japanese served as volunteers and fought against the French. Even in Indonesia which had announced its independence on 17 August, when the British and Dutch returned in September, armed Japanese were being used for civil security. When Mountbatten stepped down in May 1946, there was a total of 64 000 armed Japanese security workers throughout South East Asia, of which 38 000 were in Sumatra and Java. Around 25 000 former troops, having left the employ of SE Asian armies, sided with the nationalists and became involved in fighting the war for Indonesian independence.[39]

Notes

1. Shiryo Chosa-kai (ed.), *Taiheiyo senso to Tomioka Sadatoshi* (Gunji Kenkyu-sha, 1972), pp. 175–7; Boei Kenshujo Senshibu, *Daihon-ei Rikugunbu, Daitoa Senso Kaisen Keii*, vol. 5 (Asagumo Shinbunsha, 1974), pp. 297–311.
2. *Ishii Akiho Taisa Kaisoroku* (1956), deposited in the War History Office, National Institute for Defense Studies in Tokyo (hereafter NIDS).
3. 'Tai-Bei/Ei/Ran Senso no baai ni okeru Teikoku no Tai-Shi Hosaku', 10 November 1941, deposited in the Diplomatic Record Office in Tokyo, A1-1-0-30-33 (hereafter DRO).
4. On Japan acting as an intermediary and negotiating peace between Russians and Germans, see Ohki Tsuyoshi 'Doku-So Wahei kosaku o meguru Gunzo' Kindai Nihon Kenkyu-kai (ed.), *Nenpo Kindai Nihon Kenkyu 17* (Yamakawa Shuppan-sha, 1995); Ohki, 'Dokuso Wahei Mondai to Nihon', in Hosoya Chihiro et al. (eds), *Taiheiyo Senso no Shuketsu* (Kashiwa Shobo, 1998), pp. 51–70.
5. Ikeda Kiyoshi, 'Nihon no Tai-ei senryaku to Taiheiyo senso', in Hosoya Chihiro (ed.), *Nichi-Ei kankeishi, 1917–1949* (Tokyo Daigaku Shuppankai, 1982), pp. 89–90.

6. Please refer to Tohmatsu's chapter 11.
7. Sambo Honbu (the Army General Staff) (ed.), *Sugiyama Memo*, vol. 1 (Hara Shobo, 1976), pp. 523–4.
8. Hirama Yoichi, 'Dainiji Taisen-chu no Nichi-Doku Kaigun Sakusen: No. 2, Nihon Kaigun no Indo-yo Sakusen', *Boei Daigakko Kiyo* (Journal of the National Defense Academy in Japan), vol. 63, no. 9 (1991).
9. '*Tanaka Shinichi Chujo Kaisoroku*' (1956), NIDS.
10. Boei Kenshujo Senshishitsu, *Daihonei Kaigunbu/Rengo Kantai, 2* (Asagumo Shimbunsho, 1970), pp. 55–60; Nihon Kaigun Sensuikan-shi Henshu-iinkai (ed.), *Nihon Kaigun Sensuikan-shi* (Tokyo, 1979).
11. Ohta Hiroki, 'Biruma no Dokuritsu Undo to Kokubu Shozo', *Kagoshima Daigaku, Shiroku*, vol. 19, no. 3 (1987).
12. Boeicho Boei Kenshusho Senshishitsu, *Biruma Koryaku Sakusen* (Asagumo Shinbunsha, 1967), p. 72.
13. Ishii Akiho, 'Nampo Gunsei Nikki', NIDS.
14. Ibid. and *Biruma Koryaku Sakusen*, pp. 445–51.
15. Nagasaki Nobuko, 'Indo Kokumingun no Keisei', in Nagasaki Nobuko (ed.), *Minami Ajia no Minzoku Undo to Nihon* (Ajia Keizai Kenkyujo, 1980), pp. 13–19.
16. Ibid., pp. 20–8; Fujiwara Iwaichi, *Fujiwara Kikan* (Hara Shobo, 1966), pp. 183–4.
17. Gunji Shigakkai (ed.), *Kimitsu Senso Nisshi*, vol. 1 (Kinseisha, 1998), entry for 17 June 1942.
18. Nagasaki, 'Indo Kokumingun no Keisei', pp. 38–43; Milan Hauner, *India in the Axis Strategy: Germany, Japan and Indian Nationalists in the Second World War* (Stuttgart: Klett-Cotta, 1981), pp. 490–3.
19. Hauner, *India in the Axis Strategy*, pp. 486–90; *Sugiyama Memo*, vol. 2, pp. 137–8.
20. Hauner, *India in the Axis Strategy*, chapters 3 and 4.
21. Hatano Sumio, *Taiheiyo senso to Ajia Gaiko* (Tokyo Daigaku Shuppankai, 1996), pp. 40–1; Hauner, *India in the Axis Strategy*, pp. 476–504; *Sugiyama Memo*, pp. 137–8.
22. 'Tai-In Shisaku ni kansuru iken', 15 September 1942, *Ishii Shiryo*, No. 2, NIDS.
23. Boei Kenshusho Senshishitsu, *Daihonei Rikugunbu*, vol. 5 (Asagumo Shinbunsha, 1973), pp. 69–72; Hauner, *India in the Axis Strategy*, p. 597.
24. Hauner, *India in the Axis Strategy*, p. 597.
25. For details, see Nomura Minoru's 'Taiheiyo senso no Nihon no Senso Shido', Kindai Nihon Kenkyukai, *Kindai Nihon Kenkyu*, vol. 4, *Taiheiyo Senso, Vol. 4, The Pacific War* (Yamakawa Shuppansha, 1982), p. 39.
26. Boei Kenshusho Senshishitsu, *Daihonei Kaigunbu Rengo Kantai*, vol. 4 (Asagumo Shinbunsha, 1970), pp. 451–9.
27. 'Kawabe Nikki Sho', 22 March 1943, NIDS.
28. *Kimitsu Senso Nisshi*, entry 23 December 1943.
29. The total dead of 163 000 is based on Boei Kenkyusho materials. According to Louis Allen, the war dead of British Forces was estimated at 71 200 compared to 106 100 Japanese; Louis Allen, *Burma: the Longest War* (London: Dent, 1984).
30. Rikugunsho Gunjika, 'Saiaku Jittai ni shosuru Kokubo Ippan no Kenkyu', 25 September 1944, *Kokubo Taiko kankei Juyo shorui*, NIDS.
31. Takagi Sokichi Shiryo, NIDS.
32. Asada Sadao, 'Genbaku Toka no Shogeki to Kofuku no Kettei', *Taiheiyo Senso no Shuketsu*, pp. 195–222.
33. Kouseisho Engokyoku Shiryoshitsu, 'Shusen no Keii' (Details of the End of the War) (1946), pp. 146–8.

34. 'Wahei Chokugo no Tai-Shi Shori Hoshin, 18 August 1945', *Gendai-Shi Shiryo*, vol. 38 (Misuzu Shobo, 1973).

35. Eto Jun (ed.), *Senryo Shiroku*, vol. 2 (Kodansha, 1995), pp. 566–73.

36. From 14 August 1945 the jurisdictional area of the Supreme Commander South East Asia covered the whole of South East Asia, with the exception of the Philippines.

37. Peter Dennis, *Troubled Days of Peace: Mountbatten and South-East Asia Command, 1945–46*. (Manchester: Manchester University Press, 1987), pp. 89–162 and 226–7.

38. Kibata Yoichi, 'Youroppa kara mita Ajia Taiheiyo Senso', in Nakamura Masanori et al. (eds), *Sengo Nihon – Senryo to Sengo Kaikaku*, vol. 1: *Sekaishi no naka no 1945 nen* (Iwanami Shoten, 1995), pp. 81–92.

39. Dennis, *Troubled Days of Peace*, p. 227.

14

British Assessments of Japanese Naval Tactics and Strategy, 1941–1945

Philip Charrier

The sinking of the *Prince of Wales* and *Repulse* on 8 December 1941 by bomber aircraft of the IJN, a prelude to the loss of Singapore two months later, saw the RN humiliated by a competitor it had underrated for several decades. Since the turn of the century successive British governments and the Naval Staff had struggled to retain a dominant position for the RN in the Far East in the context of the emergence of Japan as a major sea power. However, alliance politics, arms limitation diplomacy and the adoption of new strategies could not overcome the twin problems of expanding global responsibilities and shrinking budgets.[1] More than just a strategic failure, the disaster at Singapore revealed that Britain's relative power in Far Eastern waters had faded since the glory days of the nineteenth century.

For the remainder of the war the Royal Navy almost ceased conceptualizing itself as a force with Far Eastern interests and capabilities. Between 1942 and mid-1944 Admiralty planners carried out no systematic analyses of the Japanese enemy, and reports and comments on Japanese naval tactics and equipment were sporadic and brief. Since the outbreak of war in Europe in 1939, necessity had driven the service to concentrate upon anti-submarine warfare in the Atlantic, and it could but weakly fly the flag in other areas. With Pearl Harbor and American entry into the war, it became possible to leave the problem of the Imperial Japanese Navy to the Americans. Only in the autumn of 1944, following Winston Churchill's decision to commit the main fleet to the Pacific, did the Naval Staff again take serious interest in Japanese naval activity and capability. But by then the war was into its final year.

However, for those Royal Navy officers who were stationed in the Indian Ocean and the Pacific between 1942 and 1945, Singapore and Pearl Harbor did not produce the same change of perspective that it did in London. From an Asian vantage point, the Imperial Japanese Navy remained not only the principal obstacle to the reassertion of British power in the Far East, but also a bitter enemy whose acts of aggression against British vessels and territory needed to be avenged. The reports they filed on Japanese naval tactics and technology, though small in number in the context of British naval records for the Second World War, are worthy of attention for two reasons. First, they show an appreciation of the resourcefulness of the Japanese enemy and the sophistication of his combat capability that had been absent in earlier estimates of Japanese naval power. Second, they highlight the increasing technological focus of Royal Navy during the Second World War in the assessment of other navies.

Japanese naval aviation, 1942: superior training, superior weapons

During the inter-war period there had been considerable debate within the British military establishment as to whether aircraft would develop sufficient range and striking power to pose a serious threat to capital ships on the high seas. The devastating Japanese attack on Force Z (during which the *Prince of Wales* and the *Repulse* were sunk within two hours of the start of the attack) demonstrated not only that aircraft had become a highly effective offensive naval weapon at sea, but that the Japanese had developed this weapon beyond all expectations. In the first half of 1942, the British were faced with a serious situation in the Indian Ocean, leading Admiralty leaders to appreciate the full power of the Japanese carrier striking force and dispel the myth that the Japanese were unable to make good aircraft or produce skilled fighter pilots.[2] The loss of Singapore placed the ports and naval bases of India and Ceylon within easy range of the Japanese Fleet. A 'new' Eastern Fleet based in Trincomalee had been hastily created after the fall of Singapore to defend British interests in the Indian Ocean. But this command consisted of a jumble of mostly antiquated ships and aircraft, and was inadequate for the task.[3] Indeed, on 3 April 1942, a large naval force led by Admiral Nagumo Chuichi entered the Indian Ocean and in a period of nine days inflicted serious naval losses upon the British. These consisted of the bombing of Colombo and Trincomalee, the sinking of the heavy cruisers *Dorsetshire* and *Cornwall* and the light carrier *Hermes*, and the sinking of 23 merchant vessels. Much of the devastation was carried out by Japanese carrier-borne aircraft, and the skills of their pilots and the performance of the aircraft led naval leaders in the theatre to be overawed by the force and precision of the IJN's air arm. Admiral Sir James Somerville, the C-in-C of the Eastern Fleet, concentrated on the disparity of the British and Japanese equipment, judging the British planes at his disposal to be no match for their Japanese counterparts.[4] The captain of the *Dorsetshire* was impressed with the skill with which the Japanese naval airmen overcame British anti-aircraft defences. He reported that the 'dive bombers came down out of the sun making anti-aircraft defence difficult' and in addition flew down 'from rightahead, which is the ship's blind spot for A.A. defence'.[5] Captain A.J.S. Crockett of the light carrier *Hermes* was even more impressed with the efficiency of the pilots. He said that the attack on his ship 'was carried out perfectly, relentlessly and quite fearlessly, and was exactly like a highly organised deck display'.[6] The report by the Air Staff in Ceylon on the aerial bombardment of Trincomalee left no doubt that Japanese pilots were determined, tactically-minded and masters of their superior machines. Like Captain Crockett, the air experts in Ceylon reported that the bombing 'was extremely accurate, and the pattern very close' and that the Japanese pilots were courageous and highly disciplined, pressing home their attacks even 'when closely engaged by heavy anti-aircraft fire'.[7] The reports made it clear that the British aircraft sent up to defend Colombo and Trincomalee had been heavily outnumbered by Japanese aircraft; nevertheless, the overwhelming success of Admiral Nagumo's raid caused much consternation in London about the possible superiority of Japanese tactics and equipment and the effect of this on morale within the Eastern Fleet. The reports on the sinking of the *Dorsetshire*, *Cornwall* and *Hermes* suggested that Japanese dive bombers could dive more steeply than other known aircraft of the same type, could release their bombs later in the dive, and carried bombs that possessed 'special damaging powers'. After much analysis of the reports, it was decided that none of this was in fact true. The bare facts were that the Japanese pilots were 'highly trained' and that the devastation they caused was the result of being able to score large numbers of hits on their targets in a very short time.[8]

Shortly after these reports were received, the pressure on the Indian Ocean eased with the successful American counter-attack in the Pacific. British naval planners recognized that the Battle of Midway had direct consequences upon the IJN's ambitions in the Indian Ocean. In a report on the strategic requirements for Indian Ocean bases prepared in February 1943, the Director of Plans argued that it was pointless to expend resources on strengthening naval facilities in the Indian Ocean when the 'possibility of the Japanese gaining naval superiority over the Americans is considered to be remote'.[9] In addition, in late 1942 and early 1943 US Navy reports on the Japanese air attacks that formed part of the first big carrier-to-carrier encounters in the Pacific in 1942 began to undermine the aura of invincibility that surrounded the naval wing of the IJN. The Admiralty also received first-hand reports of this kind from British naval officers who acted as observers on American ships. Lieutenant H.A.I. Luard, for example, was on attachment to the US Pacific Fleet and witnessed the Battle of Santa Cruz from on board the USS *Hornet*. Despite the fact that the *Hornet* was sunk during that campaign, Luard painted a picture of Japanese aircraft being effectively blocked from carrying out their missions by US defensive fighters and anti-aircraft fire, and suggested that IJN aircraft and their pilots were being sacrificed in far larger numbers than American ones. More specifically, Luard indicated that though the Japanese aircraft were fast and manoeuvrable, they and their pilots were poorly protected against enemy fire. He wrote: 'The Japanese aircraft appeared very light and vulnerable. They have a high proportion of magnesium in their alloy and no armoured protection for they burnt easily.'[10] In September 1943 Commander B. Wilson, who was attached to Western Sea Frontier, noted that new US Navy fighters like the F4U Corsair and the F6F Hellcat were becoming increasingly heavy and powerful in comparison with the Japanese Zero.[11] By late 1943, even a civilian like Sir Robert Craigie noted 'the rather poor showing of the Japanese air forces in the S.W. Pacific when operating against American warships possessing full fighter cover'.[12]

Japanese torpedoes and submarines, 1942–45: sophisticated weapons, unconventional tactics

In the first years after the Japanese entry into the Second World War, British interest in Japanese torpedoes and submarines was slight compared with its interest in comparable German weapons. The Japanese used their submarine fleet fairly effectively against merchant shipping in the Indian Ocean; but the scale of the problem was small compared to the serious threat posed to the British war effort by German 'wolf pack' attacks in the Atlantic. Not until 1944, when the British Fleet was being prepared for engagement in the Pacific War, did the Naval Staff take an interest in Japan's submarines and torpedo-attack tactics. By that time the IJN's offensive capability had been greatly weakened, and the effectiveness of such secret weapons as the Type-93 'long lance' torpedo and the midget submarine had been neutralized by more significant American developments such as fire control radar and high-resolution surface search radar. Nevertheless, because of the RN's anti-submarine emphasis during the Second World War, Japanese submarine and torpedo technology and tactics did occasionally attract the interest of Admiralty planners before 1944. Two particular cases are noteworthy.

In late 1943 and early 1944, a debate took place in the Admiralty about the effectiveness of Japanese air-launched torpedoes in comparison with other known types – in particular, their British and American equivalents. Had the Japanese developed an especially powerful warhead for their 'Type-91' air-launched torpedo?[13] As had been the case with the discussion about Japanese dive bombing planes and their bombs the previous year, the Naval Staff took an interest in the issue because there was a direct connection with the sinking of British ships, in this case the *Prince of Wales* and *Repulse* in December 1941.[14] It was quickly established that the warheads on some Japanese torpedoes were in fact more powerful than the equivalent British and American weapons.[15] But the Naval Staff failed to agree on whether this gave Japanese torpedo bombers a decisive advantage.[16]

At about the same time, a US translation of a captured document issued by the Japanese Torpedo School generated considerable discussion by the Naval Staff.[17] It was known at the time that the Japanese had carried out a number of very successful torpedo attacks in the Solomon Islands campaign,[18] and it was hoped that some secrets about the equipment and techniques used would be revealed. In fact, the document was highly misleading in these areas, begging the question of whether it had been specifically created to confuse the enemy. For example, the Torpedo School document began by stating that '[t]he ironclad rule of torpedo attacks is to press home the attack to close quarters' when in fact since the late 1930s the IJN had based its tactics around the concept of 'long distance concealed firing'.[19] The translated document gave no hint that the navy possessed a trackless torpedo,[20] when in fact the Type-93 was just such a weapon. Finally, it made reference to Japanese torpedoes running on a mixture of compressed air, fuel and water when in fact the 'secret' behind the Type-93's tremendous speed and range was the fact that it used oxygen rather than air. The Director of Torpedoes and Mining considered that the document's emphasis upon attacking from close range was 'in accordance with Japanese character' and accepted it as an accurate guide to IJN torpedo tactics.[21] However, the Director of Training and Staff Division noted quite perceptively that reports from recent Japanese night campaigns in the Solomon Islands suggested that the IJN had developed the ability to 'fire torpedoes in radar control at long range'. This, he argued, might make the contents of the captured document not only obsolete but also 'misleading'.[22] In fact, Japanese radar was still in its infancy in 1943 and the IJN never succeeded in developing fire control radar. But it was certainly the case that the Type-93 torpedo, fired with the benefit of the highly effective Omori method of torpedo fire control, made it possible for Japanese naval units to strike targets accurately far beyond the range of other navies of the day. Later reports continued to rate Japanese torpedoes quite highly and also considered Japanese torpedo detection capabilities to be good.[23]

During 1944 and 1945, following the decision to create a British Pacific Fleet based in Australia, the Directorate of Naval Operational Studies in London began to focus its attention on the Pacific War. The Battle of the Atlantic had turned largely on devising technologies and tactics to foil the German submarine offensive; not surprisingly, when the Navy's tacticians first studied the Pacific campaign, they were still focusing on 'submarines'. The reports they produced are interesting from a number of points of view. It was noted, for example, that Japanese submarines almost never surfaced during depth-charge attacks, but rather exploded underwater, leaving traces of debris. This, it was assumed, was probably 'connected with the known Japanese preference for death rather than capture'.[24] However, for the purpose of this chapter, the reports are noteworthy primarily because they took the view that the Japanese use of submarines for tasks other than attacks on merchant shipping was not necessarily misguided. (This was probably due in part to the fact that the RN used its own submarine fleet in such auxiliary roles as reconnaissance and minelaying rather than in anti-commerce patrols.)

In August 1944, a Directorate of Naval Operational Studies report noted that in the early stages of the war, Japanese submarines were used 'in connection with offensive operations of the Japanese fleet' and for attacking merchant shipping, but that subsequently they came to be used primarily for 'intelligence purposes in defence', co-operation with German submarines and in transporting military personnel 'to and from their bases'. The report assumed that the Japanese submarine fleet – which never numbered more than 187 boats during the war – 'was probably playing a vital role in these respects'.[25] Another report, issued a year later, agreed that the Japanese submarine fleet had been used to accomplish 'various useful tasks other than sinking merchant vessels'.[26] Both reports made the point that when IJN submarines did target Allied personnel and supply ships – as they did with devastating effect in the Indian Ocean in 1942 and 1943 – their rate of effectiveness was roughly comparable to that of American submarines in the Pacific and German submarines in the Atlantic.[27]

In the last years of the war the Admiralty showed considerable interest in areas where the IJN's submarine fleet had benefited from technology transfers from the Germans.[28] Captured German documents, as well as interviews with German Navy personnel, indicated that Japan had received information about 'Schnorkel' and other scientific developments that had been important in the Atlantic; but this transfer of technology was believed to have come too late to be of much use. The intensive bombing of Japanese cities was seen to have greatly weakened the scientific/industrial infrastructure of the country, making it difficult to incorporate the information into the production of new weapons.[29]

The *Kamikaze* threat, 1944–45: tactics of desperation

In September 1944, at the Allied conference in Quebec, the British committed themselves to sending a fleet which included four fast carriers, two light carriers, two fast battleships, eight cruisers and 24 destroyers to the Pacific by the end of the year. The principal problem encountered in establishing the promised British Pacific Fleet was the urgent need to create from scratch a fleet train capable of supporting a large carrier task force in operations up to 5000 miles from its main base in Australia. Following the appointment of Admiral Sir Bruce Fraser as C-in-C BPF in November 1944, the challenge of finding the necessary supply shipping remained; but a new problem also loomed on the horizon, a deadly new Japanese weapon which was so effective against warships that it could only be discussed in tight secrecy: the *Kamikaze* attack.

In December 1944, before the BPF had reached Australia, Fraser advised the Admiralty that with the virtual destruction of the Japanese carrier fleet, the main threat to the BPF would be shore-based air attack, and in particular *Kamikaze* attack.[30] The following month, Fraser returned to the issue of the suicide air attack. His memorandum referred to *Kamikaze* raids as 'the most dangerous form of air attack so far developed' and understood the development of the weapon to be the result of the disastrous Japanese performance in the Battle of the Philippine Sea, which cost the IJN four carriers and more than 500 aircraft and their pilots. Japanese torpedo bombers and their fighter escorts clearly no longer stood a chance against US anti-aircraft defences, with instances being reported of 'a complete wave' of attacking aircraft being shot down at once.[31]

Although the *Kamikaze* strategy was understood to have been developed to deal with a desperate situation, it was not in the beginning interpreted as a blunt instrument swung by an incapacitated opponent. Neither was it seen by contemporary naval officers as a tactic belonging to 'uncivilised races' – as the *Kamikaze* attack has recently been described in the Navy's multi-volume history of the Far Eastern war.[32] A Naval Staff report of 15 March noted that '[e]nemy tactics have been characterised by a high degree of co-ordination in the approach, in order to confuse the radar warning and fighter defences'. These tactics contributed to suicide attacks being ten times more effective than non-suicide air attacks.[33]

As *Kamikaze* raids became better understood, the sophistication of their planning and execution became ever more apparent. Reports indicated that at least four different approaches were being used by suicide pilots, that they handled their aircraft with great skill and craftiness, and that they had 'complete understanding of the capabilities and limitations of Allied radar'.[34]

Between March and July 1945, the BPF provided support to the US Fifth Fleet in the Battle for Okinawa by carrying out sustained attacks against Japanese airfields on the Sakashima Gunto and Formosa, as well as being involved in operations against the main islands of Japan.[35] A British task force consisting of an aircraft carrier, five cruisers and five destroyers also successfully bombed the Japanese base at Truk in the Carolines. During that time the carriers *Indefatigable*, *Formidable*, *Indomitable* and *Victorious* were all subjected to *Kamikaze* attacks. However, British naval servicemen benefited from the fact that their ships had armour-plated flight decks; also by the summer of 1945 *Kamikaze* tactics had stabilized and the Americans had developed effective counter-measures, the details of which had been 'widely promulgated'.[36]

In July 1945, less than a month from the end of the war, the War Office estimated that the Japanese still had at their disposal about 3700 combat aircraft and 3600 training planes which could be used for suicide attacks against ships. Even at this late stage, when the effectiveness of the *Kamikaze* attack had plummeted sharply, these planes and their pilots were not underrated. It was believed that the armament and speed of Japanese fighter aircraft was increasing, and that the use of flying bombs was likely to be developed.[37]

Despite the fact that the Japanese Fleet had been reduced to a small 'unbalanced' force by the summer of 1945, the War Office expected that IJN ships would soon begin to be used as vehicles for suicide attacks. Estimates indicated that the IJN had 60 submarines, large numbers of midget submarines and various other small vessels that could be sent out on desperate one-way missions to resist the approaching Allied invasion of the home islands.[38] Bold, industrious and tactically-minded even on the brink of defeat, it was noted that the IJN was developing a large, fast (24 knots) midget submarine for possible use as a suicide craft. This was viewed as 'capable of inflicting severe damage'.[39]

In conclusion, it appears that two general influences were of considerable importance in shaping the RN's assessment of the IJN during the Second World War. The first was the powerful and lasting impression made by Japanese naval airpower in South East Asia and the Indian Ocean in 1941–42. Detailed reports of the highly sophisticated carrier-based attacks on the *Dorsetshire, Cornwall* and *Hermes,* as well as on Colombo and Trincomalee, led to a substantial adjustment in the RN's assessment of the equipment, training and tactics of its former pupil. For the remainder of the war, the fortunes of the air arm of the IJN became, to a certain extent, representative of the fortunes of the Navy as a whole. It is notable that even in the last grim days of the war, when the *Kamikaze* attacks were failing in a tragic fashion to curb the Allied air and sea attacks on the main Japanese islands, British naval leaders were careful not to underestimate the determination and tactical inventiveness of their Japanese counterparts.

The second important influence was the change of mindset brought about by the intensely technological and tactical dimension of the Battle of the Atlantic during the period 1940–43. This was characterized by a tendency to think from the point of view of 'equipment first' when looking at other navies. Whereas in the earlier decades of the century, the RN had concentrated on the men of the IJN – their strengths, weaknesses, training and facility with the equipment of modern naval warfare – during the Second World War it tended to look more at the equipment and tactics of the organization.

Notes

1. See Christopher M. Bell, *The Royal Navy: Seapower and Strategy Between the Wars* (Stanford, CA: Stanford University Press, 2000) and 'The "Singapore Strategy" and the Deterrence of Japan: Winston Churchill, the Admiralty and the Dispatch of Force Z', *English Historical Review*, vol. 116 (2001), 604–34.
2. John Ferris, 'Double-Edged Estimates: Japan in the Eyes of the British Army and the Royal Air Force 1900–1939', chapter 6 in this volume.

3. ADM 1 14803 'Strategic Requirements for Indian Ocean Bases, March 1943' by the Director of Plans, 1 March 1943. Only after January 1944, when the Eastern Fleet was reinforced with ships released from the Mediterranean, was it possible to strike at Japanese naval targets in Southeast Asia.

4. Correlli Barnett, *Engage the Enemy More Closely: the Royal Navy in the Second World War* (London: Hodder & Stoughton, 1991), p. 864.

5. ADM 199 623 'Report of Sinking of H.M. Ships DORSETSHIRE and CORNWALL', letter by Captain A.W.S. Agar (Commanding Officer of H.M.S. DORSETSHIRE), 8 April 1942.

6. ADM 199 623 'Japanese Dive Bombing Tactics', Extract of report by Captain A.J.S. Crockett of H.M.S. HERMES, undated.

7. ADM 199 623 'Japanese Air Attack on Trincomalee on 9 April 1942', Air Staff C.I.C. (Ceylon), 24 July 1942.

8. ADM 199 623 Minute by Director of Gunnery and Anti-Aircraft Warfare, 24 June 1942; Minute by Director of Naval Air Division, 5 July 1942; Minute by Director of Naval Construction, 13 November 1942.

9. ADM 1 14803 'Strategic Requirements for Indian Ocean Bases, March 1943'.

10. ADM 199 1289 Report by Lieut. CDR H.A.I. Luard on Attachment to U.S. Pacific Fleet, 23 November 1942.

11. ADM 1 13172 'Analysis of Pacific Naval War Problem' by Commander B. Wilson (Retired), 9 September 1943.

12. ADM 1 14985 Sir R. Craigie, 'Points touched upon when in conversation with Admiral Lord Louis Mountbatten on 30 September 1943', 1 October 1943.

13. ADM 1 13172 'Analysis of Pacific Naval War Problem' by Commander B. Wilson (Retired), 9 September 1943.

14. ADM 1 13172 Minute by Director of Naval Construction (Goodall), 17 January 1944.

15. ADM 1 13172 Minute by Director of Training and Staff Duties Division, 29 January 1944.

16. ADM 1 13172 Minute by Director of Torpedoes and Mining, 5 February 1944; Minute by Director of Naval Construction, 24 February 1944.

17. ADM 1 12647 Minutes on a captured document published by the Japanese Torpedo School entitled 'Lessons Learned in Battle in Greater East Asia War (Torpedoes) Volume 1' from B.A.D. Washington, 9 April 1943.

18. ADM 1 12647 Minute by Director of Training and Staff Duties Division, 1 September 1943.

19. David C. Evans and Mark R. Peattie, *Kaigun: Strategy, Tactics and Technology in the Imperial Japanese Navy, 1887–1941* (Annapolis, MD: Naval Institute Press, 1997), pp. 266–72.

20. ADM 1 12647 Minute by Director of Torpedoes and Mining, 4 September 1943.

21. Ibid.

22. ADM 1 12647 Minute by Director of Training and Staff Division, 4 October 1943.

23. ADM 1 15713 Comments by Lieutenant Commander R.B. Lakin (RN) upon report N.A. 450 (Observers with U.S. Pacific Fleet Reports), dated 30 June 1944.

24. ADM 219 232 'The U-Boat Phase of the Japanese War', Directorate of Naval Operational Studies Report no. 27/45, 1 August 1945.

25. ADM 219 146 'Japanese U-Boats', Directorate of Naval Operational Studies Report no. 64/44, 27 August 1944.

26. ADM 219 232 'The U-Boat Phase of the Japanese War'.

27. ADM 219 146 'Japanese U-Boats'; ADM 219 232 'The U-Boat Phase of the Japanese War'.
28. ADM 219 232 'The U-Boat Phase of the Japanese War'; ADM 1 17653 'Report on anti-U-boat lessons and their applicability to the Far East', 5 August 1945.
29. ADM 219 232 'The U-Boat Phase of the Japanese War'.
30. ADM 1 17223 Telegram from C-in-C BPF to Admiralty, 31 December 1944.
31. ADM 1 18662 Memorandum entitled 'Japanese Air Attack' from Fraser to Admiralty, 21 January 1945.
32. Ministry of Defence (Navy), *War with Japan*, vol. 1 (London: HMSO, 1995), p. 80. For an analysis of the origins of the *Kamikaze* strategy in the context of the evolution of the IJN's wartime strategy, see Yoichi Hirama, 'Die Einflusse von Sun Tzu und Tosenkyo in der Kaiserlichen Japanischen Marine. Rationalismus und Emotionalismus im Zweiten Weltkrieg' in Jorg Duppler (ed.), *Seemach und Seestrategie im 19. und 20. Jahrhundert* (Hamburg: Mittler, 1999), pp. 225–40.
33. ADM 219 263 'Suicide Attacks' Directorate of Naval Operations Studies Report no. 61/45, 15 March 1945.
34. ADM 1 18646 'Report of Suicide Tactics' Notes on U.S. Naval Methods no. 10, 23 March 1945.
35. On the battle of Okinawa, see Ian Gow, *Okinawa 1945: Gateway to Japan* (London: Grub Street Press, 1986) and Simon Foster, *Okinawa 1945: Assault on the Empire* (London: Cassell, 1994).
36. ADM 1 18646 Letter from Bruce Fraser to Admiralty enclosing 'Notes on U.S. Naval Methods', 22 June 1945.
37. WO 203 5040 Telegram from Air Ministry to All SICTEL addressees, SICTEL no. 120, July 1945.
38. Ibid.
39. ADM 1 17653 'Report on anti-U-boat lessons and their applicability to the Far East'.

15
British Policymakers and the Prisoner-of-War Issue: Perceptions and Responses

Sybilla Jane Flower

Between the end of December 1941 and March 1942 approximately 67 000 British servicemen were captured by the Japanese in the Asia-Pacific region. Of this number over 40 000 surrendered at the fall of Singapore, with the majority of the remainder taken prisoner in Hong Kong, the Netherlands East Indies or at the Battle of the Java Sea. It was known in general terms where most of the prisoners of war (POWs) began their captivity, the two principal exceptions being those who escaped from Singapore to Sumatra caught before securing a passage to safety, and Royal Navy personnel from ships sunk. Many of these POWs were dispersed in workforces to Japan and to the Japanese-occupied territories; the largest concentration of British POWs was held in Thailand, where more than 30 000 of them were employed between June 1942 and October 1943 in the construction of the Thailand–Burma Railway. This essay examines how the British government obtained information about POWs held in Hong Kong, Singapore and Thailand during the period 1942–43 and their response to the distressing picture which emerged about their conditions under the Japanese. The initial response of the British government was twofold: first, to attempt to secure the nominal rolls of those who survived the final days of the fighting and entered captivity; secondly, to establish the view of the Japanese on the provisions of the Geneva Convention. Diplomatic negotiations were hampered in the early months of 1942 because British interests in Japan and the Japanese-occupied territories were represented by the government of the Argentine Republic. (At this stage of the war the Swiss represented British interests only in occupied China.) The recalcitrance of the Japanese in forwarding to the Allied governments nominal rolls of those in captivity (only 6500 names has been officially received to November 1942)[1] meant the fate of many POWs remained unknown until the end of the war. This was not incompetence. The nominal rolls of POWs that survive indicate the bureaucratic efficiency of the Japanese POW Administration at least until 1944 when the POWs became more widely dispersed, often in remote areas. The testimony of the POWs themselves describes the monotonous insistence on roll-calls during their captivity. These returns were forwarded from the camps to the POW Control Bureau within the War Ministry in Tokyo, but the release of this information was subject to the strictest censorship so that nothing of strategic value could be deduced from it.

A comparison between the details provided by the Japanese on the POWs in Hong Kong and those in Thailand clearly illustrate this policy. Hong Kong, once secured, had no further strategic significance for the Japanese. Accordingly the Japanese found no difficulty in releasing the nominal rolls of the POWs held there and the identity of most of them was known to the Allies by the end of 1942. In Thailand, on the other hand, selective lists were released but the total number of POWs was never revealed.

Hong Kong was the only territory where British POWs, at least in the first 18 months, had reasonable escape prospects. Escapees' testimonies, together with information from the British consulate in Macao, furnished the earliest intelligence about POW conditions, quickly dispelling hopes that Japanese handling of captives would prove benign. The practical and diplomatic policies relating to POWs were formulated by the British government during 1942 in the light of what was known to have occurred in Hong Kong.

At the time of the surrender of Hong Kong on 25 December 1941, the British garrison comprised approximately 14000 men, the majority of whom had some experience of life in the colony – excepting two Canadian units who arrived three weeks before the end. The two British infantry battalions had been in Hong Kong from 1936 and 1937 respectively. Among the 1700 personnel of the Hong Kong Volunteer Defence Corps who went into captivity were Chinese, Indian and Portuguese company personnel and expatriate Europeans with mercantile or professional backgrounds. Thus a good proportion of this garrison knew local customs, geography and languages and had reliable contacts outside the POW camps.

The most significant escape from Hong Kong was made by Lieutenant-Colonel Lindsay Ride, who commanded the Field Ambulance of the HKVDC during the fighting. He was well-known, having occupied the chair of physiology at the university since 1928. On 9 January 1942 Ride, with a Cantonese member of the corps and two British naval officers, left the POW camp of Shamshuipo in Kowloon before the nominal roll was compiled and made their way to Waichow, headquarters of the front-line division of the Chinese Nationalist Army. Ride journeyed on to Chungking, arriving on 17 February.

Ride's evidence on Japanese atrocities during the fighting was not the first to reach the government, but he was able to confirm and amplify the account given by two civilians: Miss Harrap, an official in the Colonial Secretariat in Hong Kong who had escaped to Macao on 27 January, and Jan Henrik Marsman, a Dutch-born merchant based in the Philippines, who had taken refuge in the Repulse Bay Hotel and witnessed the surprise Japanese invasion of that part of the island before making his way to Chungking.[2]

Miss Harrap's statement, which reached the Foreign Office by telegram from the British vice-consul in Macao, had been received in London with some scepticism.[3] However, Ride's account, including details of the massacre of medical officers and nursing staff at St Stephen's Hospital, corroborated hers completely. Ride was also able to provide intelligence about the earliest stages of the Japanese occupation and the principal POW camp at Shamshuipo.

The information which arrived in London from Chungking and Macao presented the British government with a dilemma. It was agreed that a detailed statement of facts would not only cause distress to the families of those in Japanese hands but could also undermine morale, particularly in India, Burma and Ceylon. Publicity at a delicate stage in the diplomatic negotiations with Japan over the treatment of POWs and civilian internees was also undesirable. But there was no united stance among the Allied governments. On 23 February the British Foreign Secretary, Anthony Eden, pointed out to the War Cabinet that it would be difficult to ask the Chinese to suppress information about what had occurred in Hong Kong when their earlier policy had been to give frank details of Japanese outrages in their own country.[4]

At the end of February Lord Halifax reported from Washington to the Foreign Office that the State Department had received details of the treatment of American POWs in the Philippines, but that no decision on whether or not to publicize these had been made because of the fear of inciting the feelings of Japanese living on the west coast of the USA. But the hands of both governments were forced by accounts given by escapees which appeared uncensored in the American press.

On 10 March, Eden made a statement in the House of Commons on Japanese atrocities in Hong Kong and on 21 March a press release from the State Department summarized in graphic form the experiences of American captives in Japanese hands.[5] The apprehension on the part of the British government that these disclosures could prejudice negotiations with the Japanese and provoke hostility towards the captives was soon justified. The civilians repatriated from Hong Kong in September 1942 were able to describe the manner in which the Japanese camp staff reacted to the Eden statement. They insisted that any information provided by them to the authorities should not be made public – this in an effort to protect those remaining in captivity. Confirmation of Japanese attitudes towards the POWs was provided later in 1942 by survivors of the transport *Lisbon Maru* which left Hong Kong in September in convoy bound for Japan. The ship, carrying 1800 POWs together with Japanese troops and ammunition, was torpedoed by an American submarine on 1 October off the coast of Chekiang. Some of the POWs were rescued by the Japanese and a few survivors made their way to the island of Chusan. Among these were three British POWs from the camp at Shamshuipo who had served in China, one a former chief inspector of police in Tientsin.[6] Through their knowledge of Chinese dialects the three were able to negotiate passage to Nationalist China then to India for debriefing. The testimony of these three articulate men – including details of the conditions in the hold, Japanese attempts to prevent POWs reaching the deck after the ship had been attacked and the raking by gunfire of survivors struggling in the water – was reported in the British press.[7]

As the details of the sinking of the *Lisbon Maru* had been provided by a readily identifiable, first-hand source with no intelligence implications, the British government sent a formal complaint through the Swiss government to the Japanese. The British protest, dated 26 March 1943, was answered by the Japanese more than four months later. It refuted the account given by the government and outlined the Japanese response to the emergency which resulted in the rescue of more than 900 of the original POW complement of 1800. Calls for a court of inquiry were rejected out of hand.[8]

When Colonel Ride arrived in Chungking, he lost no time in presenting to the Military Attaché at the British Embassy his ambitious scheme to assist POWs in Hong Kong. This involved liaison with Nationalist Chinese military commands and British units in South China, and also the Chinese Communist guerillas controlling approach routes to Kowloon, some of whom had aided Ride in his own escape. With the approval of Chiang Kai-shek, Ride, with an initial allowance of £15 000 per month, set up the British Army Aid Group (BAAG) under the Director of Military Intelligence at GHQ9 New Delhi but administered by the Military Attaché at Chungking. Ride's instructions stipulated his role was to effect the rescue of Allied POWs from camps in Hong Kong and Canton, set up an evasion organization for Allied airmen forced down along the China coast and, as MI19 representative, interrogate escapees and collect, collate and disseminate intelligence.[9] Links were established between the BAAG and a network of Chinese operating in Hong Kong and Macao. Contact was made in October 1942 with the POW camp in Argyle Street where the officers were detained, and for some months exchanges were made on an almost daily basis. Through this channel nominal rolls and information on POWs were forwarded to New Delhi together with detailed intelligence on Japanese strengths, location of defences, movements of shipping and aircraft, and the results of American bombing raids. Plans for a mass breakout of POWs were advanced just at the moment that the Japanese succeeded in infiltrating the BAAG network. In July 1943 arrests were made in the POW camps and at Stanley, the camp holding the civilian internees (where security was poor). Six POWs and a large number of civilian internees were apprehended, including Lieutenant-Colonel L.A. Newnham, who had taken on the role of chief liaison officer between the BAAG and the Argyle Street camp. They were charged with receiving and sending messages but not with espionage. The execution of three British officers including Newnham, one Indian officer and more than thirty civilians between October and December 1943 ended the direct link between the BAAG and the camps in Hong Kong.[10] A report on the work of the BAAG written towards the end of 1944 concluded,

> As an escape organization B.A.A.G. has fully justified its formation . . . it has enabled 21 white men, including U.S. pilots, and 120 Indians to escape . . . Intelligence provided by B.A.A.G. is, according to G.H.Q., India of the greatest importance in connection with the protection of the Indian Army, and of India as a base, from Japanese subversive efforts and espionage. B.A.A.G. also provides intelligence to the U.S.A.A.F. operating from China.[11]

The discovery of contact between captives in Hong Kong and the BAAG resulted in the Japanese taking repressive measures on a scale and with a ferocity that led the senior POWs to discourage any further attempts to establish intelligence links outside the camps or to organize escapes. But the insight obtained into POW conditions in Hong Kong in 1942–43 enabled the British government to formulate a policy and to proceed with caution in all diplomatic initiatives or public pronouncements about POWs. Government efforts were directed away from diplomacy towards the provision of cash, medicines and other supplies for the POWs.

Singapore

There are several reasons why the POWs in Singapore were unable to initiate similar plans to those adopted in Hong Kong. The Japanese occupation of Singapore island was more stringent, reflecting its importance as a naval and military base. The island was also geographically isolated. Changi, where most of the POWs were initially confined, was 17 miles outside town. Whereas most of the troops in Hong Kong had local experience and knowledge, the largest military formation to surrender in Singapore was the 18th Division, which had arrived from Europe a matter of weeks or even days before the capitulation, and consisted of territorial battalions recruited in mostly rural areas of Britain. But there were also over 1000 residents of Malaya or Singapore who served in the Volunteer units, many of whom had worked before the war in government service or for mercantile houses or banks. As the POWs were allowed to retain their pre-captivity military structure, Malaya Command continued to function in the camp at Changi, albeit in a severely limited form, and the senior POW officers sought the local expertise of these men. British officers who had belonged before the outbreak of war to the Intelligence branch of Malaya Command or had knowledge of particular value to the Japanese – for instance, the Chinese 'stream' of the Malayan Civil Service – rejoined where possible the units from which they had been seconded, and thus assumed a cloak of anonymity. In the early weeks at Changi the greatest threat to the safety of anyone in clandestine activities was probably being recognized and reported to the Japanese by Sikhs who had guarded the offices and military installations under the British, and then transferred their allegiance. For these officers at risk and for others who were returned from the Netherlands East Indies (such as Colonel A.F. Warren of the Oriental Mission of the Special Operations Executive), the work parties which left Singapore for Japan or Thailand offered an 'escape' route which some opted for with alacrity. Although too dangerous for these men to resume intelligence-gathering in captivity in Changi, their former role was taken up by members of the Volunteer units. Their work was made easier when the Japanese began to move parties from Changi into town to clear bomb damage and commence rebuilding the infrastructure. Some of the Eurasians who had worked in the public service and taken part in the fighting were ordered by the Japanese to return to their jobs to restore electricity and water to the town. The officers of Malaya Command, isolated at Changi, decided to concentrate their efforts on acquiring as much information about the Japanese occupation of Singapore as was possible from these sources and to retain within the camp the headquarters staff of the 18th Division and enough divisional troops to form the nucleus of a force either to fight their way out of captivity or to assist an Allied invasion.

The intelligence-gathering exercise in Singapore was successful within limits. One member of the Straits Settlements Volunteer Force (G.E.D. Lewis) spent four months from August 1942 at the Japanese HQ acting as a Malay interpreter. Carefully selected for this assignment, the former schoolmaster was ordered by his colonel in Changi to begin by reporting on the presence of Japanese warships in the harbour.[12] Efforts were also made to discover the whereabouts of the Indian troops who had been segregated immediately after the capitulation and subjected to intense pressure to join the Indian National Army. Contact was made with Indians who had refused to renounce their allegiance to the British.

The intelligence gathered from all over the island and from Johore was analysed at Changi. But in the early months at least, there were no means of forwarding it to any Allied power. In April–May 1943 the Japanese call for more work parties from Changi for the Thailand–Burma Railway (the Japanese allowed the POWs to make up their own parties) forced Malaya Command to send HQ 18th Division and the troops so carefully retained as a fighting force. By that date links had been forged between the POWs and officials of the neutral powers in Thailand and intelligence agents working in Bangkok. Through these channels a certain amount of information on Singapore reached the British government though by the time it arrived much of it was out of date. For those Europeans from neutral nations living in Singapore, there were few opportunities to assist the Allied captives. For those in official positions it was a matter of choice. H.R. Arbenz, honorary consul for Switzerland up to his death in 1944, took no interest in the POWs or civilian internees. He was also hostile towards his fellow Swiss, Hans Schweitzer, who played a heroic role in raising money for the POWs in 1942–43 and subsequently in the purchase of food and other supplies for the civilian internees.[13] Hans Schweitzer was manager of the Singapore branch of the Zurich-based company, Diethelm & Co Ltd. At the time of the surrender of Singapore until early 1944, he occupied the position of honorary vice-consul of the Argentine Republic. This role gave him access to Japanese officialdom largely through acquaintance on the pre-war consular circuit with Shinozaki Mamoru. Formerly press attaché at the Japanese consulate, Shinozaki was responsible during the occupation for citizens from neutral countries as Director of Education and later Head of the Welfare Department. Soon after the outbreak of war, Schweitzer was appointed to act as the delegate of the International Committee of the Red Cross, an appointment which the Japanese refused to recognize – although a compromise was later reached whereby he acted as 'Neutral Agent'. Schweitzer was able to negotiate loans to assist the POWs at Changi, forwarding to the camp between November 1942 and July 1943 the sum of $100000. Although the Japanese continued to allow him to supply food and medicines to the civilian internees until 1945, his efforts to help the POWs were abruptly halted as a result of the Anglo-Australian commando night raid on Singapore harbour which took place on 26 September 1943. The Japanese could not accept that this was unaided, suspecting an intelligence circuit directed by the civilian internees in Changi Jail had initiated and carried out the attack on Japanese shipping with Chinese assistance. For the citizens of Singapore, the POWs and the civilian internees the raid was a tragedy resulting in torture and repression. For a time Schweitzer's initiatives were stifled, though he was later able to resume supplies to the civilian internees and telegraphic communications with Geneva.

Thailand

Among the 1000 members of the volunteer forces of Malaya and Singapore who went into captivity, there were men who had worked in Bangkok or elsewhere in Thailand because it was customary for the mercantile houses and banks in South East Asia to rotate their managers and juniors between the major towns. As a result there were probably 10–15 POWs among those sent north from Changi who were familiar with Thai language and customs. There were others proficient in Chinese dialects. The international companies which traded in Thailand before the Second World War worked through a network of Chinese commercial agents based in the towns and villages. Soon after the advance parties of POWs arrived in Thailand in June 1942, at the start of the construction of the Thailand–Burma Railway, one of these Chinese agents recognized among the POWs a former British employee of Anglo-Thai. The Chinese relayed the news to interested parties in Bangkok, where Japanese intentions towards the POWs were becoming a matter of increasing concern. Nowhere was this felt more keenly than in the camp which held the Allied civilian internees. This camp was administered by the Thai Army on behalf of the Japanese and, though confined within the camp, internees were allowed to receive visitors. Within a matter of months two circuits within the camp were in operation, independent of each other but with the same objective; to collect intelligence about the POWs and send aid to them in money and medical supplies. Their emissaries were Eurasians, Thais or Chinese. The principal personal contacts outside the camp were a Swiss national, Albert Tanner, who worked for Anglo-Thai, the wife of one of the French consuls in the Vichy Legation whose husband had been asked by General de Gaulle to remain at his post in Bangkok and a group of Anglophile Thais who had received some of their education in the United Kingdom or made the acquaintance of Europeans in Bangkok. Apart from the diplomatic and the commercial elements, the principal European institutional presence in Thailand in the 1930s was the Roman Catholic Church. When the POWs alighted on Thai soil the first building they saw opposite the station of the small market town of Banpong was a Christian church. This housed a community of Italian Salesian fathers whose local work was charitable and educational. As Italians there were no restrictions on their movements until late 1943 and the Superior decided to gather as much information as possible on the POWs and then travel personally by train into Bangkok to deliver the information to the Swiss consulate. Although the construction of the railway and thus the POWs themselves moved away from Banpong and out of the orbit of this community, the initial information was invaluable, leading to a visit from a member of the Swiss consulate whose secret observations were duly communicated to London.

The information gathered from and about the POWs by these various contacts through the Swiss consular staff in Bangkok on what was happening to the POWs caused increasing concern. From March 1943 rumours about the working conditions on the Railway, the sickness, lack of medicines, medical equipment and food, circulated in Bangkok. The arrival of two reports written by POWs (one a medical officer and the other a journalist) – smuggled out of the camps and carried to Bangkok by Thai or Chinese emissaries – forced the Swiss consulate to take action. At great risk to themselves, to those who were helping in Bangkok and indeed to the POWs, the information was relayed to London on the understanding that the communication was sent in the strictest confidence.[14] The British government decided that, despite the likely Japanese reprisals, there was no option but to send a protest. A note of 5 July 1943 drew from the Japanese government 'an uncompromising and cynical reply' (dated 8 August),[15] insisting that the POWs were fairly treated. Accounts of the ensuing diplomatic exchanges, which included an interview between the Swiss Foreign Minister and the Japanese Minister at Berne where the threat of Allied 'reprisals' was mooted, were received with dismay in London.[16] However well-intentioned, the protest, a victim of language difficulties as much as clumsy diplomacy, had tragic consequences for the POWs. In mid-1943, the construction of the Thailand–Burma Railway was running behind schedule, and military and naval reverses elsewhere provoked the War Ministry in Tokyo to send the strictest orders to the railway engineers and the Japanese POW organization in Thailand that the work must proceed more rapidly whatever the cost in lives. The major security failure revealed to the Japanese by the British government protest brought an influx of *kenpei-tai* reinforcements into Thailand. The Japanese determination to discover the source of the information and how it reached Bangkok resulted in a chain of torture and a tightening of rules and regulations, making POW life even more hazardous. One concession that the Japanese made at this time was to agree in September 1943 to allow the Swiss delegate of the ICRC (whose position was never recognized by Tokyo), to make limited issues of money, food, medical supplies and cigarettes to the POWs, although distribution was to be left entirely in the hands of the Japanese military authorities.

In April 1944, the War Office in London drew up a list of protests and representations made to the Japanese government concerning POWs and civilian internees in response to a similar list made by the American State Department. The Americans listed 89 representations compared with 52 by the British, a disparity which an official in the Prisoner-of-War Department of the Foreign Office deduced that 'the Americans have been more rigid in protesting against all breaches of the Prisoners of War Convention' but 'to the best of our knowledge have not achieved any greater result than ours have done'.[16]

Eighteen of the 52 protests related to the Japanese failure to provide nominal rolls; other protests related to the inhuman treatment of POWs in Rangoon jail and conditions in the camps in Formosa, Java, Indochina and Japan as well as Thailand. Replies were received to only 17 of the British protests, and the charges relating to the treatment were summarily dismissed. After the diplomatic setbacks of 1943 the British government directed its energies to channelling money, medical supplies and food to the POWs through the ICRC, with varying success country by country.[17]

Whereas the Foreign Office's diplomatic initiatives on behalf of POWs were failures due to the intransigence of the Japanese, the clandestine links forged by the POWs themselves with various individuals or agencies – government or otherwise – in countries such as Thailand played a vital part in survival. The sudden capitulation of the Japanese and subsequent British government censorship of intelligence material has ensured these initiatives remain largely unknown.

Notes

1. 'Protests to the Japanese Government on Matters connected with Prisoners of War and Civilian Internees in the Far East': Public Record Office, Kew (hereafter PRO): FO916/1089.
2. Jan Henrik Marsman, *I Escaped from Hong Kong* (Sydney, 1943).
3. Sir R. Campbell (Lisbon) telegram to Foreign Office, 2 February 1942; Foreign Office memorandum signed by Lieutenant-Colonel S.J. Cole, 4 February 1942: PRO: CO980/521.
4. Extract from conclusion of a meeting of the War Cabinet, 23 February 1942: ibid.
5. Ibid.
6. WO235/999.
7. *The Times*, 23 December 1942.
8. PRO: FO916/1089.
9. Edwin Ride, *BAAG: Hong Kong Resistance, 1942–1945* (Hong Kong, 1981), pp. 61–2.
10. Report by Major-General C.M. Maltby: PRO: WO32/14550.
11. Memorandum signed by E.J. King-Salter, 2 November 1944: PRO: HS1/166.
12. G.E.D. Lewis, *Out East in the Malay Peninsula* (Petaling Jaya, 1991), pp. 83–5.
13. H. Schweitzer, typescript: 'Experiences of a Delegate unrecognised of the International Committee of the Red Cross during the occupation of the Japanese of Singapore and Malaya, 1941–1945': Imperial War Museum, London.
14. Memorandum from Swiss Federal Political Department, Berne, 6 April 1943: PRO: WO224/2009.
15. Memorandum by the Secretary of State for War, 21 October 1943: PRO: FO371/359899.
16. FO916/10891.
17. J.H.U. Lambert (F.O.) to Lieutenant Colonel H.J. Phillimore (W.O.), 27 April 1944: PRO: FO916/1089.

16
Changes in Perception: British Civil and Military Perspectives on War Crimes Trials and Their Legal Context, 1942–1956

R. John Pritchard

Within Japan, it is generally believed that British and other Allied war courts were conceived in anger and bitterness, that the Allies were reckless in identifying and punishing war criminals, and that their courts (and sentences) were harsh and unfair. This essay reveals British official thinking about the B/C class trials from conception until the release of the last convicted Japanese war criminal for whom Britain had responsibility.

Between January 1946 and December 1948, British military tribunals held 308 war crimes trials, conducted by 12 separate courts in fixed locations or on circuit throughout South East Asia.[1] A total of 967 accused were tried, 291 death sentences were pronounced, 564 were sentenced to periods of imprisonment ranging from one day to life, and 112 were acquitted (some purely on technicalities).[2] These figures mask complicating factors. At least 30 convictions were set aside by the Confirming Authorities. Forty defendants stood trial more than once. Only 220 (75 per cent) of those condemned to death were executed.[3] In addition, a small number of Japanese, Koreans and Taiwanese (at least eight and possibly as many as ten) were prosecuted through the territories for felonies corresponding to war crimes: no records of those proceedings have been found.

It was understood from the outset that war criminals brought to justice would constitute only a fraction of those against whom there was compelling evidence. These trials, and further proceedings carried out by other Allies on the strength of British investigations, were outcomes of huge efforts by the British Army to screen 708 000 members of the Japanese Armed Forces and enemy civilians in South East Asia in order to identify and punish individuals concerned with war crimes. It proceeded with remarkable expeditiousness. Within four months of convening their first trial, 71 per cent of British war crimes prosecutions in the Far East were concluded.[4] Thereafter the number of prosecutions fell rapidly, to a trickle by late 1947.

When the creation of these courts was first considered in London, two War Crimes Bills were drafted to be laid before Parliament in 1943 and 1944. This proved troublesome. Those responsible soon accepted it would be unfair and wrong to apply national law to members of the armed services of a foreign state without prior consent. Some argued it would breach international law. On seeing the Parliamentary Counsel's first draft of the War Crimes Bill in October 1942, William Malkin of the Foreign Office wrote:

> If there is one rule of international law which is well-established, it is that the members of a hostile invading or occupying army are not subject to the municipal law of the country concerned or to the jurisdiction of its civil courts . . .

> It is suggested accordingly that war criminals should not be tried for offences against the municipal law of the invaded or occupied country where the act was committed, but for breaches of the laws of war . . . for once the jurisdiction of the State concerned is claimed as resulting from its rights under international law and not from its territorial jurisdiction, the question of what courts it should employ for the purpose of applying international law to cases where it possesses this jurisdiction would seem to be a matter which each country is entitled to decide for itself.[5]

The Judge Advocate General, Sir Henry MacGeagh (the Army' s top legal adviser), agreed. They resisted the Parliamentary Counsel, Lord Chancellor, Attorney General and Treasury Solicitor. MacGeagh had no objection to legislation that might grant British criminal courts with jurisdiction over crimes of violence committed on British subjects overseas, but he was utterly opposed to the idea that such jurisdiction should be extended to war crimes or made retrospective. MacGeagh maintained that

> The true basis of the liability to punishment for war crimes is not that the war criminal has offended against the peace-time criminal law of the invaded country or of enemy nationals but that he has committed violations of the rules of warfare as agreed or recognized [emphasis added] among civilised nations . . .

> The question of a war crime is whether or not the act complained of can be justified as an act of legitimate warfare. This is a question involving military considerations, upon which military tribunals would be specially qualified to judge and which would appear to be unsuitable to leave to the decision of a jury.

> All belligerent forces recognize, or ought to recognize, that they are liable to be tried for war crimes by military tribunals, and in that sense no retrospective legislation would be required . . .

On the other hand, members of belligerent forces would not regard themselves as subject to the peace-time criminal law of enemy countries or nationals, and to make them so subject retrospectively would appear to offend against the principles of natural justice, which it is unnecessary to do if the other basis of liability is adopted.[6]

After protracted internal debates, MacGeagh prevailed. At his suggestion British trials of war criminals were established through an obscure Royal Prerogative, by a Royal Warrant[7] authorizing British military commands to hold war crimes courts at which common law rights were denied the accused. Those rights, however, have never formed part of international law. MacGeagh explained, 'This also applies to the Warrant issued at the commencement of this and previous wars for the maintaining of discipline among prisoners of war after capture. The power to issue these Warrants and to hold trials and inflict punishments . . . is incidental to the power of waging war.'[8]

The Royal Warrant and Regulations brought into effect under it empowered these courts to take judicial notice of international laws and usages of war, effectively incorporating such laws even where they had never received the assent of Parliament. 'In any case not provided for in these Regulations such course will be adopted as appears best calculated to do justice.' The Court of Appeal would determine in 1946 that until supervention of a peace treaty, Britain and Germany remained at war despite the cessation of hostilities and no enemy alien had legal rights to apply to any British civil court for a writ of habeas corpus.[9] The same would hold for Japanese. Officials could not anticipate these future developments, but the constitutional throwback produced tribunals beyond reach of Britain's domestic courts of appeal. These considerations, however, were never uppermost: fairness and conformity with international law were.

After hostilities ended, Japanese Surrendered Personnel (JSPs) in British custody were processed and guarded in PoW camps until arrangements could be made to ship them to Japan. The vast majority of JSPs were 'whitewashed' rapidly: they returned home as soon as circumstances permitted. About 0.5 per cent of JSPs were segregated in military prisons as suspected war criminals or detained as war crimes witnesses. Another one per cent of JSP were held in British civil gaols pending trial: these prisoners were detained in Siam, Borneo, Burma, the Andaman and Nicobar Islands, French Indochina, the Netherlands East Indies, Formosa, Hong Kong, India, Malaya and China (Shanghai). The number of suspects in civil custody reached a peak of about 7500 in June 1946 and declined rapidly thereafter. Within 18 months it had fallen to about 2000.

Early on, 17 British war crimes investigation teams gathered evidence which was evaluated by legal officers to determine whether to initiate prosecutions. The policy adopted by Britain in the Far East was to prosecute only when judges advocate anticipated a 100 per cent probability of conviction on extremely serious charges. For a short time, lesser crimes were brought before the courts, too, but as the greater part of British forces in the Far East rapidly demobilized in 1946, the number of courts declined rapidly. A policy was to prosecute only in cases involving a capital charge or where upon conviction the accused were likely to be sentenced to at least seven years' imprisonment. There was no practical alternative: the administrative legal machinery and war crimes courts were operating to capacity. This largely explains why higher percentages of British war trials ended in conviction than those of other countries: higher conviction rates do not indicate that British courts were harsher. Of those convicted by the British, the mean determinant sentence passed was 5.82 years of imprisonment. Taking life sentences into account (on their equivalency to a 'quantum' of 21 years) only raises that to 7.15 years. The supreme penalty was reserved for only the most extreme crimes.

National prosecutions, unlike international prosecutions, follow procedures in most respects similar to the courts martial by which armies uphold internal military discipline. British proceedings in the Far East, remote and undeflected by public pressure or media interest, had little interference from politicians back home. There was, however, co-ordination between London and 'War Crimes' in South East Asia: Brigadier Henry Shapcott, the former Military Deputy of the Judge Advocate General, recollected afterwards,

> In the early stages of war crimes in the Far East it was decided that it was not practicable or desirable that the final minutes of advice should be prepared in London in cases where the accused were being interrogated on the other side of the world. I therefore confined my functions to questions of policy and general supervision and also to the collection of evidence from repatriated prisoners of war ... More than 2000 affidavits were obtained and forwarded to the Far East where they were used in proceedings to corroborate the evidence of the witnesses who were called in person at the trials. As in Europe accused persons were of course not tried on affidavit evidence alone.[10]

Local colonial officials occasionally sought to control or influence these proceedings and enlisted support from the Colonial Office, but were blocked by the War Office and, later, by the Foreign Office.

The judges and prosecutors of these tribunals gained no career advantages by remaining in 'war crimes' for any considerable length of time. On the contrary, many sought an early release in order to resume their civilian occupations. Others who wished to remain in military service were impatient to be posted to duties where they could build a more stable future within slimmed-down peacetime armed forces. The generals responsible for convening war crimes courts and for confirming convictions and sentences tended to take these matters in their stride without bowing to external pressures.[11]

Notwithstanding the often terrible atrocities committed by suspects tried and convicted by British war crimes courts in Europe and the Far East, successive British governments came under considerable pressure to terminate these trials quickly and to release those convicted long before they had completed their sentences.

In the first trials, British officers familiar with courts martial procedure represented the accused as defending officers exactly as provided for at that time in trials of British servicemen. The rapid dwindling number of legally qualified officers made it imperative to adopt another system. British defending officers were phased out. In their place a pool of 39 Japanese defence counsel were retained. At first the Japanese lawyers (and 33 defence interpreters) were treated little better than ordinary JSPs, but conditions gradually improved. They were given meagre allowances of money, furniture, military escorts (their movement was subject to varying forms of restriction) and transportation facilities. Thereafter, except when individuals elected to employ and pay for their own civil counsel, expenses incurred in providing, equipping and maintaining the pool of Japanese counsel were debited against the Japanese account. After September 1946, Japanese counsel were paid directly by the Japanese government with pay credited to them in Japan. Allowances were paid to them in South East Asia by British command quartermasters which would be recovered from the Japanese government. It remains unclear whether the Japanese paid that bill, however, or whether it was held over until the Peace Treaty.

The British also provided defendants with Defence Advisory Officers (DAOs) to assist the accused and their Japanese counsel throughout the trial. Care was taken in selecting DAOs. They were expected to become thoroughly familiar with all aspects of each case to which they were assigned; to attend interviews; to arrange any interviews with possible witnesses; to serve as a liaison link between Japanese counsel, the convening authority and the various sections of 'War Crimes'; to ensure the attendance of witnesses required by the Defence; to remain in court throughout the trial; and to advise Japanese counsel on British military procedure. DAOs normally prepared the Closing Address for the Defence or at least put it into idiomatic English. Following death sentences, DAOs attended executions as mandatory witnesses, a prospect none faced without blanching. I know of no instances where these advisory officers did not do their utmost to assist the defence wherever possible. Their duties were framed by the authorities so it was clear nothing less was demanded.

Upon conviction for war crimes, prisoners ceased to be treated as Japanese Surrendered Personnel. After sentences were confirmed, they were sent to civil prisons for confinement like ordinary convicts. About 200 of those convicted of war crimes served relatively short terms, former war criminals joined with Japanese Surrendered Personnel returned and publicly complained that they had suffered ill-treatment or indignity in British captivity and became increasingly outspoken in proclaiming their innocence. Public petitions signed by hundreds of thousands of Japanese, presented to the British Embassy in Tokyo, begged London to cease allegedly degrading, inhumane treatment of people for a war which all now deplored. The treatment of war criminals became a litmus test of the recent Allies' professed trust and cordiality towards post-war Japan. An official mused, 'I am afraid that this mentality is not confined only to the Japanese. Criminals who are punished by a victorious enemy become heroes whatever the nature of their crimes.'

Beginning in 1948, British officials in London preparing recommendations concerning clemency received Special Branch reports compiled by censors who monitored correspondence between convicted Japanese war criminals in Malayan prisons and their families in Japan. These reports did not lead officials to a more sympathetic approach. Sir Esler Dening remarked, 'It is interesting – but not surprising – to find that the leopard has not after all changed its spots.' All recognized the importance of Japanese public support for the early release of these convicts.

During the first two years after the war, convicted war criminals received no remission whatever for good conduct. The pace of change, when it came, was driven by differences of opinion within the British Occupation Forces in Germany. The War Office decided that individual sentences should not be reviewed separately from time to time but that as soon as possible after the trials ended altogether, there should be a careful review of the cases of every convicted war criminal held in custody.

The Judge Advocate General was invited to prepare a paper on the subject and the views of the Attorney General, Sir Hartley Shawcross, were sought. Two weeks later, MacGeagh was commanded by Secretary of War Shinwell to create two Review Boards – one for Europe and the other for the Far East:

> Each Review Board would consider all cases . . . where the sentences were un-expired. They would examine the Proceedings of each case, any Petitions that may have been submitted and the reports of prison governors on the conduct and health of the prisoner. They would compare the circumstances of similar cases. On completion of their task these advisory Review Boards would recommend what action you might take by way of remission . . . to ensure that the punishment should so far as possible be appropriate and uniform in existing circumstances, bearing in mind that such punishments were imposed not for reformative purposes but by way of retribution.

This was agreed.

Thus, in June 1948, more than two years after the trials had opened, before the last trials came to an end, and well before the orchestrated campaign for the early release of war criminals became a major issue in Japan's relations with the Allied Powers, the War Office took steps to institute Review Boards. It took longer than expected, and it was not until January 1949 that the Number 2 War Crimes Sentences Review Board (Far East) was formed – a body which became known as the 'Lynch Board' after its president, Brigadier E.F. Lynch.

One of the most interesting documents to come to light from the Lynch Board's work was a table from which the Members of the Board were to determine what punishment should be applied in particular instances. This Board was a novelty in terms of British justice. It did not sit as a 'Court of Appeal'. Brigadier Lynch was instructed it should not do so. The merits of cases, the soundness of convictions, were not considered. The Board was only to review and harmonize sentences. Since it lacked the powers to increase sentences, the inevitable result was a lowering of tariffs, inappropriately in many instances. Brigadier Lynch was advised by Brigadier Henry Shapcott, now Director of Army Legal Services, to flag dubious cases bring into play other review processes.[12] The Court Martial (Appeals) Act, 1951, as it appears in the 1951 edition of the British Manual of Military Law, shows that convicted war criminals were given far more scope for review than British appellants in ordinary courts martial proceedings during the same period.[13]

The punishments considered appropriate were roughly comparable to those prescribed in Japanese military criminal codes. Take rape, for example, classified in the Lynch Board table (Table 16.1) as 'Gross and/or indecent torture'. There were variations in patterns of sentences, but the earliest editions of the Japanese Army's Martial Law Code in the Meiji era, heavily influenced by western manuals of military law,[14] held that on conviction by courts martial, officers in charge should be imprisoned for between seven years and life if they or their men were concerned in rape, depending on the circumstances and degree of direct involvement.[15] (There can be no more clear-cut application of criminal responsibility for breaches of command responsibility than this.) In the Japanese Army, as in others, commanders often turned a blind eye to war crimes even though such actions degrade military discipline generally, but murder or maltreatment of prisoners and civilians, or thefts of personal property for private gain, were matters strictly prohibited and dealt with severely under Japanese martial law codes.[16]

Under the Lynch Board's recommendations, 109 of 441 sentences expiring on or after 30 September 1949 (25 per cent of the total number) were reduced by the Secretary of State for War under the Royal Warrant. The Adjutant General advised the presidents of review boards that for purposes of remission all sentences of life imprisonment (unless further reduced in particular cases) meant 21 years. The result? War criminals were treated more leniently than British criminals serving time for similar offences, and these

Table 16.1 No. 2 War Crimes Sentences Review Board (Far East) Standard Scale of Punishments Evolved by the Board for War Criminals Not Awarded the Supreme Penalty

	Major Responsibility	Intermediate Responsibility	Minor Responsibility
1 Ill-treatment of prisoners of war or civilians causing death.	Life	10 to 15 years	5 to 7 years
2 Gross and/or indecent torture.	Life	10 to 15 years	5 to 7 years
3 Concerned in killing of prisoners of war or civilians.	Life	10 to 15 years	5 to 7 years
4 Gross and/or prolonged ill-treatment of prisoners of war or civilians.	Life	10 to 12 years	4 to 6 years
5 Unlawful arrest, trial and execution.	Life	10 to 12 years	3 to 5 years
6 Execution of alleged subversives without trial.	Life	10 to 12 years	3 to 5 years
7 Inefficiency in control and/or administration causing death and/or acute suffering.	14 to 16 years	8 to 10 years	2 to 3 years
8 Minor torture (e.g. beating, etc., not sufficient to cause severe injury).	3 to 5 years	1 to 2 years	–

Major Responsibility:
Those responsible for initiating and/or entering whole-heartedly into the commission of war crimes.
(NOTE: **Any** person who enters whole-heartedly into gross and/or indecent torture is normally guilty under this heading).
Intermediate Responsibility:
Persons of some status, e.g. officers, warrant officers and senior N.C.O.s who, on the orders of their superiors, were concerned in the commission of war crimes.
Minor Responsibility:
Persons of low status or intelligence who, on the orders of their superiors, were concerned in the commission of war crimes.

changes made 'Lifers' eligible for release after serving 14 years with good behaviour.

Clemency was high on Japan's agenda at the San Francisco Peace Conference. It was agreed that Japan would review and make recommendations to the detaining Power for clemency where appropriate. By the enactment of Law 103 of 1952, Japan established a National Offenders'

Prevention and Rehabilitation (NOPAR) Commission to take over these administrative responsibilities.

The War Office was not equipped to cope with the political ramifications of Japan's escalating pressure concerning clemency. Between May and June 1952 the War Office and the Foreign Office agreed to transfer responsibility from the War Office to the Foreign Office for recommendations to the Monarch concerning all exercises of the Royal Prerogative of Mercy on behalf of war criminals. The Foreign Secretary, Sir Anthony Eden, felt constrained to accept the burden: 'I would much rather not . . . there is no escape, I most reluctantly concur', he wrote. These decisions were made by men putting the past behind them.

Over the following months the Secretaries of State for War and Foreign Affairs – and the Cabinet – made determinations on these matters in growing expectations that convicted war criminals would *invariably* obtain remission of one-third of their sentences for supposed 'good conduct' in prison.

There was a general feeling that Britain must soon reach agreement with the other Allied Powers on how to deal with these cases, on their merits or otherwise. When the British first began to prepare for handling Japanese recommendations for clemency as provided for under the Peace Treaty, Ambassador Sir Esler Dening wrote with great bitterness on 11 August 1952 that

> Before the Peace Treaty took effect, it was customary for these petitions to contain at least some perfunctory expression of regret for the crimes committed. Such pretence at compunction has now been largely discarded and the language of the petitions is becoming increasingly mimatory and insolent. The recent entry into force of the Peace Treaty between Japan and Nationalist China, as a result of which some 88 war criminals sentenced by Chinese Courts have been released, has increased this tone of arrogance and some of the released felons have seen fit to call at this and other Allied Missions to 'advise' us to follow the noble example of the Formosan regime. This 'advice' has been echoed in certain sections of the Japanese press, which claim that the continued imprisonment of Japanese nationals at the behest of alien Powers is derogatory to Japanese sovereignty.

After reciting evidence from which he concluded that the campaign had been orchestrated by the Japanese government, he forecast,

> I have no doubt that the Japanese will use every opportunity which presents itself to attempt to evade their responsibility under Article 11 of the Treaty of Peace and . . . they will exert [the] strongest pressure on whichever Allied Governments they consider most vulnerable . . . I suggest that we must avoid maintaining a stand without the support of other Powers.

One Foreign Office mandarin noted,

> I do not think it has ever been suggested that our clemency recommen-
> dations (or indeed any clemency recommendation anywhere) ought to
> be based solely on juridical considerations. Clemency cannot be based
> solely on such considerations and there is nothing improper in political
> or other considerations entering into it. Indeed, it is inevitable that they
> should.'

On 9 November 1952, there was further pressure on Britain when the
Japanese Ambassador met with Sir William Strang, Permanent Under-
Secretary of State for Foreign Affairs, and formally requested clemency for
all Japanese 'major' and 'minor' war criminals. By this time the Japanese
were evidently aware that the British, French and United States governments
had agreed a common line. The United States had already appointed a
tribunal to review individual applications for clemency and the French had
indicated that they would take parallel action. With greater reluctance, especially after recently accepting all of the Lynch Board's recommendations,
the British government grasped this nettle again.

During October 1952, conscious that the campaign to secure the repatriation and early release of Japanese war criminals serving time in foreign
gaols was orchestrated by the Japanese government and enjoyed widespread
popular support in Japan, Britain complied with a request by the Japanese
authorities that each prisoner's sentence should be calculated for the purposes of 'good conduct' remission from his date of arrest rather than date
of conviction. This was intended to be in line with Japan's new Law 103.
The British, however, had already done more, as John Chevalier O'Dwyer of
the Foreign Office later explained to Colonel Gerald Draper of the Judge
Advocate General's Office: 'Japanese war criminals are getting the best of
both worlds. Under the British system we reckon their sentences concurrently and under the Japanese system, to which we have agreed, we calcu-
late the commencement of sentence from the date of arrest.' Even more
irksome, it later emerged 'that the Japanese authorities themselves, by means
of a complicated formula, reduced the period of good conduct remission to
one-fourth of the original sentence'. The British felt duped by the Japanese
but politically could not reverse course, not even where prisoners serving
time for convictions by two or more British courts effectively gained a
reprieve of 100 per cent discount for all of the lesser of their sentences.

As the NOPAR Commission approached individual former Allied Powers
with recommendations for clemency from January 1953, the British Foreign
Office began what Anthony Nutting described as 'this odious task'. At first,
officials at the War Office and the Foreign Office responded cautiously. The
Lynch Board had already adjusted the sentences of those still in custody on
a basis of equity and harmonization. The new review by the Foreign Office

went further than any Court of Appeal. The grounds on which the Foreign Office team recommended that the Queen should exercise clemency took into account usages in the United Kingdom, Germany, Italy and the practices adopted by SCAP in Japan during the recent Occupation period. At its broadest, one or other of these countries took into consideration compassionate grounds, including health and age and the financial or other circumstances of the prisoner's family; mitigating factors such as superior orders (invariably also appraised by the original court before sentencing); fresh evidence that might tend to suggest that the original conviction was unsafe or had produced a substantial miscarriage of justice, and the effect upon public opinion in the countries concerned. It was finally decided that in making recommendations for clemency the Foreign Office would consider *all* of these factors in every case: customary International Law trumped Britain's domestic criminal procedure.

The records in all 115 remaining cases were scrutinized painstakingly. For a time, great care was taken to examine each application on its merits. As of 2 September 1954, eight years after the trials had begun, only 56 appeals for clemency had been examined in this way. In 45 cases, the responsible minister found no grounds for further clemency: recommendations made by the Japanese NOPAR panel were noted but rejected. In the 11 remaining cases, only 'a slight reduction of sentence has been approved or recommended'. Where necessary, special enquiries were made through political authorities or Special Branch officers in Malaya and elsewhere. The work was slow and officials had little or no enthusiasm for it.

Change, when it occurred, resulted from a relaxation in the German political climate, rather than as a result of the unremitting pressure from Japan so resented by British officials. In Germany the number of war criminals for whom the United Kingdom was responsible had declined more rapidly: of 678 originally convicted, only 40 remained in British custody by the end of 1954. Thirteen were due for release in 1955. In mid-April 1955, Harold Macmillan accepted his Western Department's advice to endorse a unanimous recommendation recently made by the Anglo-German Mixed Consultative Board on War Criminals, lowering the 'quantum' for 'Life' to 20 years. Macmillan's move came ten days into a general election campaign. The election having been won, it was decided to bring the Far East cases into line with the changes the Western Department had so effectively railroaded through. The arguments in favour of change were entirely political. They did not proceed from concerns about particular cases.

Publicity was shunned to minimize Japanese reactions and avoid any uproar in Britain. Parliament had been assured Britain would not grant any general clemency. If Japan learned there was to be a blanket ceiling of 20 years, less an automatic one-third remission, Tokyo would likely press for further general reductions. Crowe suggested applying the new rule without making any admission that it existed. In the end there was no finesse in calculation: the older policy that Japanese cases should be considered *only* on individual merits was unsustainable after the decision to apply a twenty-year rule in the German cases.

In July 1955 all yielded to the dictates of international politics. The twenty-year capping and other reductions in sentences recently conceded had not removed this thorn from Anglo-Japanese diplomatic relations. The Cabinet instituted a tariff of 15 years' imprisonment for life sentences, except in politically hypersensitive cases. With an automatic one-third remission on presumptions of good conduct in every case, the 15-year rule made lifers eligible for release ten years after falling into British hands. That would overcome the problem within about a year. This decision to meddle with the administration of justice, like earlier decisions by ministers to impose a 21- or 20-year quantum for 'Life', was taken purely for international political convenience.

Changes in the spring and summer of 1955 produced a helter-skelter rush. Convinced that they were participating in misapplications of the Prerogative amounting to a perversion of justice, officials suppressed their feelings about particular cases, pushed through paperwork, and no longer took account of the enormities for which these men were convicted nor examined whether perpetrators had become rehabilitated during imprisonment. By April 1956, the Foreign Office reviews of the NOPAR Commission's recommendations were concluded. The last Japanese war criminal for whom Britain remained responsible was released on 30 January 1957 after clemency was approved in December 1956.

The issue of Japanese war crimes ended as a catastrophic failure for international humanitarian law. In Japan, the misconception that the national war crimes trials were unfair had taken root, nourished by campaigns for the early release and rehabilitation of the felons. Efforts by Britain and her former Allies to re-establish harmonious relations with Japan were compromised by that. When the trials ended, the Secretary of State for War rightly declared, 'There can be little doubt that this most distasteful task was carried out with much skill and those concerned deserve our appreciation.' Ten years on, the system put war crimes victims out of mind. For them, and for all who once looked for such trials to re-establish respect for the laws and customs of war, haste and political expedience led by degrees to unqualified injustice.

Notes

1. A more extended analysis with detailed citations from the archival records may be obtained from the author at pritchard@international-law.org.uk.
2. DALS/1/28Q, DALS/0185/416, Minute by Shapcott, 23 November 1948, WO 311/646.

3. Of persons identifiable by name, 76 per cent of death penalties were executed.
4. Hence, demi-official note from George W. Lambert to Sir Basil Newton, 1 April 1946, TS 26/85; Brief for Capt. M.V. Argyle by Lt.-Col. G. Barratt, 6 May 1946, WO 311/541.
5. Note by Malkin, 7 October 1943, LCO 2/2662.
6. Note by MacGeagh, 3 January 1944, LCO 2/2662.
7. Royal Warrant 0160/2498, Army Order 81/1945, 14 June 1945 (subsequently amended), WO 309/1. For a useful introduction, see A.P.V. Rogers, 'War Crimes Trials under the Royal Warrant: British Practice, 1945–1949', *International and Comparative Law Quarterly* (British Institute of International & Comparative Law, London), vol. 39 (October 1990), pp. 780–800.
8. Memorandum by MacGeagh, 30 July 1946, TS 26/906.
9. Ibid., citing *R. v. Bottrill ex parte Kuechenmeister*, 62:17 *The Times Law Reports* (1946) 374. See R. John Pritchard, 'Casual Slaughters, Accidental Judgments', *Criminal Law Forum* (Amsterdam: Kluwer Academic Publishers, 1999), vol. 10, no. 2 pp. 505–21.
10. DALS/1/28Q, DALS/0185/416, Minute by Shapcott, 23 November 1948, WO 311/646.
11. Sentences imposed by British war crimes courts were not legally valid until confirmed by the commanding general on whose convening order the trial was authorized. The effect of non-confirmation was substantially a verdict of Not Guilty. Pritchard, 'The Quality of Mercy', in Peter Dennis (ed.), *2nd Criminal Law Forum: War and Peace in the Pacific* (Canberra: Australian War Memorial, 1999), pp. 147–98.
12. DALS/A/87, Demi-Official Note from Shapcott to Lynch, 4 March 1949, WO 311/567.
13. *Manual of Military Law* (London: Her Majesty's Stationery Office, 1951 edition).
14. Toyama Tanji, *Gunpô Kaigi Hôron* (Tokyo, 1924), p. 13 et seq.
15. See, for example, Article 86 of the Army Military Law Code (Tokyo, 1908 edition) in the Boei Kenkyujo Toshokan, Tokyo. I am grateful to Kibata Yoichi (University of Tokyo) for facilitating access to these records and for the invaluable services of Tago Atsushi as my research assistant.
16. Articles 86 and 88 of the Army Military Law Code (Tokyo, 1936 edition) in D.1.5.0.2, *Taikoku Gunji oyobi Gunji Saiban Kankei Zakken* [Imperial Military and Military Trial Legal Affairs] (miscellaneous papers), at the Gaiko Shiryokan Tokyo.

17

The Japanese Military's Attitude Towards International Law and the Treatment of Prisoners of War

Yoshito Kita

The nature of Japanese war crimes

The famous scholar of international law, Sir Hersch Lauterpacht, has characterized the war crimes committed during the Second World War in the following terms: 'The Second World War witnessed war crimes, on a scale unprecedented in history, on the part of Germany and, to a lesser extent, of some of her allies. . . . on the part of Japan the main source of war crimes lay in her inhuman treatment of Prisoners of War.'[1] After the war, the Allied Powers established 49 war crimes courts based on Article 10 of the Potsdam Declaration, which promised that stern justice would be meted out to all war criminals, including those who had mistreated prisoners of war (POWs). Among the 5472 Japanese war criminals brought to justice by these tribunals, 4353 were found guilty, and 920 were sentenced to death.[2] In 36 per cent of these cases, the tribunals made their charges on crimes related to the killing, mistreatment, and mistreatment causing the death of POWs.[3]

The British Armed Forces arrested about 4000 Japanese on suspicion of war crimes, and prosecuted 933 of them. The British tribunals executed 222, sentenced 53 to life imprisonment, and condemned 514 to imprisonment for definite terms.[4] Of the 306 cases, 83 related to the treatment of POWs and involved 342 accused individuals.[5] The US Military Commission, founded in Yokohama by the US Armed Forces, tried the cases of illegal acts against the Allied POWs interned in Japan. Some 242 cases out of 307 and 542 individuals prosecuted out of 841, related to POW camps.[6]

During the war, Japan's POW Information Bureau processed 83 Allied protests and inquiries regarding inhumane treatment of POWs.[7] In addition, a considerable number of protests, demands, and inquiries regarding POWs and civilian internees were directed to Japan through the Protecting Powers and International Committee of the Red Cross.[8]

Inhumane treatment of its POWs, however, was not a part of Japan's official policy in waging war. To comply with international law, immediately after the outbreak of hostilities Tokyo set up the POW Information Bureau and legislated various domestic laws, such as the POW Treatment Regulations, the POW Camps Regulation, the POW Work Regulations, and the POW Maintenance Regulations. The POW Treatment Regulations provided that prisoners had to be treated humanely, and should not be insulted or abused (Article 2). The War Minister, the head of the POW Management Office of the War Ministry (a position held concurrently with heading the POW Information Bureau), army commanders, and POW camp commandants from time to time instructed their personnel to treat POWs decently. For example, on 23 June 1942, War Minister Tojo Hideki told new camp commandants that POWs must be treated according to the various regulations in order to show the fair attitude of Japanese Empire to the Japanese and international communities.[9]

It is appropriate to establish the dimensions of the POW problem for the Japanese. During the Second World War, Japanese forces took 167930 American and European military and medical personnel as POWs and interned them in 17 major POW camps in Japan and overseas. Of these, 38 135 POWs died due to illness and other causes.[10] According to the International Military Tribunal for the Far East (IMTFE), 132134 American and British servicemen became prisoners, and 35756 of them died in captivity. Compared with the death rate of 4 per cent among American and British POWs captured by Germany and Italy, the death rate of 27 per cent in the Japanese camps was extraordinarily high.[11]

Changing Japanese attitudes towards Japanese POWs

The primary reason that Japan's military mistreated POWs derives from a perception of POWs that was unique to the Japanese. Among western military services, a soldier surrendering to his enemy despite his best efforts does not shame himself as a soldier or as a citizen. The soldier still sees himself as honourable, and his country accepts its enemy's report of his capture. In contrast, the Japanese military understood honour as demanding that a serviceman continue to fight and to die even under desperate circumstances without prospect of victory. The Japanese held that those who intentionally surrendered to the enemy and those captured while unconscious were equally shamed.

The Field Service Code (*Senjin-kun*) of 8 January 1941 officially formalized this negative view toward POWs. By outlining the essence of the Japanese soldier's moral duty in plain language, the Code was originally intended to deal with the increasing problem of misconduct by Japanese servicemen in China. The Code also discouraged soldiers from becoming POWs. It stressed:

> To be strong, understand honour and shame. For the honour of your native community and your family name, meet their expectations by making your best effort. Do not disgrace yourself by becoming a prisoner;

do not leave behind a name soiled by becoming a prisoner (*Senjin-kun*, Chapter 2, No. 8, 'Honour One's Name').

Such instructions urged a soldier to sacrifice himself rather to become a POW. In his Commentary for the Field Service Code (*Senjin-kun Kai*), approved by the Information Section of the War Ministry, Colonel Sasaki Kazuo clearly stressed that being captured alive in itself brought shame; therefore, a soldier had to avoid it by all means.[12]

This contempt towards becoming a POW, however, was not an ancient Japanese tradition. With the rise of the *samurai* class, the Japanese had developed procedures for surrender, such as displaying a soldier's camp hat on top of a spear during a battle.[13] From the time of the Sino-Japanese War, however, some Japanese commanders had occasionally issued oral instructions forbidding their soldiers from surrendering. Notwithstanding this, to the end of the Second World War, neither the Army nor Navy penal codes contained any clause prohibiting Japanese soldiers from surrendering or demanding that former POWs be ostracized.[14]

In light of this, when and how did the Japanese develop their ideology of 'never surrender' and their antagonism toward POWs? Professor Hata Ikuhiko has studied in some depth how military authorities have treated former Japanese POWs since the Sino-Japanese War, as well as how civilian attitudes towards them. He asserts that the unique Japanese attitude towards POWs, later encapsulated in the *Senjin-kun*, first developed among individuals as an ethical standard. These ideas gradually spread as an accepted ethical norm in the military organization and finally grew to bind all Japanese as the social code.[15]

In Japanese society, negative attitudes towards war prisoners emerged after the Russo-Japanese War during which, for the first time in Japanese history, large numbers of the Japanese soldiers had become POWs. Military authorities brought 2083 returned POWs to the POW Inquiry Commission in accordance with the Regulations for the Treatment of POW Returnees. Instead of blindly condemning them for having been taken as prisoners, the Committee investigated how these Japanese soldiers had become prisoners and tried to determine if they had given their best fighting effort.[16] While officers received more severe penalties, no one was court-martialed. In some cases, indeed, the former POWs were honoured with the Golden Kite, the highest order for Japanese servicemen.

Although the military authorities had treated former POWs rather leniently, the public rejected the returnees. When former POWs returned to their military units or to their home towns, many suffered discrimination. They often found themselves ostracized in their communities. In one case, although a former POW had been honoured with a medal for his wartime ordeal, his home village still ostracized him, and village children bullied his children. Consequently, many former POWs gave up living in their home towns and migrated to big cities or overseas. Some POWs preferred not to return to Japan and spent their lives hiding in Manchuria. In some disturbing incidents, lower-ranked soldiers refused to salute higher-ranked, former POWs in their units.[17]

Bushido, the code of *samurai*, played an important role in forming Japanese abhorrence towards surrender. *Bushido* is the code of moral and ethical principles by which the *samurai* class professionally served and conducted their daily affairs. According to *Bushido*, duty, bravery, benevolence, courtesy, sincerity, honour, and loyalty were considered to be basic virtues. The conception of these virtues gradually spread from the *samurai* class to the rest of Japan's population and became established as the national moral standard.[18] Placing an excessive emphasis on the concept of honour, the view emerged that choosing an honourable death – suicide – was better than suffering shame by being captured. The *Hagakure*, an early eighteenth-century compilation of *samurai*-clan ethics and theories of *Bushido*, taught their essence:

> The Way of Warrior (*bushido*) is to find a way to die. If a choice is given between life and death, the samurai must choose death. There is no more meaning beyond this. Make up your mind and follow the pre-determined course. . . . At that very moment, if he misses his objectives and continues to live, as a samurai he must be regarded as a coward. It is difficult to draw an exact line. If he misses his objectives and chooses death, some may say he dies in vain and he is crazy to do so. But this must not regarded as a shameful act. It is of utmost importance for *bushido*.[19]

This passage greatly influenced the development of Japanese views on life and death.

The trend was that 'anti-surrenderism', which repudiated the very idea of becoming a POW, penetrated not only military personnel but also the general public. Needing to create strong military forces and to supplement Japan's material shortages with spiritual strength, military authorities conceivably followed and supported this public trend.

During the Taisho period, two incidents greatly influenced the formalization of Japanese views toward POWs: the First World War and the Nikolaevsk Incident of 1920. The large number of military personnel taken as POWs on the European front – about eight million from both sides – shocked Japanese military authorities. To tighten discipline in his department, Major General Nara Takeji, the Chief of Military Affairs Department, emphasized the differences between Japanese and western servicemen:

> From ancient times, *samurai* did not expect to return alive from battle-fields. The only choice for these warriors was either to annihilate the

enemy or to sacrifice their lives. Even when a soldier loses his combat ability, there is no excuse for surrendering to his enemy.[20]

The Nikolaevsk Incident of March 1920 occurred in the small town of Nikolaevsk at the mouth of the Amur River. When Russian partisans demanded that the Japanese garrison in the area disarm, the Japanese Army attacked the Russians. The Japanese stopped fighting at orders from the brigade and surrendered their weapons. The surviving soldiers were then imprisoned and massacred two months later. The number of Japanese casualties, including Japanese residents in the region, reached 122. The incident became a turning point. In addition to the well-established notion of surrender as shameful, from then on Japanese also feared that brutal murder was likely to follow surrender. During the Showa Period, to exalt militarism the military had publicized heroic stories of Japanese soldiers and officers who had chosen suicide over imprisonment by their enemies. The most famous of these involved Major Kuga Noboru during the First Shanghai Incident (1932). The Major, severely injured and captured by Chinese forces, was told that he could be exchanged and that he could return to Japan after a truce. Out of an overwhelming sense of shame, he instead chose to kill himself at the very place where so many of his men had been killed. The press played the story as a great heroic tale, and it was made into a popular stage play. Professor Hata suggests that the Kuga Incident heightened popular sentiments against those war prisoners.[21]

Following the Nomonhan Incident (1939), the Soviet Army returned 294 Japanese POWs. On their return home, the Japanese military tried them in the special courts martial. All of the officers were given pistols and forced to commit suicide. Among the NCOs, those who had been captured because they had suffered injury were acquitted. Those who had sustained no injury were charged with 'desertion in the face of the enemy' for their lack of will either to resist or to kill themselves. Reportedly, 567 Japanese servicemen remained in the Soviet territory, because they were ashamed for having surrendered.[22]

During the Sino-Japanese War, returnee POWs received harsher treatment. Even those former POWs who had escaped courts martial still suffered stern disciplinary measures. Some faced compulsory duty in the Retraining Unit, and many were sent overseas after they had completed their punishments. The longer the war continued, the more Japanese servicemen surrendered to become POWs. Military authorities seemed to have taken these decisive measures in order to shore up the increasingly demoralized discipline in the Japanese Army in China.[23]

During the Pacific War, Japanese soldiers who returned to Japan after having surrendered to the enemy received discriminatory treatment. Senior officers, of the rank of captain and above, were often forced to commit suicide. Lieutenants and second lieutenants were pressured to choose either suicide or life –those choosing life, however, were granted opportunities to be killed in combat. This treatment, designed to protect the honour of a serviceman, was commonly understood as an act of great benevolence for one's subordinates.[24]

In keeping with this view, during the last stage of the war Japanese commanders often quoted the *Senjin-kun* to their men before their final attack, admonishing them not to surrender and beseeching the severely wounded to commit suicide rather than falling into enemy hands. As a result, the number of Japanese POWs during the Pacific War remained relatively small. In contrast to the number of deaths, 1 932 300, according to Professor Hata's study, the number of POWs – including those on the Chinese mainland – were little more than 50 000 by the end of August 1945.[25]

Japanese attitudes towards POWs were reflected in the ratification question of the Geneva Conventions for the Protection of Prisoners of War (Geneva POW Conventions) of 1929. Although most Allied Powers ratified the treaty, Japan failed to follow suit because of opposition from its military. A letter from the deputy naval minister to the deputy foreign minister clearly stated military sentiments at the time: 'While Japanese servicemen do not expect to become POWs, foreigners think quite differently. Therefore, despite its bilateral appearance, this treaty in reality places a unilateral obligation on Japan.'[26] Second, the Geneva POW Conventions provided for a level of treatment of POWs, which was, in fact, better than that received by Japanese servicemen. Japan's ratification of the Conventions inevitably would have required the revision of the Naval Penal Code. Any such revision seemed detrimental to maintaining military discipline. The Japanese Army shared the same view, as evidenced by War Minister Tojo's testimony to the IMTFE.[27]

Japan's 'never surrender' policy forced soldiers to continue fighting to the death and promoted the spiritual strength of Japan's military. On the other hand, it also fed the contemptible behaviour of Japanese military personnel towards enemy POWs – behaviour that led to numerous acts of mistreatment of POWs. Believing that surrender was shameful, the Japanese were surprised and disgusted with enemy POWs who asserted their rights as POWs under international law or who asked that their families at home be notified of their survival. Any Japanese taken prisoner, even when unconscious, was shamed and lost his honour as a Japanese citizen. The Japanese did not understand why Allied prisoners were not similarly ashamed of their POW status.[28]

Knowledge of international law among Japanese servicemen

Historians have suggested a lack of knowledge and awareness of international laws as one of the major reasons why Japanese military personnel committed war crimes such as the murder and mistreatment of enemy

POWs. According to the survey conducted among war criminals by the Japanese Ministry of Justice after the war, many of them replied that they did not know international law and that they had not been educated regarding international laws.[29]

A study of Japanese treatment of enemy POWs, at this point, requires an examination of two questions: whether or not Japanese servicemen had been educated regarding the provisions of international, law including the rights of POWs, and whether or not Japanese military authorities had compiled manuals to explain the essence of international laws.

Japan's War College was founded in 1882 for senior and staff officers, and it began teaching international law in 1891. Although the number of classes in this subject varied from year to year, at least ten and as many as 43 classes were offered every academic year. Each class consisted of 105 minutes in summer and 95 minutes in winter. It was said that first-class scholars in the field of international law and the laws of war taught these courses through the use of case studies. Specific instruction on international law for the protection of POWs, however, was merely listed as 'Laws and Customs of War on Land' in the teaching programme of 1907. It is difficult to assess the coverage of this instruction as neither textbooks nor teaching materials have been found. It seems, moreover, that military education regarding international law was suspended in 1937 when the educational term was shortened because of the Sino-Japanese War.[30]

Since its founding in 1888, the Naval Staff College had taught international law. In 1935, for instance, sixty classes on international law and forty more on the laws on maritime war, each ninety minutes long, were scheduled. As in the War College, leading scholars of international law taught these subjects. Materials relating to the treatment of POWs, however, have not yet been found. The laws of maritime war undoubtedly remained the primary focus in these courses. After the Marco Polo Bridge Incident of 1937, which brought open hostility between Japan and China, the admission of students became biannual and was eventually cancelled after 1941.[31]

Among various ranks, junior- and middle-grade officers tended most frequently to encounter problems on the battlefield regarding international law. Around 1922, the Military Academy began teaching international law as a part of its legal studies programme. The actual number of lessons given, each of fifty to sixty minutes, was limited, however, to only two to three by the end of the Pacific War. Extant textbooks offer some insights into the contents of those lessons. For example, the textbook of 1934 defined POW status very much in keeping within the parameters and even the language used in the Geneva POW Convention:

[When a combatant enters the territory under his enemy's control, he becomes a prisoner of war. A prisoner must be treated humanely and follow the laws and orders of the Army that has captured him. These forces can detain such prisoners and impose on them work of a non-military nature.

The textbook, however, did not explain the rights of POWs. The 1943 edition offered little change from the 1934 edition beyond adding a commentary on the POW Information Bureau.[32]

The Naval Academy started including international law in its curriculum surprisingly late – in 1905. Athough the education manual of 1934 contained a section on 'Summary of International Law and Maritime Law', no classes on international law were offered.[33] Volume three of the Reference Book on Military Administration (*Gunsei Sanko-sho*) of 1941 discussed international law and took two pages to explain the meaning of POWs, their status, the escape of POWs, and the termination of POW status. Concerning the rights of POWs, it reads,

> When one captures a person with certain criteria, the captured must be treated as a prisoner of war. The prisoner will lose his freedom and be placed under certain restrictions. The captor must not mistreat the prisoner and he must give the prisoner treatment equal to that for servicemen of the detaining country . . . A POW will be placed under the authority of the detaining government and receive humane treatment.

The reference book, however, neglected to explain the working conditions and other details for the proper treatment of POWs.[34]

The remaining textbooks of wartime cadet education reveal a lack of instruction necessary to conceptualize the rights of POWs. It is possible that Japan's military feared that by learning details of the rights of and fair treatment for POWs, Japanese servicemen might too easily choose to surrender. While education in international law for officers and officer candidates was quite limited, it is conceivable that the education regarding international law for NCOs was totally absent during the Showa period.

A formal lack of education regarding international law in the curriculum, however, did not necessarily mean that Japanese soldiers should be kept in the dark. Military authorities, who were responsible for the treatment for the many POWs inevitably captured, could have summarized the basic provisions of international law that had to be observed. They could have compiled them into a field manual, which soldiers would then have used to guide their actions on battlefields. The Convention respecting the Laws and Customs of War on Land signed at The Hague in 1907 (The Hague Convention), Article 1, bound each signatory to issue instructions to its army to comply with provisions respecting the laws and customs of war on land. The Japanese Army, however, failed to give such instructions, including those regarding POWs. During the Meiji and Taisho periods, a commentary on the Red Cross Treaty was published, but even this commentary did not give any instructions about the rights of POWs.

The *Senjin-kun* defined the treatment of surrendered enemy combatants, of enemy property, and of enemy civilians. Although such passages concerned international law, they enunciated only abstract principles. For example, the *Senjin-kun* stated that

> Even though force may compel the enemy to submit, should a lapse in virtue occur by the striking of those who do not resist or by failure to show kindness to those who surrender, it cannot be said that such an army is perfect. (Chapter 1, No. 2);

> Be mindful to protect enemy property and resources. Requisitions, seizures, and the destruction of goods and similar actions must be executed in keeping with the regulations and always under the orders of your commanding officer. (Chapter 5, No. 1, 6);

> and Be gentle to and protect innocent inhabitants in a spirit of benevolence in accordance with the true ideal of Imperial Army. (Chapter, 3, No. 7)

In its one section on 'Basic International Laws Applicable during Wartime', the Manual of Wartime Service (*Senji Fukumu Teiyo*), compiled by the Superintendent-General for Military Education in 1938 for junior officers, briefly explained POWs status, the fundamental principles involved in treating POWs, and the punishment of POWs. It did not mention, however, the rights of POWs. While the Excerpts from the Geneva Conventions (*Sekijuji Jôyaku Bassui*) were again compiled by the Superintendent-General for Military Education in 1937, a commentary for the 'Regulations Respecting the Laws and Customs of War on Land' (Hague Regulations of War on Land) supplement to the Hague Convention was not published.

Regarding the Navy, the Laws of Naval War of 1914 in Chapter 20, 'Treatment of the Crews and Passengers of a Prize', defined POW status. The provision, however, was limited to the humane treatment of the crews, passengers, and POWs of seized ships and to the protection of their property (Article 121) as well as describing POW status. Naval authorities in 1937 issued the Commentary of Wartime International Laws (*Senji Kokusai Hoki Koyo*) and distributed it to the appropriate departments for use in teaching the duties of naval officers. The Commentary contained explanations of penal codes for naval, air, and land warfare. POWs were to be under the authority of the hostile country, not under the authority of an enemy military unit. They were to be treated humanely (Regulations for War on Land, Article 4). In addition, Chapter 2, which detailed the treatment of POWs, fell short of explaining their right beyond mentioning the 'newly' signed Geneva POW Conventions of 1929. In any case, Japan had not ratified them. The Navy, after the outbreak of the war, published and distributed to fleet units the Supplement to the Commentary of Wartime International Laws

(*Senji Kokusai Hoki Koyo Tsuika Hen*), which contained the Geneva Convention on POWs.

These measures clearly could not guide servicemen in treating POWs. It stands to reason that the Army authorities, who were responsible for managing vast numbers of POWs captured in the war on land, should have created a manual concerning laws and customs of war on land or at least a textbook including clauses of treaties regarding POWs. There were also practical matters that greatly hampered the proper treatment of POWs.

Supply and medical care issues

The absence of adequate provisions for the board, lodging, and medical services for POWs under Japanese control invited significant criticism from the Allied Powers. According to Article 7 of the Hague Convention Respecting the Laws and Customs of War on Land, in the absence of special agreement among the belligerents, POWs were entitled to receive the 'same treatment' in lodging, board, and clothing as did the military personnel of the government detaining the POWs. Article 11 of the Geneva Convention carried the same provision.

The POW Maintenance Regulation of 20 February 1942 provided that officers who became POWs had to receive the same maintenance as did Japanese officers of corresponding ranks (Article 2). Soldiers, warrant officers and below, were to receive rations comparable to the basic rations for Japanese servicemen (Article 5). Each POW camp purchased food for the prisoners within the limits of a fixed amount.

As the military situation deteriorated, Japanese POW camps suffered from a lack of food and medical supplies both in Japan and in the South East Asia area, also known as the *nanpo chiiki* (Southern Area). The sinking of Japanese cargo ships seriously hampered the movement of freight between Japan and South East Asia and consequently caused much hardship in the POW camps. Even in 1942, the traffic of basic supplies for Japanese field units in the area received only 76 per cent of its requests. In 1944, the satisfaction of needs fell to a mere 56 per cent and in 1945 to zero. By the final stage of the war, Japan's transport capacity had decreased to 21 per cent of what it had been before the war. In order to secure minimum food supplies for Japan's population, Tokyo forsook importing raw materials for manufacturing weapons.[35] While food supplies inside Japan declined, supplying distant camps in South East Asia was even more difficult. Depending on the road conditions, only a half or one-third of allocated rations reached those camps.[36]

Research into the supply conditions at the Osaka POW Camp in 1945 shows that the average ration of staple foods (rice and barley) was 705 grams for a POW, 705 grams for a Japanese serviceman, 570 grams for a heavy civilian worker, 390 grams for a light civilian worker, and 330 grams for a common citizen. For calories, it was 3000 kcal for a POW, 3000 kcal for a Japanese serviceman, 2200 kcal for a heavy civilian worker, 1800 kcal for a light civilian worker, and 1400 kcal for a common citizen. In addition, meat, fish, vegetables, soybean paste, soy source, edible oil, salt, sugar, and ox bones were supplied. Among those, Japanese servicemen received a little more animal meat – 5 grams for a POW vs 7 grams for a Japanese serviceman – and of sugar – 5 grams for a POW vs 7 grams for a Japanese serviceman. The POWs, however, received more edible oil and salt than did Japanese servicemen, while ox bones were given only to POWs. Meat and sugar indeed were hardly available among the civilians.[37]

Thus, according to the research, POWs in Japan received almost the same food ration as Japanese servicemen. Moreover, recognizing their more meat-oriented eating habits, camp authorities endeavoured to supply animal meat to POWs. Sick POWs in hospitals were also fed with the highest quality bread, milk, and eggs, which were all nearly impossible for the Japanese civilians to get.[38]

Faced with a critical situation in food supply, on 7 February 1945 the chief of the POW Management Office in the War Ministry sent a letter to all POW camps. This requested that all camps encourage gardening and other self-supporting work among the POWs, to 'increase self-sufficiency and ensure proper food supplies' for the prisoners. The employers of prison labour, at the request of the camps, supplemented food for the POWs at work places. For instance, Asano Dock of Japan Steel (Nihon Kokan) in Yokohama at first provided prisoners with a cup of noodles at lunchtime, 'despite the most difficult conditions for obtaining any supplies'. After their stock of noodles ran out, the company distributed dried noodles. When this ran out, the company purchased vegetables and anything available as a supplement. It also supplied POWs, 'especially because of the physical characteristics of the Westerners', with ox blood, viscera, black tea, cigarettes, salt, and vegetables.[39]

The Construction Plan for the Siam–Burma Connecting Railway of August 1942 by the Railway Unit of the Southern Army shows the POW situation in the Japanese camps overseas. It determined the distribution of staple foods: 800 grams for a Japanese serviceman vs 550 grams for a POW; 210 grams vs 50 grams of meat, and 600 grams vs 100 grams of fresh vegetables. The amount of supplies was to be increased for POWs engaging in heavy labour: staple foods to 750 grams, animal meat to 150 grams, and vegetables to 500 grams.[40] Although the amounts allocated for food for Japanese servicemen exceeded by a little that given to POWs at heavy labour, there was no severe discrimination against the POWs. When the transport of supplies ceased due to the rainy season in the Siam–Burma border area, the only food supplies left were cooked rice with a sprinkling of sugar or salt. Needless to say, POWs complained about the 'rice only' ration, even while Japanese servicemen bore the same menu.[41]

Not only food, but also medicines and medical supplies were in serious shortage. As the battles in the Southern Area took place in unsanitary and undeveloped areas, many POWs suffered from malnutrition and contagious diseases. In addition, the 3381 POWs, or 10 per cent of all the POWs transferred to Japan from the Southern Area, died because they did not adapt to Japan's cooler climate and environment. Most of them died from respiratory diseases, beriberi, and digestive disorders. Concerned for the health of their prisoners, the camp authorities endeavoured to supply bread, meat, vitamins, yeast, and so on. They also transferred sick POWs to warmer areas, while they tried to improve installations to protect POWs against cold.[42]

Japanese military authorities furthermore were conscious of sanitary conditions in the camps. Sick and wounded prisoners received the same medical treatment as Japanese servicemen. The authorities endeavoured to establish hospitals for the POWs. They also opened Japanese Army and civilian hospitals for POWs and generally improved medical facilities. On 2 March 1944, the Vice-Minister of War issued an order to better the conditions for POWs by supplying them with food and clothing as provided for in various regulations; by establishing sick rooms in POW camps; by using the services of medical staff among the prisoners; by arranging services of unit doctors from the Army hospitals for POWs as needed; by prohibiting heavy labour by sick or weakened prisoners; and by transferring prisoners to those camps whose climate best matched the individual POW's physical conditions.[43] Despite such efforts, the deteriorating military situation considerably aggravated health conditions, disease control, and medical treatment among the POWs, because of the lack of foods and medicines, as well as the worsening ratio of medical personnel to an increasing number of patients, hospitals, and military units. The treatment of Japanese servicemen, however, was hardly better than that provided the POWs. The Japanese did not necessarily discriminate against the POWs. Medicines not in stock already inside Japan were unattainable. Even when medicines and medical equipment could be sent, they often did not reach prisoners because of merchant shipping losses. It is said that the Navy had medicinal stocks sufficient for only one year. Neither penicillin nor DDT had yet been put to practical use in Japan.[44] The Japanese tried to make up for the lack of medicines for POWs by purchasing from civilians and encouraging donations from the employers of POWs. Camp staffs themselves made an effort to pick medicinal herbs in the hills and fields.[45]

Overall, deficiencies in the Japanese supply system for medicines and food were closely related to the Japanese philosophy of life and death. Facing death, the Japanese typically believed that it was honourable to accept it. Under such a mentality, the Japanese in general paid little attention to caring for the sick and wounded. As the Imperial Precepts to Soldiers and Sailors (*Gunjin Chokuyu*) stated, 'bear in mind that duty is weightier than a mountain, while death is lighter than a feather'. Japanese soldiers were taught not to value their lives above their duty to the State and the Emperor. This mentality fed the tendency to 'place priority to the transport of weapons, ammunition, and machine parts, while making light of equipment and medical supplies for medical units . . . as a consequence, medical activities became extremely difficult'.[46] Further, during the Second World War, the Japanese military did not allow its sick and wounded to remain on the battlefield with medical staff or to retreat alone. The policy was to leave the sick and wounded in the care of the enemy's armed forces. This attitude toward the sick and wounded, evolving from Japanese philosophy, did decisive damage to its treatment of the enemy POWs.

The origin of unauthorized corporal punishment

Public slapping by the Japanese guards most antagonised and offended Allied POWs. Physical punishment such as slapping and beating was, in both the military and also in civilian homes, a common and accepted discipline in Japan at that time. Although military authorities prohibited unofficial punishment of this sort, slapping even for trifling misconduct, approved by Japanese custom, persisted in the POW camps until the end of the war. In general, Japanese tend to be short-tempered and easily provoked by trivial things. Most cases of beatings of enemy POWs, based on spontaneous agitation, were exercised to reform delinquent and disobedient behaviour among POWs, behaviour that often derived from problems in communication and differences in customs. There were only a few cases of unauthorised punishment administered as expressions of personal hostility and malicious intent to cause pain and insult.

Even these few instances, authorities tried to curb. On 26 February 1943, Major-General Hamada Taira, director of the Army POW Management Bureau, made a speech at a conference of POW camp chiefs. He said:

> unauthorised punishment, which can happen based on a slight change of temper of the attacker, will be recognised in the world as a common exercise among our people, instead of the result of faults in an individual's personality. When these POWs return home and spread bad publicity of unauthorized assaults by the Japanese servicemen, its negative affect will be unmeasured.

He instructed the camp personnel to 'propagate my instruction and to treat our POWs fairly'.[47]

Unauthorized corporal punishment was meant as punishment. The Japanese, however, commonly believed that to atone for crimes and violations of regulations unofficial beatings were more lenient and paternalistic than official punishments determined by a legally constituted procedures. Westerners failed to understand this cultural difference. Japanese guards often resorted to beatings in lieu of confining offenders to the guardhouse to punish prisoners for stealing food and medicines. The Allied Powers saw this as ill-treatment of POWs.

Many such cases were brought as B/C-class war crimes to the post-war Allied tribunals, not always fairly. Lewis Bush, a reserve officer of the Royal Navy, had taught English in a higher school in Japan before the war. He witnessed an incident when a Dutch prisoner had concealed a radio in his quarters at the Japanese POW Camp in Hong Kong. Bush testified:

> If Lieutenant Wada had told the *Kempeitai* the Dutch naval Lieutenant would have been beheaded. He was, however, released after merely being beaten. A Japanese sergeant gave the punishment, and it looked rather cruel at that time. Nevertheless, I must say that the punishment would have been incomparably heavier if Lieutenant Wada had been a cold-hearted man.[48]

Doubtless, the unofficial corporal punishments were an unfortunate custom in the Japanese armed forces and reflected badly as a national characteristic. Interestingly, British armed forces also used corporal punishment against POWs. Yuji Aida, who spent two years in the Alon POW Camp, frequently witnessed British soldiers striking Japanese soldiers who had stolen food.[49]

Absolute obedience to a superior's orders

Last but not least, the Japanese military tradition of absolute obedience to superior orders was another significant cause of the maltreatment of POWs. In war crimes trials, many of the accused Japanese entered a plea of not guilty to crimes of ill-treatment of POWs on the grounds that they had merely followed the orders of their superiors. Many Allied war crimes trial regulations, most notably Article 6 of the Charter of IMTFE, clearly rejected this 'plea of superior orders' as an acceptable defence.[50] Most accused of the ill-treatment of POWs were severely punished.

In every country, military discipline is a primary concern. In order to maintain the chain of command, every military organization demands absolute obedience to orders from its soldiers. This relationship between orders and obedience was especially rigid in Japan.

The *Gunjin Chokuyu*, the Articles of War (*Tokuho*), and the Internal Regulations (*Guntai Naimusho*) defined the relations between orders and obedience in the Japanese Army up to 1945. The *Gunjin Chokuyu* was issued to Japanese soldiers and sailors in the name of Emperor Meiji on 4 January 1882. Any order from a superior, according to the rescript, was to be interpreted as an exercise of the Imperial prerogative. As a result, Japanese soldiers developed a fixed idea of orders from their superiors as being direct orders from the Emperor, 'the living god'. It was, therefore, inconceivable that any order could be illegal.

While the *Gunjin Chokuyu* was an Imperial precept from above, the *Tokuho* was a self-disciplined oath of servicemen. Until the early Showa period, a new recruit was to pledge his allegiance based on the *Tokuho* at the time of joining a unit. The Japanese government originally issued the *Tokuho* in 1871 and revised it in 1882 just after promulgation of the *Gunjin Chokuyu*. Article 3 of the *Tokuho* provided that a Japanese soldier must obey an order from his superior regardless of its content and must not refuse or object to it. The *Guntai Naimusho* of 1881 summarized various military duties and was reissued in a completely revised form as the *Guntai Naimurei* in 1943. It recognized military discipline as the 'lifeline' of the military organization, and saw obedience to orders as essential in maintaining military discipline. Therefore, it demanded sufficient training for soldiers that they would acquire the habit of unquestionably obeying and carrying out their orders (Principle 5). In order to secure this behaviour, soldiers were never permitted to argue the propriety of, or to ask the reason for, a superior's orders (Chapter 2 'Obedience', Nos 9 and 11).

Even in the Japanese military, illegal orders were theoretically invalid, and servicemen were not obligated to obey them.[51] In reality, however, it would have been exceptional for a Japanese serviceman to ignore the 'religious inviolability' of his duty to obey orders, even when such orders were illegal.[52] In return, the Japanese military customarily exonerated those who carried out illegal orders from legal liability.[53] The *Guntai Naimurei* explained that a subordinate could initially refuse to carry out an illegal order and ask for its reconsideration. At his superior's insistence, however, the subordinate was not permitted to argue the propriety of the order any further. And once the decision had been made, the subordinate was to ignore the difference of opinion and was obligated solely to make every effort to execute the order (Chapter 2, No. 12). The Army Penal Code severely punished protests and insubordination: capital punishment, lifetime imprisonment, or imprisonment for more than ten years for insubordination before the enemy; one to ten years' imprisonment for offenses committed during operations or in an area under the martial law; and five years' or less imprisonment under any other circumstance (Article 57).

Based on various military regulations and severe punishments, the Japanese military nurtured customs demanding absolute obedience to orders, regardless of their content. It was almost impossible for soldiers to refuse any order even if he recognized its illegality. The notion that a superior's orders were absolute indirectly – and directly – led to the war crimes, including inhumane treatment of POWs, committed by Japanese military personnel. The notion of absolute obedience to superior orders, thus, became an indirect cause of war crimes.

The British Manual of Military Law of 1914, Article 443, stated that a soldier who violated recognized laws of war while following an order from his government or his superior was not a war criminal and should not be punished by his enemy. Britain revised the manual in April 1944. Under these new instructions, an accused who had committed war crimes pursuant to orders could not avoid having those acts characterized as war crimes, nor could he avoid criminal prosecution and punishment by the injured power. The revision, made when the war's outcome was clear, was doubtless intended to deprive Axis war criminals of the opportunity to avoid prosecution by making a plea that they had merely been following orders.

Consequences of common animosity towards POWs

After Japan's unconditional surrender, its servicemen's unwillingness to surrender and their lack of knowledge of international laws concerning POWs ironically affected the treatment of Japanese servicemen under the authority of the Allied Forces in various parts of the world. The treatment of surrendered Japanese servicemen by the British forces was typical.

With the acceptance of the Potsdam Declaration, about 633000 Japanese officers and men of the Southern Army surrendered to the South East Asia Command (SEAC), which was composed largely of British armed forces. The British treated these servicemen as Japanese surrendered personnel (JSPs), rather than as POWs protected under international law. In other words, the Allied Powers assigned to them an unprecedented and special status, different from that of POWs under the protection of conventional international law. They were now Japanese servicemen who had fallen under the control of hostile powers after Japan's surrender.[54]

After the surrender, military authorities at the Imperial Headquarters, who had virtually prohibited Japanese servicemen from surrendering during the war, declared that they would not recognize any Japanese military personnel and employees as POWs. The Japanese Southern Army Headquarters argued that Japanese servicemen ought not be treated as war prisoners and demanded 'honour and special treatment' from SEAC for the surrendered servicemen. In response, SEAC recognized this status of 'surrendered personnel' for the Japanese. The order of 28 August 1945, by Major General F.C. Scott, Chief of the General Staff for Allied Land Forces in SEAC, clearly described the difference in status between POWs and JSPs Entitled 'Concerning the Relations between Japanese Surrendered Personnel and Enemy Civilians', it stated that those POW officers under full British control would be isolated from their men and interned. They, however, would receive treatment according to the Geneva Conventions in every respect, including the preservation of their lives based on the high British levels of supplies allocated for POWs. JSPs, in contrast, remained under the control of their original officers and in their units. Japanese commanders would be held responsible for maintaining discipline, conduct, and maintenance of their subordinates among JSPs. Because of these differences, British armed forces did not treat JSPs according to the Hague Land War Regulation and Geneva POW Convention. Furthermore, British forces in particular failed to fulfill Article 9 of the Potsdam Declaration, which said, 'The Japanese military forces, after being completely disarmed, shall be permitted to return to their homes with the opportunity to lead peaceful and productive lives.' After July 1946, when most of the Allied Powers (except the Soviet Union) had completed the return of JSPs to Japan, the British forces continued to detain 105 960 JSP throughout South East Asia and imposed various tasks on them for the purposes of post-war recovery and to increase food production. Only at the end of October 1947 was the last JSP repatriated from Singapore.

Compulsory labour for JSPs included much dangerous and unhealthy work, including dropping ammunition into the sea, quarrying, cutting trees, sewage cleaning, and excrement and urine disposal. Some tasks, such as loading coal into shipholds filled with coal dust and carrying 100 kg bags of rice and salt, were physically demanding and unsuitable for Japanese, who were generally small in stature. Such dangerous work inevitably produced many casualties. Causes of death included automobile accidents, electrocution, and falls. Some JSPs were crushed to death while cutting trees and transporting machinery; others were blown up while disposing of ammunition, and some suffered methane gas poisoning while cleaning sewage. There was even a case of 'death in action', suffered while guarding one British quarters from bandits.[55] Further, the British assigned JSPs to loading and unloading weapons and ammunition at the Singapore naval port for the British to use against Indonesian forces fighting for independence. This clearly violated international law.[56]

Former JSPs commonly recall the limited rations and monotony of the diet. SEAC fixed the amount of general rations for JSPs at less than 2000 kcal – most likely from 1600 to 1700 kcal – with nutritional balance per person. When the British commanders approved, a JSP prisoner with a heavy workload would received additional 50 per cent to this general ration.[57] Compared with the K-ration – the standard for British military personnel of 3300 kcal per day – JSPs received only about a half. According to one former JSP prisoner, who had worked in Southern Malaya until October 1947, the average ration for JSPs in 1946 was typically 64 per cent of that for Indian soldiers: for lunch, six pieces of biscuits for each, one small can of fish for five prisoners at working places, and a little more than two bowls of rice per day. Even in the summer of 1947, the general ration for the Japanese prisoners reached to a mere 1998 kcal per person per day.[58]

On the solitary island of Rempang, southeast of Singapore, the British isolated and detained about 80 000 JSPs from October 1945 to late June 1946 when repatriation was completed. At the beginning of the transfer, the prisoners suffered from a severe shortage of food and had only 1100 kcal as their average ration. Furthermore, the ration was based on a self-supporting system by the prisoners, which forced the JSPs to consume much of their physical strength cultivating the land. Many suffered from diseases such as malaria, amoebic dysentery, food poisoning, beriberi, colitis, acute nephritis, A-type paratyphoid and tuberculosis. By the time of the completion of repatriation, 137 prisoners died of sickness.[59]

The British forces paid no wages for the work done by JSPs until June 1947. From the beginning, the British had announced that its forces would not pay wages to JSP prisoners, because they were not POWs.[60] Even when private companies employed JSP as workers, these companies paid JSP salaries to the British authorities, who initially refused to hand them over to the Japanese.[61] After repeated Japanese requests and only right before the completion of the repatriation of all JSPs, did the British agree to make payments. The British, moreover, surrendered the payments only to the Japanese government so that it could distribute wages to the individuals after their return. The hourly wages were 1.5 pence for skilled labour, and 0.75 pence for unskilled, which was about $\frac{1}{32}$ of the average wage in England.[62]

Poor sanitary conditions in the British camps, including poor quarters, malnutrition, forced labour under scorching sun or in the rain, and excessive and unhygienic tasks, caused outbreaks of tuberculosis, beriberi, and other acute diseases. Although some lived in warehouses as their dwelling quarters, most lived in tents loaned by the British forces, grass-roofed huts, hovels, or log cabins. Because of the lack of construction materials, a number of living quarters had neither side walls nor floorboards. Consequently, the rates of sickness in Japanese military units on average was twice that compared to that during the war.[63] In Malaya and Singapore, monthly figures for new tuberculosis patients after August 1946 rose to five times that seen during the war.[64] In addition, the British military limited the percentage of JSPs allowed to report sick in each unit: 5 per cent in Malaya, 5 per cent in Keppel, 3.5 per cent in Seletar, 1 per cent in Tengah, and 3 per cent in Java. While British Army doctors diagnosed and hospitalized Japanese prisoners, the Japanese military was informed that the length of hospitalization would be curtailed. Except on holidays and for internal camp workers, 85 per cent of all prisoners had to work.[65]

Forced labour under such harsh conditions resulted in 8971 deaths between the end of the war and 10 October 1947. Of these, 1243 were accidental.[66] The number of casualties during camp work registered 373 deaths by September 1947 and 20084 were wounded.[67] In Burma, for instance, 52 per cent of the total deaths of 1624 by November 1946 had been caused by labour duties.[68] The fact that such a large number of deaths was related to labour indicates the possible mistreatment of JSPs in those camps.

International law obliged the detaining power to provide the same rations in quality and quantity to POWs as to its own servicemen. The detaining power also had regularly to the supply, repair, and exchange of commodities like clothing and shoes. It was prohibited to use POWs for unhealthy and dangerous work. Officers were not to be subjected to physical labour. Work in POW camps had to be properly compensated according to the average wage for the servicemen of the detaining power for doing the same kind of work. Accommodation for POWs had to be sanitary, and the detaining power was obliged to make every effort to prevent epidemics. After the war, the Allied Powers punished many Japanese servicemen as war criminals because they had not provided proper treatment for the POWs in accordance with international law.

There is some doubt as to whether the Allied Powers ensured appropriate treatment for JSP throughout their camps. Japanese servicemen after the surrender were in actuality POWs. They were not permitted to leave isolated areas and their money and other commodities were confiscated. As it was impossible for the JSPs to support themselves in these camps, there was little difference between the status of 'surrendered personnel' and that of 'war prisoners'. There was no clear difference, beyond the timing of their captivity, between the military man who became a POW taken in battle and the military man who came under his enemy's control because his home country had surrendered. The British forces, in running JSP camps, were inevitably responsible for observing the fundamental principles of the Hague and Geneva Conventions to guarantee the humane treatment of surrendered servicemen. The 1947 report by the International Committee of the Red Cross criticized British treatment of JSPs on the grounds that agreements between belligerents may regulate certain matters, but could not neglect, in toto or in part, the fulfillment of the Convention's provisions on the treatment of POWs. One country was entitled neither to create less favourable regulations nor to determine unilaterally the rights of war prisoners.[69]

The sufferings and hardships for JSP prisoners resulted from Japan's Southern Army Headquarters' thoughtless acceptance of the status of 'surrendered personnel', in order to avoid the title of 'prisoner of war'. If the Japanese had been knowledgeable about international law, they could have asserted the rights as POWs for their servicemen in their surrender negotiations with the SEAC. The British took advantage by treating Japanese servicemen as surrendered personnel rather than as war prisoners. Major-General Scott's order indicated that it would be more beneficial, convenient, and safer for the British forces to treat a large number of prisoners as surrendered personnel, rather than as POWs (Clause 7). In other words, the British intended to lessen the financial and human costs of caring for surrendered Japanese servicemen by retaining the Japanese command structure and committing the control of the Japanese servicemen to the Japanese forces. Nor was repatriating JSPs to Japan a priority for the British. The shortage of transports, some say, caused the delay in the repatriation process. The British Chiefs of Staff in England consented to retaining the 105 960 surrendered Japanese soldiers in South East Asia.[70] Only the Supreme Commander of SEAC, Lord Mountbatten, could have promulgated this decision. Although the purpose of retention was for post-war reconstruction and to increase food production, work related to these purposes reportedly was 50 per cent at most in 1946 and about 20 per cent in 1947. The bulk of the work consisted of odd jobs.[71]

Treatment of the JSPs by the British forces was not 'fair'. Especially in the year following the end of the war, many British servicemen wanted revenge for the cruelties the Japanese Army had visited upon British POWs during the war. The mistreatment of JSPs can also be seen in the near-total lack of supplies of clothing and commodities, the long working hours from early morning to midnight without even one day off at the beginning, and the unreasonable orders and violence towards the prisoners. Memoirs by former prisoners and reports by various labour unit headquarters vouch for these facts. Even worse, SEAC rearmed Japanese military personnel to suppress Communist guerrillas in French Indochina and Malaya, to protect and rescue Allied POWs and civilian internees in Java, and to maintain order against armed bodies in Indonesia. Many JSPs were killed 'in action' in these operations.

The cruelty on POWs by the Japanese military, in many aspects, cannot be excused despite Japanese traditions and national characteristics. In general, Japanese servicemen during the war undoubtedly acted with barbarity and inhumanity, some by nature and many by circumstance. This fact, however, can neither counterbalance nor excuse the British treatment of JSPs, which was incompatible with the spirit of international law and humanity. International law prohibits reprisals against war prisoners. Just as the memory of captivity and mistreatment by the Japanese military during the war still casts shadows on some former British POWs, there are former surrendered Japanese, retained in the British work camps after the war, who still are bothered by the nightmare of those years.

The responsibility of the Japanese High Command for the mistreatment of Allied POWs

While the IMTFE admitted that at the beginning of the Pacific War the Japanese government had organized a system to deal with POWs and civilian internees, the tribunal condemned Japan for flagrantly disregarding the customary and conventional rules of war designed to prevent the inhumane treatment of war prisoners.[72] The judgment at the Tokyo trial concluded that Japan had failed to ratify and comply with the Geneva Conventions, because the Japanese military had prescribed a policy of 'mistreatment of POWs' by inculcating in its soldiers a spirit of contempt toward Allied prisoners.[73] In reality, the Japanese leadership had issued no instructions or regulations to treat POWs inhumanely.

It is also true, however, that War Minister Tojo had advocated tough measures towards Allied POWs. For instance, at the POW camp commandants' meeting mentioned above, he instructed them not to let the prisoners lie idle every day and to use their labour and skills in order to increase Japan's productivity. Even though he added the condition, 'as long as such treatment does not conflict with a sense of humanity', this attitude could lead to the abuse of POWs.[74] Furthermore, even in the absence of a central policy to persecute war prisoners, some local Japanese forces issued orders to eliminate disobedient individuals among the POWs and to kill prisoners in case of an Allied invasion.[75]

However, such mistreatment of POWs never became a consistent policy throughout the units and POW camps. There are former Allied prisoners who have testified regarding Japanese kindness in POWs camps both in and outside Japan.[76] Indeed, much testimony and documentation praises Japanese camp guards who made their best efforts to obtain food, medicines, and medical treatment for the prisoners. It is impossible at this moment, with the limits on perusing historical materials related to war crimes, to examine various causes of mistreatment by inductively researching each incident. However, it can be assumed that the treatment of POWs varied due to circumstances like the natural setting of the camps and individual characters of the commanders, chiefs, and guards who controlled those camps.

The treatment of POWs by the Japanese military also derived from cultural differences embodied in the negative view of Japanese soldiers towards surrendering, and differences in national power, which caused shortages of food and medicine. It would have been a flagrant contradiction if the Japanese military had treated its enemy prisoners well while prohibiting its soldiers from surrendering. As no Japanese could theoretically become a POW, Japan's military did not have to treat enemy POWs well in order to avoid retaliation against Japanese POWs, nor did it have to educate its officers and soldiers about the rights of POWs as provided for under international law. Moreover, while Japanese citizens themselves were starving from the material exhaustion of the Sino-Japanese War, Japan's national power was totally incapable of looking after the large number of prisoners whose previous standard of living greatly exceeded the Japanese.

The report from the International Committee of the Red Cross, issued after the war, also points out some of these unintentional causes for the mistreatment. First, it pointed out that the Pacific War was an ocean war, which made the transportation of supplies difficult on both land and sea. Even if Japan had complied strictly with the 1929 Convention, POWs and civilian internees under Japan's control would have been worse off than in Europe or America. Rations that were sufficient to sustain Japanese servicemen meant starvation and illness for westerners. Living conditions and discipline, to which the Japanese servicemen were accustomed, meant indignity and humiliation to western prisoners. While this was sufficient to explain Japan's treatment of POWs, the report explained, Japan's general view of POWs certainly aggravated the situation.[77]

Even while giving due attention to these points, it is regrettable, however, that military authorities lacked any clear intention to obey international law. Given that the Japanese military had committed war crimes in addition to those related to POWs, the military authorities should have emphasized the importance of international law to all units and should have taken all necessary measures. The authorities should have thought how these crimes could drive Japan into a corner internationally and fan hostility in a belligerent. There is, however, no evidence that such efforts were made. Japanese military authorities, despite national feelings towards POWs, from a humanitarian standpoint, should have paid the closest attention to the treatment of POWs, following their own examples in the Sino-Japanese War, the Russo-Japanese War, and the First World War. At a minimum, officers should have been taught international law, including the rights of POWs. Furthermore, manuals explaining the basics of international law should have been distributed to all servicemen. If all these measures had been taken, presumably the number of illegal acts on POWs, including acts carried out under direct orders, would have been considerably reduced. This means that neither those Japanese who had abandoned common human love and had intentionally treated POWs cruelly, but also military authorities cannot escape from their responsibility.

Notes

1. Oppenheimer-Lauterpacht, *International Law*, vol. 2, 7th edn (London: Longmans, 1952), pp. 576–7.
2. *Homu Daijin Kanbo Shih-Hosei Chosabu, Senpan Shakuho Shi* (1967), pp. 20–3.
3. Chaen Yoshio and Shigematsu Kazuyoshi (eds), *Senpan Saiban no Jisso*, vol. 2 (Fuji Shuppan, 1987), pp. 11–12.
4. Chaen Yoshio (ed.), *BC-kyu Senpan Eigun Saiban Shiryo*, vol. 1 (Fuji Shuppan, 1988), p. 10.
5. Ibid., pp. 100–35 and 137–215.
6. Chaen Yoshio (ed.), *Dainihon Teikoku Naichi Furyo Shuyo-jo* (Fuji Shuppan, 1986), p. 10.
7. Of these protests and inquiries, 35 were about the treatments of POWs in general, 7 about the treatment of specific POWs, 4 about punishments, 3 about relief goods, 17 about maintenance and food supply, and 9 about medical treatment. See Furyo Joho-kyoku, *Furyo ni kansuru kogi ni kanshi furyo joho-kyoku oyobi furyo kanribu ga shochisitaru kotogara wo kirokusiaru shorui no utsushi* (1945). The document is compiled in Utsumi Aiko (ed.), *Furyo Toriatsukai ni kansuru Shogaikoku karano Kogi-shu*, intro. Ubukata Naokichi (Fuji Shuppan, 1989).
8. *Kyokuto Kokusai Gunji Saiban Sokkiroku*, no. 148, pp. 9–24.

9. Chaen Yoshio, *Furyo Joho-kyoku, Furyo Toriatsukai no Kiroku* (Fuji Shuppan, 1992), p. 59.
10. Ibid., p. 35.
11. *Kyokuto Kokusai Gunji Saiban Sokkiroku*, Judgment: no. 148, p. 182.
12. Colonel Sasaki Kazuo (ed.), *Senjin-kun kai* (Buyo-do, 1941), p. 94.
13. Fukiura Tadamasa, *Kikigaki Nihonjin Horyo* (Tosho Shuppan-sha, 1987), p. 14.
14. Hata Ikuhiko, *Nihonjin Horyo-Hakusukinoe kara Shiberia Yokuryu made*, vol. 1 (Hara Shobo, 1998), p. 20.
15. Ibid., p. 21.
16. Ibid., p. 17.
17. Ibid., pp. 16–17 and 19.
18. Nitobe Inazo, *Bushido*, trans. Yanaihara Tadao (Iwanami Bunko, 1938), pp. 26–7 and 130.
19. Watsuji Tetsuro, *Hagakure*, Furukawa Tetsuji revised, vol. 1 (Iwanami Bunko, 1940), p. 23. English translation from David J. Lu (ed.), *Japan: a Documentary History*, vol. 1 (New York: M.E. Sharpe, 1996), pp. 262–3.
20. Nara Takeji, 'Oshu-Taisen ni okeru Furyo no oki wo mite Kanari', *Kaiko-sha Kiji*, no. 527 (1918), p. 9.
21. Hata, *Nihon-jin Horyo*, pp. 24 and 44.
22. Ibid., pp. 81 and 98.
23. Adachi Sumio, 'Kokusai Jindo-ho Saininshiki e no Michi', *Ho to Chitsujo*, no. 74 (1983), p. 30.
24. Ibid.
25. Hata, *Nihonjin Horyo*, p. 530.
26. 'Furyo no Taigu ni Kansuru 1927-nen 7-gatsu 27-nichi no Joyaku', *Gohijun-kata Sosei ni Kansuru Ken Kaito* (Secret File of Secretariat No. 1984–3, 15.11.1934); Chaen Yoshio (ed.), *Daitoa Senso Furyo Kankei Gaiko Bunsho Shusei*, vol. 1 (Fuji Shuppan, 1993), pp. 152–4.
27. 'Tojo Hideki Sensei Kyojutsu-sho', in Asahi Shinbun Hotei Kishadan (eds), *Tokyo Saiban*, vol. 2 (1962), p. 893.
28. Ruth Fulton Benedict, *Kiku to Katana*, trans. Hasegawa Matsuji (Shakai Shiso-sha, 1967), pp. 47–50.
29. Yokomizo Mitsuteru, *Showa-shi Henrin* (Nihon Keizai Shinbun-sha, 1974), pp. 309–10.
30. Kita Yoshito, 'Nihon Rikugun no Kokusai-ho Fukyu Sochi: Shoko ni Taisuru Kokusai-ho Kyoiku no Kento', *Nihon Hogaku*, vol. 63, no. 2 (1997), pp. 260–4.
31. Kita Yoshito, 'Kyu-Kaigunsho Gakko ni Okeru Kokusai-ho Kyoiku', in Chaen Yoshio (ed.), *BC-kyu Senpan Rabaul Saiban Shiryo* (Fuji Shuppan, 1990), pp. 260–4.
32. Kita, 'Nihon Rikugun', pp. 135–53.
33. Nanbu Nobukiyo, a recruit in the 'Class of 61' at the Naval Academy, enrolled in 1930–33. He recollects that there was a subject called, 'Outline of International Law' within the course of 'Law and Economics'. However, he has no memory of having lectures on diplomatic history, international law, and the Geneva Conventions. Nanbu Nobukiyo, 'Kaigun to Kokusai-ho', *Suiko*, vol. 63, no. 5 (1988), p. 14.
34. Former Commander Okumiya Masatake entered the Naval Academy in 1927. He says that he never received a formal education on POWs up to the end of the Pacific War in 1945. See Okumiya Masatake, *Watashi no mita Nankin-jiken* (PHP, 1997), p. 135. Fukiura Tadamasa, after interviewing Japanese naval officers who had become POWs, paints a different picture. He asserts that many naval officers had general knowledge of the Geneva Conventions. Fukiura had the impression

that the Naval Academy had taught about POWs. Fukiura, *Kikigaki Nihonjin Horyo*, pp. 24–5.

35. Testimony of former Navy Captain Watanabe Yasuji of the Inspector-General's Department of IJN, in *Kyokuto Kokusai Gunji Saiban Sokkiroku*, no. 266, pp. 1–2.
36. Chaen, *Furyo Toriatsukai no Kiroku*, pp. 99–100.
37. Ibid., pp. 232–5.
38. Testimony of former Colonel Suzuki Kunji, Commandant of the Tokyo POW Camp, in *Kyokuto Kokusai Gunji Saiban Sokkiroku*, no. 261, p. 10.
39. 'Furyo Shiyosha yori Kyoyosareta Hoshoku Jokyo', in Tokyo Saiban Shiryo Kankokai (eds), *Tokyo Saiban Kyakka Miteishutsu Bengo-gawa Shiryo*, vol. 7 (Tosho Kankokai, 1995), pp. 452–5.
40. 'Taimen Rensetsu Tetsudo Kensetsu Keikaku-sho', in Hiroike Toshio, *Taimen Tetsudo: Senjo ni Nokoru Hashi* (Yomiuri Shinbun-sha, 1971), p. 411.
41. Ito Masanori, *Teikoku Rikugun no Saigo-Kessen-hen* (Bungei Shunju-sha, 1960), p. 279.
42. Chaen, *Furyo Toriatsukai no Kiroku*, p. 58.
43. 'Furyo Kanri Kaizen ni Kansuru Ken', ibid., pp. 89–90.
44. Testimony of former naval doctor, Captain Arima Gen (Chief of Section 1, Navy Ministry Medical Bureau) in *Kyokuto Kokusai Gunji Saiban Sokkiroku*, no. 262, p. 13.
45. Testimony of former Colonel Odajima Kaoru (Senior Clerk of POW Information Bureau and Senior Staff of the War Ministry POW Management Office) in *Kyokuto Kokusai Gunji Saiban Sokkiroku*, no. 266, pp. 7–8.
46. The Ground Self-Defense Forces Hygiene School (eds), *Daitoa Senso Rikugun Eisei-shi*, vol. 1 (GSDF Sanitation School, 1971), p. 580.
47. Chaen, *Horyo Toriatsukai no Kiroku*, p. 84.
48. Lewis Bush, *Okawaisoni: Tokyo Furyo Shuyo-jo no Eihei Kiroku*, trans. Yoji Akashi (Bungei Shunju-sha, 1956), p. 117.
49. Yuji Aida, *Alon Shuyo-jo* (Chuko Shinsho, 1962), pp. 82 and 86.
50. For instance, Article 6 of the Charter of IMTFE provided as follows:

    Neither the official position, at any time, of an accused, nor the fact that an accused acted pursuant to order of his government or of a superior shall, of itself, be sufficient to free such accused from responsibility for any crime with which he is charged but such circumstances may be considered in mitigation of punishment if the Tribunal determines that justice so requires.

    Senso Hanzai Saiban Kankei Horei-shu, vol. 1, Homudaijin-kanbo Shiho Hosei Chosa-bu (eds), (1963), p. 43.
51. Dai Ichi Fukuin-sho Homu Chosa-bu, 'Meirei to Sekinin ni Kansuru Kenkai', (1945), 9, in Kanno Yasuyuki, *Zotei Rikugun Keiho Genron* (Shokado, 1943), pp. 425–6.
52. Ibid., p. 423.
53. Dai Ichi Fukuin-sho Homu Chosa-bu, 'Meirei to Sekinin', p. 9.
54. ICRC, *Report of the International Committee of the Red Cross on Its Activities during the Second World War: September 1, 1939–June 30, 1947*, vol. 1 (1948), p. 539.
55. 'Eigun Sagyo ni Kiinsuru Shishosha Chosahyo', in Nanpo-gun So-shirei-bu, 'Doreiteki Sagyo Hokoku Tsuzuri', January 1947 (in the possession of the *Boei Kenkyu-sho*) and 'Sagyotai Hensei irai no Shibosha Renmeibo', 1.4.1947, in Shingaporu Sagyotai Shirei-bu, 'Shingaporu ni okeru Sagyotai no Jokyo ni Tsuite', March 1947 (in private possession).
56. Honda Tadanao, *Marei Horyo Ki* (Tosho Shuppan-sha, 1989), p. 42.

57. Kosei-sho Hikiage Engo-kyoku Shiryo-shitsu, *Nanpo-gun Fukuin-shi* (1957), p. 53.
58. Magota Ryohei, *Nenko Chingin no Shuen* (Nikkei shinsho, 1980), p. 11.
59. 'Rempang-to, Galang-to Eisei Gaikyo', in Southern Army Medical Department, 'Zanryu Eisei-shi' (in the possession of *Boei Kenkyu-sho*), Supplementary Chart No. 7, 'Shusengo Shibosha Ichiranhyo', in ibid., Supplementary Chart No. 11, and Yamamoto Tatsuo, *Kyokugen no Shima 'Rempang'* (private printing, 1979), p. 67.
60. Article 7(b) of the Instruction from Major-General D.D. Gracey, Chief of Saigon No. 1, Administration Committee, to General Terauchi Hisaichi, Commanding General of the Southern Army, 'Kofusha ni shite Shieki wo Meizeraretaru-mono ni Taisuru Chingin no Shiharai ni Kansuru Ken', stated that no wages were to be paid to JSPs ordered to work. See Dai Ichi Fukuin-kyoku Somu-ka Beppan, 'Nanpo-chiiki ni Okeru Nihonjin ni Taisuru Fuho Toriatsukai Jirei', 5.8.1947, Nanpo-gun So-Shirei-bu, 'Doreiteki Sagyo Hokoku Tsuzuri', Document 1, Part 2.
61. Chapter 1, No. 5(a) of SEAC's directive of 31.7.1946, 'Kofuku Nihonjin no Koyo no Ken', stated that civilian employers of JSPs were to pay wages, according to work classifications, at an average rate comparable to the current civilian wages of the labour-supplying authorities (the army). Clause (c) continued that no wage or gratuity should be given to JSPs. Nanpo-gun Soshirei-bu, 'Tonan Ajia Rengo-gun Kanri-ka Chiku ni Zanchisaretaru Juman-mei no Sagyo-tai', August 1946 (in the possession of the *Boei Kenkyu-sho*).
62. Magota, *Nenko-Chingin no Shuen*, p. 13.
63. Kosei-sho Hikiage Engo-kyoku Shiryo-shitsu, *Nanpo-gun Fukuin-shi*, pp. 68–79.
64. Ibid., pp. 81, 86 and 92.
65. Ibid., pp. 94–5 and 110.
66. 'Fuhyo Dai Juichi: Shusengo Shibosha Ichiran-hyo', in Nanpo-gun Gun-i-bu, 'Zanryu Eisei-shi'.
67. 'Sagyo-chu ni Okeru Shishosha Ichiran-hyo', Kosei-sho Hikiage Engo-kyoku Shiryo-shitsu, *Nanpo-gun Fukuin-shi*, p. 113.
68. Dai Ichi Fukuin-kyoku Somu-ka Beppan, 'Nihonjin ni Taisuru Fuho Toriatsukai Jirei', Document 2, Part 5 (2).
69. ICRC, *Inter Arma Caritas: the Work of the International Committee of the Red Cross during the Second World War*, pp. 110–11.
70. S. Woodburn Kirby, *The War against Japan*, vol. 5, p. 506.
71. Kosei-sho Hikiage Engo-kyoku Shiryo-shitsu, *Nanpo-gun Fukuin-shi*, p. 108.
72. *Kyokuto Kokusai Gunji Saiban Hanketsu Sokkiroku*, p. 186.
73. Ibid., pp. 202–3.
74. Hata, *Nihonjin Horyo*, p. 139.
75. The former was in the Instruction of the Commander of the 16th Division (April 1944), in Chaen, *Dainippon Teikoku Naichi Furyo Shuyo-jo*, p. 7. The latter is in 'Dai Juichi Butai Sanbocho ate (Taifukei Dai 10-go): Furyo ni Taisuru Hijoshudan no Ken Kaito' [Addressed to the Chief of Staff, 11th Unit (Taifu kei No. 10): Reply on the Emergency Measure for POWs], in *Kyokuto Kokusai Gunji Saiban Sokkiroku*, no. 148, p. 9.
76. For example, in his book, *Okawaisoni*, Lewis Bush testified not only to food shortages and cruelties by camp guards, but also to fair treatment from Colonel Suzuki, Commandant of the Tokyo POW Camp, and his subordinates, as well as the kindnesses rendered by Japanese citizens.
77. ICRC, *Inter Arma Caritas*, p. 103.

18

The British Commonwealth Occupation Forces in Japan and its Association with the Japanese

Takeshi Chida

Formation and reorganization of the British Commonwealth Occupation Forces

Formation of the British Commonwealth Occupation Forces

Prior to the formation of the British Commonwealth Occupation Forces (hereafter BCOF) there were a number of disputes concerning the process of unifying a British Commonwealth Force to invade mainland Japan. However, on 4 July 1945, with Japan on the verge of defeat and in anticipation of the invasion of Japan by American forces, the British Prime Minister, Winston Churchill, contacted the Australian government requesting the participation of their air, ground and naval forces in the formation of a Commonwealth Force.[1] Nevertheless, differences between the two governments, which were in part due to the early surrender by the Japanese but also reflected the fact that Australia wished to form its own independent invading force whilst the United Kingdom wished to have a composite force, meant that Churchill's proposal was not initially brought to fruition.

On 13 August 1945, the British government informed the Commonwealth governments concerned of British post-surrender policy for Japan and called for co-operation. Australia wished to stick to its position of forming its own independent force. After some very difficult negotiations between the Australians and the British, an agreement was finally reached on the formation of an Occupation Force. BCOF was eventually formed under Australian leadership with an Australian C-in-C and Australian principal staff.

On 18 October 1945 negotiations opened between the Americans in Washington and Australia who were insisting upon ensuring the independence of BCOF representing the British Commonwealth. However, the US expressed its great concern, which was that the Soviet Union might exert pressure to participate in the occupation under the same terms as BCOF.

On 18 December, after some tortuously difficult negotiation an interim agreement was formalized between General MacArthur, SCAP, and Lieutenant General Northcott, C-in-C, BCOF.[2] This was formally announced on 31 January 1946. The terms outlined in the agreement established that BCOF would be a component of the Allied Occupation Forces under the command of General MacArthur, SCAP. However, although operationally under the command of the US Occupation Forces in matters relating to administration, including policy, maintenance and personnel, BCOF independence was secured.

In Australia, an organization was established to command and control the complex BCOF administration. The Joint Chiefs of Staff in Australia (abbreviated as JCOSA) consisted of Chiefs of Staff from Australia and Chiefs of Staff representing the other Commonwealth countries.[3] Australian opposition to Britain's original wish to form an occupational force with a British force as its core, and the US post-surrender policy for Japan, based on US world strategy, thus resulted in the establishment of BCOF. Under Australian leadership, and under the command of SCAP, BCOF became an integral part of the Allied Forces.

For the other Commonwealth countries, in particular the United Kingdom, BCOF was not so highly valued since they took no direct part in the 'Military Government' controlling Japan. BCOF was assigned the Hiroshima Prefecture and its vicinity as its Occupation Area and this offered little prestige. However, it did have prestige for the British Commonwealth since BCOF was assigned to an area of occupation and permitted to be an administratively independent force.

It was thought that the UK contrived the formation of BCOF in order to 'promote British prestige and influence in the Far East, in the face of persistent economic difficulties and scepticism from the United States and Australia'.[4] 'After World War II, faced with the changes on international politics, the UK needed cooperation from the Commonwealth/Empire.'[5] The British, being obliged to stand on the sidelines during the negotiations which took place in Washington between the USA and Australia regarding the specific role of BCOF, appointed William MacMahon Ball as the Commonwealth Representative for the Allied Council in Japan, and William Webb as the Principal of the International Military Tribunal for the Far East. Along with Northcott as C-in-C, BCOF, this meant that three key appointments were all Australians.

Seeking to pursue its national interest and using the influence of BCOF, Britain placed its hopes in the Australians. It hoped that they would in fact play the role of influential Commonwealth spokesmen at international meetings and that the Commonwealth spokesman would strengthen Britain's position.[6] However, such wishful thinking on the part of Britain soon proved unfounded when Australia gained in prestige and was given top priority discussions.[7] This in turn, coupled with the shortage in British manpower and its own stringent economic circumstances, led to the early withdrawal of British troops from BCOF.

BCOF disembarkation at Kure and deployment

Following the arrival of an advance party on 26 September 1945, US transports with 41st Division, 10th Corps of the US Sixth Army, in convoy entered Hiro Bay near Kure, in the Chugoku and Shikoku area. This was later garrisoned by BCOF as its Occupation area. Early on the morning of 7 October 1945, troops began to disembark in Hiro.[8] Later the 10th Corps of the US Sixth Army were also deployed in the Chugoku and Shikoku district, excluding the Yamaguchi Prefecture.

On 18 December 1945, under the MacArthur–Northcott Agreement, the Hiroshima Prefecture and its adjacent areas were assigned to BCOF as its area of Occupation. This provoked protest by the UK. They requested garrisoning in the Kobe and Osaka areas, which were seen to have more prestige and which had once had strong economic ties with the UK. In response, SCAP readily agreed to the stationing of a detachment for guard duty in Tokyo. As far as garrisoning in Kobe and Osaka was concerned, however, it was not until 15 October 1946, that a much reduced 'British Commonwealth Sub-Area in Kobe' was allocated.

In February 1946, after BCOF had commenced deployment in the Hiroshima area, General MacArthur, requested Lt. General Northcott to extend the assigned BCOF area to include other parts of the Chugoku–Shikoku area. Northcott, who had sufficient manpower for his garrison in the Hiroshima Prefecture, and wanted to utilize additional airfields and further accommodation, accepted these additional areas. On 1 February 1946, its advance party and the Royal Navy port party entered the Port of Kure.[9] On 13 February 1946, the first full scale units, including the 34th Australian Infantry Brigade and BritCom Base Units, arrived at the Port of Kure. On 1 March 1946, the first advance party of the BritCom Air Force arrived in Kure and set up BCAIR HQ on the same day.

As soon as the US Army was relieved of its duties in the area, rapid expansion into the new areas by BCOF troops followed. For most of the troops, subsequent movements were quite complex. 2nd New Zealand Expeditionary Forces, which landed in Kure on 19 March, were required to settle in Yamaguchi by 23 March,[10] while British Indian Divisions had to carry out a 'musical-chair'-like deployment over a large area. Of the First Echelon, including 5th British Infantry Brigade Groups, which disembarked on 5 April, 2nd Battalion, Dorset Regiment settled in the Shimane Prefecture while the rest of the group were garrisoned in the Hiro area. After this, the Second Echelon, including 268th Indian Infantry Brigade, which arrived in Kure from 18 May onwards, were lucky enough to move directly to Shimane and Tottori Prefectures, whilst its rear party moved to Okayama.[11]

During this time, 5th British Infantry Brigade, temporarily stationed in

Hiro and the Shimane Prefecture, were reassigned to the four prefectures on the island of Shikoku, and its rear party to Okayama. This coincided with the movement of the HQ 34 Australian. Infantry Brigade, which left Kaitaichi and was redeployed in Hiro on 11 July.

Reorganization of BCOF

By May 1946, the initial movement of BCOF troops was almost completed. In July further movement occurred as a consequence of the ever-expanding area of occupation. As of 31 December 1946, the total strength of the BCOF force amounted to 37021, made up of 11918 Australians, 10853 Indians, 9806 British and 4444 New Zealanders.

However, as early as October 1946 the withdrawal of British troops was being scheduled. The main reasons for this were manpower shortages and financial difficulties. The withdrawal was finally carried out during February and March 1947. By June, half of the New Zealand component had also returned home and India, on attaining its independence, withdrew its component completely before October of the same year. This drastic reduction in BCOF strength by 1947, only one year after its deployment, entirely changed the original character of the force. These withdrawals continued throughout 1948. As a result, the reduced strength as of April 1948 was 12009: 8203 Australians, 2455 New Zealanders (of which 2052 returned home between July and September 1948) and 1351 British. On 28 April 1948, faced with such an exodus, Australia made a decision to reduce their strength in BCOF by 2750 and this was reluctantly approved by the US on 7 February 1949. After April 1948, BCOF steadily declined in numbers until 17 December 1948, when the Occupation responsibility of BCOF – then an Australian force – was reclassified to a restricted area including the Hiroshima Prefecture and the 'Iwakuni Police District' in the Yamaguchi Prefecture – a far cry from its original Chugoku and Shikoku areas of responsibility. Finally on 19 May 1950, it was announced that BCOF was to be withdrawn.

In the early hours of 25 June 1950, the Korean War broke out, and the British Commonwealth countries, including Canadian combat troops, found that they had a new role to play in a force known as the British Commonwealth Forces Korea (Abbreviated as BCFK), who were to fight in Korea as a component of the United Nations Forces in Korea. The BCFK were garrisoned at their base at Kure, Japan until they were finally disbanded on 22 November 1956.

BCOF and the Japanese populace in its area of occupation

Japanese attitudes as viewed by BCOF/BCFK British soldiers

As a result of four years of intensive propaganda during the Pacific War, most Japanese viewed their enemy – the British and the Americans – as 'Brutal Beasts from Hell'. However, these attitudes were echoed in the Allied views of the Japanese. Gordon Parker, an Australian in his late teens, who later married a Japanese woman, pictured the Japanese in the following manner:

> He [Sapper Gordon Parker] spent the last two years of his teens restless and unsettled by war. Like most Australians he burned with fury and loathing when he heard of the atrocities the Japanese had wreaked on the doomed Australian prisoners-of-war of the Burma–Siam death railway; in Borneo; in Changi prison camp. He joined the Australian Imperial Force believing all Japanese were filthy, cruel and inhuman. BCOF volunteers were lectured on Japanese habits and customs. They were riddled with disease, disgusting and un-Australian.[12]

The American view of the Japanese seems to have been little different from that of Commonwealth people (excluding the Indians), even though the attitude of most Americans stemmed from the surprise attack on Pearl Harbor and the atrocities inflicted by the Japanese on American POWs. In fact the only difference which existed between the Americans and the Commonwealth troops, if any, was due to the fact that the Americans regarded themselves as victors, who completely defeated the Japanese enemy. By contrast, the British and Australians were affected by the fact that their enemy had surrendered before their own armies had proved their superiority and been victorious in the final assault. Therefore, it is significant that strong sentiments of revenge remained amongst all ranks prior to the Occupation. The following is a collection of 'personal details' regarding 'BCOF Service in the Kure Area' which was gleaned from approximately 140 British veterans of BCOF from 1993.

> Impression of Japan as a country . . . 'beautiful, fascinating and picturesque countryside' . . . are a great majority of the replies . . . which was followed by . . . 'vast destruction by ordinary bomb raids'.
> Impression of the Japanese . . . 'Friendly first of all', followed by 'helpful and sincere'.
> There were some reservations such as ' . . . surprised at no animosity shown by the general public . . . bearing in mind what had taken place in the recent past, I got on well with people of all ages'.
> However, there were also such replies as . . . 'I had a feeling of suppressed hostility . . . and whilst a lot of people forgive and forget, I cannot forget'. 'Dock area destroyed, shortage of food, fearful disaster of earthquake and typhoons' . . . were among the various 'Unforgettable Memories'.

The following personal details from the BCOF service were written and summarized by Mr Wilfred Aldridge, a UK member of BCFK:

> Former British Commonwealth Servicemen who were stationed in the Kure area, have almost without exception, stated that they found the

Japanese people to be very friendly, polite, hardworking and honest. Even those who entered Kure immediately after World War II had ended, expressed similar feelings, and said how pleasantly surprised they were, after all the cruelty encountered in the prisoner-of-war camps, supervised by the Japanese military during hostilities.

   Although fraternization was strictly forbidden in the early days of the post-war Occupation, numerous servicemen were able to meet with Japanese families in their homes and several lasting friendships were struck up. This happened especially where Kure civilian staff worked alongside British Commonwealth personnel in the military establishments.[13]

These favourable views may have been a little diplomatic since the accounts were given long after the soldiers had returned home, and were forwarded at the request of the citizens of Kure via Mr Aldridge. In fact there were a few replies, which were not to be overlooked by the Japanese, as follows:

Having heard from shipmates of mine who had been taken POW in Japan, I found that they seemed to be well treated by the Japanese Navy, but once they came under the Army, they were diabolically ill treated. Some of my shipmates were taken to Hiroshima, and how they survived the treatment there, I don't know. The stories they told me were unbelievable. So I will never forgive them for that.[14]

Finally, among the many memories on record, the following give suggestions as to how to reach mutual understanding through the misery of the last war.

One who had visited Kure could not possibly have forgotten the devastation they were met with, this was nothing new to me, as I had already suffered the same act. This did not mean that I did not have sympathy for others, it was always the ordinary everyday folk that suffered the sins of the few, the folk that I met ashore seemed to be gentle folk and very polite. They had suffered the same as our folk, losing their loved ones. I talked to two families who had lost a son with the navy, they grieved the same as we would.[15]

Japanese attitudes towards BCOF/BCFK

Each of the Allied Forces advanced into Japan with their own different perspective about the Japanese. How did the citizens of Kure respond to the American Forces, the first soldiers to arrive in Kure City? 'When I saw a convoy of American jeeps and heavy vehicles, stretching endlessly into the distance, I thought, now I understand the reason why we lost the war.'[16]

   The incoming 'endless' convoy of American jeeps, together with gigantic 'bulldozers', with which the American forces demonstrated their effortless manoeuvrability, proved an effective means to foster in the Japanese the idea 'How could the Japanese defeat such a force outfitted with such *matériel* and equipment.'[17] These initial fears the Japanese citizens entertained were quickly mitigated, however, when the children made first contact with American troops, who were cheerful and generous. After this, small gangs of Japanese girls quickly threw themselves at the Americans and some became notorious in the eyes of the general citizenry.

So how were the BCOF troops who landed after 1946 perceived? BCOF was composed of various nationalities, including British, Australians, New Zealanders and Indians. A citizen who worked as a clerk for BCFK recollected that 'the main body of troops were Australians who wore large hats like cowboys and who were poorly paid as compared to their GI counterparts. The uniform was not so fashionable. I thought there were some who were not so well educated and disciplined'.

> Compared to some of the Australians who first landed in Kure, many of the British who came later were disposed with a distinctive privileged attitude and seemed better educated. What impressed me most was the Americans with their enormous equipment, and the British who came later with distinctive arrogance, although they behaved in a gentlemanly way.[18]

BCOF, mainly composed of Australians at the outset, was concerned over the tension that existed between the Japanese labourers and their Australian supervisors, who still harboured hostile feelings towards the Japanese. However, even though the relationships were not amicable at first, as the Occupation progressed, understanding between them gradually grew. Another clerk who worked for a UK unit of BCFK in 1951 later recollected that 'all ranks of the unit behaved with a sense of pride, and appreciated their orderly and gentleman-like attitude, being worthy subjects of the Queen's own Royal Army'.[19]

The Allied Forces thus left a deep impression on the citizens of Kure. The varied impressions reflect the diverse conditions experienced by the Allies, albeit coloured by their own distinctive national characteristics. While, from the outset, the Americans, with their abundant *materiel* and resources, acted in a friendly way, it can be said that BCOF, under the 'Non-Fraternization Policy' adopted at the beginning of the Occupation, behaved in a rather awkward way at first. Later, however, they gradually came to form a relationship with the people of Kure and this grew as the Occupation progressed. During the first 11 years of the post-war period, Kure was indeed an international city, which hosted garrisoned Allied Forces from various countries. It should be said, however, that this was also quite an unusual and difficult period for the City of Kure. However, as the then Mayor of Kure put it, 'Kure was lucky enough to have had the opportunity during the Occupation, to be able to encounter and establish friendships with people from various nations'.[20]

There were many BCOF personnel who attempted, from an early stage of the Occupation, to involve themselves in the numerous citizen's cultural exchange programmes. This was at the risk of violating the strict Non-Fraternization Policy, or through the guidance of BCOF Education Department. Farsighted officers included Major Arthur W. John,[21] and Lieutenant MacGee, the Chief of the Education Service, who, at the last stage of the Occupation, was someone who devoted himself to such activities. He provided reading classes and lectures for the Japanese, thus earning great respect from the people of Kure.

BCOF's socio-economic effect on Kure

Employment of Japanese labourers and associated problems

During the period when the American forces were garrisoned in Kure, approximately 3000 Japanese labourers were employed by the Allied Forces in Kure. According to the sources of the Chugoku newspapers, as of 23 March 1946, the number totaled 7978 in Hiroshima Prefecture, including those in Kure City. After BCOF deployed its New Zealand contingent and the British Indian Divisions throughout the Chugoku–Shikoku area, the workforce grew enormously. Between April and May, the daily average of employed personnel was 13 391; between June and July some 22 126 were employed; and as of 19 October, the number reached a peak of 42 270 people.[22] It was also reported that 'labourers employed in Kure where HQ BCOF was situated amounted to approx. 20 000'.[23]

From this point, the number of Japanese labourers gradually decreased until just before the Korean War broke out. The number employed by BCOF as of 1 June 1950, was 7758, of which 6450 worked in Kure (approx. 83 per cent) and 1907 (25 per cent) were women. The labourers who were still employed at the end of the Korean War were reported as being between 12 000 and 13 000 (70%–80% of the reported number were employed in Hiroshima Prefecture, of which around three-quarters employed in Kure City).

Working conditions under BCOF, which provided 'meals' and employment, were quite attractive for towns and cities in the area of occupation, especially for the City of Kure, which had lost the IJN – its most important former employer. BCOF, with its HQ, had taken its place as the most important new employer and was providing a fundamental lifeline for the city. This role played by BCOF was considered most effective at its early stage of occupation. Even as late as 1953, during the final stages of BCFK, it provided such a positive effect that the Kure City Council went so far as to state that 'more than 10 000 labourers are still working with BCFK, thus the Occupation contributes to the city some 3.2 billion yen (approximately 40% of the total income of 7.5 billion yen)'.[24]

The contribution of income by UN Forces garrisoned in Kure was extremely influential. In fact, employment was to be severely affected by the anticipated withdrawal of forces. The headquarters of the Force repeatedly appealed for the postponement of the dismissal of its labourers.

Crimes by BCOF/BCFK (British Commonwealth Forces)

Crimes committed by the Commonwealth Forces cast a shadow over the BCOF/BFCK's relationship with the citizens of Kure, many of whom were enjoying increasingly friendly relationships with the troops. The annual numbers of cases as shown by official records and other sources were: 492 in 1946; 348 in 1947; 168 in 1948; 104 in 1949; 67 in 1950; 695 in 1951; 453 in 1952; 319 in 1953; and 137 in 1955. According to the above, although there were many crimes which occurred at the outset of the Occupation, the number gradually decreased. However, after the Korean War broke out in 1950 there was a period in which BCFK and UN forces staged replacements and allowed soldiers from the Korean theatre on furlough in Kure City and its vicinity, thus permitting full use of its logistics and maintenance base. In this period many crimes occurred in Kure and it was labelled the 'reign of terror' by the media.[25]

It has been assumed that the reason that such a large number of cases, reportedly largest in 1946 and in 1947 and considerably lower than the number of cases occurring during 1951 and 1952, is due to the fact that the American Press Code suppressed the release of such crimes by Occupation Forces. This can be proved by comparing the above figures with a BCOF record titled 'Activity Report, Oct.–Dec. 1946' which includes all social disturbances that occurred in this period.

It seems that a smaller number of crimes were committed by members of the BCOF against the Japanese than those committed by the Japanese against members of the BCOF. The possible reason for this is that there were many crimes committed by BCOF for which there were very few arrests. It was reported to JCOSA in December 1946, that 'in just three months there were 312 BCOF personnel arrested for crimes against the Japanese', which may substantiate the facts stated above. 'Major Investigations' carried out by 'BCOF Special Investigation Branch Sections' gives a general idea of the nature of crimes that occurred during this time. This report listed 16 cases: seven cases of thieving and illegal dealing of goods (including cases which were under the control of Japanese bosses in Fukuyama City near Kure), three cases of rape by Australians against women in Kure, and six cases of murder (including a case where an Australian soldier shot a Japanese man and injured a woman).[26]

After the San Francisco Peace Treaty came into effect, 'Judicial Jurisdiction' – the right for the Japanese to hold their own trials – was restored.

However, it was not until after 29 October 1953, under a revision of the American–Japanese Administration Agreement that 'Criminal Jurisdiction' for the Japanese was allowed. This clause in the agreement also applied to the BCFK.

On 17 February 1954, the first case involving BCFK troops was tried at the Kure Branch of the Hiroshima District Court. Three BCFK sailors were accused of 'robbery with violence', the ringleader being sentenced to serve a minimum of five years with a maximum of eight years, another for four years with a maximum of five years, and another who was a minor being sentenced to serve a minimum of three-and-a-half years with a maximum of five years. This decision by the Court shocked BCFK and from that time, the amount of criminal activity declined.

How did the Non-Fraternization policy work?

During the war, 'Non-Fraternization' was never a matter that required serious consideration by the Allies. After the formation of BCOF, however, it became a central problem. In a JCOSA meeting held on 30 January 1946, Major General Haydon, a representative of the British Chief of Staff suggested that 'the question of Fraternization Policy should be clarified as soon as possible'[27] and the idea of issuing instructions to BCOF troops prior to their arrival in Japan was later approved by BCOF member countries.

This idea was enforced from March 1946 when the C-in-C BCOF issued an instruction to all troops prohibiting fraternization with Japanese outside of Occupational duties. In June, following this order, a 'Policy Regarding Marriage – BCOF' was formalized. The policy specified 'it was generally *ultra vires* to prohibit marriage by order' of BCOF soldiers. However, the ban was justifiable for the sake of 'security reasons'; if the woman was considered to be a 'notorious bad character'; or if both parties' lifestyles differed so greatly that a successful marriage would seem unlikely. If such a situation prevailed, formal permission for a BCOF soldier to marry would be denied. Subsequent to this, in September 1946, BCOF HQ issued BCOF Administration Instruction 39: 'Marriages in Japan'. This instruction specified that 'under no circumstances will approval be given'[28] regarding marriage between a member of BCOF and a Japanese citizen. In the interim, BCOF went so far as to order the local Japanese registrar in the Occupation Area not to receive any applications for marriage by local law, without first obtaining approval from the applicant's commanding officer. Despite all these efforts by BCOF to prevent contact between the BCOF soldiers and Japanese women, relationships between them soon became widespread. As previously mentioned in this report, at its peak BCOF employed some 42270 Japanese locals in essential positions, including a large number of women who worked as housegirls, interpreters and typists. In the early 1950s, BCOF soldiers and their families were not alone in attending BCOF church services. They were often joined by a number of interested Japanese. Contact and relationships between the two naturally spread, some on friendly terms, some developing into romance and even marriage. Clandestine relationships and marriage were maintained with the help of friends. However, when the facts became known to the BCOF authorities, many of these relationships ended in personal tragedy. Soldiers were sometimes dismissed and forcibly repatriated and many Japanese wives were deserted, being banned from entering Australia. Some ex-servicemen, back in Australia, however, continued to apply for approval for the admission of their families. In time, favourable press reaction in Australia to these mixed marriages meant that the situation became a matter of some controversy. Many argued that it was a denial of basic human rights to men who had risked their lives on the battlefield for their country. BCOF itself felt that there was a need to make an alteration to the 'Non-Fraternization Policy' when GHQ/SCAP requested BCOF's abolition of the policy, and to change the character of the Occupation from that of military to a more friendly and protective force. BCOF feared it would be isolated if it rejected SCAP's Occupation Instruction.

On 19 February 1952, at a Commonwealth Immigration Conference, the then Minister for Immigration, Mr Harold Holt, called for and had accepted the idea of accepting those Australian soldiers' wives and granted them permission to enter Australia. The Australian Cabinet approved this on 27 March. Under the headline 'Ban Off Jap Wives', *The Sun*, an Australian newspaper, reported this decision and the news that the first approval 'would be almost immediately granted for Gordon Parker' to return to Australia with his Japanese wife and two children. The government reasoned that they had previously signed a 'Peace Treaty' with Japan and that the Army did not have the same large numbers of troops in Japan as it had earlier.[29]

On March 1959, the *Chugoku Daily*, published in Kure, carried an article 'The Story of International Marriages' from Kure City, where 866 marriages were reported as having been applied for and approved during the previous six years. All wives were thus admitted to their husbands' country – 650 to Australia, 95 to Canada, 87 to Britain and 34 to New Zealand. In 1957, the year BCFK withdrew from Japan, the largest number of marriages, 363, was recorded. This was followed by 176 marriages in 1952, the year in which Japanese wives were granted permission to enter Australia; in 1955, there were 96 marriages recorded and in 1953, 89 marriages. The reported figures were from Kure City, which would have probably dealt with almost all of the applications in the BCOF/BCFK area.[30]

During war people are indoctrinated to see the belligerent race as a hostile enemy. However, it is clear from the large number of marriages between BCOF soldiers and Japanese women eventually granted in this period after the war that human beings cannot live by hatred alone. Young men and young women managed to meet, and were drawn to one another at a time when feelings towards the 'enemy' were still hostile. The sincere love shared between such couples gave them the courage to face whatever difficult barriers might confront them. In challenging the Non-Fraternization Policy they fulfilled their own desire to be permitted to marry the person they loved. But in addition they also played an important role in challenging racial prejudice in the respective countries where they made their home.

It is also to be noted that from 1946 onwards, many linguists from the School of Oriental and African Studies (SOAS) in London and other institutes arrived in Kure to assume their vital role as Japanese Language Specialists. Professor Ian Nish, who pursued his prominent academic research on Japan, later recollected his BCOF days when he served at the Combined Service Detailed Interrogation Centre (CSDIC) near Point Camp in Kure.[31]

The remarkable role played by these 'Japan hands', together with the role played by the many British BCOF personnel, both during and after the BCOF period, contributed greatly to the re-enhancement of the Commonwealth/ British Empire's prestige in Japan, as well as the promotion of Anglo-Japanese friendship.

Notes

1. British Commonwealth Occupation Force – Summary and Date History, 3/1946, ANA, CRS a5954.
2. General Headquarters Supreme Commander for the Allied Powers, Memorandum for Record, 18 December 1945, ibid., Appendices, 3/1946 (ANA: a5954).
3. On the controversial issue of the role played by JCOSA refer to D.C.S. Sissons, *Accommodating General and Commonwealth Partners in Sir Frederick Shedden's Australian* 'Higher Defence Organization – with Particular Reference to the JCOSA (Joint Chiefs of Staff in Australia) Experiment', 1945–47, 1988.
4. Roger Buckley, *Occupation Diplomacy: Britain, the United States and Japan, 1942–1952* (Cambridge University Press, 1982), p. 42.
5. Kibata Yoichi, *Teikoku no Tasugare – Reisenka no Igirisu to Ajia 1947–55* (Tokyo Shuppankai, 1996), p. 12.
6. David Horner, *High Command: Australia's Struggle for an Independent War Strategy 1939–1945* (Allen & Unwin, 1982), pp. 429, 430, 523.
7. Alan Rix, *Intermittent Diplomat: the Japan and Batavia Diaries of W. MacMahon Ball* (Melbourne University Press, 1988), pp. 268, 270.
8. Kure Chinjufu 'Shinchu Nisshi' No. 1 8 October 1945, Kure Chinjifu File, NIDS.
9. War Diary, 13–14/2/9/1946, 34 Australian Infantry Brigade War Diary or Intelligence Summary, 1–2/1946, 52 8/2/33, AWM.
10. Historical Narrative of 2 NZEF (Japan), History of BCOF, AWM 114 130/1/23.
11. History of BRINDIV, History of BCOF, ibid.
12. I.R. Carter, *Alien Blossom: a Japanese–Australian Love Story* (Lansdowne Press, 1965), p. 10.
13. W. Aldridge, *The Rise and Fall and Rise Again of Kure City, Japan*, 1995.
14. L. Furness, In Reply to Questionnaire, Personal Details etc. of Service in Kure area, edited by W. Aldridge, Japan, 1994.

15. R. Storey, ibid.
16. Ota Noboru, *Kanreki Zakki* (privately printed, 1986), pp. 24–5.
17. *Chugoku Shinbun*, 5 July 1946.
18. Ota Noboru, *Kanreki Zakki*, pp. 26–7.
19. Suzuki Takeo, Churyugun Rodo no Kaiso nitsuite (Shuki) (8 March 1994).
20. Matsumoto Kenichi, '*Yutori*', in Kure-shi Kyoikiu no Iinkai (eds), *Kure no Kyoiku*, no. 1 (November 1953) (Kure City, 1953), pp. 36, 37.
21. Arthur W. John, *Uneasy Lies The Head That Wears A Crown* (The Gen Publishers, 1987).
22. History of BCOF – Labour Service, History of BCOF, Part 3, AWM 114 130/1 23 pt 3.
23. Demoto Isao, 'Shinchu Toji no Romu', *Chugoku Nippo*, 21 August 1955.
24. Council Minute, Kokurengun Hikiage Taisaku Kyogikai Tekiroku, 3 August 1955, Kure City Archives.
25. *Mainichi Shinbun*, 31 July 1952.
26. History of BCOF Provost Service, 2 April 1948, AWM 114 803/5.
27. JCOSA Minute No. 62: Fraternization Policy for BCOF, 30 January 1946, British Commonwealth Occupation Forces: Fraternization – Marriages, ANA: a5954/1.
28. British Commonwealth Occupation Force Administrative Instruction 39: Marriages in Japan, 28 September 1946, AWM 114/130/31.
29. *The Sun*, 28 March 1952.
30. *Chugoku Nippo*, 27 March 1959.
31. Ian Nish, 'Early Experiences in the British Commonwealth Occupation Force in Japan', *The Japan Society Proceedings*, no. 128, Winter 1996.

19
The Anglo-Japanese Relationship after the Second World War

Yasuaki Imaizumi

War responsibility and Anglo-Japanese naval relations

When we consider Anglo-Japanese military relationships we should bear in mind that it is now 400 years since the visit by William Adams. Moreover it is 100 years since the conclusion of the Anglo-Japanese Alliance which created a close alliance relationship covering almost two decades. The Imperial Japanese Navy (IJN), from the mid-nineteenth century to the 1920s, also developed with the help of the Royal Navy and became the world's third sea power in the world in the years following the First World War. In the century since the Alliance was formed, Japan and Britain fought together as comrades in the First World War and worked together during the Cold War, but they fought each other as enemies during the Second World War. This war lasted only for 3 years and 8 months from December 1941 to August 1945 but left deep and lasting wounds around the subjects of POW atrocities and war crimes.

However, the development of the Cold War gradually brought Japan and Britain together again. In the years immediately after the end of the war, strict restrictions were placed on the rearmament of Japan – in part due to the wariness of Australia, New Zealand and Canada against Japan. However, the outbreak of the Korean War and the commencement of the Cold War changed the Anglo-Japanese relationship completely. During the Korean War, the Shipping Route (Mine) Sweeping Department of the Maritime Safety Agency, the forerunner of the Maritime Self-Defence Force, co-operated with the Royal Navy in carrying out sweeping of sea mines at the Korean Sea Area.[1] Also, it was the rear support facilities in Kure base of the former IJN that provided support for the British Commonwealth Forces dispatched to Korea. The former IJN Naval Hospital and supply warehouses, as well as the repair and refitting capabilities of the IJN, were made available in the area occupied by British Commonwealth Forces, and such supports were highly valued. One commentator stated 'Should the British Commonwealth Forces not have been stationed at Kure Area to take advantage of the capacities available there, it would have been difficult for the Commonwealth Forces in Korea to carry out successful operations.'[2]

As previously stated, the Japan–Britain relationship was initiated through maritime connections as both island nations had naval traditions at the core of their national security. The restoration of relations and Japan–Britain reconciliation after the Second World War was also helped by naval associations. It was a letter to the editor of the *Japan Times* by John S. Rubin, living in the city of Barrow, where Vickers Shipyards, which had produced the battleship *Mikasa*, is located that revived the broken thread again.[3] This led to a recollection of the history of the Japan–Britain alliance, and cast new light on the relationship between the Royal Navy and the Japanese Maritime Self-Defence Force. Rubin, who was operating a jewellers' shop in Barrow during the period when the *Mikasa* was under construction, took the opportunity of visiting his daughter and her husband who had been dispatched to Yokohama in the fall of 1955. He visited the *Mikasa* in the city of Yokosuka, remembering the days when the citizens rejoiced in the victory in the Battle of Tsushima as the pride of the city of Barrow. However, what he found there was a ruinously dilapidated ship. It had not only been been clumsily disarmed but, in addition, the mast and the turret had been removed and the interior of the ship was in a terrible state. Rubin was astonished, upset and angry. He sent a grief-stricken letter to the editor, writing 'Was not *Mikasa* a symbol of glory for Japanese like the Battleship *Victory* for the British? What is this miserable desolation, making us avert our eyes!' His letter provided an opportunity to let many Japanese know the state of the *Mikasa* and triggered a fund-raising effort for its restoration, bringing the *Mikasa* to the status of a national monument like HMS *Victory*.[4]

Even during the worst days of the war fought between Japan and Britain there was mutual respect and friendship between the mariners who fought for their countries in the service of their respective navies. This respect and friendship, developed during the war, although not a major development, provided some warmth at times to compensate for the cold relationship between the two countries in the aftermath of the war and also contributed to the rebuilding of good relationships. Sir Samuel Falle, who joined the British Foreign and Commonwealth Office after his release from military service and later became the Ambassador to Sweden, was the gunnery officer of the destroyer *Encounter*. This ship was sunk in the Battle of Java Sea and he was picked up by the destroyer *Ikazuchi*, while adrift at sea. He sent a letter to the editor of the *US Naval Institute Proceedings* which was printed in January 1987 under the title of 'Chivalry' to express his appreciation of the admirable behaviour of the IJN during the war.[5] Falle stated that the IJN spent one full day rescuing survivors. In particular, the destroyer *Ikazuchi*, which rescued Falle, stopped the ship as it discovered and picked up one single survivor despite the risk of a possible attack by a submarine. It finally rescued 300 survivors by itself. Falle wrote of this experience in that letter.

He told of the survivors being given clothes, shoes, foods and even cigarettes, and said that the only order they received was not to smoke on deck
at night since this might bring about a submarine attack. Furthermore, Falle
sent the following letter to the editor of the *Times* on 29 April 1990, as he
may have been apprehensive of anti-Japanese speeches and behaviour by a
group of former British POWs as the date of the visit to the UK by the
Emperor approached:

Dear Mr. Editor
Sir, as a former prisoner of war of the Japanese, may I explain why I am
interested in reconciling with our former enemies. My ship, the destroyer
Encounter was sunk by overwhelming Japanese naval force in the battle
of the Java Sea on March 1, 1942, together with *HMS Exeter*, of River Plate
fame, and the *USS Hope.*
    Japanese rescued as many survivors as they could find, taking much
time over the operation. When my shipmates and I . . . over 300 in
all . . . scrambled aboard the small Japanese destroyer *Ikazuchi*, weak after
24 hours in the water and covered in oil, we were given an astonishingly
friendly welcome, . . . rescued. Japanese sailors cleaned the oil off, and
gave us clothing, cane chairs to sit on, hot milk, bully beef and biscuits.
Ikazuchi's captain came down from the bridge and spoke to us in English:
'You have fought bravely. Now, you are honoured guests of the Imperial
Navy. I respect the British Navy'. He lived up to these words, and for the
24 hours we remained aboard we could not have been better treated.[6]

In addition, Peter Smith, a British writer and researcher on the history of
naval battles, although not a former serviceman, sent an article entitled
'UK–Japanese relationship as seen from the British Navy side'[7] to the editor
of the *Mainichi Daily News* on 28 May. In this article, he wrote in his introduction 'The visit to Britain by the Emperor and Empress of Japan has
aroused some hostility, . . . In the 20th century, governments decide on
whether to go to war or not, not kings, queens, or emperors.' He then looked
back on the UK–Japanese relationship and introduced examples of the
chivalrous spirit of the Japanese Armed Forces by writing

even during the War, one week after *Prince of Wales* and *Repulse* were sunk
on 10 December 1941, Lt. Iki Haruki made a bombing raid against the
radio station in the Anambas Islands a week or so later, his route took
him over the site of the battle, and he dropped two bouquets over the
site of the two sunken giants in respect for the dead of both sides. Also,
when 'carrier *Hermes*, cruisers *Cornwall*, *Dorsetshire* were sunk in the
Indian Ocean, the Japanese airmen made no effort to disrupt the rescue
of the carrier's survivors, and indeed, on their way back to their 'carriers
they came upon the British hospital ship, *Vita*, and sent her details of the

precise location of the sunken ships. This humanitarian act enabled her to rescue over 600 men from the shark-infected waters.

And he urged the necessity of reconciliation by saying: 'In War, terrible things occur. They should never be forgotten or glossed over or ignored. Nonetheless, not everyone should be tarred with the same brush. If British refused to speak to every country she had fought with, for centuries, we would probably only have friends in Tibet and Chile . . .'

Language officers – a bridge between Japan and Britain

The language officers comprise a small group who received Japanese-language training to better understand their partners as a result of the conclusion of the Anglo-Japanese Alliance plus those officers who received short-term intensive training in the Second World War to meet the needs of knowing the enemy's language. A typical pre-war language officer who learned Japanese was Major-General F.S.G. Piggott. Piggott came to Japan when he was five years old accompanying his father, who was then legal counsel to the Japanese government. He then graduated from the British army officer academy and visited Japan from 1904 to 1906, being attached to a Japanese army unit. He made a third visit to Japan from 1910 to 1913 as an assistant resident army attaché at the British Embassy. He went to the front in the First World War. He was assigned for the visit by Prince Hirohito (Emperor Showa) to Britain in 1921 as a member of the official reception committee and this created an opportunity for him to build a close relationship with the Japanese royal family. However, the relationship between Japan and Britain did not develop in the way Piggott had hoped. He attended the Washington Conference of 1921/2 as an aide to Sir Arthur J. Balfour, the British delegate, and felt the cancellation of the Anglo-Japanese Alliance as 'killing my own child'. After that, he came to Japan on 1921 as Assistant Military Attaché in the Embassy, with an expectation from his own government of helping to secure a favourable improvement in the deteriorating Japan–Britain relationship and stayed in Japan until 1926. After he was promoted to major general in 1935, he came to Japan for the fourth time in 1936, once again serving as Military Attaché at the Embassy. He returned home in 1939 gravely concerned over the worsening Japan–Britain relationship and then closed a lengthy military career. Major-General Piggott was widely known as the most pro-Japanese Briton and a Japan-sympathizer in England. 'His speech and behaviour in favour of Japan had been a legend.'[8] The Pacific War started in spite of all his efforts and he became involved in Japanese-language teaching as a special staff member of the specially initiated Japanese-language course in the School of Oriental Studies at London University. However, when the war ended he immediately started working for the restoration of he Japan–Britain relationship that had been shattered by the war. Piggott reopened the Japan Society of London and served as the president of the Society from 1958 to 1961, working to form a bridge between Japan and Britain. Clearly, Piggott's recognition and evaluation of Japan was not altered by the tragedies of the war.

On the other hand, training in the Japanese language, which had been essential in understanding the enemy, continued from 1942, the second year of the Pacific War, to 1947 in the School of Oriental Studies of London University. A total of 648 students received training during this five-year period. The language officers who received the training in this School worked in India, Burma and other places in South East Asia and then in occupied Japan. When the war ended, they left the military services, and many of them became specialists on Japan, enjoying lifelong relationships with Japan, as scholars, businessmen and diplomats. Typical of such individuals is Sir Hugh Cortazzi, who first came to Japan as a language officer. When he was discharged from military service he returned to London University again where he obtained a degree. He then embarked on a career as a diplomat, and became Ambassador to Japan in 1980, contributing greatly to the resolution of trade friction, the lifting of self-imposed export controls, the opening of Japanese markets, the promotion of Japan–Britain industrial co-operation, and other such matters. During more than twenty years in Japan he studied the country's society and history, writing books such as *Japan as Seen by a Diplomat's Wife*, based on the records made by the wife of a British diplomat who served in Tokyo in the mid-Meiji period. In 1984 he wrote *Island Country in the East, Island Country in the West*, which contained essays, theses, newspaper articles, and speeches made at various cities during his three years as the Ambassador to Japan. In addition, he translated *The Ogre and Other Stories of Japanese Salaryman* and *The Lucky One* by Genji Keita, and in doing so he has made a tremendous contribution to introducing and explaining Japan to the outside world.[9]

Another important figure who left a great impression on the relationship between Britain and Japan is R.P. Dore. Dore gave lectures in various Japanese cities in the 1970s when trade friction was at its height, and sent letters to the editors of the *Times* and the *Financial Times*, appealing that the causes of such friction were also rooted in the industrial practices of European countries and America. He wrote many books including *Sociology of Trade Friction, Taking Japan Seriously* and *Flexible Rigidity – Structural Change in Japan*. Such scholarly works were recognized in 1975 when he was selected as a Fellow of the British Academy, and in 1982, he created the Institute for Anglo-Japanese Comparative Studies at London University. Thus Professor Dore has exhibited a continuing and deep enthusiasm for studies of Japan. He went on to write books such as *Shinohata: a Portrait of a Japanese Village, Land Reform in Japan, City Life in Japan, Education in Tokugawa Japan, Aspects of Social Changes in Modern Japan* and *British Factory, Japanese Factory*. Another Japanophile was the late Louis Allen of Durham University who wrote a number of war records such as *Prisoner of the British* (a translation into English of *Arlon Concentration Camp* by Yuji Aida), *Japan: Years of Triumph, Sittang: The Last Battle, Singapore, The End of the War in Asia* and *Burma – the Longest War*. Through these works, he made a substantial contribution to a more balanced assessment of the war. In addition, we should also mention Professor Geoffrey Bownas, the founding Professor of the Centre for Japanese Studies at Sheffield University, and Professor Ian Nish of the London School of Economics, a world-renowned authority on Anglo-Japanese relations. Sadao Oba, author of *Japanese Language School in Wartime London*, wrote: 'An appreciable number of these students, who had learnt the Japanese as an enemy language to defeat Japan, were turned to be captured by the Japanese culture, and Japan benefited substantially from their activities.' They made an invaluable contribution implicitly and explicitly to mitigating the anti-Japanese sentiment in Britain after the war and provided a more balanced and realistic picture of Japan to the world. This historical transition is well expressed by the Japanese proverb: 'Yesterday's Enemy – Today's Friend'. Many other students from the Japanese courses at SOAS have contributed to strengthening Anglo-Japanese relations and continue to do so even to this day.[10]

Japan–Britain relations after the war

The creation of the Self-Defence Forces and influence of Britain

On 10 May 1952, the National Police Reserve and the Maritime Safety Agency were reorganized as the National Security Force and in 1954 they were again reorganized as the tri-service Self-Defence Forces. Around this time, the position of Japan was changing along with the intensification of the East–West confrontation and Japan was increasingly expected to take some responsibility in the defence in Asia. This contributed to a gradual improvement in the Japan–Britain relationship. What is particularly noteworthy in the Self-Defence Forces at their creation days was that Shigeru Yoshida, a former Ambassador to Britain and therefore familiar with things British, became the Prime Minister. Around this time the National Safety Agency was created as the forerunner of the Self-Defence Forces. Yoshida believed that the new defence organization must be one which understood British-style liberty and democracy. He therefore selected as a military adviser former Lieutenant-General Tatsumi Eiichi, who was Military Attaché at the time Yoshida was the Ambassador to Britain and served there for a number of years. Eiichi served in London twice as Military Attaché to the Japanese Embassy in London and was well known to many senior British military figures. Yoshida also selected Maki Tomo, a graduate of Cambridge University, as Superintendent of the Defence Academy where key officers of the Self-Defence Forces were trained. Yoshida wished to appoint an individual who had received an education in England to lead the Academy. In addition, Yoshida selected ex-Colonel Matsutani Makoto, who once served as Assistant Army Attaché to the Embassy in England, and appointed him as Director, Training with responsibility for ground forces.[11] Yoshida was apparently thinking of the relationship between the British armed forces and British people which he saw when he served in Britain as an ideal form when he stated: 'I was surprised to see barracks in England had very well prepared facilities', and such facilities 'will make soldiers aware that they are supported by the reliance and love of the people', and that the members of the Self-Defence Forces 'must not be made to feel uncomfortable or wanting'.[12]

Exchanges of personnel and information

The military interchange between Japan and Britain after the end of war has not been as active as that with the USA or with nations in the Asia-Pacific region. Nevertheless a close relationship has been maintained as far as the Maritime Self-Defence Forces are concerned. This is due to the teacher–student relationship together with the common features of seagoing spirit as fellow Blue Water navies. This is best exemplified by the overseas training cruise, the Rim-Pac Exercises, personnel exchanges in education and training and also observation visits, together with the introduction of weapons, equipment and munitions and so forth from Britain.

In particular, during the years of the Cold War, Japan was situated at an important geographical position to monitor the three straits which provided outlets for the Soviet Pacific Fleet into the Pacific Ocean. Therefore the Japan–Britain relation was classified as quasi-allies comparable in some ways to the closer ally relationship with the USA. Thus the information exchange between Japan and Britain was of quite high quality.

As to military attachés, one attaché from the Royal Navy plus one or two assistant attachés from the British Army or Royal Air Force have been assigned to the British Embassy since the 1960s. It was in 1957 that the Maritime Self-Defence Force was permitted to dispatch resident defence officers overseas, and the first resident defence officer dispatched to England. It clearly shows how much importance the Maritime Self-Defence Forces have placed on Britain.[13]

The personnel exchange between Japan and Britain comprises long-term stays at various military academies plus short-term assignments. The places to which students from Japan are dispatched for long-term stays include the Royal College of Defence Studies, Military Staff Colleges for Army, Navy and Air Forces, intelligence school, submarine school and engineering schools. Short-term assignments include exchange students dispatched to the military academies of the British Army, Navy and Air Force from the Japanese Defence Academy. By contrast, the number of British exchange students is rather limited due to the language problem, although some British officers have received training in the Japanese language. Students are sent from time to time to the Staff College of the Maritime Self-Defence Force and the

National Institute of Defence Studies. Compared with this, the policy conferences starting with top defence level had not been too active during the Cold War era because of the contentious issue of 'collective self-defence'. However, after the fall of the Iron Curtain and the end of the Cold War various conferences have been actively promoted in a number of fields as a part of efforts for building mutual trust. These conferences utilize a variety of channels and different groupings at differing levels such as the PM (politico-military) conference between the Foreign and Commonwealth Office, Ministry of Defence and the Japanese Ministry of Foreign Affairs, Defence Agency, staff talks between the army/navy/air forces and each self-defence force (ground, maritime and air). Staff talks between Royal Navy and Maritime Self-Defence Forces are particularly active, alternating between Japan and Britain since 1990.

Reciprocal naval visits are also ongoing and contribute considerably to the development of mutual understanding and friendship, and of the number of naval ships visiting Japan, British ships visited Japan more than any other country except for the USA. As of June 1998, 208 British ships, which represents about half of the number of foreign naval ships, had visited Japan. These have included HMS *Invincible*, a light aircraft carrier which visited Yokosuka in 1992; the Royal Yacht *Britannia* at Tokyo, Nagoya, Kobe and Naha in 1997; and HMS *Illustrious*, an anti-submarine aircraft carrier that visited Tokyo in 1998. Whenever these ships visit Japanese ports, an escort ship is dispatched by the Maritime Self-Defence Force as a host ship to provide various support services. On the other hand, visits by the Maritime Self-Defence Force have been limited – a training squadron visiting Britain once in every four years. They did, however, enjoy a warm welcome including a reception held in the official cabin of Admiral Nelson on HMS *Victory*.

The introduction of equipment and munitions

While exchanges of information on equipment and munitions are made as a result of the Equipment & Munitions Exhibition of the British Army and Royal Navy operated by the British Ministry of Defence, the weapons system of Japan is now predominantly American as a result of the very close working relationships that have been developed through the US–Japan Security Treaty.

Nevertheless the Self-Defence Force have been introducing British equipment from Britain as they continually seek high-quality, efficient products. Of the three Self-Defence Forces, the Maritime Self-Defence Force imports the highest proportion of weapons and equipment from Britain, starting with torpedo boats in 1957. Aircraft engines, marine propulsion engines, and mine warfare systems are either imported or produced on licence.[14] The Air Self-Defence Force also imports aircraft engines, and the Ground Self-Defence Force also imports or produces howitzers, mortars, tank guns and shells under licence. Rolls Royce engines for aircraft and marine engines are fairly well established in the Maritime Self-Defence Force and the Air Self-Defence Force. They naturally require a continuous supply of parts for maintenance and upkeep for the foreseeable future. Thus a close relationship and reliance in these aspects is expected to continue at a very high level.

Co-operation in the peacekeeping operations (PKO) field

The dispatch of minesweepers by the Maritime Self-Defence Force to the Persian Gulf even after the Gulf War ended gave an opportunity for the Maritime Self-Defence Forces to make international contributions under the United Nations banner. Starting with the dispatch of the first PKO troops to Cambodia, Japan is now actively involved in many countries on UN PKO duties. The exchange of information and views with Britain in this area has been greatly strengthened and the following PKO conferences have taken place to date:

May 1994: British PKO presentation team visited Japan.
June 1994: One man participated in the PKO map exercise held at the Staff College in England.
January 1995: Staffs in charge of PKO from the British Ministry of Defence visited Japan.
October 1995: The British PKO presentation team visited Japan.
September 1996: Staff in charge of PKO from the British Ministry of Defence visited Japan.
August 1997: Japan–British PKO seminar (Tokyo).
February 1998: Participation in the United Nations Logistics Course sponsored by the British Ministry of Defence (one man).

There is therefore a general trend that the requirement for interchange of personnel and exchange of information will increase from now on as Japan continues to be more and more involved in co-operation for the securing of international peace. The despatch of Japanese personnel to British training facilities with their greater knowledge and experience in PKO as well as the military exchange of information between Japan and Britain will undoubtedly grow through activities such as PKO.[15] In addition, there is a growing need to co-operate in confronting global problems which are becoming more urgent in recent times, including the contamination of oceans and the depletion of fishing resources. Furthermore, there is an increasing number of cases of unlawful acts of piracy which contribute to the instability in the South China Sea. When the fact that the number of pirate actions reported in 1999 was 309 in the entire world, but that 114 cases occurred in the waters of South East Asia is considered,[16] this represents a serious threat to the economic activities of trading countries such as

Japan and Britain. One proposal to resolve such matters is to organize Ocean Peace Keeping (OPK) in order to strengthen maritime security and order and prevent wrongful acts.[17] Maritime powers such as Japan and Britain from the East and the West need to co-operate in exchanging intelligence on pirate activities and in forming international patrol units and therefore close co-operation between the Royal Navy and the Maritime Self Defense Force will be vital.

Furthermore, there is a necessity for a maritime trading power such as Britain operating over a vast area covering the Asia-Pacific to seek closer co-ordination with a maritime Asian power such as Japan from the viewpoint of multilateral security in the economic and diplomatic sphere. On the other hand, it is necessary for Japan to strengthen mutual co-operation with Britain and with British Commonwealth countries such as Australia and New Zealand not only in economic matters but also in the military security areas. Thus, co-operation between Japan and Britain is indispensable for the stability in the Asia-Pacific area. In seeking to achieve these ends there is clearly an agenda for an Anglo-Japanese 'Global Partnership' for promoting reform and investment for the future; a strengthening of Asia–Europe relations and the realization of a better global society. This was confirmed when Prime Minister Tony Blair visited Japan in January 1998 and made a joint declaration with Prime Minister Hashimoto Ryutaro which was entitled 'A Common Vision for Japan and Britain for the 21st Century'. Thus for Japan and Britain, these two island countries, linked through their continuing maritime traditions and evolving security roles, can look forward to a bright future of fruitful collaboration

Notes

1. Takeo Okubo, *Muteki Nariyamazu* (Kaiyo Mondai Kenyukai, 1984), p. 310.
2. J. Grey, *The Commonwealth Armies and the Korean War* (Manchester: Manchester University Press, 1988), pp. 31–41.
3. Title of F.S.G. Piggott, *Broken Thread – 60 Years of Anglo-Japanese Diplomacy* (London: Gule and Ploden, 1951).
4. Ito Masanori, *Daikaigun wo Omou* (Bungei-Shunju, 1955), pp. 273–8.
5. Sir Samuel Falle, 'Chivalry', *US Naval Institute Proceedings* (January 1987), pp. 86–9.
6. Sir Samuel Falle, 'Japan's Former POWs', Letters to the Editor, *The Times*, 29 April 1990.
7. Peter C. Smith, 'A Naval View of Anglo-Japanese Relations', *Mainichi Daily News*, 28 May 1998; 'Historic UK–Japanese Naval Ties Highlight Mutual Respect', *Mainichi News*, 29 May 1998.
8. Piggott, *Broken Thread*, p. 201.
9. Sir Hugh Cortazzi, 'Japan and Back and Places Elsewhere: Memoir of Hugh Cortazzi', *Japan Economic Journal* (1998), p. 27.

10. See Oba Sadao, *Senchu Rondon Nihongo Gakko* (Chuko-shinsho, 1988).
    Businessmen and diplomats who have contributed much to Anglo-Japanese relations:
    Sir Peter Parker, Chairman of British Rail
    L. A. Radbourne, General Manager, Dodwell Japan
    Paul Bates, Shell Oil
    Terry Townsend, Japan Branch of Akzo Science
    Bill Henderson, Shell Oil
    Kenneth Slatcher, Consul-General at Osaka
    Russell Greenwood, Consul-General at Osaka
    Scholars and researchers:
    Ian Nish, Professor, London University (Studies of Japanese History)
    J.R. McEvan, Professor, London University (Studies of Ogiu Sorai)
    Patrick O'Neill, Professor, London University (Studies of Drama in Japan)
    Charles Dunn, Professor, London University (Studies of *Bunraku* and *Kabuki*)
    Douglas Mills, Professor of Cambridge University (Studies of Medieval Japanese Literature)
    Kenneth Gardner, Assistant Manager, Oriental Books Department, the British Library
    Ivor Watts, Tokyo Branch Manager, British Culture Promotion Association
11. Shigeru Yoshida, *Kaiso Junen*, vol. 4 (Shinchosha, 1957), p. 37; Matsutani Makoto 'Mako Gakucho Sensei no Hitogara', in the book, *Maki Sensei* (Maki Tomo Sensei Tsuisohensarkai, 1972), p. 45.
12. Yoshida Shigeru, *Sekai to Nihon* (Bancho Shobo Ltd., 1963), pp. 206–7.
13. Suzuki Kenji, *Zaigai Bukan Monogatari* (Fuyo Shobo, 1979), pp. 232–5.
14. Asagumo Shinbunsha-hen, *Buki Sobi Nenkan* (Asagumo Shinbunsha, 2000).
15. Kamiyo Takahiro, *Kokusai heiwa Kyoryoku Nyumon* (Yuhikaku, 1997), pp. 162–4.
16. Kaijo Hoancho-hen, *Kaijo Hoan Hakusho* (Okurasho Insatsu-kyoku, 2000), p. 18.
17. Takai Susumu and Akimoto Kazumine, *Kaijo Boeiryoku noigi to Aratana Yakuwari* (Boei Kenkyujo Kenkyn Kiyo), vol. 1, no. 1 (1998), pp. 116–18.

Index

Subheadings are listed largely in chronological order. Readers are referred to the List of Abbreviations on p. xii.